THE PHOENIX COMPLEX

THE PHOENIX COMPLEX

A Philosophy of Nature

MICHAEL MARDER

The MIT Press
Cambridge, Massachusetts
London, England

© 2023 Massachusetts Institute of Technology

This work is subject to a Creative Commons CC-BY-NC-ND license.

Subject to such license, all rights are reserved.

The MIT Press would like to thank the anonymous peer reviewers who provided comments on drafts of this book. The generous work of academic experts is essential for establishing the authority and quality of our publications. We acknowledge with gratitude the contributions of these otherwise uncredited readers.

This book was set in Adobe Garamond Pro by New Best-set Typesetters Ltd. Printed and bound in the United States of America.

Library of Congress Cataloging-in-Publication Data is available.

ISBN: 978-0-262-54570-9

10 9 8 7 6 5 4 3 2 1

For Luis, part of our "infinite conversation"

I am that great phoenix [*bennu*] which is in Heliopolis [*Annu*], the supervisor of what exists.

Who is he? He is Osiris. As for what exists, that means his injury. *Otherwise said*: That means his corpse. *Otherwise said*: It means eternity and everlasting. As for eternity, it means daytime; as for everlasting, it means night.
—*The Ancient Egyptian Book of the Dead* (Spell 17)

[There is] a fable which says that among the first medicines was one from the ashes and nest of the phoenix, just as though the story were fact and not myth. It is to joke with mankind to point out remedies that return only after a thousand years.
—Pliny the Elder, *Natural History* (29.viii)

You have seen everything that has ever been; you testify to the passing and turning of the ages.
—Claudian, "The Phoenix" (27.104–105)

Every combustion process is a sacrifice of individuality. When the sun represents the ideal principle in relation to the earth, the earth, as it were, sacrifices itself to the sun, as it does in the volcanic process, although, like a phoenix, it again revives from the ashes by the power of its indwelling individuality and binds itself in a relation to the sun anew.
—F. W. J. Schelling, *System of Philosophy in General and the Philosophy of Nature in Particular*

One need only remember how the regimes of the one and nature gave way to the disparate which dislocated them, beginning with their respective establishments, to understand that their destitutions were always a phoenix's tale. From the ashes of the Greek hegemony, the Latin hegemony emerges, and from the ashes of the latter, modern self-consciousness emerges. There is a thetic relapse without which no new regime could be put into place (yet which does not take up the destituted positions in any synthesis).
—Reiner Schürmann, *Broken Hegemonies*

Contents

Preface: Is a Philosophy of Nature Still Tenable? *xi*

1   **THE PHOENIX COMPLEX** *1*

2   **PHILOSOPHY'S THIRD PATH: PLATO/LEVINAS** *29*

3   **ON PHYSIOPSYCHOLOGY–LIFE AND ENERGY: ARISTOTLE/HEGEL** *59*

4   **UNITY AND UNIVERSALITY: PLOTINUS/SCHELLING** *89*

5   **THE PHOENIX ACTS: HILDEGARD/SPINOZA** *127*

6   **DEATH, REBIRTH, AND BEYOND IN HINDU TRADITIONS** *149*

7   **GENERATIVITY AND GENERATIONALITY IN CONFUCIANISM** *175*

8   **UNIVERSAL RESURRECTION IN RUSSIAN COSMISM** *197*

9   **POLITICAL RENAISSANCE FROM THE ROMAN EMPIRE TO THE THOUGHT OF HANNAH ARENDT** *219*

    AFTERWORD: ASHES TO ASHES . . . *241*

Notes *247*

Index *279*

Preface
IS A PHILOSOPHY OF NATURE STILL TENABLE?

Essence, truth, nature—these concepts have been highly suspect, to the point of being tabooed, in Continental philosophy circles since the second half of the twentieth century. *Nature* is, by far, the most prominent of the three, particularly because its semantic and conceptual drift affects essence and truth alike. So, essence may be understood as the inner nature of things, while truth can be defined as the accordance of a statement with their outer nature, or, in a word, with reality.[1] A lot rides, then, on the undercutting of nature, whether in its inner or outer aspects: when it erodes, its companion terms promptly follow suit. Rejecting this concept for a slew of reasons (including its atavistic connotations, hierarchical presuppositions, and blindness to cultural and social constructions), we proudly declare our membership in the vanguard of criticism and our liberation from the symbolic yoke of the past we would much rather forget. Nonessentialism and post-truth are the badges of honor that go along with this membership.

The thesis that nature does not exist has found adherents of every stripe. The nineteenth-century distinction between *Naturwissenschaften* and *Geisteswissenschaften* (natural and human sciences), which had served as the cornerstone of the modern university system, has imploded, rendering both terms in the contrast meaningless. Roughly at the same time that the spirit (*Geist*) at the pinnacle of the humanities has lost its credibility, the nature (*Natur*) at the base of the hard sciences has been divested of its significance.[2] At the hands of natural scientists, nature dissolves into organic and inorganic chemical and molecular components, quantum mechanics and wave oscillations, condensed matter and thermodynamic processes. In the context of such dissolution, a unified notion of nature sounds like a specious abstraction.

Along with nature, life too becomes an outdated concept after it has been reduced to protein structures or energy and signal transduction, enzyme catalysts and metabolic pathways, genes and their expressions. Having fallen victim to these and countless other reductions, the life of life sciences turns out to be all but dead. Furthermore, the connection between life and nature should not be viewed as that between an organic part and the whole made up of organic as well as inorganic components. At its Latin etymological root, *natura* derives from *nascere* (to be born), or, more precisely, from the verb's past participle, *nato*. Nature is natality, the movement of birthing, of a beginning of life that keeps rebeginning and that, perpetually in statu nascendi (in the nascent state, which does not at all exclude death and dying), gives rise to future life out of the remnants of the past: of rivers and mountains, plants and animals, stones and humans, bacteria and an oxygen-enriched atmosphere. It is a movement, the dance of coming to appearance—by hatching or germinating, emerging from the birth canal, or undergoing fission—of (1) that which comes to appearance as an effect; (2) that from which the appearing comes, including the Aristotelian formal and material causes; and (3) that wherein that which appears emerges. Coming to appearance, for its part, is not covered by either the classical or the modern types of causality. Rather than merely phenomenal, it indicates that the movement of birthing is phenomenaliz*ing* (in fact, self-phenomenalizing, which is not quite the same as autopoietic) and, as such, it both precedes and succeeds scientific explanations.

The objective devastation of nature, threatening, beyond any given species, the ostensibly inexhaustible stream of birthing indicated by the word itself, finds its corollaries in nature's subjective and epistemic destruction. Let us take just two recent paradigmatic examples.

Timothy Morton spots in nature a transcendental principle that needs to be done and over with for ecology and ecological thought to flourish: "The very idea of 'nature,' which so many hold dear, will have to wither away in an 'ecological' state of human society. Strange as it may sound, the idea of nature is getting in the way of properly ecological forms of culture, philosophy, politics, and art."[3] Why, though, constrain nature to an idea, and one detained in scarce quotes at that? Are birth and birthing that nourish its sense equally amenable to idealization? A similarly unjustified epistemic mutilation of nature is evident in Lorraine Daston's recent book *Against Nature*. While admitting that "like all truly interesting words, 'nature' is a *mille-feuille* of meanings,"[4] Daston narrows its semantic range down to order, if not the (transcendental, once again) assurance of order; for her, "specific natures guarantee an order of things."[5] The load-bearing point in the argument converts nature into a static category, ignoring the dynamic strands of birthing. But, should one insist on this formulation of the problem, nature is both an order and an ordering, which implies a persistent *re-* and *dis*ordering of things. As such, it can guarantee nothing but change, turmoil, and disruption.

Whereas nature promises an ostensibly limitless outpouring of births, our philosophical, scientific, and technological outlooks are spellbound by death. I have already mentioned how, decrying life for being a metaphysical delusion, as atavistic as nature itself, biological sciences study life phenomena in terms of their substantive biochemical or biophysical substratum, rendering them as good as dead.[6] Analytic philosophy, aspiring to a scientific standing, inflicts the same fate on the life of the mind, laid out on the Procrustean bed of formal or symbolic logic. Nonanalytic philosophy, heavily influenced by Martin Heidegger and existentialism, is enthralled with death. Technology implements prevalent scientific and philosophical perspectives on a planetary scale, seeding death everywhere. Nature is accessible to our understanding as an a priori lifeless "sum total or aggregate of natural things."[7] The default condition of our thinking, if not of our being, is a *necroepistemology*[8] that sees the world through the prism of death cleansed of life, the death, which nonetheless passes for life itself, plus the cutting-edge research on how to delay aging and to satisfy the ever-growing demand for immortality (for the ultrarich). Even the apocalyptic sentiments of the "endism" pervading our zeitgeist belong within this scheme.

The original articulation of nature as birthing not only feminizes the *figure* or the *figuration* of nature but also zeroes in on a phase of life conventionally identified as its beginning. The beginning that is birth is highly peculiar: it coincides with the moment of coming to appearance, of emerging into the light, while leaving in the shadows life's covert development, incubation, or gestation that have been unfolding prior to that moment. The end of a life in death is a counterpart to its beginning at birth, but, unlike the coming to appearance at or in the beginning, death is not a disappearance: the dead body, the corpse, remains. Moreover, these remains themselves undergo further changes, decomposing and becoming compost for the nourishment of new life. The past participle form of *nascere* (to be born) that yields *natura* (nature) starts making sense, in the first place, not in the light in which those born make their appearance, but in the darkness from whence they emerge and whither they recede. The overall birthing that is nature does not exclude either dying or the dead, without whom the future-oriented trajectory of birth would not have been possible.

Although, at the subterranean level of being, death is not opposed to birth, the two moments have been treated as the extremes of a life, its end and beginning points. At the same time, death looms as the other of life itself; it is the sole notion I know of that participates in two binary relations at once (death/birth; death/life). If death is the contrary of a beginning of life *and* of life as a whole, is that because life is always at its beginning (which is also an unsurpassable middle), born or reborn from itself as much as from its other? While saluting Hannah Arendt for the important work she undertook with respect to natality, we have no choice but to admit that this concept is still poorly understood. Through an appreciation of its relation to life and to death, we might get a little closer to deciphering some of the meanings of nature.

The thinking of nature did not, of course, commence with *natura*, which privileged a coming to appearance in birth. In ancient Greece, it started with the pre-Socratic conception of *phusis* that, undeniably more vegetal than animal, meant "not only that out of which things grew or of which, in the last analysis, they are constituted. . . . *Phusis* included the law or process of growth exemplified in all things."[9] *Phusis* is a noun obtained from the verb *phuein* (to grow, to appear). It is the same verb that gives rise to the Greek for plant, *phuton*—a word with many other meanings, including

xiv　　*Preface*

"child," "descendant," or "creature." Taken together, the growing, that out of which, and that toward which things grow amount to *phusis*. The ground of growth is not substantively different from the growing: it is made up of the traces of past growth, decayed into the soil they fertilize. Nor is *phusis* an ever-expanding polymorphous extension, but a swelling and contracting ellipsis. Growing, coming to appearance, living—these are all rooted in death, which is why all life is an afterlife, all growth is an aftergrowth. Self-grounded, *phusis* is radically ungrounded, abyssal. Its thinking cannot be outmoded, because what it holds in store (and what it thereby invariably withholds in its variegated modes of coming to appearance) is always yet to come.[10]

If, rooted in the past, *phusis* belongs to the future, then it is an enigma. The pre-Socratic, whose thinking will energize us throughout this book, Heraclitus, observed in Fragment 123 that "nature loves to hide [*phusis kruptesthai philei*]." To translate otherwise: the growing coming-to-appearance has a predilection to self-encryption, to concealment and nonappearance. Reformulated this way, the unity of opposites, a theme winding through virtually all Heraclitan fragments, comes into a spotlight. Insofar as there is an order of things said to be natural, it is hidden; its successful elucidation conflates it with the appearing-growing entities and, therefore, misses the mark. In a similar vein, the Delphic maxim "Know thyself" (*gnōthi seautón*) does not culminate in secure knowledge of the objective kind; were it to have done so, it would have missed the very self to be known.

The paradox of Heraclitan nature may be attributable to a plethora of causes, for example, to the hunch that the ground for growth and appearing does not grow but decays and withdraws from the world of appearances and visible forms, or to the fact that the *coming* to appearance is nowhere to be found in the sphere of what appears. That said, what attracts me in these three Greek words is not the hiding but the loving. It is impossible not to love this love. The love (*philia*) of nature puts it on a par with philosophy: just as nature is the love of hiding, so philosophy is a love of wisdom. (Tongue in cheek, we might call nature *philocryptia* by analogy with *philosophia*.) So, what else can we glean from the nexus of philosophy and nature formed by *philia*?

xv   *Preface*

Compare the darlings of philosophy and nature, the respective objects of their love, namely wisdom and concealment. At first glance, it seems that they are worlds apart: wisdom discloses reality as it is, the essence and truth of being; concealment denies us such a disclosure. A closer second look, however, will reveal a cardinal difference between knowledge (the absolute knowledge, even) and wisdom. The former is pure eidetic light shed on every corner of existence; the latter is a highly elusive thing, slipping from everyone's grasp, as Plato's dialogues amply demonstrate. It follows that nature and philosophy share, besides love itself, the love for the fugacious, for what is difficult to track down and impossible to catch, for an object that is axiomatically absent, because it is yet to come.[11]

Friedrich Schelling, who, resonating with the deep impulses and vibrations of ancient thought, was exceptionally attuned to nature as an activity, was entirely correct in his assertion that "to philosophize about nature means *to create* nature."[12] We should free this pithy statement of any and all idealist undertones. This is not a manifesto of the social construction of nature avant la lettre. In keeping with Schelling's logic and our own initial foray into the subject matter, nature is not created at will by the philosopher philosophizing about it. The philosopher who *creates* nature does not manipulate it as an object of theoretical understanding and practical construction, but joins, always belatedly, its own active force and a tradition of others who in the past endeavored to interpret this force, channeling the love of wisdom toward *phusis* that loves to hide.

The question posed in the title of this preface (Is a philosophy of nature still tenable?) is, thus, misplaced. In our hurried, half-baked judgment, philosophy of nature is a thing of the past, part of a naive approach unaware of the intricate comingling of nature and culture, nature and artifice, nature and technique. We do not take either the time or the care necessary to distinguish a philosophy of nature, capable once again or for the first time of relating to nature *as such*, from natural philosophy (*philosophia naturalis*), which uncritically carried out the activity of natural sciences before they became independent disciplines with well-defined domains of knowledge and their corresponding methodologies. In light of this *in*distinction, it would be better for philosophers to refrain from meddling with the scientific study of

xvi *Preface*

nature, lest they smuggle archaic metaphysical prejudices into the rigorous knowledge production and verification procedures of the natural sciences.[13]

If, on the contrary, there is anything we can learn from the *phusis* of the pre-Socratics (hence from nature before its formalization in Aristotle's philosophy), it is that no one can justifiably lay claim to and conceptually corral it. Nature is indomitable, despite our technologically substantiated illusions of total mastery and control over it, despite all the routines of cultivation, domestication, and manipulation; it has never been kept at bay, firmly maintained in any theoretical or practical grasp. Nor, by the way, has philosophy been tamed enough to be transformed into intellectual property, regardless of the drive toward systematization, subjection to logical rules and procedures, methodological regularization, and so forth. Here, Schelling's assertion about nature (that to philosophize about it is to create it) finds a more general supplement in Gilles Deleuze and Felix Guattari's suggestion that "the object of philosophy is to create concepts that are always new. . . . Concepts are not waiting for us ready-made, like heavenly bodies. There is no heaven for concepts. They must be invented, fabricated, or rather created."[14] Nature and philosophy participate in a synergy of creation, instigated by the wild, untamed, and untamable, love at the heart of both.

A philosophy of nature is yet to come, yet to be invented, to be created or cocreated in the twinned birth of nature (including of birth as nature and of nature as birth) and philosophy. Creation does not happen ex nihilo; it requires the use of materials already at hand. We must, therefore, contend with the following in the multilayered creative effort ahead: factors that, at our present environmental, political, and economic conjuncture, condition the creative endeavor; the selection process for the sorts of materials to be deployed and inheritances to be received; and a malleable form that could grow from the selected materials.

All three points have to do, in fact, with limits to creation, limits that are historical, material, and formal. The *historical* limits are the most pressing: the assertion that philosophy of nature is yet to come, to be invented, needs to be contextualized within the actual exhaustion of ecosystems; the accelerating loss of biodiversity; the elemental mutations of water, air, and soil under a massive influence of industrial by-products released into the environment. Nature as the power of perpetual rebirth, and philosophy as the promise of a future-oriented conceptual self-recreation; nature *and* philosophy as expressions of a boundless love of concealment or of wisdom; philosophy *of* nature as a unique synergic crossing of two loves—all must be vigilantly held against the background of "finite finitude" (of nonrenewability) that is being unfurled right before our eyes, ears, noses, and minds in the twenty-first century.

The *material* limits for our creative exercise cannot stop at the history of Western metaphysics. Given how profoundly ingrained, if barely recognized in their original form, certain mythological figures and narratives governing our representations of and involvements with nature are, it would be unpardonable to exclude them from a nascent philosophy of nature. Considering the cross-cultural universality of the theme, it would be similarly inexcusable to keep to the Western tradition alone, not least because the philosophical West is a flimsy and artificial construction, propped up by support beams from North African and Arabic-speaking worlds among many other formally non-Western places. Bearing in mind the elusiveness of nature and its ontological (rather than ontic) reach, it would also be unjustifiable to restrict the scope of this work to the staple themes of natural philosophy, while keeping topics in ethics, politics, or aesthetics out of the discussion.

The project's *formal* limits are not those of a purely abstract discourse on nature. Broader than that, they admit as legitimate mythic, non-Western, and premodern figures, together with figuration as such, which depends on imagistic, imaginal, and imaginative thinking. What, at any rate, would be a form appropriate to a fugacious intersection of two wild loves, of philosophy and of nature? How could this dynamic form be expressed in a lively (interdisciplinary, cross-cultural, and at times colloquial) fashion? In what sense might it spring up hylomorphically, from the materials themselves? These are the guiding questions of the formal aspects of the work at hand that inherently deformalize it, returning over and over again to its historical and material conditions.

In the interplay of the historical, material, and formal limits, *The Phoenix Complex* comes into being. The figuration of nature proposed in the book is the phoenix, which gives birth to itself from the threshold of death. This book relies on materials that include ancient Egyptian, Greek, and Roman mythology, philosophy, and literature; Hinduism; Confucianism and neo-Confucianism; early Christian theology; nineteenth-century *Naturphilosophie*; Russian cosmism; and contemporary Jewish thought. The topics covered herein are the quest for immortality, periodic renewals of political power, the ethics of alterity, the cycle of reincarnations and liberation from its machine-like rhythm, hopes for (human and nonhuman) resurrection, the nourishing potential of death and of what strikes one as disgusting, the stretching out and the condensation of time, and the possibilities of transcendence within immanence. The list goes on, but, without exception, these and related themes are set against the historical horizon of what I have referred to as finite finitude—an apparently unprecedented disruption of the routines of rebirth; the loss of the fecundating, fertile or fertilizing capacities of death; the incompatibility of eternity realized (say, in nondecomposable materials or nuclear residues) with the regeneration of plant, microbial, fungal, human, linguistic, cultural, political existences; the reproduction of life *as* death.

The structure of *The Phoenix Complex* exemplifies (or, better yet, performs) the subject matter of the book. In the chapters that revisit texts and ideas from the Western canon (chapters 2–5 and, to some extent, chapter 8) you will find pairings of two thinkers from historical periods that are often separated by thousands of years: Plato and Levinas, Aristotle and Hegel, Plotinus and Schelling, and Hildegard and Spinoza. It is, therefore, a book as much on philosophies of nature as it is on the history of philosophy, which is more or less visibly anchored in thinking nature. Curiously enough, the ideas of ancient philosophers (above all, on issues related to reproduction and substitution, life and death, the same and the other that are fundamental to the phoenix complex) make a comeback and are reborn in the guise of modern systems of thought. Their comeback gives a lie to the default account of modernity as a radical break with the past and, more importantly, corroborates the hypothesis that not only the content of ideas but also their originating impulse is reactivated time and again. Reiner Schürmann's astute

xix *Preface*

observation on the destitution and reinstitution of hegemonic modes of thinking finds its confirmation in this tendency, which Schürmann himself expressed in terms of "a phoenix's tale."[15]

*

The tragic rift of our times is the persistence of the ideological and, for the most part, unconscious conception of nature as a phoenix, which has either become or is in the process of becoming practically inoperable, incompatible with today's realities. For millennia now, humanity has been interpreting the cyclical regeneration of nature as a sign of its infinite capacity for rebirth from the ashes of destruction. (Correlatively, the idea of phoenix-nature itself has been returning—across centuries, geographical and cultural divides—in the otherwise heterogeneous currents of philosophy of nature.) Hoping that this would continue indefinitely, we keep literally burning the world down, while awaiting its phoenix-like resurgence. The same is true, on a smaller scale, of our attitudes toward our own bodies that are supposed to bounce back and regenerate after having suffered horrific accidents, starvation, torture, and mutilation, or, less obviously, after having been subjected to the slow but steady influence of cancerogenic food additives, radioactive isotopes, or air and water pollution.

Both singly and in groups, as consumers and corporations, states and energy companies, we continue to think and to act as if nature were safe and sound in the face of the irreparable devastation of biodiversity and the planet's fragile ecosystems: as if it (and we, ourselves) were a miraculously resilient phoenix. No wonder that *resilience* is one of the ideological keywords of the day! Nevertheless, what is being and has been annihilated for some time now can no longer regerminate. It cannot be rejuvenated from the ashes, receiving a new lease on life from death. The ashes of our age are not fecund; they are the sterile signs of the death of death, not to be confused with immortality. These ashes, or these signs, include soil degradation and depletion, spent nuclear and nonbiodegradable materials, desertification and the expansion of hypoxic areas in the oceans, the catastrophic melting of Arctic and Antarctic ice, the suffocating smog filling the atmosphere. Any future philosophy

xx *Preface*

of nature must bear the realization of environmental finitude as a birthmark on the body of its thought.

In what follows, we delve into the rift between the already-surpassed limits to regeneration, on the one hand, and the economic and political, theological and secular ideologies that still make us believe in infinite regenerability, on the other. We will seek a philosophy of nature in the continuities and contradictions between traditions that, in disparate epochs and geographical regions, shape the phoenix complex and, with and through it, our tragic predicament in the twenty-first century.[16]

1 THE PHOENIX COMPLEX

The phoenix complex: we are all suffering from it, individually and collectively. It is in us, having become entrenched in minds and bodies over millennia, all the while we are trapped in it, our practices and infrastructures servicing its many units and component parts. Even more so, the fate of the livable world well beyond the human sphere is hanging in the balance on account of this cross-cultural and transhistorical, in equal measure psychological and political, religious and philosophical, complex. If it remains undiagnosed, it is because the phoenix complex comprises a mélange of practices, narratives, discourses, beliefs, and hopes that has not yet been formally called by its proper name. And, assuming that scholars duly recognize and classify it, this predicament will likely not be acknowledged as a problem at all, but as a blessing in the form of the infinitely self-regenerative capacity inherent in finite existence.

In the concluding pages of *Pyropolitics in the World Ablaze*, I brought up the phoenix complex with reference to "the politics of ashes." I described it as follows: "In the twenty-first century, the myth of the phoenix continues to bewitch us. We still think of ashes as fertilizers, nourishing new growth. After destructive flames have done their work, the sun's creative blaze will give a sign of resurrection to the plants it will call forth from the residues of past burning. Between the two fires, life and hope will resume. Vegetation will spring from the earth and strive skywards afresh."[1]

The invocation of the phoenix complex in *Pyropolitics* was a playful riff on Gaston Bachelard's elaboration of the Prometheus complex and the

Empedocles complex in *The Psychoanalysis of Fire*.[2] Bachelard sees the complexes he identifies as two sides of the same flaming coin. (Gold, by the way, has a privileged relation to the cosmic flame, to which Heraclitus analogizes it in Fragment 90.[3]) The active Prometheus complex is an expression of "the will to intellectuality," replete with "all those tendencies which impel us *to know* as much as our fathers, more than our fathers, as much as our teachers, more than our teachers."[4] The Empedocles complex is its passive counterpart, the condition, in which the "fascinated individual hears *the call of the funeral pyre*."[5] The phoenix complex is, conversely, on the hither side of knowing and fascination, while embracing both of these poles. Instead of choosing between the imperative "to seize fire" (Prometheus) or "to give oneself to fire" (Empedocles), the phoenix seizes fire by giving herself to it, surrendering her past self in order to gain a foothold, or a winghold, in the future.

Why does the self-sacrificial logic of the phoenix triumph, even and especially in an age that prides itself on its secularity? This question will shadow every hypothesis and every conclusion to come. One possibility is that humanity has not yet learned how to deal with and, above all, how to think otherwise about the finite transcendence of finitude that yields an image of infinity. Fecundity, regeneration, procreation, the beginning of life after an end of other lives: every facet of vitality, with its ruptured continuities tracing the outlines of survival, is sieved through the mesh of sacrifice and self-sacrifice. A religious framework exchanges finite existence for life everlasting; hence the leap of the pre-Socratic philosopher, Empedocles, into the active crater of Mount Etna in an attempt to become godlike. A secular outlook, for its part, trades finite existence for another finite existence, meant to extend life past the predecessor's expiration date. In both instances, fire is the preferred medium of these transactions.

The idea that humanity must burn the earth in order to renew it is as old as humanity itself. Slash-and-burn agriculture or shifting cultivation (known as *jhum* in India; *milpa*, *conuco*, or *roza* in Latin America; *shamba* or *chitemene* in Africa; *rai* in Sweden, etc.[6]) has been practiced since the Neolithic period as a way to fertilize the soil with the ashes of vegetal matter that has gone up in flames. Plants, fungi, microbes, insects, and other animal

2   *Chapter 1*

species are set ablaze in order to give room to the future, to stimulate the growth to come. On this view with thousands of ramifications, the world and life itself are constituted in and by fire, including, among other things, the practices of burning, or "fire-fallow cultivation," and whatever is cultivated on burnt grounds. The more and more frequent forest fires ravaging a warming planet with drier climates and monoculture tree plantations extend the phenomenon of slash-and-burn agriculture beyond what is humanly intended. No one believes that the green phoenix[7] rising from the ashes of flaming biomass would be eternal. But everyone thinks and acts as though the series of resurrections it heralds would never come to an end. Nothing could be further from the truth. Land degradation soon depletes the soil of nutrients necessary for plant growth.[8] It is not only that the present is sacrificed for the sake of the future; the longer-term future is placed on the altar of the shorter-term one.

The phoenix complex is predicated on hope—the hope that death will not have the final word, that life and its slow-burning fires will resume in the ashes of past existence, that the earth and plants will stay fecund. But it is a hope that drives on a spiral of hopelessness (it is not by chance that, at the bottom of Pandora's box, there was hope, among the other evils the box contained). With every twist, it becomes less and less objectively justifiable, and yet its strength is undiminished. The road to hell is paved with good intentions, and the road to environmental destruction is paved with hope, which is shaped like a phoenix. In various languages, there is a saying, "Hope dies last."[9] We should hear the truth of this expression in a literal key: hope will have buried all of us along with a liveable planet before it, itself, dies out. It would have been better (more honest, more constructive) to adopt a stance of absolute hopelessness, not of a paralyzing variety but of a translucent kind that works as an antidote against the surfeit of self-deception. Such hopelessness could finally prompt us to care for the world, irrecoverable in any future iteration of expected growth. It could prompt us to care, if our hands and minds were not tied by the millennial bonds of the phoenix complex. And if someone dares write a utopian treatise for the twenty-first century, then an appropriate title for it would be (*contra* Bloch) *The Nonprinciple of Hopelessness*.

3   *The Phoenix Complex*

But what, exactly, is the phoenix complex? That no univocal definition of the term is possible is indicated by the word *complex*, which *per definitionem* eludes definitions. A mix of affects, ideas, images, and associations, it retains an *effective identity*, bolstering the claim to a widespread, generalizable (if not universalizable), and rapidly self-propagating, reproducible, stable *and* highly mobile mode of thinking and associated practices.

Before Bachelard, Sigmund Freud introduced the Oedipus complex in his 1899 *The Interpretation of Dreams* and further developed it in, among other books, *Totem and Taboo*. Psychoanalytically explained, a complex is a network of cathexes, of the bound quanta of libidinal energy that form a recognizable pattern of dreaming, feeling, thinking, and relating to oneself, to others, and to the world. As Freud puts it, emphasizing the affective component, "In the case of a psychical complex which has come under the influence of the censorship imposed by resistance, the *affects* are the constituent which is least influenced and which alone can give us a pointer as to how we should fill in the missing thoughts."[10] And, still prior to Freud, Baruch Spinoza gave us hints as to the formation of a complex in the fifth part of his *Ethics*, where he postulated that "the greater the number of other images with which an image is associated, the more often it springs to life [*quo imago aliqua pluribus aliis iuncta est, eo saepius viget*]" (V.xiii).[11] The image of the phoenix boasts a wealth of such associations, which is why it not only frequently springs to life but also outlines the contours of that which we think of in connection with life and, by elision, with death.

Arrested, repressed, or pent-up affects form the grid of a complex in a manner similar to the conceptual grid of the schemata in Kant's philosophy. No longer identifiable in their incipient form, myths that used to express, obliquely, these repressed libidinal forces (the myths of Oedipus, of Electra, of Prometheus, or of the phoenix) dissolve into the fabric of culture and the psyche. As myths shed their narrative identity, their power and effectiveness do not diminish; on the contrary, their hold on us, as well as on countless generations before and after us, grows stronger.[12] The reproducibility of any complex, its resurfacing with each new generation, lends it the characteristics of a psychocultural phoenix. So much so that we might say that the phoenix

4   *Chapter 1*

complex is the complex of the complex, the apparatus (*dispositif*) by means of which every complex works, sets itself to work, or, even prior to that, is prepared for being put to work across temporal and spatial divides.

In contrast to the other protagonists of fire complexes, the phoenix is not a human, but a mythic bird. Its speciation and sexuation (which is—let us admit it already—highly unstable and multifarious, weaving together divine elements, animal and plant species, as well as male, female, and asexual specimens, while being inscribed in the phallic frame of masculine desire[13]) are the likely reasons for its relative obscurity, at least in Bachelard's oeuvre, compared to Prometheus and Empedocles. Whereas Prometheus stole fire from the gods and, with this theft, gave rise to technique, the phoenix, in an act of autocombustion, paves the way to life's regeneration. Thus, we are faced with technology, on the one hand, and nature, on the other. But fire is kindled in each of these "hands" or wings that are hard to keep apart, since life is not without its techniques (its mechanics and machinations), and technology is not without its reproductive capacities.

A figuration of nonhuman nature, the phoenix is a singular universal. The earliest cultural documents, where the creature is mentioned, starting with the Egyptian story of the bird *bennu* who is an incarnation of Atum, the ancient god of Heliopolis,[14] announce that the phoenix is so rare as to be one of a kind. Sixth-century Spanish theologian Isidore of Seville relates that "in the entire world, the phoenix is singular and unique [*sit in toto orbe singularis et unica*]." "The Arabs," he continues, "call someone singular a phoenix [*singularem 'phoenicem' vocant*]" (*Etymol.* 12.7.22). That is how singularity universalizes itself: it translates the proper name of a species into a common name, the word for singularity as such.

The phoenix is a species of one, as the Neoplatonist Porphyry argues in his commentary on Aristotle's *Categories*: "The bird species phoenix is not said to belong to several things differing in number, if indeed only one phoenix ever comes to be. If it is said of several things, they differ by succession [*diadochē*], not in number."[15] Isidore probably draws on third-century North African author Lactantius, who similarly highlights the uniqueness of the bird, inscribing her in the feminine: "*unica phoenix*" (*De ave phoenice*

31). Ambrose, the fourth-century Bishop of Milan, likewise considers the phoenix to be "one sole bird [*avem unicam*] not allowed to perish" (*Exaemeron* 5.23.79).

It is, furthermore, the singularity of the phoenix that permits her, him, or it to stand in the place of the universal, representing the whole of nature. The universalization of the singular proceeds along three paths.

The *first path* depends on the erasure of boundaries between different classes or types of beings in conventional systems of classification. Although the phoenix is a bird, the origins of its name are rather murky. Lactantius indicates that the territory of ancient Phoenicia (present-day Lebanon) shares its name with the phoenix and that, moreover, date palm (*Phoenix dactylifera*) is so called because the phoenix must die in a nest built on that tree.[16] "The aged bird," he writes, "directs her swift flight to Assyria, upon which Venus herself bestowed the name Phoenicia [*Phoenices nomen cui dedit ipsa Venus*]" and "chooses a palm tree with the top towering high in the air, a tree which is so named thanks to the bird [*sublimem vertice palmam, quae gratum Phoenix ex ave nomen habet*]" (*De ave phoenice* 65–70). Two centuries prior to Lactantius, Roman philosopher Pliny the Elder, on the contrary, deduces the name of the bird from the tree: "The bird phoenix, who receives his name from a palm tree, dies together with it and is reborn of itself [*phoenice ave, quae putatur ex huius palmae argumento nomen accepisse, intermori ac renasci ex se ipsa*]" (*Historia naturalis* 13.ix.42). What is striking in Pliny's description is that the tree must die together (*intermorior*) with the bird who bears its name; more effectively than this very name, it is a shared death (intermortality, as we may baptize it in Latinized English) that succeeds in blurring the boundaries between the representatives of vegetal and animal kingdoms. In Fragment 3 of his *De natura*, third-century Pope Dionysius of Alexandria goes so far as to claim, in the spirit of catachrestic conceptual translation we have already detected in Isidore of Seville, that the appellation *phoenix* is a fitting one for all "long-lived creatures, be they animals or plants [*ta de makrobiōtata zōa te kai phyta*]" (Eusebius, *Praep. Evang.* 14.25.4).

From this brief sampling of classical sources, it becomes apparent that, despite its singularity, the phoenix participates in heterogeneous regions of existence: plant and animal worlds, the sun and other astronomic entities such as the comets, the land of the creature's birth or death, dry high ground (*Benben*) and the watery abyss (*Nu*),[17] and the divine realm, from the Egyptian god Atum to Jesus of Nazareth, which explains the intense interest of early Christians in this symbol of resurrection. The indeterminacy of classical mentions of the phoenix is not a token of their failure to delineate its sense better, more clearly;[18] such indeterminacy is faithful to the central and overarching role prepared for the phoenix in the imagination of nature. The name also has a contribution to make here: whether common or proper, it is already a juncture of the singular and the universal, of a unique being so named or so designated and all other beings bearing the same appellation. As it names someone or something utterly singular, one of a kind, *phoenix* initially muddles the difference between proper and common names and goes on to level distinctions between types of beings, while preserving its own singularity. Out of this essential, irreducible confusion, it spreads out to all of nature and beyond—to supranatural being, the divine.

The *second path* to the universalization of the singular intersects with the first and activates the operations of synecdoche. In rhetoric, *synecdoche* is a figure of speech, through which a part represents the whole and, vice versa, the whole is condensed into one of its parts. Via a synecdoche, the phoenix does not gradually encroach on domains outside its own, but, as an exception to the general order of things, momentarily, in the bright flash of self-incineration, stands in for all organic being and even the inorganic elements. With some classical authors convinced that the phoenix is an actually existing creature, others persuaded that it is a figment of human imagination, and others still affirming its rarity and *probable* existence, the phoenix hovers between reality and fiction, something that grants it the privilege of a representative part, achieved, precisely, by its subtraction from the whole it represents. Throughout, the exceptionality of the phoenix enables synecdochic exchanges.

In a work by fourth-century Latin poet Claudian, the phoenix is a singular witness to the whole history of being: "You have seen everything that has ever been; you testify to the passing and turning of the ages [*vidisti quodcumque fuit; te saecula teste cuncta revolvuntur*]" (*Carmina minora* 27.104–105). In his *De carnis resurrectione*, second-century Christian author Tertullian develops a complex synecdochic economy, where the whole is gathered in a part and a part manifests the whole with regard to the phoenix: "If the whole world faintly figures resurrection [*Si parum universitas resurrectionem figurat*] and if, moreover, there is no other such sign as this . . . , then take a most complete and unassailable symbol of our hope . . . I refer to the bird, which is peculiar to the East and famous for its singularity [*de singularitate famosum*], marvelous for its posthumous life, renewed from voluntary death" (13.1–6). While all of creation is a poorly perceived sign of resurrection, the phoenix is a glaring sign, a spectacular part that, jutting out from the rest, represents the whole.[19]

In the synecdoche of the phoenix and nature, the world or the universe, which Tertullian designates with the Latin *universitas*, is, like the mythic bird, one of a kind. And, also like the phoenix, it is periodically reborn from the ashes that remain after its incineration. The difference between the organic and the inorganic domains is flattened by fire: the fire of life itself, shooting off myriads of sparks that are the living, who engender similar new sparks; the cosmic fire of the sun and of other celestial bodies that enlivens and brings everything to appearance; and the inner fire of the earth, taking care of the gestation of metals in their ores and of the volcanic formation of mountain ranges. Heraclitan fire is everything that exists as well as the medium of exchange of the singular for the universal and of the universal for the singular: of death for a new life. The faint and inherently ambivalent figuration of the world—the world as a figure at once for itself and for something other than itself, namely for itself *othered*, refreshed, reborn—comes into visibility in the synecdochic light cast by the flames that consume the aged body of the phoenix.

Another dimension of the phoenix–nature synecdoche is epistemological, rather than *stricto sensu* ontological. In his study *De natura animalium*, the second-century Roman author Claudius Aelianus praises the phoenix's exceptional wisdom, astute mathematical skill and geographical knowledge. "The phoenix," writes Aelianus, "knows how to count five hundred years without the aid of arithmetic, since it is the disciple of all-wise nature [*mathētai phuseōs tēs sophōtatēs ontes*], so that it has no need of fingers or anything else to aid it in the understanding of numbers" (6.58). The bird

8 *Chapter 1*

also knows where Egypt is situated and uses this knowledge to transport its predecessor's remains for burial in Heliopolis. While, as Aelianus emphasizes, humans (priests and scientists alike) bicker about the appropriate methods for counting years and while prized human wisdom deals with such things as "the affairs of the market, armaments, and other schemes of human mutual undoing [*ta agoraia kai ta enoplia kai tas allas tōn antrhōpōn eis allēlous te kai kat allēlōn epiboulas epoumen sopha*]" (6.58), the phoenix is imbued with the knowledge of nature as the embodiment of nature's own self-knowledge. The closest "disciple" of nature, the phoenix is a part of the whole, concentrating in itself the self-relation of that whole.

The epistemological facets of the phoenix–nature synecdoche contribute to the dismantling of the distinction between reality and fiction. There is no need to be "astonished" with the inclusion of the phoenix in serious naturalistic and historiographic works by the likes of Pliny the Elder, Tacitus, or Gaius Julius Solinus.[20] As a part of the whole it expresses, the phoenix both exists and doesn't exist in actuality, a symbolic supplement of the totality, which does not come into being as the totality that it is before this event of supplementation. If the phoenix's presence among crocodiles and eagles and oysters is unusual, it is not so due to the creature's purely invented, fantastic character but due to the phoenix's special status vis-à-vis nature, compared to other creatures. It is a part that stands apart from the rest and, thanks to this apartness, is able to reflect the whole.

The *third path* to universalizing the singular traverses the terrain of reproducibility, repeatability, and replaceability. Lactantius conveys many of the promises and ambiguities latent in the self-reproduction of the phoenix, in her replacement by herself as other to herself, female and male: "She is her own offspring, her father and her heir [*Ipsa sibi proles, suus est pater et suus haeres*]. . . . The same indeed, but not the same; the very one, yet not the one [*Ipsa quidem, sed non eadem, quia et ipsa, nec ipsa est*]" (*De ave phoenice* 165–170). With these words, Lactantius echoes Tertullian, who notes that, reborn, the phoenix is "once more where just now there was none; once more himself, but just now out of existence; another, yet the same [*iterum phoenix ubi nemo iam, iterum ipse qui non iam, alius idem*]" (*De carnis resurrectione* 13.8–9).

9   *The Phoenix Complex*

The confluence of sameness and otherness in a flaming reincarnation is the crux of the phoenix complex as far as its environmental and philosophical dimensions are concerned. The body and the life of the phoenix are, despite their uniqueness and inimitability, replaceable—by no one but the phoenix her-, him-, or itself. If there is neither time nor a good reason to mourn the loss of a weary life ebbing away from the aging bird, that is because self-replacement in the other, who is and is not the old self, is assured. The gap between different iterations of the same existence ("once more where just now there was none") is a minor interval illuminated, scorched, and immediately hidden, swept under the rug of being by the powers of fire. Generations upon generations of living (and dying) creatures are understood on the basis of this same otherness: the next generation is both next and not next; this one is and is not the preceding one. "Once more" existence recomposes itself, replacing itself by itself as other. That is what comes next, if it indeed comes.

Given the identification of the phoenix with the whole of existence (in particular, with the whole of nature), its recovery from the clutches of death no longer belongs squarely to the realm of the fantastic; this event comes to describe, instead, our millennia-old relation to and representation of nature's reproduction or self-reproduction. In the best of scenarios, when its loss is not altogether ignored, biological life is mournable only when it is not replaced, or, rather, not replaceable, by itself as other to itself. The psychological weight of mass extinction balances on (or falls with) the irreplaceability of the lost species. Yet, even here, mourned irreplaceability is diluted and reintegrated into the logic of the phoenix complex via suggestions to create genetic databanks (in the case of plants, seed archives), the DNA archives of endangered species that can be resurrected from the stored blueprint of their basic makeup at will. The classification of biofuels—for instance, ethanol, distilled from sugar cane, or biodiesel, derived from soybean oil—as renewable sources of energy alongside solar, hydro, and other elemental energy alternatives is the phoenix complex at its purest, seeing that the reproducibility (*renewability*) of the burnt elevates this mode of energy production to an ideal environmental practice.[21]

From Plato to twentieth-century French Jewish author Emmanuel Levinas, philosophers, too, have trodden the third path toward the

10   *Chapter 1*

universalization of the singular so frequently that it has, by now, become a metaphysical highway of sorts.[22] According to the philosophical recipe whether directly or indirectly inspired by the tale of the phoenix, the unique can be replaced by itself as other to itself by means of either or both biological and cultural reproductions. Seeking the infinity that dwells in finitude, as the word *infinite* already intimates, philosophers tease out that in a living being which temporally, conceptually, physically, or psychically exceeds this very being, the excess granting it the quality of aliveness in the first place. From the speech of Diotima, which Socrates reports in Plato's *Symposium* (208a-b), to Levinas's notion of fecundity and ethical substitution, the "mechanics" of overcoming finitude and mortality have been, for all intents and purposes, unchanged. In keeping with the phoenix's spectacular resurrection and the cunning of reason it encapsulates, everything finite keeps itself by letting go of itself, by losing its identity and recovering what has been lost in a new version of the same existence, "another, yet the same."

*

At this point, I am obliged to interrupt the relatively smooth expository flow of the phoenix complex so as to consider an issue that, apparently secondary, needs to be addressed from very early on, because it will be the touchstone of subsequent discussions. The issue is that of sexual difference.[23] Lactantius is one of a handful of classical authors who writes about the phoenix in the feminine. Earlier still, first-century CE Roman geographer Pomponius Mela observes that the phoenix is "always unique," *semper unica* (the adjective in the feminine), and that she "is not conceived by copulation nor born through parturition [*non enim coitu concipitur partuve generatur*]" (*De chorographia* 3.72). This qualification plainly presages the immaculate conception of Jesus, but it also raises the question: Why should the bird be male or female if it does not reproduce by sexual means? How does the gendered adjective in the Latin assertion of the phoenix's absolute uniqueness both contradict and intensify that very assertion?

The thread of sexual difference is tied in a knot with those of mortality and individuation. The asexual reproduction of organisms by cell division renders them virtually immortal and less individuated than those that employ

11 *The Phoenix Complex*

sexual reproduction; the awareness of an impending death bestows on us the most intense, painful individuality and, drawing attention to the body and its finitude, puts us face-to-face with the reality of sexual difference; individuality as a dialectical achievement requires a negation of a simple identity, the negation that mimics the nullifying effects of death and confronts us with another sex (or with other sexes). In the story of the phoenix, the three threads in this conceptual knot are both present and absent, affirmed and denied, acknowledged and repudiated: the phoenix is both mortal and immortal, unique to the point of being a *she* and (asexually) reproducible, the same and the other. The technical psychoanalytic word for the simultaneous acknowledgment and repudiation of something is *disavowal*.

By dint of disavowal, then, the phoenix complex is put to work, at the same time affirming and denying death, sexual difference, and individuality. It does so on the largest scale imaginable, since the phoenix is a synecdoche for nature. In our deeply ingrained attitudes toward the worlds of plants, animals, and bacteria, and to the milieus of the earth, the atmosphere, and the oceans, we disavow the finitude, individual uniqueness, and sexual differences of actors in the ecological drama. Lulled by the cadences of natural cycles, long since fatefully disrupted, extended, or contracted, thanks to the artefacts and by-products of human industry—the cycles that include those of birth and death—we deem existence invariably reproducible either in itself or in the other. Everything happens as though death did not have the final word at the levels of the genes, the ecosystems, and the elements that are also supposed to "regenerate." It is this *as though*, a fiction we keep telling ourselves without the least awareness of reproducing *it* at the expense of the world, that provides the essential ingredient for the disavowal that sets the phoenix complex to work.

Since Greek antiquity, philosophers have singled out two types of reproduction: in oneself and in the other. Hegel only gave these types and their interrelation the crispest expression in his *Philosophy of Nature*. The phoenix, for his part, reproduces himself in himself as in the other and in the other as in himself, not mediating but compressing the extremes of sameness and otherness, as well as life and death, into each another. Refracted through the Hegelian prism, such reproduction is colored in distinctly vegetal hues.

12   *Chapter 1*

According to Hegel, in the world of plants, "The process of formation and of reproduction of the *singular* individual in this way coincides with the process of the genus and is a perennial production of new individuals."[24] The individual and the genus are immediately one, as they are when it comes to the phoenix. The life of plants is their constant rebirth, their survival of themselves as others and of others as themselves. Following from this is an equally constant reinvention of nature, of *phusis* or *natura* as the overall movement of burgeoning-birthing. A perennial renaturing of nature, perhaps. Magnified and reprojected onto biological existence in general, vegetal "perennial production" yields a model for the resurrection of the biosphere from the ashes, to which it has been reduced.[25] The phoenix is always green.

Not by accident, the phoenix is reinstated in her vegetal incarnation. The synecdoche plant–nature, upon which I have commented elsewhere,[26] mirrors the synecdoche phoenix–nature. And there is more: the temporary erasure of individuality and sexual difference allows for the elimination of the third thread that invariably accompanies them, namely mortality. But the dismissal of sexual difference is bound to fail. Has this difference not initially arisen in the kingdom of plants that have both sexual and asexual methods of reproduction at their disposal? Doesn't the indeterminacy of vegetal sexuation, also evident in the figure of the phoenix, apply not only to the question *Which sex is it?* but also, and above all, to the question *Does it have a sex at all?*

The indeterminacy of sexual difference in plants and the phoenix alike points toward a similar equivocation with respect to their individuation and finitude. In sexual reproduction, some of the main protagonists are seeds or the seed, straddling the divide between plant and animal classes of being. (See the first path toward the universalization of the singular.) Soon after noting that the phoenix is utterly unique, Ambrose goes on to say that it "reproduces itself from its own seed [*resurgentem eam sui semine*]" (*Exaemeron* 5.23.79). The Latin *sēmen* can mean plant seeds as much as semen. In other versions of the myth, the rebirth of the phoenix is made possible by the fire of the sun that symbolizes the male side of the sexual relation. Twelfth-century Byzantine poet Johannes Tzetzes writes that the phoenix "builds its nest of delightful smell on trees / And when it dies, is born again as a worm

13 *The Phoenix Complex*

from that tree / And then is nourished by the heat of the sun [*thalpomenos hēliō*] and turns into a phoenix once again" (*Chiliad* 5.390–393).[27] Being born again from the tree that has served as its last habitat, the phoenix is also nourished in the manner of plants by solar energy that substitutes the flames, in which the bird is reborn in keeping with the widely known storyline. With its belonging to the plant or animal kingdom rendered more indeterminate than ever before, the individuation of the phoenix is also unfixed.

The ambiguity that envelops the phoenix's finitude complements the indeterminacy of its sexuation and individuation. While some depict the rebirth of the new phoenix from the ashes of the old, other authors, such as Tzetzes (but also Pliny the Elder and first-century CE Roman historian Tacitus), stress her resurrection through the spontaneous generation of a single worm or of maggots from her dead flesh. (The relative oblivion, to which the latter narratives have been subjected, is yet another symptom of the operations of the phoenix complex.) Be this as it may, a place of dwelling, a tomb, and a womb for renewed existence converge on the nest, which the ageing bird builds for herself at the end of her long life. Second-century CE Greek poet Dionysius Periegetes, notes that the phoenix "makes itself a pyre for death or a nest for life [*puran tina tēs teleutēs hē kalian suntithēsi tēs zōēs*]" (*De aucupio* 1.32). Sixth-century Gallo-Roman historian Gregory of Tours writes that the phoenix "builds for itself its nest or grave [*construit sibi seu nidum sive sepulchrum*]" (*De curso stellarum ratio* 12).

Confusion about the receptacle for life or for death further escalates when Tacitus treats it as an actual womb, from which the young phoenix will emerge. In this rendition of the myth, the phoenix "builds a nest in his own land and then pours forth his genital force into the nest, from which the fetus arises [*suis in terris struere nidum eique vim genitalem adfundere, ex qua fetum oriri*]" (*Annals* 6.28). The vital fluid (*vis genitalis*, i.e., the semen) reveals that the phoenix is male, but, more interestingly, Tacitus is evoking a situation, in which the seed of an animal impregnates a feminized vegetal structure that is the nest. With the addition of the sun, which Tzetzes endows with a fiery and phallic function, or of the lightning that strikes the old phoenix with its "life-giving dart" in Claudian (*Carmina minora* 27.57–60), impersonal

14   *Chapter 1*

environmental forces and objects participate in the bird's reproduction on the suspended edge of life and death.

The crux of the matter is that disparate accounts of the phoenix's sexuation, life, death, and individual attributes do not (only) contingently clash with one another owing to the heterogeneous traditions and historical strata they belong to, from the Egyptian *bennu* and the earliest extant Coptic text on the phoenix to classical and late antiquities. Rather, the inconsistency of these accounts is an effect of the equivocal triple knot, tied in the figure of the mythic bird, who is both mortal and immortal; individuated to the point of absolute uniqueness and utterly generic; male, female, and sexless. By means of the synecdoche, in which the phoenix relates to all existence as a part that condenses the whole, the equivocations (three in one and one in three) reflect on *us*—on our relation to the outside world and to ourselves. Our hitherto undiagnosed phoenix complex does not permit us to be at a safe distance from the plants, the earth, and the atmosphere consumed by the flames. In them and as them, we, too, are burning, alongside the past and the future that are not ours. We, too, are the phoenix.

*

Already in Heraclitus, fire is the element of transformation. *Puros tropai*, the turns or turnings of fire, mentioned in Fragment 31, are the revolutions of becoming, through which every element is eventually sifted. Fire's turns or turnings, in their turn, should make sense in the light of Fragment 30, which speaks of "fire everlasting, kindling in measures and going out in measures [*pur aeizōon, aptomenon metra kai aposbennumenon metra*]."[28] The phoenix is, on this view, a spark of cosmic fire, which, on an exceptional basis, makes fire's turnings in general phenomenally accessible and which, in the spectacular display of its rebirth, hypostatizes the passage from going out in measures to kindling in measures.[29] The measured extinguishing and reigniting of her life testify to the ever-living (*aeizōon*) nature of the fire she seizes by delivering herself to it: the fire of vitality, infinite across its finite instantiations, infinitely self-regenerating past the term of each living being and its milieu. And, because the microcosm and the macrocosm are the mirror images of one another, the periodic lighting up and dimming down of the world's ensouled body would be transposed onto our own bodies and lives, their fires not to be snuffed out once and for all.

The transformation of the phoenix in fire, or with the help of the fire released by the sun or by lightning, is the passage from a threadbare life through death to a fresh life. His death is, far from the end, a strange detour from life to life, a bright flash, after which the body of the bird is reconstituted not in the yonder of heaven, but here below. It is for this reason that the early Christians, of the likes of Tertullian, saw in the phoenix the answer to the problem of resurrection *in the flesh*.

Claudian expresses the notion of a fiery death as a break and a continuation in the chain of lives with beautiful discursive economy: "The adjoining twinned lives are separated in the exact middle by a burning fire [*geminae confinia vitae exiguo medius discrimine separat ignis*]" (*Carmina minora* 27.70–71). In a breathtaking fashion, he articulates life and death as the varying modalities and intensities of the same fiery life (just as day and night are articulated in the same unity of *one day*, a twenty-four-hour cycle). A brief flaming interval is wedged between the past and the future existences of the phoenix, distinguished from one another by virtue of this wedge. The effacement of death happens, tellingly, before the instant of resurrection, in the very moment of death, construed in terms of an elemental figuration of life in and as fire. Death is rid of its sting to the extent that it is deprived not of its finality but of its being-death: fire, which discriminates between lives, is itself a living, moving, growing, decaying, propagating animal or plant, Heraclitan *pur aeizōon*. The break between two lives is not a break; it is a sublime continuation of life in a different, cosmic or elemental, register, where *puros tropai*, the turnings of fire, turn death inside out into life.

Here is how Lactantius narrates the turnings of fire in the phoenix's death-birth: "Meanwhile her body, by birth-giving death destroyed [*interea corpus genitali morte peremptum*], grows warm, and its heat itself births a flame, and from the ethereal light from afar it conceives fire" (*De ave phoenice* 95–98). A "birth-giving death" is another way of saying the "phoenix complex." This gnostic-sounding formulation implies both forgetting death and reveling in it, living under the illusion of one's immortality and running

16   *Chapter 1*

or flying toward death as toward a gateway to the future. Transfixed by the phoenix, we forget death, because it is nowhere to be found and because it happens all around us, to others, whether human or not. At the same time, and equally mesmerized by the phoenix, we revel in death. When it is contemplated at all, assuaging the fear it awakens in us, it takes the shape of another life, suffused with "ethereal light" and "heat," *calor*, or of a birth into another life, perhaps a better one: refreshed, reinvigorated, more independent inasmuch as self-given.

The blurring of boundaries between distinct kinds of beings and the apparatus of synecdoche that, each in its own way, universalizes the singularity of the phoenix signal that the phoenix's life and death (or nondeath) are life and death *as such*. When contemporary science focuses on genes instead of their carriers, it is still wandering in phoenix's tracks or following her flight paths. Triumph over death at the level of individual bodies translates into an analogous triumph at the level of ecosystems. Although nuclear flames block the rebirth of whatever they touch, there are plenty of ideologically laden attempts nowadays to present Chernobyl as a magnificent phoenix reborn from the nuclear ashes. Isn't plant and animal life making its comeback in the "exclusion zone" abandoned by humans in the aftermath of the disaster? There is, however, very little awareness of the fact that decomposition rates in the most contaminated areas of Chernobyl are exceptionally low, given the near absence of microorganisms and soil invertebrates who carry out this process.[30] With the accumulation of vegetal matter on the forest floor, devastating fires become widespread, leading to new smaller-scale fallouts due to the resuspension of nuclear particles in the air.[31] The death of death, which the phoenix complex celebrates, is manifest in nuclear disasters and environmental devastation. That is why its philosophical investigation is irreducible to a mental exercise, bearing instead on some of the most urgent practical problems and impasses of our times.

Nevertheless, mixing the rejection and the affirmation of rotting, the phoenix complex already contains the resources necessary for working through it, the resources that await those determined to overcome cultural amnesia, itself symptomatic of heavy repression. The dominant variant of the myth involves, no doubt, a fiery death and a nearly immediate resurrection.

This variant itself is not uniform; it accommodates a plethora of reports, ranging from the phoenix entrusting herself to a blaze she did not spark to the phoenix generating fire from his own body or from his body's interactions with wood.

In its earliest (Alexandrian) rendition from the second century CE, *Physiologus* states that the phoenix "sets itself ablaze" or "kindles the fire by itself" (*kai auto to pur anaptei*) (7). Fourth-century Bishop of Salamis Epiphanius of Cyprus specifies in *Ancoratus* how, "with its wings, having beaten its own breast many times, bringing forth fire from its body [*pur hapo tou sōmatos autou propheromenos*], it sets afire the underlying wood" (84.4). Other authors, such as Claudian or Ambrose, postulate an external source of fire, be it the sun or lightning, while later texts depict the kindling of fire by an environmental force in combination with the rapid beating of the phoenix's wings.[32]

Perhaps the most interesting among these is the poetic version presented by sixth-century Christian grammarian Joannes de Gaza in his *Discriptio tabulae mundi*: "clapping its wings [*kinumenōn pterugōn*]," the phoenix who places itself opposite the sun, endeavors "to seize the blaze [*phlogos harpazein*]" of the sunray and to immolate itself of its own accord (2.215–218). A Promethean leitmotif runs through this account of rebellion, in which nature rises up against nature, unleashing a *contranatura* force within *natura*: the phoenix positioned over and against the sun, stealing the solar ray, not clinging to its waning biological vitality, and earning the right to be by renouncing its actual being.[33] But, whereas the theft of fire by Prometheus sets the scene for the technology of artifacts, producing and reproducing the prosthetic supports for a vulnerable and naked existence in this life, the capture of a sunray by the phoenix lifts the curtain on the technology of salvation, producing and reproducing life beyond death.[34] If the basic "Promethean structure" is being-for-death,[35] that is, of adjusting better to the harshness of life with the horizon of absolute finitude, the structure of the phoenix is being-for-deathlessness, or surpassing this horizon and de-absolutizing finitude.

Whatever the source of fire, in an act of self-immolation, the phoenix as synecdoche burns all of nature with the intention of reinvigorating life

18   *Chapter 1*

itself. According to the rules of the game dictated by the phoenix complex, by burning the world, we burn ourselves (unless it is the world that burns itself through us), albeit unintentionally so. A synecdoche is, after all, reversible. This act is what in theology is designated with the Hebrew word *'olah* or the Greek *holokaustos* (the whole burned), an offering, in which the sacrificial victim is entirely consumed by fire. The combustion of fossils is their rebirth, albeit without the singularity of the phoenix, seeing that they are extracted and incinerated en masse, as mass. The life–death relation is also inverted here: between the millions of years it takes to liquify, gasify, or petrify vegetal and animal remains and the eternity of *mass* extinction, there is only a flash of combustion, enlivening our technologies. The life, or the afterlife, of the fossil phoenix is but a punctuation mark between one death and another.[36]

Lurking in those phoenix narratives that emphasize the bird's immolation is the tacit desire to skirt decay. This desire is rooted in two affects, namely impatience and disgust, that are themselves correlated with time and matter. Jointly, they rebuff finitude. Claudian's phoenix realizes that he must prepare his own funeral pyre when his "bright eye grows dim [*decrescit lumen*] and the pupil becomes palsied by the frost of years" and when "his wings, wont to cleave the clouds of heaven, can scarce be raised from the earth" (*Carmina minora* 27.36–40). The decrease of the inner flame of the eye (*decrescit lumen*) calls for reanimation with external fire, the medium of the bird's rebirth. Between decline and renewed vigor, the impatience of the phoenix is double. On the one hand, he is unwilling to accept senescence and the gradual approach of death, which, while still impending, robs the body of its innate powers and capacities. On the other hand, he rejects the slowness of decomposition, impatient with what happens *after* death. Just as the bird's life in its late stages is fast forwarded to its final moment, so a transformation into a new version of its existence that follows is sped up.

The impatience of the phoenix is also ours within the complex that bears her name. With the global growth of an elderly population,[37] already at its highest level ever, geriatric care and cosmetic industries are flourishing in response to the demand to minimize and delay the onset of aging and its visible signs. A more radical demand that often goes under the name of transhumanism is to do away with aging altogether, to discover by scientific means the fountain of eternal youth, a perennial capacity for self-renewal, keeping close to the event of birth, circling back to it over and over again, and being reborn—perhaps, renatured even, reinitiated into the order of life. Stem cell therapy research, with its associated promises and risks, is tending in this direction. What our fantasies of life without senescence and decrepitude ignore is that, to skip aging, to elude death, one needs to die all the faster and more spectacularly, literally to burn oneself up. Some of the lethal side effects of experimental treatments, including stem cell therapy, are subtle reminders of this paradoxical logic.

Impatience with mortality and with the physical changes an aging being experiences goes hand in hand with the desire for unlimited energy. (Entropy is, after all, the energy equivalent of death and dying in a system.) Combustion has a central place in the energy paradigm that, breaking matter down, effects a fast release of heat and light, the fiery element of the phoenix. Energy extraction wrests potentiality from an actual body that contains it, while destroying this body, reducing it, precisely, to a mere discardable container. Similarly, the sublime mechanics of phoenix's reproduction draw the infinite from finite corporeality, abandoned as something superfluous at best and as an obstacle on the path to renewal at worst. Matter and its forms are treated as no more than shells, hiding the valuable kernel of potentiality or infinity. Fire, into which the phoenix, fossils or biodiesel, our entire planet, and we ourselves are thrown, institutes another regime of phenomenality: an unsustainable vision of the future that would repeat, indefinitely, the present.

In addition to impatience with finite time, permeating the phoenix complex is disgust with rotting, with the finitude and materiality of the flesh. At the most immediate, sensory level, the sight and smell of decomposition are obviated in the flaming resurrection of the phoenix. Virtually all classical authors, from Herodotus and Ovid to Clement of Rome, Lactantius, and Ambrose, bring up olfactory issues related to death. The phoenix builds its last nest with aromatic herbs and spices—myrrh and cinnamon, above all. Animal flesh burning with fragrant vegetal materials neutralizes the sensory evidence of death.

Fifth-century Christian poet Dracontius explains that the phoenix ignites the flames of its funeral pyre by beating against the aromatic wood of the nest with its wings: "*et verberat alas / ut flammas adsciscat avis (sic nascitur ignis) / ante alitem ambrosios iam consumpturus odore*" (*Romulea* 10.107–109). The bird gives birth not only to its future self but also to the medium of its rebirth, taking over the signature activity of nature itself. Fire is born from the phoenix (*sic nascitur ignis*) who is consumed by the flames so as to be reborn: the self-annihilating and self-generating circle of its action is closed without a glitch, without as little as a hint of decay, which is the whiff of death.

The fire raging in scented wood and aromatic herbs muffles the smell of decomposition, but that is not the only reason for choosing it as the element of resurrection. As the Hebrew term *'olah*, which I have already mentioned, indicates, flames allow a burnt offering to be lifted up in smoke, to be nearly disencumbered of the heaviness of matter and handed over to the heavens. In a Hegelian vein, we might say that fire is a material element which borders on ideality, opposing and negating, as it does, the materials it is burning in, and yet dependent on these very materials.[38] Wafting from aromatic herbs heated by the sun, fragrant smells move along a similar trajectory, foreshadowing (less violently, perhaps) the ascension of the body and of the spirit.[39] When matter is raised in and as smoke, it is almost dematerialized, and whatever is left of it is reduced to ash, which is next to nothing. The desiccated, minimal remnants of corporeal materiality dispense with the stage of decay and the revulsion that the sensory facets of decomposition tend to provoke.

In the self-generation of the phoenix who will be different from, but also the same as, her predecessor, we may spot a peculiar relation to the notion of identity and to the third path of universalizing the singular. Besides being a visceral reaction to the outcomes of decay, disgust is an affective response to the changing shape of the corpse, slowly tending toward amorphousness. There are two possible solutions to this inexorable alteration: fixing a material form in its present mold or, conversely, speeding up change. Somewhat counterintuitive, the second strategy is the one the phoenix embraces. The idea is to accelerate change so much that it will become barely perceptible, the new incarnation almost instantaneously supplanting the old. Although in the course of a gradual alteration changes are imperceptible as well, a comparison of freeze-frame shots taken at different stages of the process allows us to register them. The fiery metamorphosis of the phoenix, where everything and nothing is altered, does not afford the spectators this opportunity; in the version that has magnetized cultural imagination, little more than a bright flash, as blinding as it is revelatory, separates the old from the new.

If the phoenix is a synecdoche of nature, then the impatience and disgust it betrays are impatience with the slow pace of periodic decay-and-renewal cycles and disgust with the material transformations of the body and the outside world. The phoenix's corpse is the corpse of nature itself; its aging, conflagration, and ashes—the aging, conflagration, and ashes of nature. Furthermore, if the phoenix as the condensation of the whole of nature in a single animal-vegetal-elemental figure is both the same and not the same after its fiery revival, then there is no such thing as nature—only natures, continually dying and being swiftly reborn.

*

Supposing that, as I have already argued, the resources for overcoming the phoenix complex lie hidden in the complex itself, it is necessary to pay close attention to the alternative versions of the story that have been largely forgotten, or that, at least, do not immediately come to mind at the mention of this mythical character. The versions I am referring to welcome decay as a source of spontaneous generation or regeneration of life from the dead body of the phoenix. Here, the flesh itself, even when it is already rotting, is seen as a marvelous brooder of life.

In Ovid's *Metamorphoses*, the old phoenix arranges his aromatic nest, in which he lies down and puts an end to himself: "*se super inponit finitque in odoribus aevum*" (15.400). Then, "a small phoenix is reborn from the body of the father [*corpore de patrio parvum phoenica renasci*]" and, when he is strong enough, carries "his cradle, which is also his father's grave [*pius cunasque suas patriumque sepulcrum*]" to the city of Hyperion to be offered at the altar of the city's temple (15.402–407). The coincidence of one phoenix's grave and another's cradle is poignant in light of the reproductive potential of the dead: it is from the corpse of his predecessor that the small phoenix emanates. The city of Hyperion, to which the young phoenix takes his cradle-grave, is the city of the sun, the ancient Heliopolis (*helios huperion* [the sun up above], is a citation from Homer's *Odyssey* [12.346]) featured in the original exposition by Herodotus. The inference to be made is that the remains of the deceased bird along with the nest are burned on the altar of the sun god already after the offspring is strong enough to make an offering on behalf of the dead ancestor.

Ovid does not elucidate how the rebirth of the phoenix happens, though it definitely does not entail a flaming transformation, which is postponed until the time when the offspring is already mature. Ambrose gives a more detailed account: "When the phoenix realizes that he is coming to the end of his life, he builds himself a casket of incense, myrrh, and other aromatic plants, into which he enters and dies when his time comes [*impleto vitae suae tempore*]. From the moisture proceeding from his flesh, a worm emerges [*De cuius humore carnis vermis exsurgit*]. In the course of time [*Ac processu statuti temporis*], he puts on 'the oarage of his wings' until the bird is restored to his primitive form and appearance" (*Exaemeron* 5.23.79).

I will bring three details of Ambrose's description into sharper relief. First, the passage of time is welcomed, reiterated twice: in relation to the moment of death when "his life's time is completed" (*impleto vitae suae tempore*), and in relation to the metamorphosis of the worm into the phoenix "in due time," or "in the course of time," (*ac processu statuti temporis*). Second, rather than fire, it is the "moisture of his flesh," (*humore carnis*) that generates the worm; instead of the phallic fiery element, it is a watery substance that permits the phoenix to be reborn. There is, consequently, neither impatience nor disgust in Ambrose's account. Third, the generativity of the corpse is in line with what, well into in the Medieval period, was known as *generatio aequivoca* (spontaneous generation). The emergence of maggots or flies from rotting meat is a paradigmatic example of the phenomenon,[40] identified at least since the times of Aristotle and scientifically disproven by Italian naturalist and physician Francesco Redi as late as 1668.[41] By means of *generatio aequivoca*, the reproductive potential of the dead comes to the fore. The miraculous origination of life from a corpse obeys the logic of the phoenix in a different way, no longer allergic to the process of decomposition.

Pomponius Mela sexualizes the putrefaction fluid of the dead phoenix, implicitly equating it with the seminal liquid, with which the bird will inseminate himself in his afterlife. "The phoenix," he writes, "broods on a funeral pile heaped up with different scented plants and decomposes. Next, after congealing from the moisture of its putrefying limbs, the bird conceives herself and is born from herself [*dein putrescentium membrorum tabe concrescens ipsa se concipit atque ex se rursus renascitur*]" (*De chorographia* 3.72–73). A dead body becomes the source and the incubator of new life. By virtue of the phoenix's inscription in the feminine, as well as the mention of brooding, and the bird's postmortem self-insemination and self-conception, sexualization accomplished from the side of death acquires a richly hermaphroditic feel.

Mela's take is rather surprising when examined against Aristotle's theory of spontaneous generation. For the Greek philosopher, sexual difference accounts for the production of an offspring of the same kind (*homogenē*), whereas resorting to spontaneous generation means that the "offspring are not identical with their parents." Aristotle continues in *De generatione animalium*, "Such are the creatures which come into being not as a result of the copulation of living animals, but out of putrescent soil and out of residues" (715a). In principle, as a result of reliance on spontaneous generation, the progeny of the phoenix might not be identical to the predecessor, since this mode of procreation is much more indeterminate and open-ended than sexual reproduction (maggots and flies are born of rotting horse meat, whereas only horses are born of living horses). Nevertheless, Mela mixes the two methods—the sexual and the spontaneous—by sexualizing the phoenix's putrefaction fluid, which plays a lead role in her self-conception. With this, cross-generational identity, threatened by spontaneous reproduction, is secured, albeit at the price of the indeterminate future of fecund remains.[42]

The liquid origins of the phoenix are also conspicuous in a reference by fifth-century CE Egyptian grammarian, Horapollo. In Horapollo's encyclopedic work *Hieroglyphica*, the entry for "How Great Cyclical Renovation Happens," states, "When the phoenix is about to die, he casts himself vehemently upon the ground, and is wounded by the blow, and from the ichor, which flows from the wound, another phoenix is produced [*ex sanie vero (vulneris) defluente, alius gignitur*]" (2.lvii). The self-inflicted wound is a variation on the theme of self-sacrifice, without, however, any recourse to fire. The offspring then arises from the wounded, yet still living, body of the father, with whom he is a contemporary for a short while. The two travel to Heliopolis, where the older phoenix dies at sunrise, which is itself the birth of a new day.[43] The "great cyclical renovation" transpires when the end meets a new beginning, the one flowing into the other. Curiously, in Horapollo's implicit understanding, reproductive capacity (and, perhaps, sexuality *in toto*, though, as described, the process does not involve mating) is a self-inflicted wound, enabling the renewal of the genus at the expense of individual specimens, who fulfill their "end" in this act.

Pliny the Elder points to the bones and marrow of the phoenix's corpse as the place, whence life resprouts: "From its bones and marrow is born initially a little worm, before becoming a chick [*Ex ossibus deinde et medullis eius nasci primo ceu vermiculum, inde fieri pullum*]" (*Historia naturalis* 10.ii.4). Decomposition must be already advanced for the bones and their marrow to be laid bare and to give rise to a small worm. Further, the emergence of the young phoenix is quasi-vegetal: she is born from a hard kernel (like that of a fruit) that, in life, is wrapped in soft fleshy tissues. Seldom is the skeletal system seen as essential to anything but the support of a living body or as the remnant of a dead one verging on the inorganic. For Pliny, however, it is the innermost chamber of corporeality, holding the seeds of rejuvenated life.

The subterranean, chthonic, and "humid"[44] current of the phoenix narrative is the repressed underside of the bird's glorious resurrection. This other phoenix does not eschew the slowness of time's passage nor does it exhibit disgust toward a material transformation. As Dutch scholar of world religions Roel van den Broek reminds us, several classical authors were abreast of the existence of the two traditions (of fiery self-renewal and of emanation from a decaying body) and even tried to integrate mutually exclusive scripts in their texts.[45] Notable in this regard are Lactantius, Epiphanius of Cyprus, and the unknown author of the third-century Christian treatise *Didascalia apostolorum*. More than a mere historical curiosity or a contingent finding of intellectual archaeology interested in the myth of the phoenix, the duality in question bespeaks a complex approach to finitude, with the blindingly bright upside and the shadowy underside of its overcoming.

There are sundry cultural, religious, ideological, and phenomenological reasons for the prevalence of the narrative upside over the underside, reasons that explain the notoriety of flaming regeneration and the near oblivion, to which a slow transformation in the course of decomposition has been subject. Obviously, I am extending here my earlier argument on the equivocations of the triple knot (sexuation, individuation, and death) tied in the story of the phoenix. This addendum is important in its own right: it taps into the repressed resources that may be of some use for immanently overcoming an ecologically and intellectually pernicious set of beliefs and practices, that is to say, for working through the phoenix complex. The apocalyptic mood, which is prevalent in contemporary ecological thought on the obverse side of the complex, shows, precisely, the inability or the unwillingness to work through it, acting out its negation instead.

Whereas both traditions concern themselves with the fact and the mechanics of regeneration—of the phoenix and, hence, of nature or natures—they outline divergent means for reaching the same end. The wager of a fiery rebirth is on the ideality of self-substitution; in a slow emergence from a decaying or wounded body, the emphasis is on material metamorphoses. The ideal that the first strategy envisions is realized thanks to the contraction of time and the elimination, or sublimation, of matter in fire. The materiality of the second strategy requires tarrying with (and within) the flow of time, attending to decomposition, to the fluxes and miraculous upshots of decay that, in a variety of forms, circle back to life after the threshold of death has been crossed. Synthetic and, to some extent, syncretistic accounts, marrying strands from the two traditions, are, therefore, tantamount to efforts to reconcile the ideal and the material aspects of survival, reproduction, and rejuvenation.

In the third century CE, such synthetic accounts abounded. In *Didascalia apostolorum*, for instance, the farewell act of a dying phoenix is to "pray facing the Orient and to set itself aflame and to burn up and to become ash [*et succenditur a se ipso et comburitur et fit cinis*]; from the ashes, a worm emerges [*de cinere autem fit vermis*], and this worm grows, transforming into another perfect phoenix" (5.7.14.10–13). Upon depicting how the dead body of the phoenix catches fire due to a combination of the heat spewed

26   *Chapter 1*

from its decomposition and "ethereal light from afar," Lactantius writes that it dissolves into ashes. He continues: "These ashes gather into a pile, as though concentrated by moisture into a mass, and have the effect similar to that of a seed [*quos velut in massam cineres umore coactos conflat; et effectum seminis instar habet*]. Hence, an animal is said to arise, first without limbs, and it is said to be the milky color of a worm. It grows." (*De ave phoenice* 99–103).

This is not a poetic collage, a ragbag of two traditions, vying for the right to represent the death of the phoenix, but their careful harmonization, balancing the ideality and the materiality of regeneration and, indeed, self-regeneration. Take the body ablaze, an iconic image of matter inflamed by the power of spirit. In the context of the phoenix's incineration, Lactantius separates the powers of fire—light and heat—apportioning them to an ethereal and distant source of luminosity, on the one hand, and the very near fount of warmth emanating from the corpse, on the other. Fire itself is divided between the ideal and the material worlds, between a disembodied gleam and a heat-producing body that is a decomposing corpse. The division is a necessary precondition for a union of another kind, one where self-combustion is indistinguishable from kindling by the other. The body is no longer a passive substratum receiving the fire of spirit; it participates in the act of ignition.

Lactantius and other authors working at the uneven seams that suture the two traditions have their finger on the pulse of *the spirit of matter* and *the matter of spirit*, which will, a mere century and a half later, fascinate Augustine and instigate his own thinking. Sustainable regeneration is possible nowhere but at this double crossing, which goes far beyond the bid to sew together heterogeneous literary or theological traditions.

Aside from fire, the phoenix is nourished in its rebirth by water, the moisture that lets cinders coagulate into a mass. In effect, mass is a cipher for matter, the materiality of the remains that, losing their recognizable form, are depersonalized, rendered anonymous. Theirs is not matter devoid of spirit: in the anonymity of a mass, a power of generativity "similar to that of a seed" resides. Chaos and the makings of a novel order merge into a single hylomorphic whole.

27   *The Phoenix Complex*

Preserving the indeterminacy of a seed, which may be the vehicle for vegetal or animal reproduction, Lactantius patiently follows the movement of the phoenix from absolute singularity through anonymous massification to another such singularity. Gradual transitions from a mass of ashes to a seed, a worm without limbs, an egg, and finally a hatchling move at the pace of spirited matter, or, in other words, of materiality imbued with the energies and changing forms of spirit, which it successively gives to itself. Reproductive capacities are not the ideal and idealizing iterations of the same mediated through the genetic code and its transmissions or recombinations; they are dispersed throughout the world, generously allocated to the powers of fire and the sun, moisture and clouds, rotting, a generative mass, a seed. In them, the infinite peers out of the finite otherwise, as the spirit of matter morphing into the matter of spirit, with enough time and patience to undergo a chain of metamorphoses, yet without a guarantee that this chain would not, at some point, break, giving finitude its due.[46]

2 PHILOSOPHY'S THIRD PATH: PLATO/LEVINAS

The problem of life's finitude is a shared root of theological and philosophical thought in the East as much as in the West. Wherever we turn, we find evidence of an irresistible urge to demonstrate that life has meaning despite (but also thanks to) its inevitable end in death. The ruptured continuation of life after the end of a biological life lent itself to thinking in several guises, including reincarnation, the migration of the soul of the deceased to heavenly or hellish regions that are not in this world, and survival in one's progeny or in one's works, the material traces of one's activity.

Reincarnation is the most ecologically sensitive among the options, because it acknowledges the interconnectedness of different forms of life, while providing no certainty that in a subsequent life one would be or remain human. In Jainism, for instance, the soul (*jīva*) "sometimes is born as a worm, as an insect or as an ant" (*Uttarādhyayana Sūtra* 3.4). In Plato's most "eastern" dialogue, *Timaeus*, rebirth depends on one's actions and character in a previous human life: "and the tribe of birds are derived by transformation, growing feathers in place of hair, from men who are harmless [*akakōn andrōn*] but light-minded" (91d). The doctrine of reincarnation forces us to recognize our past or future selves in nonhuman creatures, softening the rigid boundaries set in systems of natural classification. In this sense, the ruptures that mortality represents appear as continuations from the standpoint of life itself, over and above its variegated forms, kinds, and species.

Regardless of the answers they give to the question of finitude, philosophy and theology operate within the conceptual space of the phoenix complex. This axiom holds with respect to biological life and cultural existence, and even, to some extent, erodes the opposition between "nature" and "culture." In particular, philosophy and theology tread the third path toward the universalization of the singular, which I have outlined in connection to the phoenix's reproducibility or replaceability. Except that, in the Judeo-Christian paradigm, this world is replaced with otherworldly regions in the afterlife of heaven or hell, while, according to the philosophical perspective and doctrines of reincarnation, it is the individual who is, within limits, replaceable by that which or the one who issues from her.

A programmatic formulation of replaceability, which is also at the heart of the phoenix complex, surfaces in Plato's *Symposium*, in the middle of teachings on the subject of love, with which Diotima gifts Socrates. Indeed, Socrates reports Diotima's words, replacing *her* within the structure of the dialogue as much as in relation to his own students and listeners.[1] What is the crux of her teaching? Addressing Socrates, she says, "In this way everything mortal is preserved, not by remaining entirely the same forever, which is the mark of the divine, but by leaving behind that which is growing old and passing away something other and new after the kind of the [aging] one [*heteron neon egkataleipein oion auto hēn*]. By this means [*mechanē*], Socrates, what is mortal—the body and everything else—partakes of immortality [*thnēton athanasias metechei*]; but what is immortal does so differently" (208a-b).

In these lines, Diotima sketches out the mechanics of life that lives past its end without pretending to have become either eternal or divine. The term she uses is *mechanē* (device), which is the root of machine, as much as of machination. What is at issue, therefore, is a mechanism for the reproduction of life and a machination, slipping transcendence in the place of immanence, that is, allowing one to live *beyond* the physical and temporal limits of one's biological existence.

The machine for reproducing what is growing old needs fuel: it needs to be powered by something, and, in keeping with the two senses of *mechanē*, this power is also double. On the face of it, everything is moved by the power (and the fire) of love—*L'amor che move il sole e l'altre stelle*, "Love that moves the Sun and other stars," as Dante will put it in the final verse of his *Divine Comedy*. After all, Diotima's entire discourse, as narrated by Socrates, her

30   *Chapter 2*

lover, is on love, and it is ensconced within a larger dialogue on the subject of love, which is Plato's *Symposium*. It turns out, nevertheless, that love is itself in the service of something else; love is powered by yet another force, which is the desire for the kind of immortality that is practically attainable (or, at least, participable) by mortals. Hence Diotima's conclusion: "It is no wonder, then, that everything naturally values its own offspring. This universal zeal and love [*erōs*] is for the sake of immortality" (208b).

Let me indicate, in a rather abbreviated fashion, that the interpretation of *means* in terms of mechanics and machinations befits the phoenix complex, not least because, since antiquity, the accoutrements of the phoenix have been redolent of craftiness, a sinister trick, or an insidious lie. The clearest and the most literal statement to this effect is by Pliny the Elder, who gives, as the first example of medicines that are not trustworthy, "those said to be derived from the ashes and nest of the phoenix [*ex cinere phoenicis nidoque medicinis*], as though, forsooth, its existence were a well ascertained fact, and not altogether a fable [*non fabulosum*]" (*Historia naturalis* 29.viii). Tongue in cheek, he adds, "And then besides, it would be mere mockery to describe remedies that can only return to us once in a thousand years [*inridere est vitam remedia post millensimum annum reditura monstrare*]." Those who push remedies presumably made of phoenix's ashes and nest are charlatans, and, even if they were not, a medicine made of such rare materials as to be obtained every millennium is anything but useful or widely employable. A good dose of charlatanism is also detectable in the complex that borrows its name from the mythical bird: by its means, in which mechanics and machinations merge, it is possible to replace, renew, substitute the living, as though death had no finality about it and as though nothing substantially distinct has happened with the generation of new existents. Such are the roots of our metaphysics and their deleterious effects that reverberate globally today, whether with respect to the environmental crisis or with respect to proposed energy, lifestyle, and other solutions to it.

The mechanics of replacing an aging being with a newer copy of itself operate on the basis of two machinations. First, covered with the fig leaf of wishing to keep its object forever, love appears in the place of desire for immortality on the pretext that the strivings of *eros* are directed toward the other. This is a machination, a scheming maneuver, because such a desire is, in the first and last instances, narcissistic, wishing for the preservation of oneself by means of the other. Second, the other appears in the place of the same as if there were no alterity in the other, as if *this* other were other to otherness itself. Matching the repudiation of my identity is the denial of the otherness of the other who will replace me with a younger version of myself.

The two machinations involve one another, are entwined among themselves and with the concept of transcendence within immanence, a material and ongoing resurrection of the dying or the dead. These machinations do not overlay (and, in overlaying, thwart the normal functioning of) the mechanism of life's reproduction; they are built into the mechanism as its engine, the driving force behind life's reproducibility. And isn't the intended outcome of *mechanē*, which Diotima describes by means of Socrates as her mouthpiece or for which Socrates recruits Diotima as a projection of his own quasi-mystical persona, a third machination, namely the inclusion of what is mortal (*thnēton*) in immortality (*athanasia*)?

Note that the mechanics and machinations of reproducibility and (or as) replaceability are not restricted to humans: according to Diotima, all mortals preserve themselves this way, by letting go of their simple and static self-identity in order to recover themselves in "something other and new" after "their own kind." It is not a matter of tricking the other or telling a lie to oneself, since the *mechanē* of life antedates and is independent of the apparatus of symbolization, of cogitation and speech. What Diotima touches on is the technique of life that works primarily as a technology of salvation, overshadowing the sincerity of love and altruistic self-sacrifice on the side of the human and the power of instinct and evolutionary developments on the side of the other-than-human.

The allegory of the phoenix contains, in a nutshell, the mechanics and machinations of reproduction and replacement: it is a handy rhetorical device (another instance of *mechanē*) demonstrating how a part of nature and life stands in for the whole and how each part is, like the whole, infinitely renewable. We are now in a better position to understand the avowed contradictions in the works of Tertullian and Lactantius, the former writing that the new phoenix is "another, yet the same [*alius idem*]" (*De carnis resur-rectione* 13.9), the latter—that she is "the very one, yet not the one [*et ipsa, nec ipsa est*]" (*De ave phoenice* 170). In line with the second machination, in which the other appears in the place of the same, the phoenix spans the extremes of otherness and sameness. Now, this second machination comes to light without the usual trappings and camouflages, because the first machi-nation, replacing the desire for immortality with love, is absent. The phoenix does not need a sexual partner to reproduce; at most, his sexuality is dispersed among the elements: the warmth and the light of the sun, a thunderbolt, the rain and humidity, the vegetal matter of his nest. Nor does the bird ever meet her offspring, who may be deserving of maternal affection. Far from privative, the absence of love rarefies the veil of machinations, reducing two to one and revealing with greater clarity the mechanism of life's reproduc-ibility and (or as) replaceability.

The phoenix complex juggles sameness and otherness in a relation (with-out relation) forged across the fiery divide. As a result, reproductive activity does not engage with an original and its copy: these categories simply do not apply. Fourth-century Bishop of Verona, Zeno, makes the inapplicability of such aesthetic categories clear in the part of his *Tractatus* devoted to the phoenix: reborn, the phoenix is "not a shadow, but truth, not a likeness but the phoenix itself, not the other that, though better, is still the same as the one before it [*non umbra, sed veritas, non imago, sed phoenix, non alia, sed quamvis melior alia, tamen prior ipsa*]" (*Tractatus* 1.16.9). Zeno of Verona shuns the Platonic notion of ideas, corresponding to the original phoenix, and shadowy appearances that would be derivative from them in the bird's subsequent incarnations. The mechanics of glorious rebirth, holding fresh machinations in store for us (the *machina ex deus* in place of the old *deus ex machina*), hinge on reproducibility without reproduction, an arising in truth, in the light and fire of truth, rather than as a photocopy of the lost original. In this unmediated relation between the same and the other, repeti-tion plays the role of idealization, of maintaining intact the phoenix's *essence*. The one coming after is actually better (*melior*) than—fresher, younger, filled with more vitality—but not an improvement over the predecessor, because it *essentially* remains the same.

33   *Philosophy's Third Path*

In Diotima's speech, the preservation of mortals "not by remaining entirely the same forever" nevertheless presupposes the essential sameness of the reproducing and the reproduced. The genus and the genes are, each time anew, revived in the body of the newborn, who replaces the progenitors as yet another vessel, recipient, or carrier of what has been passed along in the process of reproduction. All significance resides in this deeply concealed essence with its phoenix-like capacities; the carriers are of little consequence by comparison.[2]

While it shares some markers of Platonic ideas, the genetic *eidos* is generative and self-regenerative (rather than ungenerated and entirely static), comprising as it does the ideal blueprint of a being that is the launchpad for actual existence. Letting go of one's own identity, becoming other in one's child, is something of an illusion, when reckoned from the vantage point of eidetic material that is passed on, from a gap between lives, the abyss of death.[3] It is in this sense that the other replaces the one—that is, the one replaces oneself with the other who is not essentially other—without anything either gained or lost, with nothing laudable or mournable. By putting love out of the equation (albeit not the kind of self-love that inheres in the desire for immortality), the phoenix complex and our contemporary nihilism foster the attitude of indifference toward the actual iterations of existence. What it is *not* indifferent toward is the iterability of being, the possibility of calling upon essence to clothe itself in flesh-and-blood once again.

*

The phoenix is a synecdoche of nature; Prometheus is a prototype of technique or technology. There is, for all that and not just on account of the element of fire that unites them, something of the phoenix in Prometheus and something of Prometheus in the phoenix. Nature isn't altogether natural, inasmuch as it is filled with devices, machines and machinations, and, therefore, with technologies, say, of reproduction. In its turn, reproduction itself does not respect the nature/culture divide that is largely in our heads: it may be biological, social, or political, corporeal or spiritual, which is the thesis Diotima defends next. "Those who are pregnant in their souls [*psuchais kuousin*] even more than in their bodies, are pregnant with the kind of offspring which it is fitting for the soul to conceive and to bear. What offspring are these? Discernment and the rest of virtues [*phronēsin te kai tēn allēn aretēn*]" (209a).

Cultural conception and spiritual pregnancy are not metaphoric inventions, as some commentators are apt to believe.[4] To make this argument is to miss the point. Though standing lower or higher on the steps of the ladder of love, those pregnant in the body and in the soul are subject to the same mechanics of a finite being transgressing its spatiotemporal boundaries and overflowing toward infinity by not keeping its self-identity, by generating another. Love (*eros*) is the name of this overflow. The one pregnant in the soul becomes other in the works, which include "a harmonious ordering of cities and households [*poleōn te kai oikēseōn diakosmēsis*]" (209a).[5] *Phronesis* (discernment) and the virtues share the soul's DNA; the works have the eidetic makeup of the psyche. Becoming other in the works is not the moment of alienation that it is in much of modern philosophy. Rather, the works replace and reproduce (reproduce by replacing) the soul with its vision of beauty and the good.

The Platonic soul, too, is at least in part finite, which is why, to preserve itself, it must let go of itself, while leaving behind something or someone other and new after *its* kind. The *mechanē* of life itself functions in the body and in the psyche, with all the machinations and mechanisms of replication themselves replicated, redoubled, speculatively mirroring one another. In a shorthand, we might call these mechanics and machinations *two in one and one in two*.

When Socrates presents himself as the midwife of ideas in *Theaetetus*, he transforms himself into the medium of rebirth, occupying the structural spot of fire (or, at a slower pace, of fecund decomposition) in phoenix narratives. As he announces to his interlocutors that he is the son of a midwife, Phaenarete (the brightness, the phenomenality, the virtuous coming or bringing to light encrypted in this name cannot escape our attention), Socrates proclaims, in the case of yet another identification with a woman that taps into the sexual ambiguity of the phoenix, that he practices "the same art [*tēn autēn technēn*]" (*Theaetetus* 149a) as his mother. To the *mechanē* of life's reproduction and replacement, we must now add the *technē* of its reception, of helping along what is languishing in obscure potentiality to reach the light

35   *Philosophy's Third Path*

of day. More than this potential, however, Socrates stresses the intermediary between the one who gives birth and the birthed, the mediation that is inconspicuously there even when it seems that one is giving birth to oneself, all by oneself. Fire and a midwife are mediators, conduits from one state to another, and both are the representatives of death in life, of the emptying out, minimization, privation of properties, or reduction that is necessary to receive that which, or the one who, is about to be born in all its, her, or his singularity. There is no reproducibility and, or as, replaceability without such reception, which may, to be sure, get out of hand, the emptying out waxing absolute and inflecting with lethal indifference the mechanics of life, be it the life of the body or of the mind.

Centuries after Socrates, Zeno of Verona will contend that the phoenix's offspring is true, neither an image nor a shadow. Socrates' point, though, is that this truth needs to be ascertained in each event of birth: the definitive act of a midwife of ideas is "to discern between a true [offspring] and one that is not so [*to krinein to alēthes te kai mē*]," the latter being a mere "image offspring" (*eidōla tiktein*) (*Theaetetus* 150b). For, when it comes to reproduction, chances are that it would be of images—and not only in the sphere of cultural or psychic life. (Some parents wish more than anything to have children, who are their replicas, recognizable as the physical and behavioral images of themselves.) Provided that machinations are integral to the mechanism, which allows mortals to participate in immortality (in contemporary terms, we might say, "provided that machination is not a machine's bug, but its feature"), the substitutions they are responsible for produce one thing in the image or in the likeness of another. Love is the image of a desire for immortality, itself mediated through beauty that moves through images beyond the image; the other is the image of the same; bodily pregnancy is the image of the soul's reproductive activity, itself yielding either image or true offspring, and so forth. The self-showing of truth, ideally sheltered in the deep reserves of essence, is invariably an appearance, which doesn't preclude the possibility of it being a *mere* appearance.

Socrates views the totality of his philosophical practice as a gynecology of the soul, with a particular specialization in the arts of distinguishing between an image offspring and its true counterpart. That is his unique

36   *Chapter 2*

technē. How do the arts of psychical gynecology tally with the mechanics of life? What is the relation between the Socratic *technē* and the *mechanē* of the finite participating in the infinite?

The Socratic examination of the offspring draws a circle in speech: "We must, in truth, perform the rite of *amphidromia*, going around the offspring in the circle of our speech [*meta de ton tokon ta amphidromia autou ōs alēthōs en kuklō perithrekteon tō logō*]" (*Theaetetus* 160e). *Amphidromia* is, in fact, a ceremony of socially acknowledging and legitimizing the newborn, "a 'walking around' or 'running around' the hearth, or around the child who lay in the hearth, which was the symbolic center of the *oikos* [the dwelling, MM]."[6] During the ceremony, the midwife also had to wash her hands, signaling that the period of pollution linked to childbirth had come to an end for her and for the child's mother.[7]

When he circles the mind's issue in speech, Socrates legitimizes (or not) the ideas (or the images) that have emerged with his assistance. The critical limits of his endeavor, embodied in this circle, signal that his *technē* can do no more than perform further machinations with the machinations built into the *mechanē* of a living (self-reproducing, self-replacing) life. Socrates ultimately verifies, as he moves around the offspring of the soul, that the circle of regeneration has been completed, that the soul has properly reproduced and replaced itself with the other appropriate to it, which is to say, with the same. But his ceremonial circle, like that in the original rite of *amphidromia*, also redraws the path of the phoenix's self-reproduction, to the extent that its center is the hearth and the fire burning there, temporarily replaced, in a ceremonial setting, with the body of the newborn or with the offspring of the soul. A conservative dynamic, where roles and functions were kept constant in the procession of those who occupied them, the renewal of the household with each subsequent generation—the son or the daughter becoming the father or the mother of their daughter or son, as though nothing has changed—replayed the spectacle of the phoenix arising from the ashes. The rejuvenation of *logos*, which encircles an examined idea or image offspring, is homologous with the renewal of the *oikos*.

*

37   *Philosophy's Third Path*

The phoenix is a household and a soul, a body and an order of ideas; writ large, it is also the cosmos in Plato's constellation of texts and, above all, in *Timaeus*. Akin to the phoenix, the cosmos is unique, one of a kind (*monōsin*) (*Timaeus* 31b). It is, moreover, a unique "living being, ensouled and enreasoned [*kosmon zōon empsuchon ennoun*]" (*Timaeus* 30b). A cosmic animal or a cosmic plant, if you will. As such, this living being is "the most beautiful" and "the most perfect," "holding and embracing [*perilabon*] in itself all intelligible living beings" (*Timaeus* 30c). The cosmic phoenix, the phoenix as cosmos, is universal in its singularity and singular in its universality: it embraces in itself all life irrespective of division into kinds and species, while relying on the synecdochic power of *zōon* (a living being).

Egyptian influences, overtly mentioned in *Timaeus*, make it highly likely that, in the shape of *bennu*, the phoenix and her paraphernalia made their way into the Platonic dialogue. In the prefatory part of the text, Critias conveys that the source of cosmological speculations was Solon, who, in turn, imported them to Greece from the district of Sais in the Nile Delta (*Timaeus* 21e). Further, this dialogue includes the first mention of the astronomical interval known as the Sothic period in classical Greece, or the Egyptian Great Year amounting to 1,461 solar years. The noteworthiness of this ostensibly marginal fact is that the Egyptian Great Year is one of the presumed life spans of the phoenix, marking the beginning and the end of a cosmic cycle.[8] Finally, fire is front and center in *Timaeus*, both as the means of humanity's destruction and as the medium of its rejuvenation.

As his Egyptian interlocutor—an elderly priest from the city of Sais—tells Solon, throughout its history humanity has suffered "many and diverse destructions, the greatest of which are by fire and water [*puri men kai hudati megistai*]" (*Timaeus* 22c). These periodic destructions, however, are not total: whatever is left of civilization persists in the absence of written records and collective memory that lend a culture its age. The strange effect of fiery and watery devastation is the rejuvenation of the survivors. Speaking of and to the Greeks, the Egyptian priest says, "You are young in soul, every one of you [*Neoi este, eipein, tas psuchas pantes*]. For, in your soul, you possess not a single belief that is ancient and derived from old tradition, nor one science that is hoary with age" (*Timaeus* 22b-c). It is unclear how Egyptians managed

38   *Chapter 2*

to escape the fate of the rest of humanity and, in this case, of Greece. What is obvious, though, is that renewal and rejuvenation, repeatedly reproducing the psyche as a clean slate, follow the model of a phoenix reborn, young and essentially unchanged, from the ashes of destruction.[9]

The mythic stand-in for the phoenix in the anecdote narrated by the Egyptian priest is Phaethon, the son of Helios, the sun god. After receiving for but a single day the right to drive his father's chariot, Phaethon, unable to control it, crashed into the earth, "burnt up all that was upon the earth and himself perished by a thunderbolt." "That story," the priest continues, "has the fashion of a legend [*muthou*], but the truth of it lies in the occurrence of a shifting [*parallaxis*] of the bodies in the heavens, which move round the earth, and a destruction of all things on the earth by great fire, which recurs at long intervals [*dia makrōn chronōn gignomenē tōn epi gēs puri pollō phthora*]" (*Timaeus* 22c-d). The long intervals at which periodic destruction and renewal recur refer to the epochal changes, accompanied by the appearance, death, and rebirth of the phoenix.[10] Mixing cosmic and political events, the completion of astronomic cycles and of pharaonic or imperial reigns, the phoenix simultaneously symbolizes decline and the ascension that follows it.

But the phoenix (or its mythical substitutes) is not limited to the beginnings and ends of great cycles; rather, the phoenix is a specific condensation of cosmic fire—of cosmos *as* fire. The Chinese counterpart of the Egyptian phoenix, the *fenghuang* bird,[11] is said to have "illuminated the heavens with its flight, producing the luminous Milky Way."[12] The flickering of the cosmic blaze, its "kindling in measures and going out in measures," in the words of Heraclitus, betokens the periodicity of its everlasting life (*aeizōon*) made up of distinct phases. The qualification of the cosmos in *Timaeus* as *zōon empsuchon* (an ensouled creature) thus blends together fire, a living being, and the world.

The rhythmic brightening and dimming of cosmic fire signal the birth, life, death, and rebirth of the cosmic animal or plant. When Timaeus picks up the narrative thread from Critias, he rehashes the main traits of this animal or plant with greater precision in 32d–33a. This portrait consists of three crucial elements. First, the cosmic creature is "perfect and all its parts are perfect [*zōon teleon ek teleōn tōn merōn ein*]." The perfection of the

39   *Philosophy's Third Path*

phoenix is a mainstay of virtually all classical and early Christian accounts. Likewise, the Great Year (not necessarily coinciding with the Sothic period), which is often thought of as the phoenix's life span, is "a perfect number [*periodos . . . teleios*]" (*Republic* 546b).[13] The perfection of the whole and its parts means that all the living beings who constitute the cosmic living being are, themselves, perfect as its constituents. The part–whole relation forged in a synecdoche still holds. Second, *zōon empsuchon* is "one [*hen*], such that there is nothing left behind out of which another similar being could come into existence." The uniqueness of the phoenix, who is peerless in the world, is blown up to cosmic proportions, assuming the form of a totality. Cosmic fire and life are not only prefect and unique but also all-embracing and exhaustive, comprehending all without a remainder. The third feature of the cosmic living being is that it is "not prone to ageing and unailing [*agērōn kai anoson*]." This is where divergences from the myth of the phoenix are at their starkest.

Another way of formulating the third characteristic of *zōon empsuchon* is that it is exempt from the order of time and material decay. Despite the phoenix's aging and weakening at the end of its life cycle, the dominant variants of the myth, moved by impatience with time and disgust with decomposition, dissimulate these phenomena. With instantaneous resurrection, it seems that death did not occur, that nothing changed from one incarnation of the phoenix to the next, that time did not pass, and that life in its continuity was not disrupted. Even those versions of the myth that depict a slow emergence of the young phoenix from the decaying remains of its predecessor put an accent on the identity of the two. When the process of renewal concludes, the changes and metamorphoses that took place along the way are no longer visible and are deemed insubstantial compared to triumphal self-regeneration.

Something that happens, is granted as happening, and is treated as though it has never happened is subject to the psychological (defense) strategy of disavowal, which we have already come across. But there is more to the phoenix complex than disavowal: the noncoincidence between the third feature of the Platonic cosmos and the mythic bird indicates that the phoenix is in an ambiguous position between finite beings, who have the imperfect

40   *Chapter 2*

mechanē of participation in the infinite at their disposal, and the imperturbable nature of eternal divine vitality. This ambiguity must have appealed to early Christian thinkers, who saw in the phoenix a prototype of Christ, himself slotted between human and divine natures, or, in a word, *theandric*.

A different facet of the cosmic *zōon empsuchon* makes it fall short of the freshly generated phoenix, who is not a copy but a true original, as Zeno of Verona argues and as, before him, Socrates hopefully affirms about the child brought into the world on his watch by a pregnant soul. Timaeus conveys that the "cosmos is a copy of something [*kosmon eikona tinos einai*]" and that, moreover, it is a copy of a model (*paradeigma*) envisioned in advance of its actual production (*Timaeus* 29b). In other words, the production of the cosmos, the engendering of a perfect, unique, total, and incorruptible living being, is already a reproduction of the original that is only accessible by inferring it from the image or likeness (*eikona*) at hand. The logic of *mechanē* with its inextricably bound senses of mechanics and machinations returns with a vengeance.[14]

The cosmos need not reproduce itself because of its stable and unitary nature. *And* it does nothing but reproduce, from its very inception, a model for the life within it. The cosmos is, thus, an intermediary between the paradigm of life and the living who are part of it. Although the enormous fiery animal or plant that is the cosmos is unaging and unailing, in the logical chronology of its generation as the likeness of a previously defined paradigm it is both older and younger than itself, coming a distant second to demiurgic design.

Fire, life, and the world are so many reflections, iconic images of the thought that initially envisioned their look, their *eidos*. As a result, the perfection of cosmic *zōon empsuchon* is put in question by the very ideal of perfection it is meant to embody. The periodic destructions of humanity by water and fire and its phoenix-like regeneration, which the Egyptian priest invokes in the beginning of the dialogue, reenact the simultaneous youth and agedness of the world. Egypt occupies the historical and conceptual place of old age vis-à-vis Greece that is incorrigibly young in its soul; in addition to coming first, compared to Greece, within the historical chronology of "great civilizations," Egypt serves as the paradigm, a conceptual model for being

Greek, implemented afresh and unbeknownst to the Greeks themselves in every instance of their rejuvenation.

For the Greek world, for the cultural cosmos of the Hellenic civilization, Egypt is the idea formed prior to its actual production or reproduction. But, beginning with Rome, it was ancient Greek culture that was allotted the role of a model for the subsequent development of Western civilization. A copy became the original. Similarly, in relation to the living beings it comprises, the cosmos undergoes a veritable paradigm shift: an image (*eikona*) of the world as it is drafted in divine ideation (*paradeigma*). In addition, it is also a model for creatures created in its image. "Accordingly," says Timaeus, "seeing that that model [*paradeigma*] is the eternal living creature, he [the demiurge; "the father": *patēr*] set about making this universe, so far as he could, of a like kind" (*Timaeus* 37c-d). But divine intention hits a snag: the creatures of the world are not eternal (*aiōnios*), in contrast to the creature that is the world. Given that "this quality [made] it . . . impossible to attach in its entirety to what is generated, he contrived to make a moving image of eternity [*epinoei kinēton tina aiōnos poiēsai*]" (*Timaeus* 37d).

The "original" contrivance operative in the making (*poiēsis*) of life will be later on replicated in life's mechanics and machinations. It, too, involves a substitution of paradigmatic eternity for its image, of immovable reality for its moving imitation.[15] The moving image of eternity is time, itself expressed through "an eternal image [*aiōnion eikona*]" that is number (*arithmon*) (*Timaeus* 37d). The doubling of eternity is matched by the doubling of images, each bolstering and undermining the other. The contrivance at work in the production of life (which is, from the get-go, life's reproduction) passes, in this way, into the mechanics and machinations of self-regeneration. What is this contrivance's bearing on the phoenix complex?

In the best-known renditions of the phoenix, the preponderate, barely concealed, gnostic or nihilistic sentiments are impatience and disgust taken to the extreme: impatience with time and disgust with matter. My hypothesis is that, with its fiery death-birth, the phoenix momentarily exits the order of time and returns, rejuvenated, thanks to this egress. The phoenix complex aims to recover the paradigm of the world prior to its depiction in an image, albeit by *intensifying* the logic of the image, by compressing the

42   *Chapter 2*

fiery and eternal being of the world in a singular mythic, emblematic, iconic image. This is why the mythology of the phoenix morphs into a complex—a paradigm or a model of relating to the world and to ourselves with the same perennial fears and hopes, sentiments and objectives, as those implanted in the storying of this wonderous creature.

If the phoenix complex contemplates a leap to the state of being prior to the order of time, then, given the entwinement of impatience with disgust in the renowned versions of the myth, the same resolve must apply to matter as well. We ought to remember that a philosophical concept of matter is still absent in Plato; it will not be formulated until Aristotle's reinterpretation of *hulē*, the Greek word for wood and for the woods. Nevertheless, coming into existence, or being born (*genomenon*), according to *Timaeus*, is coming to visibility and to tangibility, becoming open to the senses of vision and touch. The material prerequisites for the becoming of whatever or whoever is born are fire and the earth, responsible for each of the two sensory aspects of a new emergence, respectively, "Drawing the beginning of all from a composite of fire and the earth [*ek puros kai gēs*], god made a body" (*Timaeus* 31b). Lending itself to and opening up the sense and the field of vision, fire is spiritual matter. Available to and inaugurating haptic sense, earth is material matter. Jointly, they anticipate the dance of the spirit of matter and the matter of spirit in Lactantius and Augustine. The composite of both fire and earth is a body, which likewise requires two intermediaries (*mesotēs*) to attain depth, balance, and synergic arrangement, namely water and air (*Timaeus* 32b). This precociously developed elemental dialectic is a prototheory of matter, explaining the production (or reproduction) of cosmic *zōon empsuchon*.

The phoenix's death and birth in fire counters the synthetic cosmogony, which Plato summarizes in the dialogue. There is no dialectic in this event, no synergies of elements, no mediation between the same and the other, birth and death. Which is to say that there is no air and very little water. The spectacle of the phoenix's consumption by and rejuvenation in the flames engages only the sense of vision; indeed, this spectacle is so spectacular that it augurs momentous events, like the birth of Christ, announced, in keeping with certain apocryphal texts, by the appearance of the phoenix on the roof of the temple in Jerusalem.[16] For Plato, a fiery constitution is the prerogative

43   *Philosophy's Third Path*

of divinity, of celestial bodies, such as the stars: "As regard the divine kind, it is made for the most part of fire [*pleistēn idean ek puros*], so that it would have the look [*idein*] of utmost brilliance and beauty" (*Timaeus* 40a). Divine celestial bodies are not pure spirits; they are spiritual matter, the "that out of which" (*ek*) of making nearly overlapping with the look or the idea (*eidos*) of what is made and how. This unbearably bright and beautiful region of being is the one the phoenix inhabits, if only for an instant, in its fiery transformation. There, matter with its earthiness and tangibility is reduced, physically broken down by the flames, and metaphysically bracketed, dropped from the formula of existence. In the grave or the cradle that is its nest, the phoenix gains a new lease on life because it (willingly) dies to the world of matter.

*

To recap, the "third path" of philosophically universalizing the singular has taken us to the *mechanē* of life's reproduction and the *technē* of its knowledge and evaluation. The making of life, its *poiēsis*, harks from philosophy back to mythology, but, insofar as it is philosophically legible, production is already reproduction, with the "technical" aspect—the art of interpretation— doubling as an overarching principle of both *poiēsis* and *mechanē*.

Along the third path we have trodden thus far, the danger of the phoenix complex has shown itself to us in high-resolution images of thought. The phoenix's enlivening flight from time and from matter traverses temporal and material reality. In philosophical jargon, this is the movement of transcendence in immanence. Transformation in fire contracts to a point, a flash, evincing unfathomable acceleration, compared to the much slower metamorphoses of decay narrated in the lesser-known variants of the myth. Combustion reduces matter to ash. And yet, time and matter are not entirely done away with: acceleration is the speeding up of time sequences, while combustion is a material process of rapid oxidation. So, we are not just dealing with an otherworldly tale that has been told since Egyptian, Chinese, Greek, and Latin antiquities and that we keep telling ourselves, usually without knowing what we are doing. Despite the mythical provenance of the phoenix, this unique creature illuminates *this* world and ourselves, to say nothing of our relation to the world and to ourselves. The many, often cacophonous, voices that have narrated the story of the phoenix, occasionally even neglecting to mention her by name, join in a chorus when it comes to swearing by the infinity of the finite, the overcoming of the world in the world, of matter in matter, of time in time.

The problem of transcendence within immanence is one of the overarching themes in the philosophy of Jewish French twentieth-century thinker, Emmanuel Levinas.[17] Although his name has become nearly synonymous with the ethics of alterity, couched in terms of the asymmetrical relation of the I to the other, Levinas has a fair bit to say on the mechanics of life's reproduction, in light of which this relation itself appears drastically altered. His magnum opus, *Totality and Infinity*, moves back in its conclusion from the ethical philosophy of an encounter with the other who is a stranger to a philosophy of biological reproduction, of fecundity that ensures the infinity of finite time.[18] Levinas describes "total transcendence" as "the transcendence of trans-substantiation," where "the I is, in the child, an other [*le moi est, dans l'enfant, un autre*]."[19] Bracketing the Eucharistic overtones of transubstantiation, the odd mechanics of such transcendence is that the I is, or becomes, the other, bridging a gap that is otherwise unbridgeable in all of Levinas's philosophy. It is the manner of this becoming other that should occupy us here, even as it brings back to mind the main turning points in the phoenix narratives.

The instability of terms in the relation of paternity (we will have something to say on the subject of gendering this relation in a moment) that is concretized in fecundity gives us the first telltale sign of a carryover from the phoenix complex. "The diverse forms Proteus assumes do not liberate him from his identity," Levinas writes. "In fecundity the tedium of this repetition ceases; the I is other and young [*le moi est autre et jeune*], yet ipseity that ascribed to it its meaning and its orientation in being is not lost in this renouncement of self. Fecundity continues history without producing old age."[20] The words of Tertullian and Lactantius resonate in this discussion of how ipseity is preserved in the other, in the son who is and is not the father; the phoenix's offspring, too, is "another, yet the same" (*De carnis resurrectione* 13.8–9) and "the same indeed, but not the same [*ipsa quidem, sed non eadem*]" (*De ave phoenice* 169). Even the Latin-derived ipseity (the French

45   *Philosophy's Third Path*

ipséité) literally echoes the Latin authors who grappled with the figure of the phoenix.

Another sign that Levinas's thoughts on fecundity fall within the purview of the phoenix complex is his treatment of death as a mere interval, punctuating the ever-recommencing chain of infinite time or infinite being. "Infinite being is produced as times, that is, in several times across the dead time that separates the father from the son [*à travers le temps mort qui sépare le père du fils*]. . . . The nothingness of the interval—a dead time—is the production of infinity [*Le néant de l'intervalle—un temps mort—est la production de l'infini*]. Resurrection constitutes the principal event of time."[21]

Rather than finitude and death, the negation of death in resurrection, the infinite surpassing of dead time, makes time what it is. Death itself is a hiccup in the temporal order, its nothingness opening up an interval across which the self-regenerative movement of generations resumes. Replacing fire with death, or, more precisely, with dead time, Levinas unintentionally takes a page from Claudian's book, especially the latter's phrase, "The adjoining twinned lives are separated in the exact middle by a burning fire [*geminae confinia vitae exiguo medius discrimine separat ignis*]" (*Carmina minora* 27.70–71). Separation unites (as opposed to the "absolute separation" between the I and the other, with which *Totality and Infinity* commences), not interfering with but actually strengthening the adjoining arrangement of the father's and the son's lives. The interval is necessary—if not to the success then to the very possibility of a leap across the dead time that stretches between the two. It is there to delimit times, to outline the ends and the beginnings of eras or generations, and, consequently, to be overcome.

Stubborn insistence on the *production* of infinite being or time in Levinas takes us back to the mechanics of life and the technologies of salvation. As we have come to expect, this production is already a reproduction, flowing from father to son. Wedged in the middle, dead time is the nonreproducible precondition for reproduction, a discontinuous threshold or verge for a phoenix-like resurgence in existence. Thus, Levinas writes, "A being capable of another fate than its own is a fecund being. In paternity, where the I, across the definitiveness of an inevitable death, prolongs itself in the other [*se prolonge dans l'Autre*], time triumphs over old age and fate by its

46   *Chapter 2*

discontinuity."[22] A secular salvation, the triumph of time is the cunning of letting go of oneself in order to recover something of oneself in the other. The discontinuity, the rupturing of time, the rupturing that *is* time, ensures the prolongation of what inevitably draws to its end. The mechanics and machinations of life converge, spilling out into salvific technologies.

The term *production*, peppering these pages of *Totality and Infinity*, may make us wonder, with an eye to the Platonic corpus, which model, which paradigm, is operative in envisioning that which or the one who will be produced and how.

On the one hand, the paradigm in question is obviously biological but also economic, in lieu of Levinas's habitual ethical model. Not so much because of the reproductive exchange of the father for the son, who represents interest on the investment that prolongs or extends the finite time of paternal life, but because life's mechanics and machinations pertain to the domain of substance, in which the I is a kind or a mode (*espèce*): "To be infinitely means to be produced in the mode of an I that is always at the origin [*se produire sous les espèce d'un moi qui est toujours à l'origine*], but that meets with no trammels of the renewal of its substance, not even from its very identity."[23] Substantiation and transubstantiation are immanence and immanent transcendence that belong within the circle or the circulation of the economy of the same. The smooth production and reproduction of the I "that meets with no trammels" in its renewal also corroborate this economic construction.

On the other hand, while also drawing on the logic (or at least on the discourse) of production, the paradigm of fecundity implies a desaturation of power and control: "Infinite being, that is ever-recommencing being—which could not bypass subjectivity, for it could not recommence without it—is produced in the guise of fecundity [*se produit sous les espèces de la fécondité*]. . . . The relation with the child—that is, the relation with the other that is not a power, but fecundity—establishes relationship with the absolute future, or infinite time."[24] A recommitment to subjectivity uncoupled from an identity dilutes the thick substantivism of renewal, which was so blatant in the economic paradigm. We, therefore, need to distinguish, in keeping with a fine filament of Levinas's text, the incessant replaying of

47   *Philosophy's Third Path*

a substantive origin, including substance's unique mode that is the I, from the ever-recommencing world of a subject. The structure of transcendence in immanence cannot help but lead to a clash between these two paradigms, veiled over by the language of production.

Yet another trace of the phoenix complex in Levinas's thought is the erasure of sexual difference in the engendering of a child, in whom the progenitor is transubstantiated. The transcendence and multiplicity that are there in existence itself are such that in fecundity "I am not swept away, because the son is not me; and yet I *am* my son [*le moi ne s'emporte pas, puisque le fils n'est pas moi; et cependant je* suis *mon fils*]."[25] Lactantius is, once again, glancing at us through the lines written by Levinas: the phoenix in *De ave phoenice* is "its own father and its heirs [*suus est pater et suus haeres*]" (167). It might be possible to explain the perspective on fecundity as paternity by the phenomenological bent of the text, whose author is a male philosopher working out of his experience.[26] But what happens when the "transubstantiated" I of the father is a daughter, or, vice versa, when that of a mother is a son? Then other kinds of complexes, which Freud enunciates, are in order.[27] Most important, the phoenix's recovery of identity across the abyss of death depends on the fact that the phoenix is either sexless or produces an offspring of the same sex. For all the inexhaustible and nontotalizable multiplicity in existence that, following Levinas, does not obey the laws of Eleatic unity, and for all the ambiguity of love he gives prominence to, the offspring is an emanation of the one (the I), instead of being the third who emerges from a relation between two. The child other is, in other words, the I othered *and* another progenitor also othered, leading to an inconsistent transubstantiation, at least when the social setting for reproduction is a heterosexual family or when the gender of the child does not coincide with that of a parent.

Finally, like the phoenix, the father and the son interlaced by the ties of fecundity are unique. "*To be* one's son means to be I in one's son, to be substantially in him [*être moi dans son fils, être substantiellement dans lui*], yet without being maintained there in identity. . . . The son resumes the unicity of the father [*l'unicité du père*] and yet remains exterior to the father: the son is a unique son [*fils unique*]. Not by number; each son of the father is the unique son, the chosen son."[28] Transubstantiation is thereby revealed

48   *Chapter 2*

as synonymous with the consubstantiality of the parent and the child: the father is in the son as substance, though not as subject, unless—and this proviso is highly significant for Levinas—subjectivity means something other than the maintenance of a self in its identity.

The uniqueness of the phoenix in classical and early Christian corpus (notably, in Lactantius, Ambrose, and Isidore of Seville) was our point of departure, as was the arduous task of reconciling without the assistance of dialectical techniques the movement of substitution with the uniqueness (the nonsubstitutability) of the being primed for substitution. Levinas's work revisits this point of departure under the heading of personal transcendence, in which the I is preserved, substantively if not subjectively, in contrast to the ancient "terrors, whereby the transcendence of the sacred, inhuman, anonymous, and neuter menaces persons with nothingness or with ecstasy [*menace les personnes de néant ou d'extase*]."[29] For their part, these "ancient terrors" go to the root of the phoenix-nature that is reborn, primordially, in the anonymity of impersonal existence. The myth of the phoenix is a fledgling attempt to put a face—a mythical face, but a face nonetheless—on this force. Yet, nothingness and ecstasy do not go anywhere; they do not disappear, staying instead behind the mask that is the face. Uniqueness makes sense only against the general backdrop of the neuter and the void.

*

It would not be an exaggeration to say that the thought of Levinas bears the stamp of the phoenix. We have studied some of this stamp's impressions in his approach to biological reproduction, but his theory of subjectivity is not free from them either. Still within the paradigm of production, "in the mode of an I, being can be produced as infinitely recommencing [*sous les espèces du Moi, l'être peut se produire comme infiniment recommençant*], that is, properly speaking, as infinite."[30] In the mode of an I, then, the subject is a phoenix, produced as infinitely reproducing. For whatever reason, Alphonso Lingis, the English translator of *Totality and Infinity*, omits the words "*sous les espèces du*" (in the mode of) and writes "in the I." Nonetheless, it is just this mode of being that accommodates the production and infinite reproduction of the being who says *I*, occasioning a conflation of the most intimate,

49   *Philosophy's Third Path*

the most unique, and the most generally abstract. According to Hegel, the indifferent welcome the word *I* gives to whomever utters it is the abstract beginning of phenomenology, in which the singular and the universal are as yet unmediated through their mutual self-negation. In this phase of the dialectic, the mode of an I is one where, in the guise of multifaceted diversity, nothing changes; where substitutions of the unique are inattentive to who or what is being substituted; where the same and the other are formally interchangeable.

In Levinas's later work, *Otherwise Than Being*, substitution is the dynamic structure of subjectivity, rather than an act *a posteriori* initiated by the subject. "Substitution," Levinas notes there, is "the very subjectivity of a subject [*substitution comme subjectivité même du sujet*], interruption of the irreversible identity of the essence."[31] It is the mechanism and the machination of subject production, that through which, in the mode of an I, being is infinitely recommencing. Substitution is the moment of transcendence inculcated into the subject's subjectivity: to be a subject, for Levinas, is to be self-transcending toward the other, that is to say, to be capable of substituting oneself for the other.

Yet, substitution is not an escape route, a way of evading responsibility by getting out of the skin of the I who could be held to account (Levinas's early and relatively understudied essay is titled *On Evasion*[32]; the responsibility and the urgency of responding to the other are variations on the theme of *t'shuvah*—repentance, return, and response, all wrapped in one word). The transcendent vector of substitution is embedded in the immanence of uniqueness, in the sense that no one else is in a position to step in and do for the other what I must do for her: "Here uniqueness means the impossibility of slipping away and being replaced, in which the very recurrence of the I is effected [*se dérober et de se faire remplacer, dans laquelle se noue la récurrence même du je*]."[33] Substitution is not replacement, in which the uniqueness of both the replacing and the replaced would be nullified.[34] Perhaps, this is the gist of the self-contradictory affirmation that the reborn phoenix is simultaneously the same as and other to its predecessor.

If substitution is the matrix of subjectivity, then the phoenix complex accounts not only for intergenerational biological or social renewal and

50   *Chapter 2*

extension of finite existence beyond its limit, but also for psychic regeneration. In each instant, the subject is reborn in its memories and inspirations, anticipations and experiences, while many other memories and so forth remain dormant—forever or until another moment of rebirth. Every time I recur in these forms of psychic life, the same as and different from the previous version of me.

"Do the being encumbered with oneself and the suffering of constriction in one's skin, better than metaphors, follow the exact trope of an alteration of essence, which inverts, or would invert, into a recurrence in which the expulsion of self outside of itself is its substitution for the other?" Levinas asks. "Is not that what the self emptying itself of itself would really mean? This recurrence would be the ultimate secret of the incarnation of the subject [*Récurrence qui serait l'ultime secret de l'incarnation du sujet*]."[35] The self perpetually dying and reborn, "emptying itself of itself" and, across the ensuing void, substituting for the other is the phoenix-subject, the subject as phoenix. Recurrence routinizes reproductive mechanics and machinations of the subject as much as of substance. Transubstantiation dovetails in Levinas's thought with transubjectivation.

Shuttling between the philosophy of nature, latent in the notion of fecundity, and a philosophy of subjectivity allows us to examine Levinas's project from an uncommon angle. The phoenix as the paradigm of the subject is *either* extrapolated from the world of nature *or* it is a mode of subjectivity equally at work in nonhuman nature. Substitution and signification (indeed, substitution qua signification) do not require any utterance on the part of the subject. Recommencement in the mode of an I is but a limitrophe case of recurrence that is not pervaded by anonymous, neuter, and terrifying powers of impersonal transcendence but that befits the subject's "uniqueness without identity [*unicité sans identité*]."[36] To say, as Levinas does, that recurrence is "the ultimate secret of the incarnation of the subject" is to undersign the vegetal, animal, and altogether unclassifiable incarnations of the phoenix, who stands for the whole of nature, precisely as subject. And it is to shift the decidedly modern discourse of the production and reproduction of life, which animates the closing chapters of *Totality and Infinity*, onto a more ancient terrain of life's incarnation and reincarnation.

51   *Philosophy's Third Path*

Admittedly, the Levinasian subject is not reducible to life: its emptying out, the voiding of self, dying (in saying *I* as well as in becoming a progenitor) point in a direction that is the opposite of life. But the emptying, voiding, and passing are in life, and they are activated for the sake of life and its continuation beyond the limits of its finitude. This is what transcendence in immanence means, occasioning at the same time various tensions and torsions in the tissue of Levinas's texts. Next, I gloss on the most salient among these and their connection to the phoenix complex.

Whereas in *Totality and Infinity* Levinas praised fecundity for its marvelous gift of "continu[ing] history without producing old age," in *Otherwise Than Being* "subjectivity in ageing is unique, irreplaceable, me and not another [*la subjectivité dans le vieillissement est unique, irremplaçable, moi et pas un autre*]."[37] The wrinkles on our skin or tree rings that spatially articulate the aging of a plant are the marks of an irreplaceable being, as much as of a subject constituted by substitution before its beginning and after its end. Further, the fast transubstantiating and transubjectivating leap of paternity is moderated, in the later work, by patience, lingering, awaiting, that are not all that different from aging: "The temporalization prior to the verb, or in a verb without a subject, or in the patience of a subject that lies as it were on the underside of the active ego, is the patience of ageing [*la patience du vieillissement*]."[38] Rather than the other of the phoenix, it is another phoenix who manifests herself in these lines, where patience, forbearance, the witnessing of a slow transformation "on the underside of the active ego" do not strive to wipe out time and matter within temporal and material reality. All these are traces of immanent resistance to the phoenix complex already present in the complex itself and, in a more literary vein, in the alternative mythical accounts of the phoenix's death and resurrection. The difference between the two mythical traditions may be, therefore, transposed onto the divergences between the paradigms we find in Levinas's *Totality and Infinity* and *Otherwise Than Being*.

The thorny issue of nature "itself" is another piece of the puzzle that is transcendence within immanence, now honed by a difficult relation of subjectivity to life. At times, Levinas understands nature in the classical sense as natality, or birthing. In this line of thinking he writes, "Rather than nature, earlier than a nature [*Plutôt que nature, plus tôt que la nature*], immediacy is this vulnerability, this maternity, this pre-birth or pre-nature [*cette pré-naissance ou pré-nature*] in which sensibility belongs."[39] Maternity, conceived following in the footsteps of Socrates as the subject carrying the other in itself, is assigned to the time of prebirth (hence of prenature), just as paternity has been designated for the time of postdeath (or postnature). Together, they complete the regenerative cycle of the phoenix, but the life in between the two is absent, because that is where mediations belong—in the middle that remains foreign to Levinas.

The immediacy of maternity that presumably precedes nature itself is contentious, above all on the terms of Levinas's philosophy: maternity is fullness and emptying out, a life and subjectivity, immanence and transcendence. In other words, maternity is already the middle, excluded from radical ethics and from formal logic alike. The grain of truth in the ascription of immediacy to maternity has to do with a lack of mediations within that sensibility which precedes consciousness and so resists the powers of representation.[40] Nature, not least in its synecdochic condensation in the phoenix, is immediate in this sense, which suggests that nature precedes nature: prenature is also nature.

Levinas himself notes as much in another section of *Otherwise Than Being*, and still in the context of maternity and the "absolute passivity" of being formed by the other—of not having one's origin in oneself: "This passivity is that of an attachment that has been already made, as something irreversibly past, prior to all memory and all recall. It was made in an irrecuperable time which the present, represented in recall, does not equal, in a time of birth or creation, of which nature or a creature retains a trace, unconvertable into a memory [*un temps de la naissance ou de la création dont nature ou créature garde une trace, inconvertible en souvenir*]."[41] Both other to and the same as itself, nature precedes itself in the manner of the phoenix, recoverable across the distance of death, dead time, or fire. Being born, however, is "irreversibly past," "a trace, unconvertable into a memory," everpresent like a trauma, the very site or nonsite for the emission of the ethical demand, the trace or the face of the other: "A face can appear as a face, as a proximity interrupting the series, only if it enigmatically comes from the Infinite and

53   *Philosophy's Third Path*

its immemorial past."[42] So Levinas's project of *ethics as first philosophy* does not exclude but, on the contrary, presupposes a philosophy of nature in the guise of the "time of birth," irrecuperable by the consciousness of the one who is born.

Among the classical myths of the phoenix, some underscore the ethical impulse, interpreted in a traditional (indeed, the most traditional) terms of a desire to pay one's last respects to the dead. This is the impulse that moved Antigone to disobey Creon and to bury her brother Polynices in violation of Creon's edict. It is also the impulse that, in those renditions of the phoenix story where the mortal remains of the bird's predecessor stay in the nest, prompts the young phoenix to gather the remains and carry them across the sea to perform burial rites with them back in Egypt. As we have seen in Ovid's *Metamorphoses*, "When time has given the offspring sufficient powers [*cum dedit huic aetas vires*]," he transports the cradle-grave with its contents to "the city of Hyperion, where he will lay this heavy burden just before the sacred doors within the city temple" (15.403–407). The tradition goes back to Herodotus, according to whom, the phoenix's offspring "flying from Arabia to the temple of the sun . . . conveys his father encased in myrrh and buries him at the temple of the sun" (*Histories* 2.73). With the phoenix–nature synecdoche in mind, it is nature that is burying the past incarnations of itself or offering them on the altar of the sun—and, thus, creating fertile soil or fossils. In this way, nature both renews itself, physically and biochemically, *and* lays the ground for ethics before ethics, coming at us from the same direction as the immemorial, unrepresentable trace of the other and the injunction it conveys.

Levinas's experiments with transcendence in immanence have led us to an odd place where biological reproduction and a theory of subjectivity, corresponding to philosophy of nature, and ethical thought, overlap. This overlap does not forge a totality, which would subsume multiple singularities within itself; it teases infinity out of finitude instead. At the same time, Levinas's optimism with regard to the perennial recommencement of youth in fecundity is tempered with his acceptance of aging, patience, and passivity more passive than a mere opposite of activity. The two classical renditions of the phoenix complex come into focus in his work: the leap that voids time in the substitution of one finite being with another (in fact, Levinas argues that this voiding of time's finitude bestows meaning on time) and a tarrying with the limited span of a life lived by an irreplaceable existent. These divergent perspectives reveal themselves as two sides of the same coin, in which life and subjectivity—"the vivacity of life" and the "event [of] . . . this permanent revolution" that is the ethical relation to the other—are "an excession, the rupture of the container by the uncontainable."[43] It is this excession and this rupture, in their sundry shapes and guises, that the phoenix complex thematizes in the image of life bubbling up and surpassing itself, its term, its limit defined in death.

*

The phoenix's rebirth from the ashes is something Levinas dithers over (vacillating unconsciously—since he does not, at least to my knowledge, couch it in these terms) after the singular catastrophe called in Hebrew with the word *catastrophe*, the Shoah.

In his interpretation of the Talmudic tractate *Bava Kamma* (60a-b), "Damages Due to Fire," Levinas asks, "Does the ultimate reason of the violence of war sink into the abyss of an extermination coming from beyond war? Or does the madness of extermination retain a grain of reason?" And, Levinas adds, "that is the great ambiguity of Auschwitz [*la grande ambiguïté d'Auschwitz*]. That is the question. Our text does not resolve it [*ne la résout pas*]. It underlines it. Our text does not resolve it because the answer here would be indecent, as all theodicy probably is."[44] The ashes of Auschwitz do not hold the promise of redemption, of regeneration. The persistence of the light of reason—the twisted reason of a logic "coming from beyond war"—in the midst of the ashes is an open question, unresolved by "our text" and by "all theodicy." To answer this question in an attempt to resolve it is to contribute, however unwittingly, to the Final Solution. With a rebuke to all theodicy, including that of a rational or rationalist variety, Levinas spurns the view of the Jewish people as a phoenix reborn from the ashes of extermination camps. (Let it be mentioned here that the phoenix is not foreign to the Jewish tradition, either: as the bird *ḥol*', it is present in the midrash *Bereshith Rabbah*, where it is said to be the only animal who refused to taste

55   *Philosophy's Third Path*

the forbidden fruit along with Adam and Eve and who was, consequently, granted a long life, its days as numerous as *ḥol*—the Hebrew for "sand."[45])

The technologies of salvation and the mechanics or machinations of life stop working in and in the aftermath of Auschwitz. Before, "the righteous could still hope that their death would save the world. But here they are, dying first, and the unjust perish with them. Holiness serves no purpose, then. . . . Useless sacrifice! [*Sacrifice inutile!*]"[46] Useless sacrifice resonates with the title of a small essay by Levinas, "Useless Suffering," the suffering undergone for nothing, totally meaningless. "It is the *impasse* of life and of being—their absurdity—in which pain does not just somehow innocently happen to 'color' consciousness with affectivity. The evil of pain, the deleterious per se, is the outburst and deepest expression, so to speak, of absurdity."[47] There is no hope of self-recovery in the other across the void of useless suffering and useless sacrifice. Dead time and the fire burning in this void are all-consuming, with respect not only to the sentient flesh but also to reason that seeks justifications, cause-and-effect chains, and even to reason's cunning that works behind our backs. There is, in the situation of useless suffering, neither a quick leap over the limits of finitude nor a gradual, patient transformation. If it brings life and being to an impasse, that is because both paths of the phoenix are blocked, and we lack the resources to deal with the meaning of being and life in any other way.

Despite Levinas's contention that biological and psychological vitality are irredeemable—that they cannot be processed by the mechanisms of the phoenix complex after Auschwitz—and despite his denunciation of "all theodicy," his approach to spiritual and political life is caught up in the phoenix complex. This discrepancy within Levinas's thought is nothing short of dithering in the face of the ashes. His defense of Judaism is thoroughly phenomenological, in that it points to the still warm and burning animating impulse beneath layers of concealment and sedimentation. "Is this worm-eaten old Judaism to be preferred to the Judaism of the Jews? Well, why not? We don't yet know which of the two is more lively [*le plus vivant*]. Are the true books just books? Or are they not also the embers still glowing beneath the ashes [*la braise qui dort sous la cendre*], as Rabbi Eliezer called the words of the Prophets? In this way the flame traverses history without burning

56   *Chapter 2*

in it [*La flamme traverse ainsi l'histoire sans brûler en elle*]. But the truth illuminates whoever breathes on the flame and coaxes it back to life."[48] The question, however, is whether the phenomenological strategies of reanimation (if not resurrection), of reduction and desedimentation are still effective after Auschwitz—the proper name for the unsubstitutable loss, which is not available to sense-making and understanding.

In the spiritual history of Judaism, bodies of meaning retain their liveliness to the extent that they are irreducible to the actual books or texts containing them. Just as the vivacity of life and of subjectivity are predicated on the excession of excess, "the rupture of the container by the uncontainable," so the sense of "old Judaism" breaks through the ashes of meaning as the embers still glowing underneath it. The phoenix effect of this slow-burning fire is its reanimation by "whoever breathes on the flame and coaxes it back to life." As a matter of fact, the fire of spiritual life is not extinguished, its flare-ups and diminutions varying in the course of a history. And, along with the fire, the phoenixes are all those who interact with it, those whose breath fans the flames. Coaxing it back to life, they are themselves revivified by it. As in the myth of the phoenix, spiritual fire is the elemental milieu of renewal, an interval between lives that is more alive than the incarnations it separates from one another. The entire millennia-long practice of Jewish exegesis is compacted in this image.

In an essay from the same collection, Levinas aligns the political history of Zionism with the spiritual history of Judaism. Having apparently forgotten the "indecency of theodicy" confronted with Auschwitz, he writes the following in "Space Is Not One-Dimensional": "The Nazi persecution and, following the exterminations, the extraordinary fulfilment of the Zionist dream are religious events [*des événements religieux*] outside any revelation, church, clergy, miracle, dogma, or belief."[49] In this spiritual-political history, the State of Israel figures as a phoenix, undertaking a "daring task of recommencement [*cette audace de recommencement*]" after exterminations, after the mass burning of European Jewry in the Nazi gas chambers. Recommencement refers to the political (and, Levinas implies, the spiritual) rebirth of the Jewish people after the physical annihilation of millions of Jewish people. "The creation of the State of Israel was produced at this level [*se produisit à*

57   *Philosophy's Third Path*

ce niveau]," Levinas continues. "It revived [*Il ressuscitait*] in 1948, scorning all sociological, political or historical improbability."[50]

"At this level": the level of spiritual history, distinguished from that of sociological, historical, and other probabilities. Spiritual revival, wrapped in the political form of the state, is the rebirth of a people from the physical ashes, into which actual lives and living bodies of people were turned. I fear that this is the "grain of reason" in the "madness of extermination," according to the question Levinas formulates and, tactfully, leaves without an answer in "Damages Due to Fire." Though useless and meaningless at the level of individual lives and biological existence as a whole, suffering is imbued with meaning at the spiritual-political level. The phoenix complex is simultaneously scrapped and bolstered, depending on the kinds of life—and death—that are sieved through fire and ashes.

And concepts? Do they renew themselves after they are thrown into the fire of history? The metaphysical concept, the very conceptuality of the concept in Western philosophy from Plato to Husserl, has been deemed immune to the forces of physical destruction. The concept's indestructibility is not merely one among its traits, but an essential feature, setting it apart from extended reality. This changes in Levinas. In a paragraph contemplating "what happened in Europe between 1933 and 1945," he writes: "There are events which burn up the concepts that express their substance [*Il existe des événements qui brûlent les concepts qui expriment leur substance*]."[51] What is the fate of these burned concepts? What, if anything, do they express? Do the incinerated concepts get a chance to undergo transubstantiation or transubjectivation across the fiery abyss of the event? Is this chance itself indexed to distinct "levels" of being—spiritual or biological, political or individual? What does a phoenix concept, neither metaphysically eternal nor destructible once and for all, look like?

3 ON PHYSIOPSYCHOLOGY–LIFE AND ENERGY: ARISTOTLE/HEGEL

Judeo-Christian tradition considers the soul immortal. The resurrection of the flesh, after an indefinite period of separation of the soul from the body beginning with death, is an event, of which the phoenix is a symbol, "a most complete and unassailable symbol of our hope," in the words of Tertullian (*De carnis resurrectione* 13.1–6). But the phoenix is not only a symbol of resurrection; in a vaster cultural, literary, and philosophical panorama, it is the symbol of the soul as such. For instance, in the so-called Hesiod's riddle (Frag. 304, preserved in Plutrach's *De defectu oraculorum*), the phoenix lives "the lifespan of nine ravens" (*De def. orac.* 11.[415c]). Since a raven is said to live 108 years, the life of the phoenix is equivalent to 972 years, which, upon a certain reading, signifies the period of the soul's peregrinations after death.[1] Similarly, in the Coptic *Untitled Gnostic Treatise* found near the Egyptian town of Nag Hammadi in 1945, the phoenix is called "the ensouled animal," *empsuchon zōon* (170.2), resorting to the same expression as the one with which Plato designated the cosmos in *Timaeus*.

As for Aristotle, who wrote a seminal treatise on the soul (arguably, one of the most important in antiquity), there is only scant circumstantial evidence of his interest in the figure of the phoenix. So, in keeping with fragments preserved by Censorianus and Cicero, Aristotle theorized that the Great Year (*magnum annum*), like terrestrial years, consisted of the periods of cooling down and warming up, a sort of cosmic winter or autumn and spring or summer (*Aristotelis fragmenta* 25). The Great Year, you might recall, was supposed to coincide with one of the phoenix's hypothetical life spans. If the phoenix stands for the soul, then she is, at the same time, the symbol of an individual soul and of the cosmic or world-soul, the macrocosm reflecting and reflected in the microcosm. The cosmic soul, too, has its term and limit, temporally marked by the length of the Great Year.

Another piece of evidence reaches us from *De historia animalium*, where Aristotle mentions birds that bring cinnamon to humans (616a.5–10). The indispensability of cinnamon for the phoenix's funereal nest, stressed by Herodotus, Artemidorus, Lactantius, Claudian, and a host of other classical authors, supports the associative link between this kind of birds and the phoenix.[2]

The third indirect testimony to the the fact that Aristotle paid attention to the figure of the phoenix may be found in Plutarch's *Quaestiones conviviales*. Discussing the "freshness and immortality" of the victor's honor, Plutarch compares it to "a palm-tree, which is the longest lived [*o de phoinix makrobion*] of any" and cites "this line of Orpheus": "They lived liked branches of a leafy palm [*phoinikōn*]" (8.4.2). In a somewhat cryptic fashion, the line harkens back to Hesiod's riddle about various life spans. Now, given the phoenix's indeterminate speciation and synecdochic representation of nature, it may, of course, be an animal, a plant, or a combination of the two as in iconic depictions of the phoenix bird sitting atop a palm tree. For our purposes, though, the word that is crucial is *makrobion*, "long-lived." This is the very word that appears in the title of Aristotle's minor text from *Parva naturalia*, "On the Length of Life [*makrobiotētos*] and the Shortness of Life." Here, Aristotle states, probably also with an acknowledging nod to Hesiod, that "on the whole, the longest-lived are to be found among plants [*ta makrobiōtata en tois phutois estin*], namely the palm tree [*phoinix*]" (466a.9–10). In its singular vegetal incarnation, the phoenix thus exemplifies the long life of plants in general. And it is to this marginal text that we should turn in an attempt to schematize the dynamics of life through the long life of a vegetal phoenix.

*

Before proceeding, it is imperative that we address an apparent lapse in argumentation. It has already been established that the phoenix is a synecdoche of nature by virtue of gathering in the same figure plants and animals, miscellaneous elements, as well as a territory and its inhabitants. It has been further pointed out that the phoenix is a synecdoche of the world, the Greek *kosmos* or the Latin *universitas*—a connection that becomes apparent through the associations of the Great Year with the phoenix's age. The new claim is that the phoenix is a symbol of the soul. How is this possible?

At the core of the question is the surprising affinity of nature and the soul, of ancient physiology and psychology. In later theologico-metaphysical systems (even those that, like Avicenna's are heavily influenced by Aristotle) the soul will appear as something supernatural, indeed as a tendency or an entity that moves *contranatura*, against the laws governing interactions of physical elements. For Aristotle, though, the soul is not an abstract metaphysical entity somehow conjugated with the body, but an activating (or actuating) principle of life, differentiated into kinds of vitality or vital movements.[3] Physiology, understood as the logos of the body, gathered or assembled in itself across its various organs, is nothing other than a psychology, provided that we hear in *psuchē* one of the senses Aristotle imbues it with, namely "the first actuality of a natural body with organs [*entelecheia hē prōtē sōmatos phusikou organikou*]" (*De anima* 412b.5). What nature/*phusis*, *kosmos*, and *psuchē* have in common is life, distributed in them along disparate scales, dimensions, and kinds (or, in some instances, touching upon the everlasting and the immortal without much of a regard for kinds and divisions between and within kingdoms, genera, species).

Let us now go back to Aristotle's *Parva naturalia* and, especially, to his text on longevity and the shortness of life. More than his approach to the duration (or the durability) of living beings, what is remarkable about this piece of writing is the efficiency, with which it stages the drama of the phoenix with respect to life, lives, living as an afterlife, and ruptures in vitality indistinguishable from its seamless continuation. According to Aristotle, "Living beings are naturally moist and warm [*zōon esti phusei hudron kai thermon*]" (466a); "by nature," life conjoins opposites in a living being. Old age and the impending death announce themselves in the weakening fire of vitality—a biochemical fire that gives life while slowly burning the living up—and in the drying up of life's moisture until the total exhaustion of these

61   *On Physiopsychology—Life and Energy*

elemental forces in a cold, dead body. Just as a fire destroys the substratum in which it burns, so "natural warmth . . . consumes the matter in which it is [*to phusikon thermon . . . analiskei tēn hulēn en hē estin*]" (466b.33–34).

At the beginning of his text, Aristotle has already made clear how futile it is to resist the mortiferous tendency of life itself on its own terms: only "the upper fire" (*to pur anō*), is indestructible because it has no contrary (465b.2–3). Seeing that life is constituted by oppositional elements, it contains the principle of its own destruction and, therefore, of death. Implicit in Aristotle's argument is the insight of Diotima that mortals cannot preserve themselves by keeping fast to their identity and sameness. The greater longevity of plants (and of the phoenix-plant, or the palm tree, in particular) is due to the fact that they "are constantly reborn [*aei ta phuta ginetai*: also, come into being]" (467a.13). Every plant is a miniature phoenix, and the palm tree is the phoenix of vegetal phoenixes. What seems to be an uninterrupted duration of their lives is actually a kindling of many new vital fires where the older ones are nearly extinguished. At the same time dying and being born (*to men phtheiromenon to de ginomenon*), a tree perseveres in being (*diatelei*), continues existing while letting go of its existence and getting a new lease on life (467a.17–18).

While Aristotle shares the argument concerning the vegetal phoenix with Diotima, the mechanics of overcoming finitude are patently his own. From the empirical observation that plants, as well as some insects and other animals, maintain themselves alive even after they are physically divided into parts Aristotle deduces the conclusion that "the plant possesses potential root and stock [*echei kai rizan kai kaulon dunamei*] in every part" (467a.23–24) and that, consequently, "the vital principle exists potentially [*archē dunamei*] in every part of the plant" (467a.29–30). Plants enjoy their longevity to the extent that they give up life in exchange for lives: this is the means (*mechanē*: mechanics and machinations) by which they are able to reignite and to keep reigniting their vital fires almost indefinitely. They are the consummate beginners, recommencing their existence time and again, imperceptibly leaping across the chasm of dead time without as much as getting out of the places of their growth. In every vegetal part, a potential root is awaiting actualization, which may never happen.

62   *Chapter 3*

Within the context of Aristotle's philosophy, the assignment of potential vitality to every part of the plant is highly charged. In the first place, the potential existence of the vital principle in every part of a plant puts it on the side of matter that, in *De anima*, is identified with potentiality in contrast to the actuality of eidetic form: "Matter is potentiality, while *eidos* is actuality [*Esti d' hē men hulē dunamis, to d' eidos entelecheia*]" (412a.9–10). In plants, the potentiality of matter—or matter as potentiality—comes into its own, also in light of Aristotle's use of a colloquial word for wood or for woods (*hulē*) in this more specialized, philosophical sense. Nevertheless, and in the second place, this very feature of vegetal vitality distances plants from the aforementioned conception of the soul as "the first actuality [*entelecheia hē prōtē*] of a natural body with organs." The first "first actuality," which is vegetal vitality in charge of organismic nutrition and reproduction (*to threptikon* and *to genetikon*), borders on potentiality. How will Aristotle cope with this source of (potential) confusion?

The answer comes into view in another text from *Parva naturalia*, titled "On Youth and Old Age: On Life and Death," where Aristotle solves the conundrum of actuality and potentiality. According to him, in plants and some insects, the divisible part "is actually one, but potentially many [*energeia men echei hen, dunamei de pleiō*]" (468a.29), which means that "the nutritive soul must be actually one [*energeia men hen*] in beings that possess it, but potentially many [*dunamei de pleious*]" (468b.3–4). If the empirical division of living beings into separate parts does not result in their death, then the metaphysical division of the activating or actuating principle of their life is equally possible. Actual unity must be sacrificed to potential plurality for the phoenix effect of spanning the gap of death to be achievable. But, together with unity and actuality, it is the *uniqueness* of the mythic phoenix and of finite existence that goes up in flames on the pyre of survival.

Heavy reliance on potentiality in the Aristotelian version of the phoenix, equated to the bodies and souls of plants and some animals, speaks volumes about the energy at work in the phoenix complex. Having coined the word *energeia*, Aristotle defines it in a roundabout way in *Metaphysics* as "the presence of the thing not in the sense which we mean by 'potentially' [*mē outōs hōsper legomen dunamei*]" (*Met.* 1048a.31–32). The association of energy with potentiality and dynamism is a quintessentially modern one, inverting the Aristotelian comprehension of energy in terms of actuality.[4] The phoenix complex is a complex of energy restricted to potentiality, including the potential rebirth of an organism or parts of an organism despite their finitude. What matters is not actual existence but its projection into the future by way of multiplication, of copying in part or as a whole the one who, as a consequence of this procedure, will become *more* than one. The mechanics and machinations that Aristotle discloses replace actuality with potentiality, slipping the many in the place of the one. The vegetal soul is responsible not only for nutrition but also for reproduction because, in itself, it is already potentially reproducible, being potentially many. The conflation of progenitor and offspring phoenixes, taken to be both the same and other, the same and not the same, one and more than one in the texts of Tertullian and Lactantius, belongs within this psychoenergetic framework.

The persistence of fire, which is a facet of vitality in Aristotle and which serves as a medium of rebirth in the dominant strand of phoenix narratives, is commensurate with the survival (indeed, the self-survival and resurrection) of plants and certain animals that gives the illusion of uninterrupted longevity. "Fire," Aristotle writes in the essay from *Parva naturalia* devoted to youth and old age, "is always coming into being [*pur aei diatelei ginomenon*] and flowing like a river, but its speed is so great that it is not noticed" (470a.4–5). Fire is plantlike insofar as it is constantly dying and being born at such a speed that its intermittencies and discontinuities are perceived as smooth, riverine flows. And plants are firelike, proximate to its vital impulse; matter is wood and the woods on fire. A flaming rebirth of the phoenix spectacularizes these events of the vegetal soul, rendering them phenomenal.

*

What is the fate of potentiality (and, hence, of the energy animating the phoenix complex) in a perpetual fiery and vegetal rebirth that guarantees longevity and survival, if not longevity as survival of oneself? A pure potentiality is as unthinkable for Aristotle as totally formless matter, which would be, similarly, mere potential. Potentiality is always of or for something (*Met.* 1049a–1049b). In the case before us, potentiality is to some extent actual

64   *Chapter 3*

when it is hemmed into the terms of a birth—an incessant rebirth of fire, plants, and the rest of phoenix-nature, defined by its activity of birthing or sprouting into being (not least from death and obscurity). Beyond their identification with causes and principles, and beyond, also, their circumscription to the "developmental" arc extending from a prior to a subsequent actuality via the detour of potentiality, *phusis* and *natura* are snarls of potentialities and actualities. In the vegetal soul and in plant bodies, this unavoidable confusion reaches its highest point, and *this feature fuels the phoenix complex.*

Debunking in *De anima* an earlier theory of the soul as a "self-moving number," Aristotle reiterates the idea that "plants and many animals continue to live even when divided, and seem to have the same soul as before [*dokei tēn autēn psuchēn echein tō eidei*]" (409a.9–10). Aristotle's point is that numeric or extensional division does not diminish the ensoulment of vegetal and certain animal beings whose bodies are fragmented: each fragment retains the same degree of vitality as that before the division. Nevertheless, his statement also has far-reaching unintended consequences.

For one thing, the vegetal soul is the site of excess, not only distributed throughout the entire body of the living being who has it but also concentrated as a whole in each part of that body. Thanks to this excess, plant matter rapidly proliferates, with reproduction being, at the same time, the function and the effect of the vegetal soul. *To threptikon* and, especially, *to genetikon* do what they do best because they are more than themselves and, in this noncoincidence with themselves, overflow into the other, whether this other is a nourished being surviving itself or a being generated afresh.

For another thing, Aristotle's statement insinuates that, in the actual existence of plants and some animals, unity is only potential, and a potential never to be actualized at that! Certainly, as he will explain in the essay on youth and old age, the nutritive soul is an actual unity and a potential multiplicity, an assertion that is repeated in *De anima* 413b. But the explanation does not sit well with the notion that "the soul seems rather to hold the body together" [*psuchē to sōma sunechein*]; at any rate, when the soul is gone, the body dissolves and decays (*De anima* 411b.8–10). The provisional unity of a vegetal body renders it nearly immortal on this view. And, furthermore, as a potential multiplicity, the vegetal soul no longer does the work of the

65   *On Physiopsychology—Life and Energy*

soul according to Aristotle, notably the work of holding the body together. Instead, potentially multiple, no longer uniting the body with itself and letting it be many bodies, this soul *is* the body, matter as the woods and as wood.

For Aristotle, the substantive sense of the soul is "a form of a natural body potentially having life [*eidos sōmatos phusikou dunamei zōēn echontos*]" (*De anima* 412a.20–21). The soul is the actualization of that bodily potential—of a body as potentially living—as a result of (a) the equation of *eidos* with actuality and (b) the "universal" definition of the soul as the body's "first actuality." In the vegetal soul, however, potential multiplicity lingers on, precipitating the potentiality *of* actuality as actuality and spawning the body of the soul itself. A soft version of the phoenix complex belongs at this level, at which vegetal vitality is indistinguishable from reproducibility in the plant itself or in another plant it gives rise to, since, in itself, it is already a host of others.[5] A hard version of the phoenix complex, skipping over the gradual movements of growth, decay, and metamorphosis, and crafting a model of energy out of pure potentiality, is alien to Aristotle. Nevertheless, it is the one we are most familiar with, be it in the form of myth or in the prevalent sources and practice of energy production.

The vegetal soul epitomizes the potentiality of actuality as actuality. While he denies the possibility that the soul is a self-moving number, Aristotle is willing to contemplate parallels between the soul and geometrical figures. He writes, "The facts regarding the soul are much the same as those relating to figures; for both in figures and in things which possess soul, the earlier type always exists potentially in that which follows [*huparchei dunamei to proteron*]; e.g., the triangle is implied by the quadrilateral, and the nutritive faculty by the sensitive" (*De anima* 414b.28–32). In other words, the earlier type of the soul, which is the body's "first actuality," leads potential existence within a later type, assuming the role and the place of psychic matter or a psychic body. This is what the nutritive vegetal faculty (*to threptikon*) becomes in an animal, and this is what the sensitive animal faculty (*to aesthētikon*) becomes in the human. In us, the vegetal soul is a potentiality twice over, having passed along the way through an animal instantiation. Rather than a confirmation of the teleological structure of Aristotle's thought, this

66   *Chapter 3*

means that the nutritive and genetic faculties proper to the vegetal soul are doubly othered in the human: the phoenix complex works by not working and does not work by working. The past becomes the future: the deeper the past (say, vegetal or animal) in the crosshairs of Aristotle's philosophical biopsychology, the more open and indeterminate the future it announces in and for the human.

On a grand scale, that which Aristotle defines as life is coextensive with the vegetal soul in its nutritive and genetic aspects. "By life we mean self-nourishment, growth, and decay [*autou trophēn te kai auxēsin kai phthisin*]" (*De anima* 412a.14–15). If so, then, in the animal and human modes of vitality, where the vegetal soul leads potential existence, life itself turns into a potentiality, the energy of life—its putting to work, actualization or actuality—converted into anti-energy. The grounds for the harsh version of the phoenix complex, sustained by pure potentiality that remains unthinkable for the Greek philosopher, are prepared by Aristotle.

Within the vegetal soul itself, which is the first actuality of a plant body, the nutritive and genetic faculties, often assimilated into a single faculty by Aristotle, are capacities, the potentialities of that actuality qua actuality: "The capacity to absorb food may exist apart from all other powers [*allōn dunaton*], but the others cannot exist apart from it in mortal beings. This is evident in the case of growing beings [*phuomenōn*], for they have no other capacity of the soul [*dunamis allē psuchēs*]" (*De anima* 413a.31–33). The fundamental *dunamis*, without which no others can exist, is not a secure foundation. In its unity, as the only capacity of living beings viewed primarily from the perspective of growth, it is already many, falling apart as it does into the nutritive and the generative faculties.[6] Now, as Aristotle has taught us, the manifold of the one *is* potentiality (recall that the body and the soul of the plant are actually one, but potentially many). The vegetal soul is, thus, in itself (in and as the first actuality of growing bodies) potential before its subsumption to other sorts of vitality.

Nourishment is the basic capacity of the soul that renders a body living. But it is also a capacity that betrays this same body as dying; hence, in the same breath, Aristotle invokes not only growing beings, but also mortals (*thnētois*). The refrain in Homer's definition of mortals in *Odyssey* is that they are those "who eat bread" (9.190–191; 10.101, etc.). In the Hebrew Bible, eating bread earned "by the sweat of your brow" is on a par with the return of one's mortal body to the earth, meted out as punishment to Adam and Eve for their original sin (Genesis 3:19). To make of death but a brief detour from life to life, as some versions of the phoenix story do, it is necessary to deal with the problem of nourishment. So, according to Pliny, the Roman senator Manilius reports that "there is no one who has seen [this bird] eating [*neminem extitisse qui viderit vescentem*]" (*Historia naturalis* 10.ii.3). In *Metamorphoses*, Ovid notes that the phoenix "lives not from fruit nor herbs but from drops of frankincense and cardamom" [*non fruge neque herbis, sed turis lacrimis et suco vivit amomi*] (15.393–394). Claudian, for his part, presents a vegetal take on the phoenix's nourishment: "He needs no food to satisfy hunger nor any drink to quench thirst; the sun's purer heat is his food [*purior illum solis fervor alit*], and he drinks the windy nutriments of Tetys, taking nourishment from innocent vapors" (*Carmina minora* 27.13–16).

Minimal or elemental nourishment is meant to extract the phoenix from the category of mortal beings, while retaining the fundamental *dunamis* of the living. The energy of the phoenix in the classical accounts is not a potentiality, but an actuality, very much in keeping with Aristotle's original coinage and interpretation. Even when eating or drinking, the phoenix lacks nothing. Energy predicated on fullness on the hither side of satisfaction or dissatisfaction is energy as actuality, and it is only fitting that it be rooted in the sun, the paragon of energetic plenum and excess. Solar heat directly supplies and supplants the fire of vitality in a vegetalized phoenix, even as "innocent vapors" transported by the wind or by drops of frankincense provide moisture—the two elements that, following Aristotle, are invariably conjugated in the living. Instead of the heat of digestion—"all food requires digestion and that which produces digestion is heat [*thermon*]" (*De anima* 416b.28–29)—the external warmth of the sun yields a fire that does not burn up the substratum in which it burns, or, at least, does not burn it up as quickly. Longevity depends on the mode of energy a living being employs and on the proximity of that energy to actuality, on the one hand, and potentiality, on the other.

68   *Chapter 3*

The reproductive capacity of the vegetal soul, sometimes assimilated to the nutritive capacity in Aristotle's writings, is also linked to longevity within the scheme of discontinuous existence. In this respect, the Platonic influences that are merely implicit in *Parva naturalia* are fully explicated in *De anima*: "Since they [living creatures] cannot share in the immortal and the divine by continuity of existence [*adunatei tou aei kai tou theiou tē sunecheia*], because no perishable being can remain numerically one and the same, they share in these in the only way they can . . . ; what persists is not the individual itself, but something in its image [*eidei*], identical not numerically but specifically" (*De anima* 415b.3–8). Emphasizing, once again, that the soul in its generative capacity is not a matter of number (a self-moving number, to be exact), Aristotle confirms that "perishable beings" share in the immortal and the divine by letting themselves go as units of life and by allowing their progeny to take their place, identical in their *eidos*, as opposed to number. When it comes to the phoenix, the identity of the offspring is, nonetheless, both eidetic and numeric: there cannot be more than one. Whereas the discontinuity of existence is accentuated in those renditions of the myth that involve gradual decay, spontaneous generation, and the burial rituals a young phoenix performs for her predecessor, a near continuity is achieved in the moment of combustion and fiery consumption of the phoenix's body, offered to fire as a medium of higher life.

What are the practical means (the mechanics and machinations) for achieving resemblance across the intergenerational gap, thus securing the eidetic-specific identity of the progenitor and the offspring? In *De generatione animalium*, Aristotle lists four hypotheses of pangenesis avant la lettre, among which is the view that "the offspring which are produced are like their parents not merely in respect of their body as a whole, but part for part, too; hence, if the reason for the resemblance of the whole is that semen is drawn from the whole [*to aph holou elthein to sperma*], then the reason for the resemblance of the parts is surely that something is drawn from each of the parts" (721b.20–24). Aristotle is ultimately skeptical about the theory, citing plenty of arguments against it—from the impossibility of assembling all the features of both parents in a child to an offspring resembling not the parents but a more distant ancestor. But the theory must have had traction in the ancient world to have made it into *De generatione animalium* and to have been carefully refuted by Aristotle. Applied to the phoenix, it explains how "genetic materials" for a new life must be drawn from the whole of nature condensed, in the manner of a synecdoche, in this singular figure. Whether in the equation of a plant-based nest with the womb in Tacitus or in the ascription of the phallic function to the sun and to lightning by Tzetzes and Claudian, we see the phoenix's pangenesis expanded to and dispersed in all of nature. Part for part resemblance is incredibly complicated when, in addition to the earlier and the later phoenix, we are dealing with an interplay of part and whole typical of synecdoche.

*

Lest we forget, the *eidos* (image or form) inherited by the offspring is not purely corporeal, seeing that the substantive sense of the soul in Aristotle is "a form of a natural body [*eidos sōmatos phusikou*] potentially having life" (*De anima* 412a.20–22). And, since the phoenix is a symbol of the soul, its form is that of the soul *as well as* of nature—"a form of the body of nature," we might say, slightly rephrasing Aristotle. The dynamic sense of the soul as a capacity for nourishment, reproduction, sensation, and thinking does not, for obvious reasons, have a visual equivalent, even though it is tied to the speciation of the being, whose soul it is and whose capacities it fittingly actualizes.[7] But, as far as the soul's *eidos* is concerned, the question of sexuation, intertwined with that of individuality and mortality, is key. Does the soul have a sex? Does it coincide with the image of a sexed body?

As the symbol of the soul *and* the synecdoche of nature, the phoenix is a composite portrait of male, female, and asexual being; she, he, and it, plant and animal, the phoenix unites sexual difference with the lack thereof and with the transposition of sexuality onto the inorganic world of the elements—for instance, the solar blaze or lightning and wind. The asexual reproduction of plants that are not angiosperms and of some animals, such as blackworms that reproduce through fragmentation, migrates into most classical accounts of the phoenix that insist on its uniqueness and singularity. Recall in this respect Pomponius Mela's observation that the phoenix "is not conceived by copulation nor born through parturition [*non enim coitu concipitur partuve generatur*]" (*De chorographia* 3.72). In early Christianity, this feature goes hand in hand with the purity of the phoenix, who is untouched by the original sin, and the asexuality of the soul. So, Ambrose writes that "the phoenix does not know corporeal coition, nor the lure of libidinal desire [*phoenix coitus corporeos ignorat, libidinis nescit inlecebras*]" (*Expos. Ps.* cxviii.19.13). And Zeno of Verona notes that the phoenix "is not born through intercourse [*non ex coitu nascitur*]" (*Tractatus* 1.16.9).

I will put aside (for the time being) the possible role of the Fall in the sexuation of the soul according to early Christian theologians. The thread I would like to follow is that of the phoenix's (and, hence, the soul's and nature's) self-conception. Ovid writes that the phoenix is the only creature that "renews and reproduces itself [*una est, quae reparet seque ipsa reseminet*]" (15.392). The verb *reseminet* means "reproduces," but, literally, it says "sows again," or "reseeds" itself (*ipsa*). Lactantius writes that the phoenix "begets itself [*se tamen ipsa creat*]" (*De ave phoenice* 78). Fourth-century Latin theologian Rufinus of Aquileia also underlines the nonconjugal origin of the phoenix, who "is always one and always follows itself, born or reborn from itself [*semper una sit, et semper sibi ipsa nascendo vel renascendo succedat*]" (*Exp. Symboli* 9).

The act of self-begetting divulges the phoenix's sex and, with it, that of the soul or of nature. Aristotle supplies a functional (or, perhaps, an energetic), rather than anatomical, definition of male and female in *De generatione animalium*: "They differ in their *logos*, because the male is that which has the power to generate in another [*to dunamenon gennan eis heteron*], while the female is that which can generate in itself [*to eis auto*]" (716a.20–22). This power, this capacity, is actualized or attains its energy *proper* in that which is generated. The phoenix's self-begetting identifies the creature as female, actualized or energized in herself as her own offspring.

That said, some variations on the myth put the phoenix on the side of the male, who generates in another. According to Tacitus, the other, in whom the phoenix is reborn, is vegetal; the phoenix "pours forth his genital force into the nest, from which the fetus arises [*suis in terries struere nidum eique vim genitalem adfundere, ex qua fetum oriri*]" (*Annals* 6.28). Fire, as the medium of rebirth, may be likewise considered the other, in which the phoenix regenerates. In "Praecepta ad virgines" (526–528), Gregory Nazianzus, the fourth-century archbishop of Constantinople, compares the rebirth of those who are dying in a flaming passion for Christ with that of the phoenix "becoming young again and in fire reborn [*neazein / en puri tiktomenon*]" (*Carmina* 1.2: "Praecepta ad virgines," 526–527). Claudian states that the phoenix's lives are "separated in the middle by fire [*separat ignis*]" (*Carmina minora* 27.70–71). And Dracontius concludes that fire is born of phoenix's actions (*sic nascitur ignis*) of beating its wings against the branches of the nest and that, afterwards, the phoenix is consumed by and reborn in the flames (*Romulea* 10.107–109).

The circularity of Dracontius's account foregrounds a problem with Aristotle's definition of male and female. To discern between one sex and the other, it is necessary, *ab initio* to distinguish self from other, generation in oneself *versus* generation in the other. We return here to the tangle of individuality and sexual difference: hyperindividuated to the point of singularity in its own genus, the phoenix is, however, infraindividual, inasmuch as she, he, or it encompasses the elemental and vegetal other by blurring the boundaries of classificatory systems (the first path toward universalization) and by standing in for the whole of nature or the soul in a relation of synecdoche (the second such path). Plus, the intergenerational difference between the predecessor and the offspring phoenix is not a given, since the reborn phoenix is often said to be both the same as and other to itself. A critical implication of these nuances is that, regenerating in fire or in the wood of the nest, the phoenix regenerates in the other that is not *entirely* other and is, therefore, feminized or, at the very least, rendered more indeterminate than ever with respect to her or his sex. In Aristotelian terms, "male" and "female" cease being the principles (*archai*) that they are in light of a clear-cut distinction between self and other (*De generatione animalium* 716b.10–11).

*

The negation of sexes as *archai*, or principles, happens at the very beginning (as and in a principle, *in principio*) of the invention of sexuality by higher plants. Hegel could not have overlooked this productive contradiction in his *Philosophy of Nature*, notably in the section dedicated to vegetal nature. In principle, plants fail to develop "the principle of opposition," defining a mature sexual relation: "The different individuals cannot therefore be regarded as of different sexes because they have not been completely imbued with the *principle* of their opposition [*sie nicht in das* Prinzip *ihrer Engegensetzung eingetaucht sind*]—because this does not completely pervade them, is not a universal moment, not a principle of the *whole* individual [*nicht Prinzip des* ganzen *Individuums*], but is a separated part of it."[8] Because flowers and other sexual parts of plants are easily detachable and apparently inessential to the vegetal organism, the sexual principle—sexuality as a principle—is still merely formal and abstract, neither self-negated in a relation to another sex nor concretely determinative for the entire individual plant. That is why the determination of sexual difference in vegetal life "exists merely as an analogue of the sexual relationship,"[9] the analogue *preceding* that which it analogizes (i.e., animal sexuality). Instead of a principle, in the beginning we find an analogue, which is what a still undeveloped principle always is from a dialectical point of view. The sexual relation in plants is a strange relation without the relata, sexual difference without the identity of individuals belonging to different sexes.[10]

In Hegel's thought, the knot, tying sexuality to individuality and mortality, is very much intact: the formally asexual character of plants, despite the means of sexual reproduction at their disposal, has to do with their nonindividuation, that is, their nonnegation by themselves. This knot, both affirmed and denied in the phoenix complex, is also disavowed in the life of plants as Hegel construes it. Sexual ambiguity (not least, the ambiguity of the difference between sexual difference and lack thereof) belongs together with the confusion between plant self and its other—a distinction, which underlies the capacities of generation and according to which Aristotle assigns to living beings their sexes. Speaking of the "process of formation," Hegel notes that the "*inner* process of the plant's *relation to itself* is, in keeping with the simple nature of the vegetable organism, immediately a relation to an outer world, and an externalization."[11] The plant finds itself in an external (elemental) other, and externalizes itself in response to this discovery. Hence, in their very life process, in the course of their own production and preservation, plants

73   *On Physiopsychology—Life and Energy*

perform a synecdoche, whereby they stand in for nature, albeit without a sharply individuated part *representing* the whole.

Given plant nonindividuation, the dividing lines between vegetal formation process and genus process are virtually nonexistent: for a plant, its production in itself is already its reproduction in the other. "Since the plant, in producing other individuals, at the same time preserves itself, the significance of this fruitfulness is not merely that the plant, by its constant budding [*Verknoten*], transcends itself, but rather that the cessation of growth, the arrest of this sprouting [*Hinaussprossen*], is the condition for that fruitfulness."[12] What Hegel refers to here, in concrete terms, is the alternation of vegetative growth and sexual reproduction, phases that are mutually exclusive in plant life. This alternation, or temporal negation, should have given the German thinker some pause and should have complicated the assertion of an immediate identity of plant self-production and reproduction. It did not. Hegel still maintains that the mechanics and machinations of overcoming finitude in plants are simple: that, in continuing to be itself, the plant already transcends itself, including its finite life span and spatial confines. The Hegelian plant is a phoenix *in each one of its parts*, a self-renewing creature that achieves this renewal by growing—indistinguishable from "producing other individuals" like it—and that, in producing other individuals, preserves itself. And yet, the "cessation of growth" serving as "the condition for that fruitfulness" indicates that negativity is not alien to vegetal self-transcendence and, therefore, that something like death forms the horizon of vegetal life.

Positing the identity of vegetal self-production and reproduction, Hegel agrees with Aristotle, who collapses the two functions of the vegetal soul into one: *to genetikon* unites under its heading the highly elaborated residues of *to threptikon*. So, the genus process in plants is "on the whole, superfluous, since the process of formation and assimilation is itself already reproduction as production of fresh individuals."[13] Even more overtly, in the world of plants, "the sex relationship should be regarded as much, or as even more, a *digestive process*; here digestion and generation are the same."[14] Life and survival are one and the same, insofar as in being lived, vegetally, life survives itself. This further undermines the logic of firm principles, which we have

74 *Chapter 3*

seen corroded with regard to sexual difference. To say (well before the advent of deconstruction) that production is, in itself, reproduction is to put repetition, replication, copying at the origin, divested of its originality, just as to brand plant sexuality an "analogue" of sexuality is to begin with similitude, an imitation of "the thing itself."

Nevertheless, the vegetal phoenix as Hegel imagines it deviates from the phoenix complex in at least one respect. As digestive and generative processes and capacities merge, the element of self-sacrifice evanesces. Comparing plant and animal reproduction, Hegel writes, "Whereas in the genus process of the animal the genus, as the negative power over the individual, is realized through the sacrifice of this individual which it replaces by another, . . . [the plant's] relationship with the outer world is already a reproduction of the plant itself and therefore coincides with the genus process."[15] There is no "negative power" in the vegetal individual–genus relation, meaning that the former generation need not pass away (or, more radically put, need not lay its own life on the altar of the future, burning itself to a life-giving death or inflicting a fecund wound on itself) in order to give time and space to those yet to come. But the phoenix complex does not tolerate exceptions. On Hegel's reading, the nonsacrificial nature of vegetal life in its individuality assigns a sacrificial mission to the plant kingdom as a whole: "The plant is a subordinate organism whose destiny it is to be sacrificed to the higher organism and to be consumed by it."[16] There are no alternatives to sacrifice: the choice is between being sacrificed to the other and sacrificing oneself (to oneself as other). The fate of a living body ruled by the digestive function is to be digested in another living body. The sacrifice externally imposed on plants by animals and humans is understood, on another plane of dialectical reason, as a self-sacrifice of vegetal nature moving along the path of a self-actualizing concept.

The enigma of vegetal "digestion," assigned the task of gathering together distinct facets of plant life and subjectivity, is that it does not assimilate nutrients to a psychic or physical inner core, wherein they would be digested; on the contrary, a plant "is drawn out of itself by light, by its self which is external to it, ramifying into a plurality of individuals."[17] We are no longer dealing, as in Aristotle, with the actual oneness and potential multiplicity of

75 *On Physiopsychology—Life and Energy*

plant souls and bodies, but with an actual (that is, energy-rich, determinate and determinative) plurality, where synthesis and analysis are one (as in the combination of *photo*synthesis with moisture and minerals osmotically absorbed from the soil). In the elemental domain, the plant is the "concept which has materialized the light principle and has converted the watery nature into a fiery one."[18] But on the plane of its subjectivity, it is an affirmation of fire as life and of its own self in the medium of fire. "The plant draws from light its specific energy [*Befeuerung*: "firing-up"] and vigor. . . . [T]he plant becomes a self to itself only in light; its lighting-up, its becoming light [*ihr Erleuchten, Lichtwerden*] does not mean that the plant itself becomes light, but that it is produced only at and in light [*am und im Licht*]."[19]

The plant's source of energy is also its self in a sense that is quite dissimilar to the usual notion of autotrophy: the means for its growth, becoming, and self-reproduction is, at the same time, the end, if only endless, unreachable as such. The implication, of course, is that the plant never reunites with its solar self, seeing that, empirically speaking, it does not contain the inner heat of life fueling animal existence. In a vegetal incarnation as a palm tree or in Claudian's account of nourishment procured from "sun's purer heat," the phoenix leads a plantlike existence, becoming "a self to itself" in the light. But in the animal incarnation, as well, external fire provides an opportunity for recharging the heat of life that is all but exhausted in the aged phoenix. If the old bird dies in order to live, that is because cosmic, solar fire is a powerful substitute—a replacement and replenishment of life's inner heat.

In keeping with Hegel's dialectics, elemental light and heat are *not* of a higher ontological rank than the warmth of animal vitality. In fact, the latter, despite its finitude, is dialectically more determinate, actualized, energetically fuller, because it has overcome the abstract indifference of the inorganic domain. But elemental fire is more significant to the story of the phoenix: since the provenance of this mythical creature is the religious cult of the sun, the part on "Luminous Essence" (*Lichtwesen*) from the "Natural Religions" section of Hegel's *Phenomenology* is particularly relevant. Assuming that Light is Life, it is vacuous until such a moment when "this swaying life [*taumelnde Leben*] must determine itself into *being-for-itself* and must give existence to its vanishing shapes [*un seinen verschwindenden Gestalten*

76   *Chapter 3*

Bestehen geben]."[20] The phoenix's fiery transformation is an act of dipping into Life itself, as light and fire. This act is tantamount to death, in which a living being sheds its shape (not this or that shape, but any shape whatsoever), actively participating in the immanent vanishing of its figure. To live again, a fresh shape must be assumed, following the thesis of Life's self-determination "into being-for-self," the being that is nonindifferent and, most importantly, nonindifferent to itself. Thus, pure Life is death without the material substratum of a living shape; existence in a living shape is dying; and it is only the speculative reflection of Life into substantive organic shapes—its self-negating self-determination—that energizes the process of living (or of living-dying).

*

Along the winding paths of vegetal vitality, plants carry the elements of water and earth up to the air and to solar fire that lends them determinate shapes, textures, colors, smells, flavors. Once the plant is "itself the movement of fiery nature within itself, it proceeds to ferment; but the heat which it gives out of itself is not its blood but its destruction."[21] The plant's "phoenix moment," if I can call it that, is the interiorization of heat, its partial becoming animal, which brings it to ruin, as Hegel does not fail to recognize, but also preserves it otherwise, as fermented spirits, for instance. Fermentation is the afterlife of vegetal life, materially crucial to the Christian narrative of resurrection: the transubstantiation of Christ's body in bread and of his blood in wine. The inner heat of a fermenting plant is, indeed, not that of animal blood; it is more akin to divine vitality. Slowly heating up from within, it is life and survival handed over to the process of decomposition in an alternative phoenix complex, not suffering of an allergy to the passage of time nor disgusted with matter.

In *Phenomenology of Spirit*, Hegel will correlate the Eleusinian mysteries of bread and wine with the religion of "a merely *immediate* spirit, the spirit of nature [*nur der* unmittelbare *Geist, der Geist der Natur*]."[22] Vegetal gods—vegetalized divinity or divinized vegetation—such as Ceres and Bacchus are not yet "the strictly higher gods whose individuality includes as an essential moment self-consciousness as such." "Therefore," Hegel continues, "spirit has not yet sacrificed itself as *self-conscious* spirit to self-consciousness, and the mystery of bread and wine is not yet the mystery of flesh and blood [*und das Mysterium des Brots und Weins ist noch nicht Mysterium des Fleisches und Blutes*]."[23] Fermentation itself needs to ferment, now in the cultural domain, rather than in the world of nature, in order to attain to the level of spirit's self-consciousness, its return to itself across the abyss of negativity and natural estrangement from itself, marked by death. After all, fermentation serves as a bridge between nature and culture, the "useless" end of a natural process taken up again into cultural works and endowed with new utility.

Hegel's 1831 lectures on the philosophy of religion will vacillate between a designation of Egyptian religion as that of "enigma" and that of "ferment" (*Gärung*).[24] Consistent with the statement we have just spotted in *Phenomenology*, however, enigma or mystery *is* ferment and ferment *is* an enigma, judging by Eleusinian rituals. The mystery, in more precise Hegelian terms, is in how spirit comes back to itself from its self-estrangement in external nature, crossing the bridge of fermentation. But it is what Hegel calls "Phoenician religion" that interests us in the present context, because it is there that the German philosopher addresses the figure of the phoenix.

"In the Phoenician religion," Hegel writes, "emphasis is placed on the defeat and estrangement of God and his resurrection." And he continues: "The representation of the phoenix is well-known [*Die Vorstellung vom Phönix ist bekannt*]: it is a bird that immolates itself in the flames, and from its ashes a young phoenix issues forth in renewed vigor."[25] Hegel selects the most well-known version of the myth, in which the phoenix is reduced to a determinate species and to a particular way of dying and being reborn. The well-known (*bekannt*) quality of this narrative will be highlighted again in the following paragraph, as well as in other works by Hegel, in which he mentions the phoenix, from *Introduction to the History of Philosophy* to *Lectures on the Philosophy of World History*. The mythic bird flashes like a meteorite through his texts, incarnating spirit, especially at the end of its wanderings through nature, in which it is alienated from itself. It is highly probable that Hegel focuses on the most popular narrative of the phoenix because he is not aware of alternative renditions of its death and rebirth. That said, we cannot help but notice certain affinities between the dialectical view

78   *Chapter 3*

of fire as the material medium of ideality, the means of idealizing matter,[26] and the bird's self-immolation in the flames, which forms a part of the "well-known" image Hegel foregrounds.

In the 1824 lectures on "Determinate Religion" the phoenix represents a "divine process" whereby death is converted into the ground of rejuvenated life: "This estrangement, this other-being defined as natural negation [*Diese Entfremdung, dieses Anderssein, als natürliche Negation*], is death, but the death that is likewise sublated, in that a rejuvenated new life arises from it. The eternal nature of spirit is to die to itself, to make itself finite in natural life, but through the annihilation of its natural state it comes to itself. The phoenix is this well-known symbol; it is not the struggle between good and evil but a divine process [*ein göttlicher Verlauf*], pertaining to the nature of God himself and proceeding in one individual."[27] Death, then, is a "natural negation" (*natürliche Negation*), which can mean a negation within nature *and* a negation of nature (and, perhaps also, the very movement of the second negation through the first). If the natural negation that is death is so polysemic, its sublation, in the course of which "a rejuvenated new life arises," has a still richer plurality of meanings. The new life that the negation of the negation yields may be the existence of future generations of the same life form, new forms of natural life arising from the "ashes" of the old, or a novel mode of the life of spirit no longer estranged from itself, having come back to itself from its otherness in the natural state. The "well-known" symbolism of the phoenix is the crossroads for these varied senses of biological negation and its negation. It will mark our and, even more so, Hegel's approaches to this religious figure with a unique sort of ambiguity.

Another significant point Hegel makes in this passage is that the phoenix is not only a figure but also a process ("a divine process," no less) folded into a singular being ("proceeding in one individual"). The process is the movement from life through death to another life, reflected into the "estrangement of God and his resurrection." The phoenix makes the procession of nature, as much as that of spirit, visible in a figure that, in addition to being well known, popularly accessible, and widely recognizable, phenomenalizes, lays out in the open subtle and barely perceptible developments, be they microscopic occurrences or, conversely, macroscale events of long duration. In the

79 *On Physiopsychology—Life and Energy*

figure-process of the phoenix, we see the movement of nature and of spirit; Hegel prefaces his brief discussion of this element in Phoenician religion with the assertion that "spirit consists essentially in coming to itself from its other-being—and from the vanquishing of this other-being—through the negation of negation. Spirit brings *itself* forth [*der Geist bringt sich hervor*]."[28] The only quandary is whether this return is "immediate" and, therefore, pertinent to the natural realm, or mediated and, hence, enabling the return of spirit to itself within nature, as culture, or both.

Hegel juggles both alternatives with reference to the image of the phoenix. When in the 1831 lectures on the philosophy of religion, he bestows yet another name on Phoenician religion as "the religion of anguish [*Schmerz*]," he hints at the dialectical means (the mechanics and machinations) of sub-jectivation through an experienced negativity that abuts but is not identical to death. While repeating the lesson from 1824, Hegel adds something else to it: the one individual, in whom a divine process of life-death-another-life unravels is a subject. "The representation of the *phoenix* [is] a death that is the reentry into a rejuvenated life—and this is what spirit is. Here we no longer have the struggle between two distinct principles but the process in regard to a *subject* itself, and not a human but rather the divine subject."[29] The two principles—life and death—no longer do battle against one another; they are shown in their mutual complementarity within a subject (the phoenix) they constitute. Such complementarity is not a dis-passionate, purely substantive fact of nature. To reach its realization, one must suffer, undergoing a pathos-laden experience of anguish, which is the material form of experience as such. Hegel brings himself to con-clude about the representation of the phoenix that "this is what spirit is," because it comprises the dialectical unity of subject and substance, more so than the co-belonging of life and death. In the same maximal sense, seven years prior to predicating spirit on the phoenix, Hegel said about the phoenix and related mythological figures that they embodied "the transi-tion, generally speaking, from vitality, from affirmative being, to death, to negation, and again the process of rising out of this negation [*der Über-gang überhaupt von der Lebendigkeit, dem affirmativen Sein zum Tode, der Negation und wiederum die Erhebung aus dieser Negation*]" as "the absolute

80   *Chapter 3*

mediation [*die absolute Vermittlung*] that belongs essentially to the concept of spirit."[30]

Even within this scheme of things, there is plenty of dialectical polysemy. The phoenix is an insignia of "actual spirit," which, "in order to be actual, must turn away from its estrangement and return to itself. However, this still pertains to the element of natural life as a process with symbolic significance."[31] In the architectonics of Hegel's dialectics, the return of spirit to itself from its estrangement in nature signals the dawn of culture. Nonetheless, he suggests in the text before us, it is still possible for this return to be included under the aegis of nature, with the added bonus of "symbolic" (i.e., culturally assigned) significance contained in the image of the phoenix. The subjectivity, which divine substance gains by handing itself over to the experience of suffering, anguish, and death, is equally multifaceted. It may refer to (1) subjects in nature—nonhuman life-forms that participate in the transition from life through death to renewed life; (2) nature as subject, synecdochally condensed in the phoenix; or (3) the subjectivity of spirit that has come back to itself through nature, as betrayed by the symbolic supplement it is loaded with.

This is how, in lectures from 1824, Hegel interprets the phoenix symbol, alluding to its connection with subjective spirit: "The eternal nature of spirit is to die to itself, to make itself finite in naturalness, but through the annihilation of its naturalness it comes to itself [*sich endlich zu machen in der Natürlichkeit, aber durch die Vernichtung seiner Natürlichkeit kommt er zu ihm selbst*]."[32] The return of spirit after its "annihilation of naturalness" entails the rise of another nature or the emergence of the other of nature, relative to the one which was other to spirit or to the one, faced with which spirit was other to itself. The moment of emptying substance—of its negation, annihilation, death—is, positively conceived, the birth of the subject at the cusp of finitude and its "eternal" overcoming. Assuming that this emergent subjectivity concerns another nature, we discover in the natural world not a totality of dumb proliferating organic and inorganic matter, but an articulation of dispersed intelligences, modes of thinking, and consciousnesses. Provided that the subjectivity in question is that of nature's other, it is no longer of nature in the immediate form, but of spirit denaturalizing itself.

I must admit that the latter reading is more conventional than the former and that Hegel's other writings bear it out as well. So, in the addition to the last paragraph of *Philosophy of Nature* (not included in the A. V. Miller translation), the rise of consciousness cannot be accommodated on nature's own turf, but requires the self-extinguishing of nature: "This [spiritual individuality that results in consciousness] is the *transition from natural being into spirit*; nature has found its consummation in living being, and has made its peace by shifting into a higher sphere. Spirit has therefore issued forth from nature. The purpose of nature is to extinguish itself [*Das Ziel der Natur ist so, sich selbst zu tödten*], and to break through its rind of immediate and sensuous being, to consume itself like a phoenix in order to emerge from this externality rejuvenated as spirit. Nature has become distinct from itself in order to recognize itself again as Idea, and to reconcile itself with itself."[33]

It is not by chance that the phoenix resurfaces here, at the very end of *Philosophy of Nature*, which is also the beginning of *Phenomenology*. The self-extinguishing of nature, revealed as nature's overall goal (*Ziel*), is its lighting up afresh in and as spirit. In the shape of the phoenix, it is finally nature that emerges rejuvenated as spirit. Nature's self-negation is its self-renewal as spirit *and* as (another) nature. Spirit denaturalizing itself is nature denaturalizing itself.

*

Hegel's lectures on religion and the conclusion of his *Philosophy of Nature* adopt a sympathetic view of the phoenix, at times turning to this mythic figure to illustrate the movement of spirit. Things are different in *Lectures on the Philosophy of World History*, which Hegel delivered in 1822–1823, less than two years before the course on the philosophy of religion. There, in the midst of a melancholy observation on the subject of constant "*change or alteration*—the supplanting of individuals, peoples, and states that arise, linger for a while, attracting our interest, gaining, losing, or sharing it with other, and then vanish,"[34] the phoenix flashes by again. The phoenix signifies the positive dimension of such an "alteration and declines [that] at the same time entail the *creation and emergence of new life*," inasmuch as "new life arises

82   *Chapter 3*

out of death." This time, though, the "striking" image of the phoenix, who "builds its own funeral pyre but arises anew from the ashes, handsomely rejuvenated and glorious," is said to relate "only to natural life [*Naturleben*]" and to be "merely Asiatic, Oriental, not Occidental [*nur asiatisch, morgen-ländisch, nicht abendländisch*]."[35] Hegel even calls this image and the insight it captures "the greatest thought the Orient has grasped [*ein großer Gedanke, den die Orientalen erfaßt haben*]."[36] But, despite its greatness, this thought, in Hegel's estimation, does not attain the level of self-conscious spirit, limited as it is to natural life alone.[37]

Predictably enough, Hegel opens himself to post- or de-colonial criticism by virtue of ascribing a "merely" naturalist metaphysics to the East compared to the spirit of the West, to which the image of the phoenix would be inappropriate. Nevertheless, we should not take this mereness for granted, above all, taking Hegel at his word. First, how do we square the presumed mereness of natural change passing through the phases of death and life, decline and new emergence, with the symbolic supplement of the image, embodying it? Second, since the matter under discussion is history (and a philosophy of world history at that), how does a merely natural life (*Naturleben*) fit within this framework? Is the process of natural life moving through death to the arising of new life a lens adopted from the comprehension of nonhuman reality to the historical understanding of the "supplanting of individuals, peoples, states"? If so, then, here too, the phoenix is already a transposition (unjustified in Hegel's view) from the realm of nature to that of human culture. Third, is change in nature insubstantial, resulting in a replication of the same shapes when life arises afresh generationally or on a much longer timescale of evolution (i.e., natural history)?

The last question is, in my view, the most consequential for Hegel's overhasty distinction between Western and Eastern metaphysics. By way of opposing the Oriental (or, more accurately, the Orientalized) image of the phoenix, Hegel states that Western spirit "does not rise out of its ashes merely rejuvenated in the same shape [*noch steht er nur verjüngt aus der Asche seiner Gestaltung auf*]" "but rather elevated and transfigured. . . . The alternations undergone do not merely return it to the same shape but rather reconstitute, purify, and elaborate it."[38]

83   *On Physiopsychology—Life and Energy*

The phoenix, on Hegel's reading, is a figure of preserving a static identity across change, even as radical as death: the offspring is indistinguishable from the predecessor. But, already in the classical sources, the problem of identity and difference is not solved in anything like a univocal fashion, nor is the natural mechanism of reproduction (particularly, of sexual reproduction) faithfully reflected in the image of the phoenix as identical to itself across the abyss of death. What Hegel is getting at, projecting his idea onto a construct of nature and Oriental metaphysics, is a certain change without change, a repetition of the same without transforming or re-elaborating that which is repeated. Whereas, in the 1824 lectures on the philosophy of religion, he is willing to grant that the phoenix represents a dialectical mediation (indeed, the absolute mediation, *die absolute Vermittlung*), in the 1822–1823 lectures on the philosophy of world history, he insinuates that the static identity across change, which it symbolizes, is only possible in a condition of pure immediacy, a dearth or a failure of determinate negations.

The ground for the earlier and rather one-dimensional conception of the phoenix was laid in Hegel's lectures on the history of philosophy, which he read in Jena between 1799 and 1806. In these lectures he also remarks on the "well-known [*bekannt*]" image of the phoenix as "one which took its origin in the East." The "universal thoughts" the image expresses remain too abstract for Hegel's taste, since they boil down "to the idea of rising up and passing away, and thus of making a perpetual circle [*auf di Vorstellung von Entstehen und Untergehen, von einem Kreislauf darin*]."[39] The reflections gathered in the myth of the phoenix indicate that "from life comes death and from death comes life; even in being, in what is positive, the negation is already present. The negative side must indeed contain it within the positive, for all change, all the process of life [*aller Proceß der Lebendigkeit*] is founded on this. But such reflections only occasionally come forth; they are not to be taken as being proper philosophic utterances [*für eigentliche Philosopheme sind sie nicht zu nehmen*]."[40]

It is easy to give in to a negative gut reaction to these statements, denying that the East (represented by the image of the phoenix) has a philosophy *proper*. There is, however, nothing to be gained from such righteous anger. We should ask, instead, what is going on with Hegel's forgetting of the image as image in his critique of abstraction, the forgetting that will find a parallel in his neglect of the symbolic supplement in relation to a purely natural life. As a mediation of abstraction, the mythic image of the phoenix in its singularity envisions a concrete universal. Lending a symbolic body to the perpetual circle of generation, decay, and regeneration, it does what the plant accomplishes within nature, becoming a synecdoche of overall self-emergence. Hegel overlooks these simple but far-reaching indications.

What happens in the intervening period of little more than one year, separating Hegel's disparate approaches to the image of the phoenix? In the summer of 1823 Hegel gave a course on the philosophy of art in Berlin. Although he had lectured on aesthetics before, at least since 1803, a mature dialectical philosophy of aesthetics was first formed in that course. It is this renewed emphasis on art that makes Hegel remember the image as image, as a mediation and a representation (a mediating representation) on the path toward thinking. According to lecture notes made by Hegel's student, Henrich Gustav Hotho, "Art in its appearance points, through itself, toward something higher—that is, toward thought [*Die Kunst in ihrem Scheinen deutet durch sich selbst auf ein Höheres, auf den Gedanken hin*]."[41] "That which we call nature," Hegel continues, "the external world [*Was wir die Natur, die äußere Welt nennen*], makes it arduous for spirit to know itself." Art resolves this difficulty: through "singular examples [*in einzelnen Beispielen*]," it presents "what cannot be explained to spirit except through images."[42] The phoenix is, in this sense, a thought-image, a singular example of nature that, through the singularity of the image, no longer appears as "the external world" but is mediated in aesthetic appearance.

*

Our overview of Hegel's tacit and manifest relation to the phoenix complex would not have been complete were we to have neglected the idea of life elaborated in *The Science of Logic*. Here, life itself, life *as such*, is reborn. At least twice. In the philosophy of nature, life "as exposed to the *externality of existence* [*in die Äußerlichkeit des Bestehens hinausgeworfen ist*]" is "conditioned by inorganic nature."[43] There is no such conditioning of life in dialectical logic, where the presupposition is the concept (corresponding to inorganic nature in the philosophy of nature) and where life is "the immediate idea [*die unmittelbare Idee*]."[44] Finally, "*In spirit*, however, life appears both as opposed to it [to spirit] and posited as at one with it, in a unity reborn as the pure product of spirit [*diese Einheit wieder durch ihn rein herausgeboren*]."[45] The rebirth of life itself (which, in its syllogism, invariably includes the genus process alongside the living individual and the life process) is a rebirth of rebirth.

As it has been before, the genus process is the philosophical site of our preoccupation, because, in it, the mechanics and machinations of reproduction contain the kernel of the phoenix complex. In the domain of logic, life as a genus process involves two moments: it is "on the one hand, the turning back to its concept and the repetition of the first forcible separation, the coming to be of a new individuality and the death of the immediate first [*das Werden einer neuen und der Tod der ersten unmittelbaren Individualität*]; but, on the other hand, the *withdrawing into itself of the concept* of life is the becoming of the concept that relates itself to itself, of the concept that exists for itself, universal and free, the transition into *cognition* [*das* Erkennen]."[46] The first movement is that of life itself turning back to its concept, in which and as which it is renewed, phoenix-like, letting one life die away and another to come into being. The concept acts as a flame, out of which the phoenix is reborn, maintaining the focus on the old and the young instantiations of life. The second movement is viewed from the middle of the concept/flame as its self-relation, which is no longer that of life (not even of life conceived on the basis of dialectical logic) but of cognition, of thought thinking itself in and through the logic of the genus process. This is a reworked version of the "absolute mediation," mentioned in lectures of the philosophy of religion.

The budding of cognition from a self-interiorization of the concept of life at the tail end of the genus process reverberates with what Hegel describes, in the addition to the concluding paragraph in *Philosophy of Nature*, as the issuing forth of spirit from nature under the sign of the phoenix. While natural life is reborn as the life of spirit, the logical concept of life is resurrected in the concept of the concept aware of itself. In each case, the transition is from externality to interiority and self-reflection: of spirit and of the concept. Whatever Hegel has to say about the figure, if not the conceptual logic of the

86   *Chapter 3*

phoenix, it is operative within the content, the form, and the transformation of life, which it both replicates and doesn't replicate, transposes onto another plane and thoroughly revolutionizes.

A copy and not a copy: this is the speculative formula of the phoenix complex at the level of the genus in Hegel's *Science of Logic*. The particularization of identity happens here as "the duplication of the individual [*die Verdopplung des Individuums*]—the presupposing of an objectivity which is identical with it, and a relating of the living being to itself as to another living being."[47] Conceived as duplication (*Verdopplung*), the genus process excludes sexual difference and rehashes the myth of the phoenix born of itself, notably born from its own death. The objectivity of the individual that serves as a self-relational mirror is "an externality in which the individual has certainty of itself not as *being sublated*, but as *subsisting* [*nicht als* aufgehobener, *sondern als* bestehender]."[48] Such subsistence without sublation echoes Hegel's critique of the "Asiatic" phoenix, which is merely rejuvenated but does not undergo any substantial changes. Its certainty is the certainty of life's immediate continuation, where it is punctuated and disrupted by death. In *The Science of Logic*, however, this development represents "the truth of life [*die Wahrheit des Lebens*], in so far as life is still shut up within itself."[49]

When the sexual relation does appear in the syllogism of life, it heralds a transition from the generative, or the self-regenerating, concept of life to the reproductive actuality of life's idea: the individualities locked in this relation "satisfy the tension of their longing and dissolve themselves into the universality of their genus. . . . To this extent, it is the individuality of life itself, no longer *generated* out of its concept but out of the *actual* idea [*nicht mehr aus seinem Begriffe, sondern aus der* wirklichen *Idee* erzeugt]."[50] In the sphere of reproduction, too, the phoenix complex does not achieve the actuality of energy, does not realize energy *as* actuality, but keeps both the reproducing and the reproduced beings beholden to the virtual reality of the concept. In its unrest, in its noncoincidence with itself, the concept (of the individual, of life, or what have you) spawns a great deal—all the ephemeral exemplars of itself that replace one another without exhausting the inner essence they exemplify. With the individuality of life generated from "the *actual* idea," another energy, contained *in nuce* in the sexual relation, becomes apparent.

87   *On Physiopsychology—Life and Energy*

The concrete universality of the genus, reflected in the actual idea, is compatible with the singularity of the reproduced life, which is a bearer of essence externalized, of energy converted into actuality.

Nevertheless, in the rebirth of life itself reliant on the sexual relation, the phoenix complex remains at work. "In copulation [*Begattung*], the immediacy of living individuality perishes; the death of this life is the coming to be of spirit [*der Tod dieses Lebens ist das Hervorgehen des Geistes*]. The idea, *implicit* as genus, becomes *explicit* in that it has sublated its particularity that constituted the living species. . . . This is the *idea of cognition*."[51] That the death of immediate life is the coming to be of spirit means two things: (1) this death is a transition to the life of spirit, (2) this death is the becoming of spirit as the other of life. Earlier in the text, Hegel anticipated this irresolvable contradiction inherent to spirit, which is both opposed to life and posited as one with it. Teasing the phoenix motif out of Hegel's formulation, we might say not only that death gives way to a new life (another life of the same kind *or* another kind of life) but also that death is endowed with a generativity of its own, when it is frozen, perhaps indefinitely, in a transition between lives, whether of the same kind or of different kinds. This depends, in turn, on the sort of energy that is deployed: the energy of actuality, nourishing a singular universality, or the energy of potentiality, promoting a lethal self-reproduction of the concept.

88   *Chapter 3*

4 UNITY AND UNIVERSALITY: PLOTINUS/SCHELLING

The absolute singularity of the phoenix, who is one of a kind, is a feature that recurs across narratives and traditions, from the earliest to the medieval. This feature places the phoenix in a privileged position with regard to the whole: it is thanks to her singularity that she comes to embody the whole. Even John Donne in his 1604 poem "The Canonization" equates "the phoenix riddle" with the phenomenon of two becoming one in love: "Call us what you will, we're made such by love; / Call her one, me another fly, / We're tapers too, and at our own cost die, / And we in us find th'eagle and the dove; / The phoenix riddle hath more wit / By us: we two, being one, are it."[1] The phoenix betokens not so much a post-factum unification as a primordial unity (also of opposites, the old *complexio oppositorum*, such as fire and water, the feminine and the masculine, sexual and asexual being, life and death, the eagle and the dove). The unity of nature—the unity that *is* nature prior to its unfolding, spreading or burgeoning out: which is to say, before and beyond what the Greeks call *phusis*; hence, a certain nature without nature—is at stake in the figure of the phoenix, who, in a burst of light and heat, incarnates the whole.

Born in Lycopolis, Egypt, which was then a Roman province, at the beginning of the third century CE, Plotinus deduces the existence of one nature from the nature of the One. Actually, the One in and of itself remains unknown and unknowable, even if it is partly available via three hypostases or emanations: the intellect (*nous*), the soul (*psuchē*), and the good (*to agathon*). The One gives itself as more than one, retreats from the giving, covers itself over with the latticework of multiplicities. The project of a return to the origin, which Plotinus undertakes in his philosophy, is that of overcoming multiple ramifications of the One, of reuniting with the principle of unity, of disclosing nature before and beyond nature (hence, nature without growth and, in some sense, without itself; nature compatible with the self-containment of a principle) in absolute simplicity, quietude, and energetic rest. The principle is solitary and unique, so much so that it must be "defined by its uniqueness [*monachōs*]" (*Enneads* 6.8.9.11), while "uniqueness comes from the principle itself" (6.8.9.13–14). The phoenix's dip into life-giving fire is an allegorization of this reunification and uniqueness, reducing material forms to the underlying ineffable One.

In the all-important Ennead 3.8, "On Nature and Contemplation and the One," Plotinus famously (and playfully) suggests that "all things aspire to contemplation [*panta theōrias epheisthai*] and direct their gaze to this end—not only rational, but also irrational living things [*aloga zōa*], and the power of growth in plants [*phutois phusin*], and the earth which brings them forth—and that all attain it as far as possible for them in their natural state [*kata phusin echonta*], but different things contemplate and attain their end in different ways, some truly [*alēthōs*], and some only having an imitation and image [*mimēsin kai eikona*] of this true end" (3.8.1.1–8). The power of growth in plants, for instance, is the vegetal way of contemplating the One, through what Plotinus will later dub "growth-thought," *phutikē noesis*. Sensation is the animal mode of contemplating the One in a "sense-thought," *aisthētikē noesis*. Ratiocination is "soul-thought," *psuchikē noesis* (3.8.8.15). Each thought, each manner of contemplation, is inseparable from a life—vegetal, animal, human. Being a plant is thinking-planthood (or growth) and contemplating the One, or being contemplated by the One, which imagines itself (through a rich and ever ramifying image) in the shape of a plant. Existing as an animal is enthinking animality (or sensation) and contemplating the One, or being contemplated by the One, dreaming itself up as an animal. Assuming the form of a human is thinking thought itself, presumably freer of images and imitations, and contemplating the One, or being contemplated by it already in the medium of pure contemplation.

When the phoenix appears on the cultural scene as a synecdoche of the soul or of nature, what emerges is an image or a symbol (which I have

90   *Chapter 4*

also referred to as a thought-image) of the whole. But, like the phoenix, the image, too, is unique. The phoenix is neither purely elemental nor vegetal nor animal nor human or divine, and all of these beings at once. The life of the phoenix is neither that of mere growing, nor of sensing, nor of abstract thinking, and yet it is all of the above. The phoenix neither incarnates the truth of the One nor is he its image nor imitation, even as he is all of these things. Through the phoenix, nature or the soul sees itself, as in a mirror—a contemplation of the contemplation that is as much sensuous as it is intellectual and growing-metamorphosing-decaying. The phoenix thus englobes the "ascents of contemplation from nature to the soul and from the soul to the intellect [*tēs phuseōs epi psuchēn kai apo tautēs eis noun*]" (3.8.8.1–2), ascents, through which contemplation becomes more intimate, more united with the contemplator, and yet also more universal.

More than an aspiration, contemplation is creative, such that the primordial unity of theory and practice is the principle of nature: "Nature . . . has contemplation in itself and makes what it makes by contemplation [*poiei dia theōrian poiei*]" (3.8.1.23–25). Theory moves the world, making it grow and change, endowing it with sentience and reflective capacities. Being, knowing, and making merge into one, because they are traceable back to the One.

Nevertheless, tucked into this thesis is a strong critique of phenomenality, of the process whereby, bubbling over itself, the One departs from itself, parting ways with itself, with its absolute rest, quietude, self-sufficiency, and plenitude. At first, "nature is at rest in contemplation of the vision of itself, a vision which comes to it from its abiding in and with itself and being itself a vision" (3.8.4.25–27). Subsequently (let us note that speaking of the "subsequent" is running into the problem of time, which Plotinus will take up separately in Ennead 3.7 on time and eternity), something comes to visibility, appears or surfaces, starts developing, leading a life that is exposed before the gaze of an outside observer. Passing into action, vision becomes generative or poietic and, in so doing, it grows weaker, just as "men, when their power of contemplation weakens make action a shadow of contemplation [*skian theōrias*] and reasoning" (3.8.4.30–32). Nature at rest, standing close to the One, gives way to a restless nature dispersed in the many. The

91   *Unity and Universality*

latter's "formative principle, which operates in the visible shape [*morphē*], is the last [*eschatos*] and is dead [*nekros*] and no longer able to make another" (3.8.2.30–32). But nature at rest, as well, is shadowy, compared to the brilliance of the intellect (*nous*), such that even the cosmos is but the intellect's "shadow and image [*skia kai eikōn*]" (3.8.11.28–29).

Plotinus borrows from Plato's *Phaedrus* (250c.4) the designation of the intellect as "pure light, pure radiance [*phōti katharō kai augē kathara*]" (3.8.11.27–28), compared to which the shining cosmic ornament is dull and dark. And he slots nature at rest, immersed in a contemplation of contemplation itself, between the two regimes of phenomenality (theoretical sight, on the one hand; physical vision, on the other). This in-between space is the space of the phoenix. Although Plotinus does not mention the bird by name, his early years in Lycopolis and a later sojourn in Alexandria surely made him acquainted with stories about this unusual bird and its Egyptian predecessor, *bennu*.[2] As a form of the sun god, *bennu* (probably transcribed into Greek as *phoinix*[3]) is a source of shining and a personification of radiance, seeing also that its name is derived from the verb *wbn*, which means "to rise radiantly," "to shine."[4] How and why, then, does the phoenix (or *bennu*) with its own glow stand between what I've just termed "two regimes of phenomenality," notably the shining of the cosmos and of the intellect, the one a shadow of the other?

If we take fire as a medium of rebirth in the widely known renditions of the myth, then it becomes clear that, delving back into fiery life, whether the flames shoot from her own body or from the elements outside, the phoenix returns to a radiance that does not give anything to sight. In fact, in Ennead 2.1, "On Heavens," Plotinus asserts that "there are fiery living beings among the spirits [*Kai zōa de purina esti daimonōn*]" (2.1.6.54–55). The passage of the aged phoenix through fire is a reunification with the spiritual realm, where visible forms are no longer necessary—the final forms (including those of the body itself) that are already, in themselves, dead, incapable of generating anything else. The theoretical and the practical, eidetic and ritualistic reduction of the body in fire is but the most literal crossing from one regime of phenomenality to another.

92   *Chapter 4*

Nonetheless, fire is not, for Plotinus, a principle of life; it is, itself, lifeless compared to the principles (the *logoi*) of vitality, through which nature is defined. Speaking of nature as "the power . . . which makes without hands [and therefore] must remain unmoved [*dunamin tēn ou dia cheirōn poiousan kai pasan menein*]" (3.8.2.14–15), he rejects the view of cosmic or elemental fire as the formative (spiritual) principle that enlivens (wooden) matter: "For it is not fire which has to come to matter in order that it may become fire, but a forming principle [*ina pur hē hulē genētai, alla logon*]" (3.8.2.25–26). The second crossing between the regimes of phenomenality is, therefore, signaled by the transition from fire to *logos*. Here, the "fast" and the "slow" transformations of the phoenix, both of them eluding in different ways bodily vision, rely on nature's "making without hands," the generativity of its contemplation—which is, in a certain synecdochic sense, the phoenix's contemplation. Plotinian nature is not a perfect artisan; on the contrary, its productive and reproductive powers betray a weakening of contemplative energy and need to be subordinated to the original impulse, which will revitalize them: "Action, then, is for the sake of contemplation and vision [*praxis eneka theōrias kai theōrēmatos*]" (3.8.6.1).

Besides the rising and setting sun or seasonal periodicity, another motif of phenomenality (closely tied to survival, if not to resurrection) in the phoenix complex is the germinating seeds. Reviving after apparent death, a seedling breaks out into the light, while remaining tethered to the darkness of the soil. The seed, in Plotinus's eyes, represents the formative principle so long as it stays quiet in its self-identity. Analogous to the soul and to nature, however, it gives in to the temptation of disquiet: "As from a quiet seed [*ek spermatos hēsuchou*], the formative principle, unfolding itself, advances, as it thinks, to largeness, but does away with the largeness by division and, instead of keeping its unity in itself, squanders it outside itself and so goes forward to a weaker extension" (3.7.11.23–27). A weaker nature is restlessly active, striving to appear in the light of day, unsatisfied with keeping itself in reserve and in the quiet energy of the principle. Thinking, which is indistinguishable from growing—from "the spreading out of life" that constitutes time (3.7.11.42), the plant, as well as the soul and nature it represents—exchanges the first

93   *Unity and Universality*

regime of phenomenality flooded with the pure brilliance of the intellect for the second regime lit with actual sunlight and the rest of cosmic fire.

This is Plotinus's ultimate rebuttal of the phoenix complex: it would be better if the cycle of rebirths were to stop, and better still if it were never to have started. The seed, the principle gathered in its absolute simplicity into the One, is incomparably more desirable than the fully developed plant that will grow from it, squandering itself (squandering the unity and unicity of the One, no less!) outside itself. The phoenix is the symbolic stain of a philosophical version of the original sin according to Plotinus, the sin of having parted with and departed from the origin.

*

The energy component of the phoenix complex fits, with some unease, the scheme Plotinus draws in his philosophy. On the one hand, he takes *energeia* in the Aristotelian sense of a quiet and complete actuality, not lacking in anything and perfectly self-contained in the One. On the other hand, *energeia* turns into *dunamis*, or potentiality—despite the efforts Plotinus exerts to differentiate between the two, particularly in Ennead 2.5, "On Powers and Actualities"—when, flowing down from the source, it drives the expansion of life *and* when it borders on pure potentiality, kept in reserve in the One. Be this as it may, for Plotinus, the reproduction of existence through copies of the original and copies of those copies, entails a weakening (exhaustion, entropy) of the initial energy the further it is pushed away from its source.

The paradox of Plotinian energy is explicable with regard to energy's doubling.[5] So, "the first part of the soul, that which is above and always filled and illuminated by the reality above, remains there; but another part . . . goes forth, for soul goes forth always, life from life [*gar aei zōē ek zōēs*]; for energy reaches everywhere [*energeia gar pantachou phthanei*], and there is no point where it fails" (3.8.5.10–15). The quanta of energy are fixed, whether in the realm above, or here below. But, because upper energy remains ever the same, it does not suffer any diminution, while lower energy "goes forth," expanding and flowing "from life to life," and is debilitated in its parts by being divided. The two energies, then, are those of the One in itself and of a unity that falls apart into a constantly ramifying multiplicity.

As for the figure of the phoenix, its reproduction follows the rules of "the first part of the soul," which, by producing a rejuvenated other as though it were the same, preserves a fixed quantum of energy without dissipating into the many. Cosmic fire and the cosmos itself combine sameness and difference in a similar fashion: "If anything was lost there through fire being extinguished, other fire [*pur heteron*] would have to be kindled; and if it [the cosmos] had this other fire from something else and that something else lost it by flux, that again would have to be replaced by other fire" (2.1.3.25–30). Such self-replacement is crucial to the myth of the phoenix, and it also reflects the activity of cosmic fire according to Plotinus, along with the view of energy that is invariable and at rest either above or beneath all its fluctuations. That nothing is lost in the process of substitution means that a formal identity has been established between the substituting and the substituted, stopping in its tracks the entropic tendency whereby energy dissipates the further it is from its source. Life itself—and, in the first and last instances, the life of the cosmos—is anti-entropic. All losses are not only accounted for but also neutralized, indemnified as though they have never been incurred, as though movement, change, metamorphosis never took place.

At the same time, Plotinus postulates a qualitative difference between the generating and the generated, such that "that which generates is always simpler than that which is generated [*tou gar gennēthenos pantachou to gennōn haplousteron*]" (3.8.9.43–44). The degrees of simplicity increase the closer we get to the origin, that is, the absolute simplicity of the One. And that is the very origin of energy's doubling, its distribution between the energy maintained forever intact and that suffering a constant weakening. "The first life [*zōē prōtē*]" is not first absolutely, "since it is the energy [*energeia*] manifest in the way of the outgoing of all things" (3.8.9.33–34). By contrast to the energy of vitality, there is also "something else, which is no more in the way of outgoing, but is the origin of the outgoing, and the origin of life and of the intellect and all things [*archē diexodou kai archē zōēs kai archē tōn pantōn*]" (3.8.9.38–40).

The absolute principle and origin, which is the One, generates all that is *but does not partake of the mode of being, the energy, the life of the generated*. It dispenses life from what is not in life, what is not itself living, but is "above

95   *Unity and Universality*

life [*huper tēn zōēn*]" as its "cause [*aition*]" (3.8.10.3). The phoenix's rebirth may be understood as a plunge into the nonliving cause of life, symbolized at the limits of phenomenality by fire. Pure Life is difficult to tell apart from Death, just as unadulterated Light is indistinguishable from Darkness. Along these lines pure actuality flips into pure potentiality, the energy (*energeia*) manifest in the outgoing supplanted with the power (*dunamis*) that remains nonmanifest in the cause of the outgoing: "What is it [that which is before all things]? The power of all things [*Dunamis tōn pantōn*]" (3.8.10.1).

Together with Plotinus, we circle back to the seed as a companion figure of the phoenix and as the semantic vehicle of the One, of its potency, which is, in a surprising reversal of Aristotle that makes Plotinus (almost) our contemporary, other and greater than energy. The One, Plotinus writes in a treatise on "The Descent of the Soul into Bodies," could not stay happily in itself, alone (*monon*) and hidden (*ekekrupto*) (4.8.6.1). Instead, it generously unfolds like a seed (*spermatos*) "from a partless beginning [*amerous archēs*] which proceeds to the final stage perceived by the senses" (4.8.6.9–10). The infinite power of the One becomes manifest, giving itself a body, an actuality (in the exact sense of *energeia*). What is in the Ennead "On Eternity and Time" rebuked as the weakness of the seed "thinking itself to largeness" is here restyled into a strength (the strength *of* weakness?) insofar as actual existence in a ramified multiplicity is the dimension that was missing from the hermetic plenitude of the One: locked in itself, it would have remained as ineffectual as a soul without a body. "Energy (or actuality) everywhere reveals completely hidden potency [*energeia tēn dunamin edeixe*], in a way obliterated and nonexistent because it does not yet truly exist" (4.8.5.34–36).

The notion of potency or potentiality in Plotinus is far from straightforward; like energy, it splits against itself and emerges as its own double. On the one hand, "one must speak of anything which is potential as potentially something else [*to dunamei ti on allo hulē tō ti*] by being able to become something after what it already is" (2.5.1.17–18). On the other hand, "potentiality understood in the sense of being able to make [*hē dunamis hē kata to poiein*] would not be described as existing potentially" (2.5.1.25–26). *Dunamis* as the capacity to become other is not equivalent to *dunamis* as

96 *Chapter 4*

the capacity to make others. The *dunamis* of the One, concentrating in itself "the power of all things," is not subject to alteration, to the vicissitudes of othering. It overflows itself and initiates the outpouring of existence without suffering any changes. Although they reflect the activity of the One, the seed and the phoenix are not exempt from the first sense of potentiality: they are the One in self-alteration, capable of becoming something other than what they already are. In the story of the phoenix, this othering is immediately negated, subsumed into the same, as in Lactantius: "The same indeed, but not the same; the very one, yet not the one [*Ipsa quidem, sed non eadem, quia et ipsa, nec ipsa est*]" (*De ave phoenice* 169–170). The phoenix is, therefore, halfway to the One, both partaking and not partaking of the first sense of potentiality, pinpointed by Plotinus.

The "power of all" is, by implication, a double-edged sword. Gathered in the One, this power is not capable of anything—provided that capacity is indicative of a deficiency, something yet to be accomplished—and it is capable of everything—assuming the second sense of *dunamis* as a making (here: through the creative self-overflow of contemplation). That said, the making (*poiesis*) as an effect of contemplation (*theōria*) is not the bustle of activity, but quietude oozing with the energy of rest, replete with echoes of eternity and the One: "The disposition of . . . that quiet life as a single whole, still unbounded, altogether without declination" (3.7.11.1–5).[6] Stillness (*hēsuchia*)—quietness, silence—marks this state before time, in which a potentiality not lacking in anything merges with actuality: *dunamis* melts into *energeia*. This is the state commemorated in the quietude of a seed, *spermatos hēsuchou* (3.8.11.23) and in the "soul of all that would be like the soul in a great growing plant [*phutō megalō*], which directs the plant without effort or noise" (4.3.4.25–30), furnishing a vegetal figuration of the One.[7]

Quiescence and stillness attained, as much as possible, in this life will later on become the cornerstones of the Greek Orthodox spiritual practice of Hesychasm, as formulated, for instance, in the writings of Byzantine theologian Gregory Palamas.[8] But what about the phoenix complex? Does it admit the quietude of energy at rest, the energy *of* rest that overcomes the restlessness of becoming within the sphere of becoming? Or does it frame life as nothing but a hamster perpetually running in a wheel in order to remain in the same place? To take up these questions, we need to discuss the Plotinian concept of time as it bears upon the phoenix complex.

*

In Plotinus's philosophical universe, time is derivative from eternity. In this, also, he subscribes to the position of Plato's *Timaeus*, where time is defined, protocinematically, as "a moving image of eternity" (37d). Eternity, for Plotinus, is being without either a past or a future, never expending anything of itself and yet, through its "infinite power [*dia dunamin apeiron*]," rendering the many (3.7.5.20–25). Eternity is the life (*zōē*; 3.7.5.23) and the nature (*phusis*; 3.7.6.1) of the One, or, at least, the "altogether beautiful and everlasting" life and nature, gathered "around the One [*peri to hen*]" (3.7.6.2). Time arises with "the restlessly active nature [*phuseōs de polupragmonos*] . . . seeking more than its present state" (3.7.11.14–16) and "the soul's unquiet power [*psuchēs hēn tis dunamis ouch hēsuchos*] wanting to transfer [*metapherein*] what it saw there [in eternity] to something else" (3.7.11.20–21). However necessary the physical extension of the One that lends it actuality and effectiveness at the price of its self-containment, time is, on this view, a whim of the soul and of restless nature (and, for Plotinus, "what is called nature is the soul [*hē men legomenē phusis psuchē ousa*]" [3.8.4.15]), symbolized by the phoenix.

Time is superfluous compared to eternity, of which it is the image: it replaces "the complete and infinite whole" with a "continuous and infinite succession" (3.7.11.54–55), an image that cannot be envisioned all at once because it is ever in the process of being made—*o kosmos eikon aei eikonizomenos* (2.3.18.16). And the phoenix complex confirms, over and over, the superfluousness of time. The aging of the bird or the tree that goes under that name is reversed, undone thanks to its rejuvenation, rebirth, or resurrection in fire or through a slower process of decomposition and spontaneous regeneration. Once the phoenix achieves its full manifestation, it is as though nothing happened, as though no time passed, as though the gap of "dead time" were bridged. Despite the language of filiality and even burial rites performed with the remains of the phoenix's predecessor in some versions

98   *Chapter 4*

of the myth, there is no substantive difference between the "before" and the "after." The myth thus abuts eternity, in which "you cannot apprehend anything as before [*proteron*] or after [*husteron*]" (3.7.6.18–19) and in which being ultimately appears "without any difference [*adiaphorōs*]" (3.7.6.14).

Time is erased in its very movement; a chain of succession disappears, bent into the circle, in which the phoenix is (remains or returns to being) one. It makes no sense to invoke what is before and what is after in a constantly rotating cycle. Similarly, in Plotinus, when the soul "leaves its activity outside eternity and returns to unity, time is abolished [*anērētai chronos*]" (3.7.12.20–22). Nature before and beyond nature is recoverable, because restless activity is a deviation from the underlying energy of rest, just as time is a (temporary) departure from the order of eternity. This is what the phoenix complex conveys. Embedded within the paradigm of "renewable" energy is the same sleight of hand that eliminates all differences between generations of growable and combustible materials, ideally interchangeable and substituting for the past without any positive or negative remainder. When the balance in this ontological accounting system is zero, time is, indeed, "abolished," the unevenness, discontinuities, leaps and rifts of a succession leveled down and neutralized. The absence of changes discernible in a fresh version of the phoenix compared to the old encapsulates the superfluousness of time, that is, the passage of time that may be brushed off with a deeply theoretical pretense that it did not pass. In short, what is in play here is an approximation of the temporally (part by part) reconstructed whole and the undivided whole of eternity, in the image of which time is generated (3.7.11.45–50).

Time in Plotinus operates under erasure, moving within and toward what is no longer or not yet temporal. Its operations amount to the technologies (the mechanics and machinations) of transferring (*metapherein*) what a disquieted soul espied in eternity to something or someone else. This transfer is as much psychic as physical, geared as it is toward the production and reproduction of the same.[9] Different existents and modes of existence are the manifold replications of the vision of the One: "The same vision is in every soul [*en pasē psuchē to auto*]" (3.8.5.32)[10] and "it is soul which contemplates, and makes that which comes after it . . . and contemplation makes

99   *Unity and Universality*

contemplation [*kai theōria tēn theōrian poiei*]" (3.8.5.25–30). Time is the duration of theory-practice that transfers the same vision (of the atemporal) to a multitude of generated beings. The formal equality of vision that is "in every soul" equalizes the generating and the generated on the primordial grounds of the One.

And yet, in the ongoing replications of the same vision through psycho-physical transfer "filling all things with contemplation [*esti pantas plērōsai theōrias*]" (3.8.7.23), something happens—something that, disrupting the self-consolidation of sameness, introduces transcription errors into the pro-gram of reproduction. These errors, like genetic mutations or small inaccu-racies in viral replication, muddle the vision of the One that still resides in every soul, such that a newly generated existence "contemplates in a more external way [*exōterō*] and not like that which preceded it" (3.8.5.26–28). Plotinus then suggests that the "failures [*amartiai*]" of the contemplators are due to their distraction from the object of contemplation, which is the One (the Greek word translated as "distraction" by A. H. Armstrong in the Loeb edition of the *Enneads* is *paraphora*, which entails going astray and aside, a slight derangement, frenzy or even madness) (3.8.7.21–24). If the phoenix reproduces itself without such errors, that is because it is not this or that soul, but the soul as such, counted among the hypostases of the One.

Self-creation, or self-re-creation (more recently recovered in the sense of *autopoiesis*), is another hallmark of the One, which it also shares with the phoenix. In an atmosphere of freedom, "he himself is the one who makes himself [*autos estin outos o poiōn eauton*]" (6.8.15.9). This is the sense of "the absolute making [*apoluton tēn poiēsin*]" (6.8.15.6), of "eternal generation [*gennēsei aidiō*]," and "self-governance [*archōn eautou*]" (6.8.15.29)—all of them qualities that come very close to describing the phoenix's activ-ity. Eternal self-generation is the only way to avoid the error of distracted contemplators: the generating and the generated, the before and the after are one and the same and, though there is movement between them, this movement is insubstantial, literally freed from the limiting conditions of substance. Pertaining to the economy of the One, "absolute making" works with parts that are not really parts, with the One that parts against itself without actually parting or departing from itself. It is worth underlining

100   *Chapter 4*

the singular mechanics and machinations of absolute self-reproduction and its place in the overall plot of the phoenix complex: with the whole at once undivided and divided on its own terms, time and eternity converge on the horizon on the One. And this convergence also has to do with "us," in those exceptional conditions when we attain unity with the One, "when we ascend to this and become this alone and let the rest go . . . having become the true life itself [*auto to alēthinon zēn genomenous*]" (6.8.15.20–25).

In addition to symbolizing the soul, the phoenix is the synecdoche of nature, which, Plotinus writes, "is time itself [*hē phusis autē chronos*]" (3.7.12.1). The bracketing, the reduction, the putting under erasure of time is, therefore, a putting under erasure of nature. The time that is the predicate of nature consists of "even and uniform changes [*metabolais*]" in a "continuous unfolding of energy [*suneches to tēs energeias*]" (3.7.12.2–3). There is no time without metabolism, the unremitting transformations of energy, which assumes the most varied shapes. The bracketing of time that, by the same token, brackets nature does away with the metabolic pathways of energy tending toward exteriority. The phoenix-like rebirth of nature without time happens on a higher plane (which is also the earlier, or even the earliest stage, if it still makes sense to speak of the earlier and the later here) of energetic rest, of being "turned around [*anastrepsai*]" and directed only to itself (3.7.12.4) with utmost attention devoid of the possibility of distraction. In the same line of Plotinian text, energy mutates into *dunamis*, the power beyond capability, gathered into the One.[11]

*

The superfluousness of time against the backdrop of the "partless whole" that is eternity finds its logical expression in the redundancy of death, which is the pivotal aspect of the phoenix complex. Plotinus makes the strongest statement to this effect in Ennead 2.1, "On Heavens": "Even if it were possible for all body to perish [*ei pan oion te sōma apolesthai*], nothing unpleasant would happen to soul" (2.1.4.31–32). The material reduction of the body does not in the least harm the soul: this metaphysical tenet presides over philosophical reflections throughout the millennia stretching from Plato to Edmund Husserl. Nevertheless, the phoenix signals resurrection of and in

101   *Unity and Universality*

the flesh, and the complex that goes under its name cannot ignore the bodily dimension of existence. This has not escaped Plotinus, who perhaps ironically suggests that, in order to achieve self-sufficiency (*autarkeia*) in matters of well-being, "one must cut off the body, and even perception of the body [*aisthēsin tēn sōmatos*], from human nature" (1.4.5.24–25). (As a result of the proposed cut, lost, along with the body, would be the vegetal soul, the plant-thinking of the One that permeates the body and is in charge of its growth, nourishment, and reproduction, as well as the animal soul, which is the perceptual contemplation of the One. Remaining after the drastic psychosurgery would be the purely contemplative, "rational" soul.) So, how should we approach the issue of the redundancy of death, and possibly of the body, in Plotinian thought?

The initial clue is contained in the same manuscript "On Wellbeing," where Plotinus muses about the possibility of cutting off from the soul the entire body and its perception. A radical cut occurs at the time of death. While it is absurd to desire the reduction of embodied existence in life for the sake of attaining happiness,[12] the event of death is not an occasion for grieving: "Even if the death of friends and relatives causes grief, it does not grieve him [a human being] but only that in him which has no intelligence [*en autō noun ouk echon*]," and "he will not allow the distress of this to move him" (1.4.4.34–36). Death performs a practical reduction on the body and on the most embodied levels of vitality (or the soul), while keeping intact the more intimate, purer self-contemplation of the One that constituted the human as human. It is this principle of human life that is reborn, reincarnated in the flesh.

In accordance with Plotinus's theory of metempsychosis,[13] influenced by the myth of Er that appears in Book X of Plato's *Republic*, "Those who guarded the human in them become human again [*osoi men oun ton anthrōpon etērēsan, palin anthrōpoi*]" (1.4.2.16). What one does in this life matters; how one has led it steers the transmigrating soul toward the shape of a future incarnation. Humanity is not a fixed identity, not a genetic code hardwired into our corporeality once and for all. It is, rather, a gift that may be easily lost and that requires to be kept or guarded (*etērēsan*: "they kept") in this life so that it would be received again in the next. The Plotinian phoenix

102   *Chapter 4*

is, therefore, not an automatic, mechanical, and *consequently* machinational process or procedure, but a conditional event, promising rebirth in the same stream of life, provided that the life deemed to be specifically human prevailed in one's former existence.[14]

What befalls those who do not guard the human in them? "Those who lived by sense alone [*de aisthēsei monon*] become animals; but if their sense-perceptions have been accompanied by passionate temper, they become wild animals. . . . But if they did not even live by sense along with their desires but coupled them with the dullness of perception, they turn into plants; for it was this, the growth-energy [*enērgei to phutikon*], which worked in them, alone or predominantly, and they were taking care to turn themselves into trees" (3.4.2.17–25). In the Hellenic context, the possibility of reincarnation in plants is already present in the thought of Empedocles; however, Plotinus does not differentiate among the species or kinds of plants, as he does in the case of animals. Nor is it spelled out, though this is implied, what happens to animals who do not guard their animality: they are, obviously, reincarnated in plants. As a rule, whatever the energy that gained an upper hand and steered the body-soul assemblage in life will be the very energy that will find an appropriate form for itself after this life is over (3.4.3.2). The intermittencies of death, death as the intermittency of life or of lives, is an opportunity for a correction, an adjustment (for this is, indeed, a matter of justice) of the predominant kind of soul to the body it receives. Plotinian metempsychosis manages a modified version of the phoenix complex, whereby the reincarnated soul may find its temporary home in a body that is not physically the same as the previous one but that is appropriate for this soul's habitual activities.

As a result, death is no more than the possibility of readjustment, of the soul's retraction from the body with which it is imbricated in this life, its return to the One, and its reenergizing plunge into a fresh and more suitable corporeal entity. Actually, since the body is what is superadded to the soul, it is "the soul [that] waits for the body to fall altogether away [*to sōma apostēnai*] from it" (1.9.2–4). As in later philosophies of immanence (notably, in Spinoza's), death is akin to a rearrangement of pieces, not to a radical break—the untying of a bond that is retied elsewhere, by other means, or

103 *Unity and Universality*

even by the same, assuming that one lived one's life in a way befitting the kind of being one was. To be sure, "no single individual thing lasts forever, but the unity of form [*to hēn tō eidei*]" (2.1.1.9–10). The phoenix is this unity of form (of *psuchē*, of *phusis*) personified, figuratively attributed to a "single individual thing." If he is born from death, that is because death is not just the dissolution but also the contrary, an occasion for further consolidating the form in its unity.

At the global level, the unity of living form conjugated with the constant flux of matter justifies the simultaneous sameness and difference of the phoenix, of the "universal living creature [*to pan zōon*] [that] would not remain the same thing, even if it remained the same sort of thing" (2.1.3.30). Within the elastic unity of form, matter is replaceable: the variability or substitutability (above all, the self-substitutability) at the core of the phoenix complex pertains to materiality. The flux of matter, however, is not chaotic: the synthesis of elements is such that "through the community of the universe [*kata tēn en kosmō koinōnian*], while remaining itself each [element] takes not the actual [other] element, but something which belongs to it" (2.1.7.15–16). Matter is, therefore, a combination of sameness and otherness, its "cosmic community" attached to the "all-embracing living creature" by means of its universality, the being-in-common of community (*koinōnia*), which resonates with "the all" (*to pan*) of the grand living creature.

Strangely, matter and the body taken in their universality corroborate the formal irreality of death in Plotinus. In the Ennead "On Heavens," which we have been reading quite closely, "the matter and body of all . . . cooperate toward the immortality of the universe [*tou kosmou athanasian*]" by "flowing in themselves; not flowing out [*rei gar ouk exō*]" (2.1.3.1–4). In his polemic "Against the Gnostics," Plotinus adds the following: "That which has nothing into which it can be dissolved will not perish" (2.9.3.15). Material forms dissolve back into matter, but matter itself does not dissolve into anything else. The phoenix principle is active here: across changes, fast or slow, the phoenix reverts back to the same because everything moves within a closed system lacking an outside. An inwardly directed flux is congruous with stasis.

104   *Chapter 4*

The last two themes to take up with respect to death and materiality in the crucible of the phoenix complex, as Plotinus configures it, are spontaneous generation and disgust.

In the Ennead "On Our Allotted Guardian Spirit" (3.4), the theme of *generatio aequivoca* is briefly addressed. The generativity of the soul in the process of division is most clearly observable in plants: "Sometimes the soul remains in the same living being and gives [life to others], like the soul in plants" (3.4.6.41). A living plant is a phoenix that generates other living beings (like it) from the threshold of death, of being sliced into parts. (Note that, for Plotinus, division into parts is already a harbinger of demise, since, by bordering on others, each part is in a tense, finite coexistence, potentially annihilated by them.) "But sometimes," Plotinus continues, "when it [the soul] goes away, it gives before it goes, as with plants which have been pulled up or dead animals, when from their putrefaction many are generated from one [*ek sēpseōs pollōn ex henos gennēthentōn*]" (3.4.6.42–44). Spontaneous generation from putrefaction is a birth from death that restages in miniature the origination of the many from the One, a source of tremendous wonder (*thauma*), as far as Plotinus is concerned (3.8.10.14). Both at the macroscale of the origin of the living as such and on the microscale of *generatio aequivoca*, there is a collaboration, a working-with, a synergetic assemblage (*sunergeia*) of the One and the many, that is, the bond holding together the power (*dunamis*) of a generative unity and the generated multiplicity: "The power of all things collaborates [*sunergein*], and the particular power which is the same here [of one decomposing body], too" (3.4.6.45). The synergy in question is also that of the One and the one in the process of decomposition, the arriving and the parting gifts of the soul.

Through spontaneous generation, the parting gift of the soul spawning life from a decomposing body rejoins the life-giving power of the One. Hence, in keeping with Plotinian logic, neither putrefaction nor death is disgusting: the former, participating in a synergic relation with the creative origin of life; the latter, a misnomer. What *is* disgusting is living matter itself at the farthest remove from the One: it is the worst (*cheiriston*), savage (*agrion*), and opaque. "Its product is a living being, but a very imperfect

105   *Unity and Universality*

one, and one which finds its own life disgusting [*kai duscherainon tēn autou zōēn*] since it is the worst of living things, ill-conditioned and savage, made of inferior matter, a sort of sediment of prior realities, bitter and embittering" (II.3.17, 20–25). In this passage, Plotinus speaks of plants and vegetal life. He ascribes to them disgust with their own kind of vitality (*tēn autou zōēn*), which means that they would have at their disposal, besides the consciousness of their life expressed in axiological notions, terms of comparison with other lives (more perfect, less savage, and so forth). In the last instance, it is the One disgusted with itself, contemplated and realized (realized by being contemplated) in vegetal form. The One reemerges as a phoenix from its every incarnation, passing judgment on itself.

*

For Friedrich Schelling, too, the One is foundational, and the whole history of existence is a myriad paths, through which one becomes all. As he puts it in his 1804 text on "System of Philosophy in General and the Philosophy of Nature in Particular," "All that is [*Alles was ist*] is to the extent that it is one."[15] And it is in the same text that the first of three extant mentions of the phoenix in Schelling's corpus may be found. There, he writes apropos of the combustion process, *Verbrennungsproceß*: "Every combustion process is a sacrifice of individuality [*Jeder Verbrennungsproceß ist eine Aufopferung der Individualität*]. When the sun represents the ideal principle in relation to the earth, the earth, as it were, sacrifices itself to the sun, as it does in the volcanic process, although, like a phoenix, it again revives from the ashes by the power of its indwelling individuality and binds itself in a relation to the sun anew [*obschon sie, dem Phönix gleich, durch die Macht der inwohnenden Individualität immer wieder aus ihrer Asche auflebt, um sich aufs neue mit der Sonne zu verbinden*]."[16]

In combustion, the universal element consumes the particular, which sacrifices itself or is sacrificed to this element (namely, to fire) by losing its identifiable figure and material form. The allocation of particularity to the earth and of universality to the sun pits them against each other, but also, by subterranean means, reconciles them. On the one hand, the inner fire of the earth, our planet's molten core, represents its inner sun, the universality

106   *Chapter 4*

hidden in the particular that occasionally breaks through and out in the "volcanic process," which Schelling cites, the process shaping and molding the landscape. The sacrifice of the earth's surface to its fiery depths, which come to the surface, evokes the phoenix simile: the burning earth cools down and revives from the ashes as fertile soil, ready to welcome vegetal growth. Its renewed relation to the sun is then mediated by plants, with respect to which, likewise, it "represents the ideal principle." The "indwelling individuality," *inwohnenden Individualität*, of the earth is not only a new relatively stable form it receives once lava flows cool, but also, and especially, the forming and generative power that enables the growth of plants and the life of everything that is. The earth is, thus, reborn both as itself (with new geophysical formations: mountain ranges, valleys, etc.) and as the other (the plants that sprout from rich volcanic soil).

The phoenix, lest we forget, is a bird dedicated to the sun: its magnificent radiance personifies (individuates) the solar deity; it dies a fiery death, following some mythic narratives, when the sun ray or lightning strike its nest; its remains are, according to other narrative strands, buried or left on the altar of the sun god in Heliopolis, the city of the sun. Even granting that the phoenix incarnates something of solar universality, her rebirth from the ashes or from the fluids of her decomposing flesh is attributable to the earthy power of "indwelling individuality." Vegetal mediators, the green phoenixes that plants are, combine the two elements in the most empirical, palpable, accessible mode: they strive toward the sun, as to the ideal principle of existence to which they sacrifice themselves, but they receive their individuality from this self-sacrifice as much as from the earth, in which they are rooted. Plants rise radiantly as they stretch in their upper portions toward solar radiance; they are the growing-metamorphosing-decaying *phenomena* (needless to say, derived from the same root as *phoenix* and earlier still, probably, the Egyptian *bennu*), partly appearing in the light and shining in and with their unique light.

So, although, as Schelling will say in his Stuttgart seminars (1810), "the element of fire is hostile to the *proper nature* or *selfhood* of things [*ist feindselig gegen die* Eigenheit *oder* Selbstheit *der Dinge*],"[17] these very proper nature and selfhood are essentially beholden to fire. The "hostility" to formed

107   *Unity and Universality*

matter exhibited by the fiery element is of a piece with its formative (if not life-giving) effects. The figure, or the transfiguration, of the phoenix, brings under its wing the ambivalent relation of fire to life.

Pure life, imagined as fire, is indistinguishable from death—it is, as Schelling notes in *First Outline of a System of the Philosophy of Nature*, "the original phenomenon of absolute fluidity [*das ursprüngliche Phänomen der absoluten Flüssigkeit*],"[18] and, hence, the flux of life without the living who could retain, however briefly, their forms or "selfhood." It is, moreover, the flux that is only temporarily dammed by living forms that retain their vivacity to the extent that they temporarily slow down, reroute, and circumscribe this fiery-living flow, de-absolutizing it. The "proper nature" of these living forms is inseparable from such slowing down, rerouting, delimitation, and so forth, which are then swept back into the fiery flux of pure life, to which the phoenix willingly delivers himself at the end of another cycle of his existence. This is what Schelling means by the footnote he appends to the definition of fire as the "phenomenon of absolute fluidity": "This being [of fire] inimical to all shape, and for this reason the favorite being for shaping—the universal *liquefying* principle, and therefore the mainspring of all formation and of all productivity in Nature."[19] Nothing guarantees that, when taken up into the biological formation process again, the unshaped, liquefied materials of past life will achieve the same form. Yet, holding out the hope of individual resurrection, the phoenix promises just that. How so?

The second extant mention of the phoenix in Schelling's work provides us with a semblance of a response. In the third draft of *The Ages of the World*, dating from 1815, Schelling describes a "backward process" (*rückgängiger Proceß*) in the free development of life that is akin to spontaneous combustion (*freiwillige Selbstverbrennung*). "But that life," he writes, "because in itself it is immortal and because it cannot not be [*jenes Leben, weil das an sich unsterbliche, das gar nicht nicht seyn kann*], always again revives itself anew out of the ashes, as a phoenix [*als ein Phönix*], and hence, the eternal circle emerges."[20] More than an individual living shape, despite all its singularity and uniqueness, the phoenix is a shaped figure of the shapeless, the eternal life that, unable not to be, returns in circular motion after the backward process of reduction to ashes has been completed. A synecdoche of nature and

108 *Chapter 4*

of the soul, the phoenix is a representation of vitality, of life's flux detained in and released from a determinate shape. This detention-and-release model produces the "eternal circle," in which immortality appears as an expression of *unfreedom*: a life that "cannot not be [*gar nicht nicht seyn kann*]." The coveted feature—immortality—becomes a sign of subjection to the necessity of life, to life as such as a necessity that blocks access to the realm of freedom.

The phoenix complex betrays its enabling limitation here: the collective or individual subject at its core is so obsessed with perseverance in being that this subject denies itself the possibility of freedom, which does not entail a choice between being and nonbeing, but which lies beyond (and, for Schelling, before) this choice. Such an obsession does not allow the subject to experience "the yearning to escape the eternal annular drive [*Umtrieb*] and to reach continuance and rest."[21] It is not that the yearning, the desire is not there to begin with: the phoenix complex merely anesthetizes us to it and to the freedom it connotes. The ruptured continuation of a circle (what Schelling calls "cision," *Scheidung*) is a memory of the yearning that is perpetually repressed, pushed down and prevented from coming to the surface, from being expressed. Schelling recalls it with the assistance of Buddhist traditions, with Hinduism and Jainism, where the notion of *nirvāṇa* (also *mokṣa, vimokṣa, apavarga,* or *mukti*) refers to a release from the necessity of being into what, perhaps, is neither being nor nothingness.[22] Schelling writes, "But in that eternally commencing life there lies the wish to escape from the involuntary movement and from the distress of pining [*Aber in jenem ewig anfangenden Leben liegt selbst der Wunsch, aus der unwillkürlichen Bewegung und dem Drangsal zu entkommen*]."[23] That wish is the obverse side of the phoenix complex.

The phoenix complex, above all as the binding-together of the expressed and the repressed, turns out to be at the heart of Schelling's investigations on the relation of freedom and necessity in nature. That is where the third, and final, mention of the phoenix in his oeuvre fits. In the 1821 Erlangen lectures "On the Nature of Philosophy as Science," Schelling summarizes the process in which "eternal freedom first adopts a particular form—an existence—and the way, proceeding through everything and remaining in nothing, it finally breaks through to eternal freedom again—as the eternally struggling, but never defeated, forever invincible force that ends up consuming each form it adopts, and, hence, rising from each one like a phoenix transfigured by its death in the flames [*also aus jeder wieder als Phönix aufsteht und durch Flammentod sich verklärt*]."[24] Schelling considers this movement as "the *content* of the supreme science [Inhalt *der höchsten Wissenschaft*]."

In light of philosophy's absolute content, life is the organic force that *expresses* eternal freedom. To be sure, life is neither eternal freedom itself nor a particular form this freedom may adapt in existence but the movement of freedom, its "proceeding through" (*hindurchgehend*), everything while remaining in nothing. This movement is one, in the course of which freedom perpetually passes over into necessity when it commits to a form of existence (the moment of freedom's self-delimitation), while necessity flips into freedom when that form is consumed by the movement itself (the moment of restoration that transfigures, surpassing a particular figure). Expression is the truth and its betrayal, the betrayal of truth and the truth of the betrayal. Life is a mediator between freedom and necessity, but its mediating activity is steeped in freedom that reigns before the circle closes and after it opens up again, as well as within the circle itself—in the cisions, that cut across every transition, not permitting transfigurations to be straightforward translations of the real into the ideal, and vice versa. Life's mediating activity *is* its expressive function, seen absolutely, within the field containing the content of the highest science. And the phoenix is an expression of that expression, a figure of transfigurations that, in addition to a long chain of other figures, points toward the other of a figure.

*

The scheme, in which freedom is the starting point (and a persistent presence, accompanying the rest of the development) of nature, is evident in Schelling's *First Outline*. Everything begins, for Schelling, with the absolute and unimpeded activity of nature, which, as pure activity, cannot have any objects or products detaining it. Everything begins, then, with a nature (as activity, the unconditioned, or subject) without nature (as "the sum total of existence," conditioned products, or objects).[25] This is a beginning that cannot surpass its initial stage. To begin developing, rather than merely to begin

110   *Chapter 4*

beginning, the unconditioned activity of nature must contract, accepting limitations (indeed, self-limitations), temporary as they may be. The sum total of existence is the sum total of such self-limitations.

But, even when it generates certain outcomes, nature's activity contains "a trace of freedom" (*Spur der Freiheit*), which cannot be fully extinguished in any one of them. So, while everything begins with absolute activity and with the self-delimitation of the infinite (similar to the self-contraction of God at the origin of the world, as conceived in the Lurianic Kabbalah[26]), the problem for human knowledge is to rediscover the infinite in the finite, or, as Schelling puts it, "the possibility of exhibiting the infinite in the finite—is the highest problem of all science [*Möglichkeit der Darstellung des Unendlichen im Endlichen—ist höchstes Problem aller Wissenschaften*]."[27]

The paradigm Schelling sketches out in his *First Outline* inverts the phoenix complex as documented thus far in this book. To be exact, it inverts the ontological side of the complex, while keeping the epistemological side relatively unaffected: the task of teasing out the infinite from the finite at the level of "science" (*Wissenschaft*) must contend with the opposite question of how the infinite delimits itself to begin with, temporarily stabilizing itself in a welter of finite products. The mechanics and machinations of finite beings projecting themselves into the future, beyond their final expiration date, through reproduction have an air of cunning only on the assumption that nature is identified with a "dead mechanism," the quintessentially modern view Schelling fervently rejects. "To philosophize about nature," he writes, "means to heave it out of the dead mechanism, to which it seems predisposed [*aus dem todten Mechanismus, worin sie befangen erscheint, herausheben*]."[28] The predisposition to reduce nature to a dead mechanism is justifiable within a theoretical and practical vision beholden to the provisionally stabilized natural products. But as soon as its original activity comes into view, nature as a collection of ingenuous devices, of equipment for living, of means (*mechanè*) dissipates, letting the first nature without nature shine through this appearance.

There are two sites, two cardinal points, at which the active and infinite impulse of nature is felt most acutely, but even they do not lead us to the purely unconditioned and absolute natural activity. I am referring to reproduction

111   *Unity and Universality*

and death. In reproduction, the organism is the "means and *instrument*" of natural activity,[29] that through which the infinite or the unconditioned acts (i.e., neither squarely the subject nor the object of this activity). Such transcendental instrumentality reinstalls the logic of life's reproduction in the "dead mechanism" of nature. In death, the organism undergoes fluidification, a loss of form, which is, however, never total, inasmuch as matter is a composite (hence, minimally "formed") all the way down.[30] Both reproduction and death thus show that the unleashing of nature's activity is coextensive with its inhibition: technicization and instrumentalization, but stopping short of utter objectification; fluidification and formlessness, but never complete. And, in fact, Schelling aims to understand "how nature could inhibit its product at particular stages of development, without ceasing to be active itself [*wie die Natur ihr Produkt auf einzelne Entwicklungsstufen hemmen könne, ohne daß sie selbst aufhöre thätig zu seyn*]."[31] The phoenix, I claim, is the imagistic or mythical filter through which the simultaneity of inhibition and activity may be grasped.

As far as its reproduction is concerned, the phoenix perfectly fits Schelling's assertion: "'The product is inhibited at a determinate stage of development' does not mean that it absolutely stops being active, but that it is limited with respect to its productions; it cannot reproduce anything to infinity except itself."[32] This inhibited activity or active inhibition is the lot of the phoenix that reproduces only itself to infinity. At the same time, modes of reproduction vary: it can be asexual or sexual, for instance. In the former mode, a potentially infinite growth of the same (implying an inhibition of possible difference, which is what we seem to witness in the case of the phoenix, at least in its vegetal incarnation) predominates. In the latter, growth stops, but the same is rendered fluid and malleable, its fixed form lost in the merging of the two progenitors (implying an inhibition of the individual that is akin to death, while something of the individual is carried over to the next generation).

For his part, Schelling proposes that sexual difference governs the development of the organic realm as a whole: "Throughout the whole of nature, absolute sexlessness is nowhere demonstrable, and an *a priori* regulative principle requires that sexual difference be taken as point of departure

112   *Chapter 4*

everywhere in organic nature [*organischen Natur auf Geschlechtsverscheidenheit auszugehen*]."[33] The types of inhibition in reproduction are, therefore, not as clear-cut as they are typically imagined to be. The ambiguity of the phoenix's sexual difference (and, in the first instance, of the difference between this difference and its lack) only highlights its irreducibility. As a synecdoche of nature, as an exceptional part that stands in for the whole, the phoenix illustrates the "*a priori* regulative principle" Schelling is discussing. Taken in and of itself, the sexual ambiguity of the phoenix combines the poles of activity and its inhibition: depending on which mode of reproduction prevails, one side or the other will predominate *within the same organism or organismic ensemble*. But if we add to this idea the phoenix's reproduction through death, by way of liquescence that involves, in keeping with Schelling, a fiery transformation and liquids properly so called (as in the life-giving emissions of the corpse), then the de-absolutizing cision of sexual difference is bolstered by the de-individuating effects of mortality.

Do de-absolutization and de-individuation fall on the side of nature's infinite activity or its inhibition? Unfixing the products of nature, these tendencies recover the productive impulse that was temporarily slowed down and detained in living forms. They free the infinite from the finite existence it became when it started to determine, delimit, and shape itself. Nonetheless, the freedom of ongoing dissolution is kept in check; its counterbalancing happens at a limit, which, delineating the spatiotemporal edges of a mortal being, signifies the common boundary of life and death. As a regulative a priori principle of organic nature, sexual difference is not self-sufficient; it must be tied in the already-familiar knot with mortality and radical individuation.

The unity and uniqueness—the unicity—of nature-qua-phoenix goes beyond individuality toward the one, or the One, in which difference is gathered. The following statement should remind us of Plotinus, who is an important precursor to Schelling's thinking of the absolute:[34] "If, according to our principles, the production of various genera and species in nature is only *one* production captured at different stages, then the formations of the opposite sexes in the *same* genus and species must be only *one* formation, one natural operation, such that the different individuals of the same genus amount to only *one* individual, but developed in opposite directions."[35]

113 *Unity and Universality*

The phoenix lives up to Schelling's deduction as a genus of genuses, representing the whole by virtue of its exclusion from assorted orders of that whole (real, biological, taxonomical, and, in another way, symbolic, mythic, or mythological). On the body of nature, the different (even, opposite) sexes form one androgynous being. The births and deaths of different individuals are nothing more than the growing of new and shedding of old skin cells. Just as an organism is "a collective expression of a multiplicity of actions [*gemeinschaftliche Ausdruck für eine Mannichfaltigkeit von Aktionen*],"[36] so nature is a collective expression of genuses that, on its immense body, correspond to multiple intraorganismal actions. This is, actually, what Schelling calls "an absolute organism" (*absolute Organismus*), an archetype "without internal difference in kind, in which individual and species coincide, which is now neither individual nor genus, but *both at once*."[37] The phoenix's multiple exclusions are vital here: without them, it could not have become such an archetype, not least because, for Schelling, no individual existent can embody the absolute.[38]

Not only in its organismic garb, but also as matter, the absolute in Schelling is phoenix-like. "*Absolute matter*" (die absolute Materie) is an infinite, self-reflected (circular) process of decomposition and recomposition: "Where it is decomposed, it must be composed anew in every moment [*wo sie decomponirt wird, in jedem Moment neu componirt warden muß*]."[39] What is absolute in absolute matter is the coincidence of activity and its inhibition (that phenomenally present themselves in the guise of analysis and synthesis), of freedom and necessity, a coincidence that is itself unconditional, not contingent on something else outside it. The absolute is not incompatible with time; it is just that, *from the vantage of the absolute itself* (be it as matter or as an organism), every moment in time replays the drama of the phoenix, burnt or rotten and reborn again from its ashes or putrefaction fluids, while, *from the vantage of individual or even species existence*, these moments are spread out across much longer time spans.

*

Besides the absolute organism and absolute matter, the atmosphere is a kind of phoenix, "daily organized anew."[40] The ongoing renewal of the atmosphere

114   *Chapter 4*

conforms to the dynamics of the phoenix to the extent that its life is each time recovered from the threshold of death, or, better yet, to the extent that its death is, in itself, life-giving, while its life is death-bearing. There are two ways in which we can appreciate these conclusions in the company of Schelling.

First, if life is understood in terms of combustion or of general combustibility, then its division into animal and plant vitalities amounts to atmospheric degradation and regeneration, death and life, in the overall life of the planet: "The animal destroys the atmosphere about itself, and preserves, increases and moves itself like the mobile, growing flame [*gleich der beweglichen, wachsenden Flamme*]. The plant returns the power of combustion to the burnt, ubiquitous substance, and returns to the atmosphere that substance which makes combustion possible."[41]

It is easy to give a species-relativist answer to the question of what constitutes life and what corresponds to death: since the respiratory processes of plants and animals are diametrically opposed (the former "inhale" CO_2 and "exhale" O_2; the latter, the other way around), any definition of a vital milieu will have to take into account *whose* milieu it is. But such relativism comes up against its limits once life is equated to combustibility, which is fostered, in turn, thanks to the life activity of plants. The atmospheric phoenix is vegetal in its rebirth and animal in its demise. The "growing flame" that is an animal (doesn't its *growing* make it, in part, vegetal?) preserves itself by destroying its own life-support systems; the flaming green growths that are plants provide the material conditions of possibility for burning twice over, both as the matter in which the flame rages and by emitting oxygen, without which there is no fire. The flames, in which the phoenix renews its existence, are the same ones that reduce its old body to ash. But fire, too, is a phoenix, enveloped by a more or less welcoming atmosphere and burning in a vegetal-animal substratum (of the bird's body, the nest, and so forth).

Second, we need to concentrate specifically on oxygen in order to realize just how the atmospheric phoenix operates on and in bodies, organic and inorganic. For Schelling, oxygen, which enables burning, is itself a remnant of the burned: "Oxygen, or an element of it, *must* itself (if it is already

115   *Unity and Universality*

a *combusted* substance [*eine* verbrannte *Substanz*]) descend again into the categories of combustible [*die Kategorie der verbrennlichen*], i.e., chemically composite substances."[42] The circular arrangement of the combusted and the combustible means that oxygen is a phoenix, preceding the phoenix's plant and, especially, animal life. And yet, a recovery of the combustible from the combusted—the recovery which, we might add, is far from assured when the phoenix complex is objectively destabilized and when the fragile conditions of life on earth are threatened—does not explain the *simultaneity* of life and death, that is, of the enlivening and the deadening in daily organismic and atmospheric organization.

This simultaneity revolves, in Schelling's estimation, around stimulation and, once more, oxygen (and oxidation). The means promoting life are the road toward the demise of a living organism: "Nature achieves its aim in precisely the opposite way than the way in which it attempted to achieve it; the activity of life is the cause of its own dissolution."[43] Steady stimulation leads to an equally steady desensitization toward the stimulus and, at the extreme, the body becoming "unreceptive to external stimulus, such that life itself is only the bridge to death."[44] Further down the page, Schelling returns to oxygen and its potentially lethal effects: to those who say "how wise it is that oxygen is not present in pure form in the atmosphere, because otherwise the vital air would consume the animals as quickly as a flame," he responds, "If the atmosphere were pure oxygen, then the organisms of the earth would have to be correlatively otherwise constituted." What is, of course, subtly implicit in Schelling's insight is how oxygen triggers the reactions of oxidation, known at least since Antoine Lavoisier coined the term in the eighteenth century, and more recently found to be involved in the production of chemicals ("free radicals") that damage cells in the body. In a very literal sense, then, "the activity of life is the cause of its own dissolution."

The atmosphere, the very air we breathe, is a phoenix both in itself—in its daily, if less and less assured, regeneration—and in us. It signals the immemorial infiltration of death into life and of life into death. In the third version of his *Weltalter* work, Schelling formulates the phoenix complex in two, apparently incompatible, theses: "There is no life without simultaneous

116   *Chapter 4*

death [*Kein Leben ist ohne gleichzeitiges Sterben*]"[45] and "There is no life without the overcoming of death [*Kein Leben ist ohne Überwindung des Todes*]."[46] To be fair, Schelling uses two different nouns in German, *Sterben* and *Tod*, both of them rendered as death in the English translation. *Sterben*, though, is a more "active" dying, as opposed to the fact of death that is *Tod*. It follows that living is dying and an overcoming of death, a living on or from death, of others and of oneself.

What Schelling describes is not ghostly survival, although in *Clara* he (or, at least, the character of the doctor as his mouthpiece) will be open to this possibility: "The true ruins are not those of ancient human splendor that the curious seek out in the Persian or Indian deserts; the whole earth is one great ruin, where animals live as ghosts and men as spirits [*die ganze Erde ist Eine große Ruine, worin Thiere als Gespenster, Menschen als Geister hausen*]."[47] Rather, living *as* dying and *as* overcoming death refers to the physiology of respiration, digestion, and reproduction. Each in its own way affirms and denies death: oxygen and oxidation; caloric intake and aging, not to mention the disintegration of the eaten; generation of another like oneself and dissolution of the individual in the genus.

The phoenix complex is lodged not only in our brains and not only in our lungs, but also in intestines and genitalia—in fact, throughout the corporeal extension and its relation to the environment. It is in part a "complex" and in part the living on of finite life, itself inventing and reinventing, dreaming up, contriving, and scrunching up again its infinitude. While full of machinations, the mechanism works, is effective; it spawns actual effects. The "inner life that incessantly gives birth to itself and again consumes itself" does not remain inner; it is, following Schelling, already an imitation of the force "concealed in everything," and it is expressed in every act and actualization of the organism. "It is the constant inner mechanism and clockwork, time, eternally commencing, eternally becoming, always devouring itself and always giving birth to itself [*das beständige innere Trieb- und Uhrwerk, die ewig beginnende, ewig werdende, immer sich selbst verschlingende und immer sich selbst wieder gebärende Zeit*]."[48] The eternal commencement is an eternal ending; always giving birth to oneself, one always consumes and buries oneself. It is the rhythms of this beginning and ending, of dilation and

117 *Unity and Universality*

contraction, that constitute time. What or who remains constant across all these comings and goings, except the mechanism itself and the Moloch of hope attached to it? The phoenix complex is a clock that runs in circles, that with every turn of the dial causes the beginning to retreat, to come to an end having barely begun, and, as a result, to begin re-beginning.

Lest any doubts linger about the relation of this mechanism to the phoenix, Schelling adds the fire of the hearth, symbolizing the inner realm of domestic and psychophysical life, as well as cosmic fire and its flickering (measured rekindling and extinguishing) in Heraclitus. "This," he continues, "is the sanctuary (*hestia*), the hearth of the life that continually incinerates itself and again rejuvenates itself from the ash [*der Heerd des beständig sich selbst verbrennenden und aus der Asche wieder neu verjüngenden Lebens*]. This is the tireless fire (*akamaton pur*) through whose quenching, as Heraclitus claimed, the cosmos was created."[49] The difference between inner and outer fires, microexistence and macroreality, is similarly reduced to ash in Schelling's depiction of the mechanism that extends finite life past its limits. But, rather than level that difference, the phoenix complex reconstitutes it anew with each rejuvenation, each reconstruction of the hearth of life and of the cosmos from the ashes of their self-incineration. Recommencement is nothing if not non-indifference, a rebellion against ash gray, a resurgence of limits and boundaries, edges and outlines, delineating another identity in the place of the one that has been consumed, irretrievably lost in its singularity.

The rotary movement of "a life that eternally circulates in itself"[50] is the sole product of the mechanism that is the phoenix complex. The organic and physiological allegories of the mechanism abound: from the universe's exhalation and inhalation, through the alternations of expansion and contraction,[51] to the pulse of the world with its systoles and diastoles representing "a completely involuntary movement [*eine völlig unwillkürliche Bewegung*] that, once begun, makes itself from itself."[52] The phoenix's self-reproduction, her generation out of herself, classically taken as a sign of freedom, is ensconced in the unwilled rotations of the circle, the runaway gyrations of mechanical repetition. The phoenix complex presents us with a peculiar mix of freedom

118   *Chapter 4*

and unfreedom that, though Schelling raises the question of the difference between mechanism and organism—should "the origin of the world system ought to be thought more organically than mechanically?"[53]—invalidates this very question. Eternally recommenced with every gyration of the cycle, the origin is as mechanical as it is organic. The world's breathing, heartbeat, expansions, and contractions are the products of a machine that, not at all separate from the world, makes the world what it is.

(In the present chapter and in the book as a whole, we too are moving in circles around the phoenix complex, starting anew every time. The book and its argument are a kind of machine—not free from the machinations that are wed to the mechanisms of argumentation—processing "philosophy of nature" through a mythico-theologico-philosophical grinder. Nevertheless, the occasional openings of the circle in excess of a mere widening, expansion, or dilation should, as I have already mentioned, point the way beyond the material at hand within this very material.)

Compared to the stoppage of what elsewhere I have christened "planetary metabolism"[54]—the stoppage that is due to the mass of undecomposable or slowly decomposing substances released into the environment—the seamless circular workings of the universal heartbeat or respiration are indubitably better. But they are not the end-all and be-all of existence and philosophy, for Schelling in the first place. So, the undecomposable remains of industrial, energy-generating, and consumer activities clog being as a result of their resistance to passing into nothing, to becoming the past. The interplay of being and nothingness—of God's negating power and affirmative potency, his eternal *yes* and eternal *no*[55]—shapes the pathways of becoming. Planetary metabolism belongs here, with its worldwide mouth and anus rhythmically expanding and contracting, and with the transformative fire of digestion mediating between the two extremes. And then, there is the beyond-being (and beyond-nothing), which Plato and Levinas, Schelling himself, Buddhist, Hindu, and Jain traditions have variously alluded to.

The phoenix complex, precisely as a *complex*, is stuck between the second and the first stages of my improvised schema: metabolic activity proceeds unimpeded, yet there is a desire for the retention of the same material form

119   *Unity and Universality*

after every turn of the wheel. For Schelling, this is not enough: "Were life to remain at a standstill here, it would be nothing other than an eternal exhaling and inhaling, a constant interchange between life and death [*Bliebe das Leben hier stehen, so wäre nichts als ein ewiges Aus- und Einathmen, ein beständiger Wechsel von Leben und Sterben*]."[56] Life as a "constant interchange of life and death" is a life that enwraps and neutralizes death, that digests death into itself, that bridges the two incarnations of the phoenix with a fire that, despite reducing organic matter to ashes, represents a higher vitality. But, no matter the efficiency with which it countervails its other, this phoenix life does not lead to infinity before and after the ever-reinitiated circle. In other words, it does not culminate in freedom.

*

We seem to have raised the question before, but every time it is raised anew it displays before us its shining and previously unnoticed facets and edges. The question is, What does freedom before and after the phoenix complex look like in Schelling's philosophy of nature?

Before the closure of the annular drive, it is the freedom of the infinite, the productive activity of which "must be inhibited, *retarded* [*muß sie gehemmt, retardirt werden*]," for finite products to appear.[57] Still, the outcomes of this inhibition or self-limitation of the infinite are going to harbor a trace of infinity within; Schelling states that they are "merely *apparent products* [*bloß Scheinprodukte*]": "the tendency to infinite development must lie once again in every individual; every product must be capable of being articulated into products."[58] On the one hand, it is this apparent nature of products and of a living finitude that is unmasked as *merely* apparent in the phoenix complex, when another creature or creatures like the initial one are released into the world. The trace of infinity develops, as though in a photographic negative, as soon as organismic life passes through the complex's machinery. But, on the other hand, this is a trace of infinity without freedom, a distorted infinity that is highly conditioned, put to the task of reproducing the living form in question. The forces of inhibition are retained in the midst of a disinhibiting movement, which allows infinity to work, breaking through its apparently finite products.

120   *Chapter 4*

The distortion (and the being-*complex*) of the phoenix complex has much to do with a disinhibiting inhibition. Schelling himself views "the condition under which the infinite in general is finitely presentable [*die Bedingung ist, unter welcher allein ein Unendliches überhaupt endlich darstellbar [ist]*]" and under which the finite projects itself forward (or back) to infinity as an "original antithesis in itself" of nature.[59] The psychological condition of disavowal, implying the acknowledgment and repudiation of a reality, is anticipated in this coincidence of acknowledgment and repudiation *in* reality itself, making reality what it is. (In his *Ages of the World*, Schelling will frame the issue in terms of the divine *yes-no*, the confluence of infinite negation and infinite affirmation, that creates the world.) The finite may open unto the infinite—indeed, may get back in touch with the infinity that is in it—from many sides and in a number of ways, echoing in each of them God's creative *yes-no*. Its specific opening through the phoenix complex, however, overlays the "original antithesis" with the clash between freedom and necessity, irresolvable on the complex's terms.

Paradoxically, the merging of freedom and necessity in the phoenix complex reenacts their coexistence in God prior to creation. "Necessity and freedom are in God [*Es ist in Gott Nothwendigkeit und Freiheit*]," Schelling writes. "Even though the God who is necessary is not the God who is free, both are still one and the same."[60] But the reenactment of the divine paradox in the phoenix complex yields directly inverse consequences. The moment of a groundless decision just before the creation of the world refers to "the eternal freedom" that "is nothing," that "is like the will that wills nothing, that desires no object, for which all things are equal [*wie der Wille, der nichts will, der keine Sache begehrt, dem alle Dinge gleich sind*]. . . . Such a will is nothing and everything."[61] The creative will is an overflow of nothing, from which everything comes into being without the least bit of desire, inclination, or predilection attributable to the cause of creation. The freedom and necessity that are in God are funneled into an absolutely free (because indifferent) gift of created existence, endowed with its own kind of (natural) necessity and determination.

The phoenix complex, conversely, activates a will that wills something very determinate, namely itself, the continuation of particular finite existence in this world after death. In a different context, Schelling notes that "each being primarily wants itself and this self-wanting is later precisely the basis of egoity [*Das Erste jedes Wesens ist, daß es sich selber will, dieses sich-Wollen ist eben nachher die Grundlage der Egoität*], that through which a being withdraws itself or cuts itself off from other things."[62] The singularity of the phoenix is, subjectivity conceived, the principle of egoity taken to the extreme: a self-wanting that cuts the phoenix (say, as a soul) off from the rest of the world and that stimulates the spasmodic movements of contraction and expansion, a calculated self-misplacement—a cunning self-sacrifice—followed by the recovery of the self (even in the other). This is the absolute narcissitic predilection for oneself at the antipodes of the divine will that wills nothing. The freedom of infinity that persists within the finite, marked by its necessarily limited life span, is channeled into an absolutely necessary reaffirmation of past identity and the will to hurl it into a future beyond death.

Freedom *before* the phoenix complex resembles Plotinus's nature without nature, without the constantly alternating expansion and contraction, without the annular drive that is at the origins of every nature.[63] Freedom *within* nature's "eternal inhalation and re-exhalation"[64] that dynamically shape the phoenix complex lies in the moments of cision, of breathlessness even, of nature holding its breath, in memory or in anticipation of a nature without nature. Freedom *beyond* the phoenix complex, which has in the meantime monopolized the beyond, is, again, a nature without nature, albeit already transformed.

In the second draft of *The Ages of the World* from 1811, Schelling imagines "the authentic future, the future as such" as "what will come after the world [*nachweltliche*]," as opposed to the authentic past as "what came before the world [*vorweltliche*]," while time and history are "just . . . a repetition within a narrower sphere."[65] The post-world that succeeds the repetitions instigated by the phoenix complex is not a post-apocalyptic reality. Or it doesn't have to be *that*. The fragment "Spring" at the conclusion of *Clara* ends with the suggestion that "even this firm structure of the world will one day turn into spiritual, but only this external form will disintegrate, the

122   *Chapter 4*

inner power and truth will persist to become revealed in a new transfiguration. The divine fire that now rests sealed within it will one day gain the upper hand."[66]

Is the sealed divine fire not the one that already breaks through the rotary movements of nature, consuming the aged body of the phoenix, just as the inner fire of the earth occasionally irrupts with volcanic lava? Gaining the upper hand, this fire will transfigure reality itself not as spirit that revivifies the flesh but as the spiritualization of matter, the liquescence of the world and the freeing up of its "inner power." As far as I can tell, the image, cursory and patchy as it is, is Schelling's vision of the post-world, of freedom beyond the phoenix complex. Whereas, currently, as the lament in an earlier passage from *Clara* goes, "The whole earth is one great ruin, where animals live as ghosts and men as spirits," the fire of spiritualization will (1) level the difference between ghosts and spirits, or animals and humans, (2) bring the ruin-earth to its true and complete ruination—the liberating disintegration of its external form, and (3) come to a crescendo in a life of spirits living on spirits and on spirit alone. The authentic future and the authentic past meet in another circle, where what is after the end (of the world) does not perfectly mirror what was before the beginning.

*

I cannot help but mention the fourth, veiled allusion to the phoenix in Schelling's oeuvre, in addition to the three with which our discussion of his writings commenced. Toward the end of the third version of *The Ages of the World*, he speaks of comets, "those enigmatic members of the planetary whole . . . in this state of fiery electrical dissolution." Comets, Schelling avers, are the "living witnesses of primordial time [*lebendige Zeugen jener Urzeit*], since nothing prevents the earlier time from migrating through a later time via particular phenomena."[67] We have heard Claudian call the phoenix, in the same vein, a witness to the whole of history: "You have seen everything that has ever been; you testify to the passing and turning of the ages [*vidisti quodcumque fuit; te saecula teste cuncta revolvuntur*]" (*Carmina minora* 27.104–105).[68] In the myth of Er, with which Plato closes *The*

123 *Unity and Universality*

Republic, having drunk of the water of forgetting in the world beyond, souls fall asleep and, in the middle of the night, are "suddenly wafted . . . upward to their birth like shooting stars [*hösper asteras*]" (621b). The Heraclitan turns of fire between the past, the present, and the future of the world also support the idea of time travel or "migration" through time via a particular phenomenon, which, in its singularity, is the crux of phenomenality, of a shining emergence, a radiant coming-to-appearance of all that is. The flame, in which the phoenix is transformed, is the fire of the absolute past held back by everything that lives, and it is given a free rein in the absolute future of the post-world.

"In all ages," Schelling insists, "human feeling has only regarded comets with a shudder as, so to speak, harbingers of the recurrence of a past age, of universal destruction, of the dissolution of things again into chaos [*einer Wiederkehr der vergangenen Zeit, allgemeiner Zerrüttung, Wiederauflösung der Dinge ins Chaos*]."[69] The "recurrence of past age" hints at the rebirth of the phoenix as an eon, an era, or an epoch, but a rebirth (hence the return of a seemingly bygone form—above all, the form of time) accompanied by and not at all inconsistent with death, dissolution, deformation. It is a sign of the co-belonging of life and death, generation and destruction, repetition and the frightening advent of the new in the conceptual, symbolic, and affective vicinities of the phoenix.

Despite all the suggestive imagery, I would have overlooked these references were it not for the book *The Phoenix: An Essay* by one John Goodridge from 1781, with a telling subtitle: *Being an attempt to prove from history and astronomical calculations, that the comet, which, by its approximation to our earth, occasioned the change made at the fall and the deluge, is the real Phoenix of the ancients*. Here, Goodridge sets out "to prove that the Comet is that so much celebrated emblem of Antiquity (perhaps of the resurrection also), the *Phoenix*," whom he calls "most certainly an Egyptian hieroglyphical representation of the Comet."[70]

More than its visual resemblance to a fiery bird streaking across the night sky, the comet's singularity gives credence to this comparison with the phoenix in light of Schelling's work: "Evidently, the individual center of gravity (the separate life [*das eigene Leben*]) in a comet is not reconciled with

124   *Chapter 4*

the universal center of gravity."[71] The comet is one of a kind, a separate life, but, as an exception from the cosmic order of gravity, it comes to represent the whole. "Comets are eccentric to such a degree that their movement can be regarded as a simple systole and diastole [*bloße Systole und Diastole*]," measured by their approaches to and retreats from the sun.[72] In its eccentric singularity, the comet gathers into itself the entire breathing or pulsing of the universe, the systolic and diastolic movements of cosmic contraction and expansion, dwindling and waning. The comet, then, as a synecdoche of cosmos, but also as a reminder of what was before the world and a preview of what will be after it.

5 THE PHOENIX ACTS: HILDEGARD/SPINOZA

Twelfth-century Benedictine abbess, mystic, and polymath, St. Hildegard of Bingen did not display any overt interest in the figure of the phoenix. She did, however, briefly mention date palm (*Datilbaum*) in her encyclopedic compendium *Physica*, which featured entries on different species of plants, animals, and minerals. The Latin nomenclature of this tree is *Phoenix dactilyfera* (finger-bearing palm), since ripe dates resemble fingers. (Nota bene: this resemblance holds for palm trees in general due to the shape of their branches and leaves reminiscent of an open hand, which is just that—a palm.) A mix of human anatomical structures, a plant specimen, and a mythical bird, this entry in Hildegard's *Physica* does not, by any means, fit the rigid parameters of scientific classification. Within a book that borrows its title from the Greek for *nature*, date palm (the vegetal phoenix par exellence) concentrates in itself various orders of natural beings and, by approximation, the entire physical realm.

Truth be told, Hildegard did not intend to lay out a taxonomic system of nature. The transversal qualities of disparate organic and even inorganic entities in her work are heat and cold, representing the soul (*anima*) and the body (*corpus*), respectively (*Physica* Praef; *PL* 197.1127a).[1] This rule of thumb applies to plants as much as to animals and stones. In the case of *Phoenix dactilyfera*, Hildegard has no doubts: "The date palm tree is hot and has moisture in it, which is as sticky as mucus. And it signifies happiness [*Datilbaum calida est, et humiditatem in se habet . . . et beatitudinem signat*]" (*Physica* 3.17; *PL* 197.1130b). Crucially, the hot nature of date palm, bespeaking its proximity to the world of spirit, is married to the quality of moistness. A combination of heat and moisture is particularly propitious to the emergence and development of life, so much so that it forms the matrix of *viriditas*, or the self-refreshing power of finite beings and of creation itself to recommence, to get a new lease on life. It follows that date palm, bearing the Greek and then Latin denomination *Phoenix*—as we have also remarked in our reading of Aristotle and Plutarch—not only epitomizes all of nature but also gathers in its physical and spiritual constitution the potentialities of revivification or resurrection, of the replenishment of life from the edges of its finitude.

Viriditas (greenness or the greening green) is one of the key concepts in the Hildegardian corpus. Bearing a stamp of the divine act of creation, it is responsible for the ongoing re-creation (indeed, the self-re-creation) of existence, despite the condition of mortality and without a direct intervention by God. In a sense, *viriditas* is the power of redemption that mitigates the veritable death sentence meted out to Adam, Eve, and their descendants for the original sin. As such, it contradicts and counteracts from within the fallenness of humanity, while entrusting the highest expression of this power to a particular kind of existence, namely to the vegetal, to plants who lend their chlorophyll-based greenness to the very name *viriditas*.

For the same reason, on Hildegard's reading, Jesus comes to renew the nearly depleted capacity for renewal; she construes his coming as the Word of God wrapped in *viriditas* within the womb of the Virgin Mary. "The eternal Father, in sweet *viriditas*, sent his Word into the womb of the Virgin for the salvation of humanity [*eterni Patris . . . pro salute hominis in suavi viriditate misit Verbum suum in Virginis uterum*]," she writes in a letter to the Archbishop of Mainz (Epist. 24.64–65; CCCM 91.68).[2] What Jesus redeems, Hildegard implies, is redemption itself, the material redemption that is engrained in the natural world and that *is* this very world with its self-reproductive dynamics. Thus, Hildegard supplements the early Christian association of Jesus's resurrection and the phoenix's rebirth with the evangelical "good news" of ever-recommencing freshness, of *viriditas* strengthened through and as Jesus. Differences between the content and the form of the

128   *Chapter 5*

message, the messenger and the addressees, the Word and the Son of God, dissolve in the warm moistness of *viriditas*.

The mix of water and fire in baptismal rituals—a spiritual rebirth that immediately follows biological birth—recalls the elemental composition of *viriditas* and of the phoenix, in the guise of the date palm, which or who serves as its synecdoche. Baptism is rebirth "from the water of sanctification and the spirit of illumination [*renascatur ex aqua sanctificationis et Spiritu illuminationis*]" (*Scivias* 2.3.27; CCCM 43.151).[3] Perhaps Hildegard sees in this second birth a genuine generation of the human from the animals that we are at first birth. But neither animal nor plant natures stand lower on *scala naturae* (the Great Chain of Being) than the human, as they do in medieval scholasticism; vegetal-divine *viriditas* steers the entire process of regeneration that is in equal measure spiritual and material. Just as the capacity proper to finite existence to refresh, to re-create, and to project itself into the future beyond its own temporal horizons disrespects the boundaries and divisions of sundry classifications, so it scrambles the ontological-axiological hierarchies that have organized Western thought for millennia.

*

Viriditas takes over the baton of the phoenix complex. As moist fire that, in a finite existent, envisions a new generative or regenerative beginning, as another kindling of a life, it is meant to carry out the work already programmed in Plato: to render operational the mechanics and machinations of self-substitution, whereby finite beings can participate in the infinite by producing copies of themselves. But that is not all. *Viriditas* is a tendency assuring, in addition to the rise of the next generations of the living, the dynamic preservation of each creature in its limited lifetime. So, like St. Augustine, who claims to have encountered God in the depths of his soul, Hildegard salutes God within her in *Scivias*, "And I will know you in the *viriditas* of my soul [*in viriditate animae meae*]" (2.5.54; CCCM 43.219).[4] The soul has its *viriditas*, or, more accurately put, it *is viriditas* as the fresh, self-refreshing bond that ties it to the body. In every instant, it keeps reanimating the body, which would have been but a corpse without it, rejuvenating and maintaining it, for instance through the capacity to receive nourishment. Differently put, the soul is the body's *viriditas*, the power caring for bodily renewal and regeneration, whether in itself (thanks to what we now call "cell division" and "tissue repair") or in another (by way of reproduction, sexual or asexual).

Readily recognizable as a Christian interpretation of the Aristotelian *to threptikon* (the nutritive principle) and *to genetikon* (the reproductive principle), *viriditas* is the conceptual legatee of the vegetal soul, which, combining these two principles, constitutes the most common, shared stratum of life, according to the ancient Greek philosopher. This feature accounts, at least in part, for the focus on greenness in Hildegard's original term. What is more unexpected is that the soul *tout court* is identified with what was "merely" a plant soul with its two-pronged faculty of nourishment and reproduction in Aristotle and that, moreover, one can commune with and *know* God in the soul of that soul, *in viriditate animae meae*. To be clear, Hildegard proposes that she knows God in her own vegetality, in the *viriditas* that is the living and enlivening aspect of her life.[5] As for rationality, it is, for the Christian mystic, an offshoot of *viriditas*; that is to say, rationality lives and puts things in motion only thanks to the *viriditas* that animates it from within, letting the soul soar, propelled by the power of fiery breath.[6]

From the abbreviated description I have just offered, it is possible to reconstruct the affinities of Hildegard's notion of the soul to the classical view of the soul as a phoenix, from Hesiod's riddle to the untitled Coptic fragment of Gnostic thought, the ensouled cosmic animal in Plato's *Timaeus*, and the Great Year of the universe's heating up and cooling down (with a direct line linking it to Hildegard's association of spirit with heat and body with cold) in Aristotle. A site of renewal and rebirth, the soul is entwined with the capacities of *viriditas*, as well as with the body, by which it is, nevertheless, encumbered as by a "heavy weight" (*durum pondus*). The body is its "dress in this life [*veste huius vite*]" (*Ordo* 1.37; CCCM 226.506).[7] As the dress that the soul wears, the body may be periodically changed, admitting the possibility of either resurrection or reincarnation, and it may even be discarded when it is too worn out. Without its bodily garment, however, the soul has no effectivity in this world, and *viriditas* is of no use; as elsewhere in

130   *Chapter 5*

Hildegard, spiritual and physical realities intermingle, each being the sign or the expression of the other.[8]

The garment of corporeal existence is constantly mended by the soul that wears it, such that nourishment and reproduction become the two aspects of this mending. It is for this reason that, with the mediations of *viriditas*, spirit is able to resist the otherwise inexorable entropic process. "Remember this," Hildegard implores, "that the fullness which was created in the beginning / need not have run dry [*memor esto, quod plenitudo que in primo facta est / arescere non debuit*]" (*Ordo* Epil. 351–352, CCCM 226.521). Christian redemption is none other than the renewal of renewal, the rejuvenation of rejuvenation by means of granting to souls the same service that they provide to the bodies they wear. (See, for instance, the striking proto-feminist depiction of Mary as "the author of life, / rebuilding salvation" [*auctrix vite, / reedificando salutem*] [*Symph*. 8.1–3].[9])

The possibilities of rejuvenation in the same and renewal in the other are arrayed by the phoenix, whose tracks are clearly visible in the notion of *viriditas*. As a result, Hildegard's theology also inherits the ethical question that goes along with the phoenix complex, the question of whether, despite their singularity, irreplaceability, and uniqueness finite existents are actually dispensable in light of the compensations promised by *viriditas*. We should put aside, at least for now, the deconstructive dictum that only the irreplaceable can be replaced. What is at stake is creaturely value indexed to the power each creature has, the potentiality to be or to stay alive (to continue being *in* life: *vita est in vita*) and to generate other creatures in one's likeness. The power (*vir*), overlapping with *viriditas*, dwarfs the creatures who have it, so much so that it is this power that has creatures in its grasp, rather than the other way around. Rooted in it, the living are in a life that will continue after they are no longer in it—continue up to the "living eternity" (*vivens eternitas*) to which their *vir/viriditas* points. If Jesus comes to redeem *viriditas* and, through it, the living, then redemption ensures above all the endurance of the phoenix complex. The Hildegardian mechanics and machinations of replacement imply slipping one life in place of another: seriality in place of uniqueness. The life, in which the living are, is in this manner conflated with the life that is in a larger living whole.

The living character of eternity anchored in *viriditas* assumes the shape of a circle, when God is said to be "like a wheel," *quasi rotam* (*LDO* 3.5.i; CCCM 92.405),[10] and "holy divinity" is "a circling wheel [*circueuntis rote*]," (*Symph.* "O Fili dilectissimi," 3–4), its energy (*virtus*)—"a circling circle, / encompassing all [*circuiens circuisti, / comprehendendo omnia*]" (*Symph.* 2.2–3). The turns of *viriditas*, returning to finite existence its youth, restituting time lost by refreshing being-in-life, replicate the rotations of the divine wheel, its circling repetition tirelessly performing infinity. With being itself refreshed, beings change, the new ones supplanting those who have aged and died. Platonic participation (*méthexis*) of the finite in the infinite is also *this*—the workings of the green and greening phoenix who restores the undying springtime of existence.

As Hildegard sees it, the greening green oozes from the creative fingers of God—"O, the greening greenness of the fingers of God [*O viriditas digiti Dei*]" (*Symph.* 42.1)—and, having percolated to the world, lets the world re-create itself all by itself. Only when this capacity is fatally undermined is redemption necessary, even though, qualitatively, its effects are the same as those of the world's self-mending or self-healing. But, as in the date palm (that is, the vegetal phoenix), moistness needs warmth to become the life-giving or the resuscitating force that it is. The cross is a symbol of this intersection of opposites, including the horizontal and the vertical planks or planes, earth and sky, humanity and divinity, water and fire, the thriving woods and dead wood. After the Fall, the cross is the crux of *viriditas*, the *viriditas* of *viriditas* similarly imagined in the shape of a phoenix-tree: Jesus is "hung on the tree of his passion [*in ligno passionis suae pendente*]" (*Scivias* 2.6.1; CCCM 43.232), which reverses Adam's tree of sin and perdition. The wood of the cross comes back to life as a tree, restoring the liveliness (or at least the equivocations, vacillating between life and death) of matter. It is a stand-in for the greening greenness of the fingers of God, redeeming not only humanity but also all of fallen nature, its Fall expressed in the rapid decline and loss of *viriditas*.

*

132 *Chapter 5*

Hildegard's poetic and visionary writings are awash in pyrological discourse that is typical of Christian theology in general and of representations of Christ as a phoenix in particular. So, Mary is "the greenest branch," *viridissima virga* (*Symph*. 19.1), on which the flower of redemption will blossom, gleaming, shimmering like a beacon to the world: "The flower of Virgin Mary / gleams at dawn [*unde lucet in aurora / flos de Virgine Maria*]" (*Symph*. 11.4–5). Further, Jesus is "the sun of justice" (*sol iustitiae*) "with the brilliance of burning love [*fulgorem ardentis caritatis*], of such great glory that every creature is illuminated by the brightness of his light" (*Scivias* 1.3.3; CCCM 43.43).

The seasonal context of flowering embeds the sublime blossom in the cycles of divine nature: it opens at the right moment, when time itself is ripe for salvation, *cum venit tempus* (when time came) (*Symph*. 19.2). And yet, at the same time outside of time, this flower leaps out of the seasonal cycle as "the strongest fruit [*fortissimus fructus*] that shall never fail" (*Scivias* 2.6.32; CCCM 43.261) and as the one begotten "in primal dawn / before all creation [*in prima aurora / ante omnem creaturam*]" (*Symph*. 7.7–8). With reference to Christ and *viriditas*, the one barely distinguishable from the other, Hildegard stages the phoenix complex as the field of transcendence within the immanence of life, atemporal within the order of time. And she does so with a language steeped in brightness and lucidity, brilliance and burning, of the dawn and the sun.

Of course, Jesus is not the only participant in the theological drama of hot and moist divine-human-vegetal *viriditas*. His mother is also a phoenix, the dawn who gives birth to "a new sun": "From your womb [*de tuo ventre*] / came another life [*alia vita processit*], / the life that Adam / stripped from his children." And again: "But from your womb, / O dawn [*o aurora*], / has come forth a new sun [*novus sol processit*] / that cleansed all the guilt of Eve" (*Symph*. 20.2a–20.6a). When Hildegard casts the salvific phoenix as female side by side with the male phoenix, who is Jesus, she replays the indeterminacy of the phoenix's sexuality already prominent in the classical sources. The Christian phoenix is not one but two: Mary and Jesus in a matrix of sexual difference that both rehashes and reverses the relation of Adam and Eve. The

133   *The Phoenix Acts*

mother and the son who renew the self-renewing capacity of creation are the mirror image of the first progenitors who are, roughly speaking, a father and a daughter (according to one of the narratives preserved in the book of Genesis that insists on the creation of Eve from Adam's rib). Incestual connotations aside, the phoenix is a complex also because sexual differences, including the difference between sexuality and its absence, are irreducible within it, not least when it comes to refreshing the self-refreshing power of *viriditas*.

As was noted in chapter 1 of the present study, mortality and individuality are tied in a single knot with sexuality. While Jesus is born of Mary in order to save humanity from the universal punishment of death meted out to Adam, Eve, and their descendants as a consequence of the original sin, the vegetal bent of redemption in Hildegard renders the theme of mortality more tortuous than would prima facie appear. Coming up with a hyperliteral interpretation of the Eucharist, she writes that God the Father is the vine out of which the wine that is his Son flows (*ut vinum de vite sudat, ita et Filius meus de corde meo exivit*), as "liquor from the sweetest and strongest fruit [*sucus de dulcissimo ac fortissimo fructu vitis*]" of "all merciful and true justice" (*Scivias* 2.6.28; CCCM 43.257). The fermentation of fruit does not cancel death, but sublimates or sublates vegetal matter and mortality. "The strongest fruit" is not immortal; it is not the one that unfailingly perseveres in its self-identity, but, rather, one that is capable of metamorphoses, converting death into another life, pointing to the *alia vita* (another life) that blossomed forth from Mary's womb.

Among heterogeneous phoenix narratives resonating in these lines from Hildegard's *Scivias*, the dominant version of the myth that emphasizes cremation and an instant rebirth from the ashes is muted down. Fermentation is in line with decomposition that does not skip over death as the uncomfortable and disgusting underside of life, but that gradually fashions the material grounds for another growth and for a livable, living future. Nonetheless, it is not without the fiery element combined with moisture in the matrix of *viriditas*. Like the vegetal phoenix *proper*, namely the date palm in Hildegard's *Physica*, the fruit of the grapevine, to which Christ is compared, has "fiery heat and moisture in it. The fire is so strong as to change its sap into a

134   *Chapter 5*

flavor that other trees and herbs do not have" (*Physica* 1.liv; *PL* 197.1244b). Given her insistence on the flaming essence of grapes that denotes their proximity to the realm of spirit, a fundamental distinction between diverse phoenix narratives turns out to be, instead of funereal/enlivening fire and the absence thereof, the speed and the intensity of the blaze: fast and fierce in combustion; slow and relatively mild in decomposition and fermentation.

The third thread—that of individuation—is hued by Hildegard's vegetal representation of the Christian phoenix. If Mary corresponds to the greenest branch and Jesus is analogous to a brilliant flower blossoming on the branch, then there is neither a strict separation nor a fusion of the two. In their singularity, the mother and the son are co-constituted by this relation, which is as much vegetal as it is psychic or spiritual: "The intellect in the soul is like the *viriditas* of branches and foliage on a tree," while "the will is like its [the tree's] flowers [*voluntas autem quasi flores in ea*]" (*Scivias* 1.4.26; CCCM 43.84). Just as the will grows from the discernments of the intellect, and just as a flower buds on a branch, so Jesus extends into the world out of Mary. Moreover, the will—bent on saving this world, even at the price of one's life—is, far from a one-time determination, a choice that is made repeatedly, regenerated out of the intellect, and reaffirmed in the face of temptation. The death and resurrection of a phytotheandric being are supplanted by the death and resuscitation of the will. The intellect and the will are the psychic phoenix reborn each time anew within the scheme of "The Similarity of a Tree to the Soul [*Similitudo de arbore ad animam*]," which is a part of the fourth vision in Book 1 of *Scivias*. They shape each other on the hither side of identity and difference.

*

In its nucleic version that becomes visible in Hildegard's oeuvre, the Christian phoenix complex involves the Virgin Mary and Christ, which is why fiery imagery is rife with regard to her as well. Mary's associations with dawn (*aurora*) or with luminous matter (*lucida materia*) are interspersed with the acknowledgment of her "brightness," *claritas*: "The supreme Father / took note of the virgin's brightness [*supernus Pater claritatem Virginis / atendit*]" (*Symph.* 21.17–18). In line with the vegetal nonindividuation of the mother

135 *The Phoenix Acts*

and the son, this quality migrates to (or, better, it is borrowed by) Jesus, in whom her *claritas* takes the form of a flower, described as "marvelously bright [*mirabiliter clarus flos*]" (*Symph.* 21.14).

The capacity of life to refresh itself is renewed thanks to the divine-human-vegetal couple who channel the dual power of fire, its light and heat, through themselves for the sake of the world. There are two vital implications to the pyrological complex of this renewal of renewal. First, fire, including its Trinitarian sense conveyed in one of Hildegard's mystical visions—"three little torches [*tres faculas*], arranged in such a way that by their fire they hold up the globe lest it fall" (*Scivias* 1.3.4; CCCM 43.43)—loses its exclusively phallic connotations and is sexualized otherwise within the framework of the Christian phoenix. Light is not shed onto abysmally deep and dark matter (as Plotinus indelibly characterizes it); it emanates from materiality, from matter's phosphorescent glow, its own luminosity and lucidity. By including Mary in the realm of fire, Hildegard is able to overturn, subtly but efficiently, the philosophical tradition, which goes back to Plato and Aristotle and according to which matter in the feminine is a dark and moist receptacle, while spirit is the life- and form-giving light and heat. The complex of sexual difference, where Mary appears in the fullness of her luminosity and brightness, also as an instantiation of the intellect, defies classical gendering and separation of spirit from matter.

Second, the discovery of light and heat proper to matter affects, in the most pronounced manner, *vegetal* matter, the plants no longer set apart from spirit or the solar blaze, which they imbibe, objectify, and transmute into growth. That is why some plants, like date palm (the botanical phoenix par excellence) and grapes, can be exceedingly "hot." But vegetal heat is by no means the sole prerogative of plants that are prominent in their capacity to host spirit. Roots, for Hildegard, are not (only) mired in the moist darkness of the soil and of the unconscious; they are aflame, binding the plant (also) to the sun: "O most noble *viriditas* / that is rooted in the sun [*que radicas in sole*]. / . . . You blush like dawn / and burn like a solar flame [*et ardes ut solis flamma*]" (*Symph.* 56.1–2; 56.10–11). The "blushing dawn" and the burning "solar flame" are Mary and Jesus within the vegetal scheme of the Christian phoenix. Unless *viriditas* is both at the same time, it is nothing at all. And

136   *Chapter 5*

unless a plant is rooted simultaneously in the sun and in the earth, it cannot develop, grow, decay, and regerminate once again nor can it give rise to new growth as compost. The womb of rebirth (above all, the rebirth of rebirth) and the indwelling of plant roots are internally illuminated, enlightened and enlightening. With the mediations of *viriditas*, Hildegard attends to the clarity and lucidity of matter (*materia*), mother (*mater*), and wood/woods (*lignum*)—the alternative trinity that shines in her work.

"What or who is this matter or mother, wood and the woods, on fire?" I inquired about Hildegard's trinity in my *Green Mass*.[11] The answer is now evident: a Christian phoenix, both mother and son, a she and a he, moist and warm, chthonic and solar. The caveat is that this phoenix is not focused on its own rejuvenation in the flames and revival from the ashes, but on the reanimation of life's liveliness, the restoration of the youth of the world, the *viriditas* of *viriditas*. What the phoenix representing the whole of nature accomplishes by means of a synecdoche the Christian phoenix achieves directly through redemptive action (or passion). Nonetheless, the moment of singular universality is still there in Christian salvation that needs to pass through the crucible of individual faith.

*

It is very odd, at first blush, to conscript Spinoza to the cause of the phoenix complex and to pair him with St. Hildegard of Bingen. Although he was excommunicated from the Jewish community of Amsterdam, the descendant of Portuguese Jews, Baruch (Benedict) Spinoza opposed the sorts of mystical interpretations of religion, such as the one advanced by Hildegard. "I found nothing expressly taught in Scripture that was not in agreement with the intellect or that contradicted it," he writes in the *Tractate*'s Preface (*CW* 392). This view is congruent with Spinoza's earliest critique of animism, which he launched in *Emendations of the Intellect*, blaming the faculty of imagination conceived as "composed of diverse confused perceptions of things that exist in nature [*compositae ex diversis confusis perceptionibus rerum in natura existentium*], as when men are convinced that divinities are present in the woods, in images, in animals, and other things" (68; *CW* 19). Were Spinoza to have mentioned it in his corpus, the phoenix would have been one of the chimeras of imaginings, in the face of which "the soul has only a passive role" (86; *CW* 24), despite the illusion that it is active and creative. The very notion of a complex is similarly anathema to Spinoza's take on substance and on God with their absolute simplicity (though, as we have seen in the preface, key ideas in his *Ethics* help us understand what a complex entails). Complexity arises only where ramifications are rife—at the level of images and their associations or passions and their confusion or the modes of substance. So, a phoenix complex would be something Spinoza would vehemently object to.

That said, a set of core concepts in his philosophy both nourish and are nourished by the phoenix complex: the universal singularity of substance, the confluence of sameness and otherness in its modes, the division between the untiringly active *natura naturans* and the created *natura naturata*, the diachronic view of nature between the perspective of eternity (*sub specie aeternitatis*) and that of affected, finite existence, as well as the masterpiece of his thought, *conatus essendi*. While I cannot, within the limits of the present chapter, offer a detailed analysis of each of these themes, I will delineate their contours as they bear on the phoenix complex.

To begin with, the absolute singularity of substance in Spinoza applies, in a strict relation of equivalences, to the singularity of nature and of God. Already in the *Short Treatise on God, Man, and His Wellbeing*, available only in an early translation into Dutch but not in the original Latin, Spinoza lays the foundations for his philosophy, deriving the unity and the uniqueness of nature and substance from the notion of God. In chapter 2 ("What God Is"), he states that "there is no finite substance [*er geen bepaalde selfstandigheid en is*], but . . . that in the infinite understanding of God no substance can be more perfect than that which already exists in nature" (1.ii; *CW* 41). Thus "all these attributes, which are in nature, are but one single being, and by no means different things [*alle deze eijgenschappen die inde Natuur zijn, maar een eenig wezen is en geenzins verscheijde*]" (1.ii.; *CW* 43). Subsequently, in *Emendations of the Intellect*, the philosopher reflecting on the "origin of nature" writes that "this entity is unique [*unicum*] and infinite, that is, it is total being, beyond which there is no being [*est omne a esse, et praeter quod nullum datur esse*]" (76; *CW* 21). The formulaic expressions *Deus sive*

138   *Chapter 5*

substantia (God, or substance) and *Deus sive natura* (God, or nature) in *Ethics* formalize these earlier insights with the utmost clarity and economy.

The singularity of the phoenix, unique in its kind, places it on the same level as nature, substance, and God in Spinoza. As a mythical predecessor of monotheism (harkening back to the Egyptian cult of the sun god, Aten, who is, like the god Atum, associated with *bennu* as one of the sun animals[12]), the figurative idea of the phoenix eventually comes to steer the philosophical expressions of a religion that posits the existence of one God, or, simply, the One, as Plotinus has it.[13] So, among the definitions Spinoza provides in his *Ethics*, we find this on the subject of finitude: "A thing is said to be finite in its own kind [*in suo genere finita*] when it can be limited by another thing of the same nature" (D2; *CW* 217).

Uniqueness implies both totality and infinity: the one God, nature, or substance encompasses *all* being (totality) such that there is no limit, at which this total being could be negated by something else and could, thereby, come to its end either in space or in time (infinity). This is the point where, while she is utterly singular and as such becomes a stand-in for the whole of nature, the phoenix diverges from the Spinozan incarnations of the One: she encompasses all a posteriori and largely in an unconscious way. Further, the phoenix is not infinite absolutely: limited in time, she perpetually overcomes this limitation by her self-iterations as the other. Finally, the uniqueness of the phoenix is that of an exception that universalizes itself not as a source of its emanations but by way of supplanting the universal in keeping with the mechanics and machinations I have been cataloging in these pages. Due to her composite nature, serial singularity, and the operations of a synecdoche, the totality and the infinity of phoenix's existence are conditional, which is why she must die to be reborn.

With these provisos, the phoenix joins the family of singular entities in Spinoza, particularly with respect to how they calibrate the relation of sameness and otherness. It was, as we already know, Lactantius who wrote about the phoenix's descendant that he was "the same indeed, but not the same; the very one, yet not the one [*Ipsa quidem, sed non eadem, quia et ipsa, nec ipsa est*]" (*De ave phoenice* 165–170). Spinoza does not reconcile the same and not-the-same under the umbrella of species being and individual specimens;

139   *The Phoenix Acts*

rather, as early as in *The Short Treatise* he notes that, whereas difference, division, and alteration, generation and death, take place in the modes of substance, they do not affect substance as such: "As regards the parts in nature, we maintain that division, as has also been said already before, never takes place in substance, but always and only in the mode of substance. Thus, if I want to divide water, I only divide the mode of substance, and not substance itself. And whether this mode is that of water or something else is always the same. Division, then, or passivity, always takes place in the mode; thus, when we say that man passes away or is annihilated, then this is understood to apply to man only insofar as he is such a composite being, and a mode of substance, and not the substance on which he depends" (1.ii; *CW* 44–45). Far from arbitrary, the example of water will crop up again in *Ethics* in connection to the same thematic cluster. In the scholium to a proposition on the identity of God and substance, Spinoza writes, "For example, we conceive water to be divisible and to have separate parts insofar as it is water, but not insofar as it is material substance. In this latter respect it is not capable of separation or division [*quatenus substantia est corporea; eatenus enim neque separatur neque dividitur*]. Furthermore, water, qua water, comes into existence and goes out of existence; but qua substance it does not come into existence nor go out of existence [*Porro aqua, quatenus aqua, generatur et corrumpitur; at, quatenus substantia, nec generatur, nec corrumpitur*]" (*Ethics* 1.xv.sch; *CW* 227).

Regeneration and rebirth are possible in the interplay between the substance and its modes, between the eternal and the finite, giving rise to the infinite. Going out of existence is a smoothening out of the wrinkles on the surface of substance that persists and that exhibits fresh wrinkles in its remodification. The Spinozan phoenix is a hinge between the substance and the modes: the same with regard to the former and not the same with regard to the latter. And, since, for Spinoza, the order of thoughts mirrors and strictly corresponds to the arrangement of extended things (as two attributes of the same substance), reinvigoration of thinking entails an analogous interplay between the same and the other. "So that all ideas may be subsumed under one [*omnes ideae ad unam ut redigantur*]," writes Spinoza in *Emendations*, "we shall endeavor to connect and arrange them in such a manner that our mind, as far as possible, may reproduce in thought the reality of nature, both as the whole and as to its parts" (91; *CW* 25). The reproduction "in thought [of] the reality of nature,"[14] just as the reproduction of the reality of thought in thought, depends on carefully (if not yet dialectically) juggling the one and the many, sameness and difference, substance and its modes. More than a mere replication of one order or regime in another, such reproduction requires connecting the immanently divisible and the indivisible, the logic of parts and wholes and what neither has nor is a whole nor parts,[15] the mortal and the immortal, the constitutively open and the self-enclosed, sealed in itself, utterly unique, idiosyncratic, idiotic even.[16] Nature and the phoenix—nature as the phoenix and the phoenix as nature—are these paradoxical connections working, despite the apparently seamless continuation of existence they promise, with and across the unconnectable.[17]

*

Anyone wishing to fully appreciate the theme of regeneration in Spinoza ought to take a close look at chapter 22 in the second part of his *Short Treatise*, titled "On True Knowledge, Regeneration, etc. [*Van de Waare kennis, Weedergeboorte enz*]." There, Spinoza pursues the classical philosophical theme of the second birth, of the phoenix-like rebirth in the most secure kind of knowledge of oneself and of the world through God. When we become aware that "the whole of nature is but one only substance, and one whose essence is infinite, all things are united through nature, and they are united into one [being], namely God," then "we may say with truth *that we have been born again* [*als dan konnen wij met waarheid zeggen weder geboren te zijn*]" (2.xxii; *CW* 94–95). Whereas God, nature, or substance are not themselves reborn because they are neither generated nor do they pass away, those who grasp their vital and essential participation in the whole these entities name achieve the sort of renewal that renders their physical death, the separation of the soul from the body, obsolete. As Spinoza explains, "Our first birth [*eerste geboorte*] took place when we were united with the body, through which the activities and movements of the [vital] spirits have arisen; but this our other or second birth [*andere of tweede geboorte*] will take place when we become aware in us of entirely different effects of love, commensurate with the knowledge of this incorporeal object, and as different from the first as the corporeal is different from the incorporeal, spirit from flesh" (2.xxii; *CW* 95).

In other words, the first birth is biological activation, the union of the soul with the body that sparks off organismic life; the second birth is spiritual potentiation that situates the body-soul unit within a much vaster divine, substantial, and natural reality, of which it is a part. In fact, the extra step, already taken in the *Short Treatise*, according to which there are no radical splits or gaps within this reality ("division . . . never takes place in substance"), means that one is of a piece with God, nature, or substance in toto, on the hither side of the usual differentiation between parts and wholes. A move more radical than the synecdoche of the phoenix, the second birth establishes an identity, as intellectual as it is amorous, between the one who is reborn and the world into which one is reborn. (Note that this is neither another world nor, even less so, an otherworldly domain, but this very world, which we inhabit, just seen from another standpoint.) In this sense, Spinoza's comparison of the difference between the first and the second births with that between the corporeal and the incorporeal, or between flesh and the spirit, is altogether material. And the double perspective—from within the phenomenology of existence and *sub specie aeternitatis*, or "under the aspect of eternity"—he wields has to do with the two births within the overall scheme of the phoenix that is in effect throughout his writings.

The path toward the second birth as Spinoza sees it bears closer resemblance to the Platonic way of love. A drastic change of perspective involves an affective alteration, which is not, in its turn, separate from "true knowledge": "Now we have said that this kind of knowledge does not result from something else but from a direct revelation of the object itself to the understanding. And if that object is glorious and good, then the soul becomes necessarily united with it. . . . Hence, it follows incontrovertibly that it is this knowledge which evokes love. So that when we get to know God after this manner then . . . we must necessarily become united with him. And only in this union, as we have already remarked, does our blessedness consist [*In het welke alleen gelijk wij nu al gezeit hebben, onse zaligheid bestaat*]" (2.xxii; *CW* 93–94). Regeneration in love, as a desire to unite with the excellent object that has been revealed to understanding (God, nature, substance), is a rebirth by means of rational desire, the desire of reason, named *amor intellectualis* in *Ethics*. That is the hinge of the Spinozan phoenix. Its end (not to be conflated with the limit or a finite condition) is the state of blessedness (*beatitudo*; *zaligheid*) that, as it will also in the concluding chapters of *Ethics* (e.g., 5.xlii), signifies the enduring fulfillment of rational desire.[18] Now, *beatitudo* is a near synonym of *benedictio*—the Latin version of Spinoza's first name, Benedictus, translating the Hebrew Baruch. Subtly, the philosopher practices the affirmative (and self-affirmative) thinking he preaches, including himself, perhaps unconsciously, within the ranks of those who have experienced the second birth.

In the sense intended by Spinoza, regeneration is a rebirth into what no longer degenerates, into what does not die: "And this may, therefore, all the more justly and truly be called regeneration [*Wedergeboorte*], in as much as only from this love and union [*deze Liefde en Vereeniginge*] does eternal and unchangeable existence ensue" (2.xxii; *CW* 95). In the following chapter, Spinoza will put this in even starker terms: "We have shown sufficiently, we think, what our love of God is and also its consequences, namely our eternal duration" (2.xxiii; *CW* 96). The spatial aspect of substance as extension without division corresponds to its temporal dimension as a time without end. The question is whether immortality in a loving union with God, substance, or nature is achieved at the expense of individuation, seeing that the one who is so reborn dissolves into these immense realities and foregoes death.

Since the opening pages of this book, I have tried to show how individuation is tied into a knot with mortality and sexual difference and how, moreover, the phoenix complex vacillates on all three issues, exhibiting the highest degree of equivocation and insecurity. Levinas was the one who put it in the most blatant terms when he raised the demand for the kind of worldly transcendence, in which the I is not lost, even though his own solution fell short of such "personal" transcendence in the relation of substitution of one's offspring for oneself. Likewise, Hegel's imperative in the Preface to his *Phenomenology* to apprehend and express "the true not as *substance* but rather even more as *subject* [das Wahre nicht als *Substanz*, sondern ebensosehr als *Subjekt*]"[19] sounds like a direct rejoinder to Spinoza and the sort of transcendence within the immanence of substance he prescribes. It is advisable to

143   *The Phoenix Acts*

proceed with caution, however, in matters as delicate and intricate as these. A merging with substance, God, or nature in Spinoza is, far from a mechanical process, a regeneration and unification mediated by love, which is itself indebted to the desire of reason. Thanks to love, the subject persists in the midst of substance when one least expects it, when the object of this love is no one else than the being or existence of this very subject. I will flesh out the consequences of this insight in the discussion of *conatus*. Of the essence in the preserving function of love is that "eternal duration" is one of its consequences, a remnant of the subject present despite its possible absence in the midst of substance. It follows that the Spinozan phoenix is not so different from Hegel's: dwelling in truth both as subject and as substance.

*

The division of nature into the ever-productive *natura naturans* and the generated *natura naturata*, also reflected in the difference between life and the living, prefigures the relation of subject and substance in Spinoza. (Apparently immutable, substance contains an excess over itself, notably the subject, who puts in motions the very things that are supposed to be at rest in substance.) In *Short Treatise*, Spinoza explains this division in terms of causality—in particular, immanent or emanative divine causality. God is "an *emanative* or *productive cause of his works*; and, insofar as there is activity, *an active or operating cause* [*een uitvloejende ofte daarstellende oorzaak van zijne werken en in opzigt de werkinge geschied, een doende ofte werkende oorzaak*]" (1.iii; *CW* 50). *Natura naturans* is another name for this cause postulated as the first of God's attributes (*Propria*). In turn, *natura naturata* is split into two, the general (*algemeene*) and the particular (*bezondere*), whereby "the *general* consists of all the modes which depend immediately on God" and "the *particular* consists of all the particular things which are produced by the general mode" (1.viii; *CW* 58). In *natura naturata* the initial division between the generating and the generated or life and the living is thereby reintroduced.

While classified as a part of *natura naturata*, the general mode stands at the intersection of *natura naturans* and *naturata*, the intersection, which has already been surveyed as the territory of the phoenix. Hildegard's *viriditas*, too, belongs here as the creative spark within creation that, thanks to this undying spark, is capable of self-renewal. For Spinoza, the general mode of *natura naturata* again bifurcates into "*motion* in matter and the *understanding* in the thinking thing" (1.ix; *CW* 58), indicative of the presence of the causing in the caused, of the cause in its effects. Tellingly, Spinoza calls both motion and the understanding "*a Son* [een Zone], *Product, or Effect* created immediately by God" (1.ix; *CW* 59). In spite of its palpable resonance with Christian Trinitarian theology (most obviously, through the figure of the Son), I hold that this characterization goes further back to the source it has in common with the figure of Christ—the thought-image of the phoenix. The dynamism of both matter and the thinking thing (motion and the understanding, respectively) is attributable to the initial creative impulse that does not die out in its effects, but lives on, re-creating them or letting them re-create themselves.

The ceaselessly productive view of nature Spinoza holds is not, for all that, reducible to productivism. As he repeats, time and again, in *Ethics*, "Nature has no fixed goal and all final causes are but figments of the human imagination [*naturam finem nullum sibi praefixum habere, et omnes causas finales nihil nisi humana esse figmenta*]" (1.app; *CW* 240). Focusing on the first cause and rejecting final causes, Spinoza understands *natura naturata* as merely derivative from *natura naturans*, without the definitive *why* orienting their course. Although contingency is out of the question (1.xxix; *CW* 234), everything is guided and steered from behind and from below, not from ahead. So, "by *natura naturans* we must understand that which is in itself and is conceived through itself [*per naturam naturantem nobis intelligendum est id quod in se est et per se concipitu*] [. . . while] by *natura naturata* I understand all that follows from the necessity of God's nature or any of God's attributes [*per naturatem autem intelligo id omne quod ex necessitate Dei naturae sive uniuscuiusque Dei attributorum sequitur*]" (1.xxix.sch; *CW* 234). What was earlier defined as the "general mode" of *natura naturata*, harboring the dynamism of the phoenix, now instigates a protodialectic of the in-itself and the for-us, of the initial cause and its effects, of potentiality and actuality, the creating and the created. And, instead of a final cause, the end of this movement lies in itself, in substance, in nature, or in God whence it derives.

145   *The Phoenix Acts*

This intermediate conclusion assigns to the general mode of *natura naturata* an essential role related to *conatus essendi* (the tie that binds beings to their being): within the creatures, creation is a repeated and repeatable re-creation of each in their identity at every single moment of their finite existence. Thus, despite having biological parents who are different from one, each one is also his own son or her own daughter, a phoenix reborn from oneself throughout the time of one's life. The striving that *conatus* expresses is none other than the general mode of *natura naturata* experienced from the standpoint of creaturely life: "Each thing, insofar as it is in itself, endeavors to persist in its own being [*Unaquaeque res, quantum in se est, in suo esse perseverare conatur*]" (*Ethics* 3.vi; *CW* 283). The persistence of each entity is by no means static: to persevere in one's own being is to keep replacing oneself by oneself, to live on, surviving oneself, after having more or less imperceptibly died to oneself. Here, finitude internally opens unto infinity, since there is no inherent limit to the mechanics and machinations of self-replacement, of *conatus* realized (without ever being accomplished) with the mediation of the general mode of *natura naturata*, involving movement, on the one hand, and understanding, on the other. Hence "the conatus, with which each single thing endeavors to persist in its own being does not involve finite time, but indefinite time [*nullum tempus finitum, sed indefinitum involvit*]" (*Ethics* 3.viii; *CW* 283). The finite is converted into potential infinity through the in-de-finite number of repeated operations of the phoenix that each is, that the finite *is* itself is.

Another conceptual link between *conatus* and the general mode of *natura naturata* (also analogous to Hildegard's *viriditas*) resides in the obliteration of differences between God's creative and preserving activity. In *Principles of Cartesian Philosophy*, Spinoza argues that "*God's action is the same in creating the world and in preserving it*" since "the same amount of force is required for the creation of a thing as for its preservation" (2.x; *CW* 204). This statement nearly levels the distinction between *natura naturans* and *natura naturata*, seeing that creation is not an event relegated to a deep past at the dawn of time, but a process, in which self-preservation is a continual creation or re-creation of the world, now with the participation of the creatures themselves.[20] Spinoza's definition of life, conceived as *conatus*, in the

146   *Chapter 5*

same work—life is "the force through which things persevere in their own being" (2.vi; *CW* 197)—implies that it is as much a productive as a reproductive activity, that which is simultaneously in-itself and for-us. It is one of God's propria and what is proper to the living beings themselves, and, as a result, the "self" of self-preservation is double, referring to the creature and the creator.[21] In line with the phoenix complex, the self is its own progenitor and offspring, the cause and the effect, divine and finite.

Without naming it as such, Spinoza includes *conatus* in the list of God's attributes in his *Short Treatise*, where providence "is nothing else than the *striving* which we find in the whole of nature and in individual things to maintain and preserve their own existence [*die poginge die wij en in de geheele Natuur en in de bezondere dingen ondervinden, strekkende tot behoudenisse en bewaringe van haar zelfs wezen*]" (1.v; *CW* 53). In our ownmost being, we are the other at the confluence of sameness and alterity in the figure of the phoenix. By binding us to ourselves, to our existence projected into the future, *conatus* ties us to others (all the other creatures, each of whom strives to preserve itself) and to the Other (namely, God). In its singularity, it is universal, ethically and ontologically. In the words of *Ethics*, "To act in absolute conformity with virtue is nothing else in us but to act, to live, to preserve one's own being [*agere, vivere, suum esse conservare*] (these three mean the same) under the guidance of reason, on the basis of seeking one's own advantage [*ex fundamento proprium utile quaerendi*]" (4.xxiv; *CW* 333). Practically speaking, striving to survive is desiring (unconsciously at first and in keeping with the precepts of reason later on) for the rest of humanity to survive (4.xxxvii; *CW* 339). This is the desire of the phoenix, extrapolated from oneself to the other human beings and, further out, to everything living. It is the red thread stitched into Spinoza's thought.

6 DEATH, REBIRTH, AND BEYOND IN HINDU TRADITIONS

As Laurence Gosserez rightly observes in his study of the phoenix, "It is not always possible to establish with clarity the exact kinship among diverse mythic birds, such as the Greek and Latin phoenix, the Egyptian *bennu*, Chinese *fenghuang*, Persian *simorgh*, the Judaic phoenix [*ḥol'*, MM] or the Arabo-Muslim *anqa*."[1] There are neither definitive lineages nor exact equivalences here, only probable influences and cross-cultural reverberations. The list of names, which Gosserez has hastily compiled, would not, however, be complete without the Indian bird Garuḍa. In the very first book of *The Mahābhārata*, *The Book of the Beginnings*, Garuḍa is said to have been born all by himself, "in all his might without help from his mother," Vinatā, the daughter of Dakṣa, one of the agents of creation (M 1(5)20.1.1–5).[2] Like *bennu*, Garuḍa is a sun-bird: "Ablaze like a kindled mass of fire, of most terrifying aspect, the Bird grew instantly to his giant size and took to the sky. Upon seeing him, all the gods took refuge with the bright-shining Bird; and prostrating themselves they spoke to him of the many hues as he sat perched: 'Fire, deign to grow no more! What that thou do not seek to burn us. For this huge mass of thine creeps fierily onward!'" (M 1(5)20.1.5–10).

The bird's connection to the sun and to fire, its self-mediated birth, its instantaneous transformation from a hatchling to a magnificent and unique specimen—all this resonates with the key shared features of various phoenix narratives. Still more impressive is the resonance between the cosmic and historical scale of the Egyptian *bennu* and the Indian Garuḍa, as attested in the hymn of praise that the gods sing to him: "Thou art the Lord, of the aspect of fire, thou art our ultimate / redemption. . . . Of thy heat that never lackest in fame we hear, / All that is future and all that has befallen. / Superbly thou shinest upon all that moves and stands, / Eclipsing the splendor of the sun. / Thou art the finisher of all that is, the lasting and the brief. . . . / Destroying and ending the revolutions of the Eon" (M 1(5)20.1.10–15).

Not only is Garuḍa a singular witness of the entire history of being (knowing "all that is future and all that has befallen"), as the phoenix will later be for Claudian, but he also marks the end of "the revolutions of the Eon," in a way similar to how *bennu*'s and phoenix's life span coincides with the Egyptian Great Year. The radiance emanating from Garuḍa and eclipsing the light of the sun finds its parallel in the ancient Egyptian root *wbn*, from which *bennu* is formed, meaning "to arise brilliantly," or "to shine." The arising is replete with phallic connotations too: "Filled with glow, might, and strength," the bird "rose like the upraised staff of Brahmā" (M 1(5)26.1.1–5). The mission Garuḍa receives from his mother shortly after his birth is to steal soma, the elixir of life, from the gods, which cannot help but be associated in our minds with how Prometheus stole fire from Olympus in Greek mythology. Encountering Viṣṇu after successfully obtaining soma, Garuḍa is granted two boons, one of them being, "May I even without the aid of the elixir never age and never die!" (1(5)29.1.15). From that time on, the bird's achievement of immortality goes hand in hand with his role as the destroyer and ender of eons.

The imbrication of life and death in the figure of Garuḍa is even more evident in his designation as "cleaver of mountaintops, drier of the water of the rivers, whirler of the worlds, awesome image of death" (M 1(5)26.1.1–5). The bearer of the elixir of life and himself immortal, Garuḍa embodies the wheel of time that rolls toward death and destruction—the "whirling" of worlds, recalling the famous dance of Śiva—which in turn prepares the ground or the stage for world-making. The mythic bird thus embodies the Hindu conception of infinite time: "Unlike the Hebrew and Christian conceptions of creation, the Indian allows for the infinity of time, and regards the universe as one of many that stretch, in cycles of creation and destruction, into the endless past, and that will stretch, in similar cycles, into the endless future."[3]

The term "Eastern phoenix" is a misnomer, which is not so innocent, considering that it extends as a model or a prototype the Greek and Latin figuration of the mythical creature to regions outside Europe. But this does not mean that what I have referred to as "the phoenix complex" is not shared by cultures in the East and in the West, still before the emergence of the phoenix properly so called. The reason for affixing a Western name to the complex is that, with all its disastrous consequences, it is most crisply implemented in the West both with regard to the natural world and with respect to the technological concretization of this way of treating nature. The actual capacity to burn the world as a whole, while hoping for its ongoing regeneration from the ashes, was realized with the industrial-scale use of fossil fuels. But the advantage of non-Western traditions, such as those thriving on the Indian subcontinent, is that, in addition to hosting modes of thinking that dovetail with the phoenix complex, or with which the phoenix complex dovetails, they untie the ideational and affective knots that "complexify" it in the first place. What Schelling struggled to express in the conceptual and natural language at his disposal, what he grappled with in terms of incipient and final freedom, can be stated with beautiful economy in the words of the *Bhagavad Gītā* (which is, probably, the most famous portion of *The Mahābhārata*) or of the early *Upaniṣads*, or, again, of certain hymns from *Ṛg Veda*—materials, to which we turn next.

*

In the *Bhagavad Gītā* the god Kṛṣṇa endeavors to allay the doubts and concerns of prince Arjuna, who is reluctant to throw his army into battle in the Kurukshetra war. His arguments, though, are not tactical; in his speeches, Kṛṣṇa explains nothing less than the nature of the self, of birth, death, and rebirth, as well as the path to freeing oneself from bondage to the cycle of reincarnations. The infinite time Garuḍa embodies turns out to be that of each creature, whether vegetal or human, animal or divine.

"Truly," Kṛṣṇa says early on, "there was never a time when I was not, nor you, nor these lords of men; and neither will there be a time when we shall cease to be from this time onward" (BG 2.12).[4] Nonbeing is illusory, so long as there is a world soul (*ātman*) essentially unsullied by the events of birth and death, the soul or breath that cannot be harmed or even touched by empirical occurrences. "These bodies inhabited by the eternal [*nityasya*], the indestructible [*anāśino*], the immeasurable [*prameyasya*] soul/breath [*ātman*] are said to come to an end [*antavanta*]."[5] Yet "he who imagines this (*ātman*) the slayer and he who imagines it the slain, neither of them understands [that] it does not slay, nor is slain" (BG 2.18–19). The phoenix exemplifies the indestructability of *ātman* traversing the gap of death; the figure of Garuḍa is more precise, in that he reveals the illusory nature of death as such. The infinity of finite creatures is assured not by virtue of producing another finite being in their likeness, but by finding *ātman* within oneself and, through this indestructible breath of life in oneself, identifying with other living beings, in whom the same *ātman* similarly dwells. Hence, Kṛṣṇa appeals to Arjuna: "Know that that by which all this universe is pervaded is indeed indestructible [*avināśi*: also, "not to be lost"]" (BG 2.17).

Already the discovery of *ātman* within oneself helps one cut the ties to individual identity that overlays this shared stratum of existence. It, therefore, represents a vector of liberation: while the phoenix complex is invested in the resurrection of the same embodied being, or of another who is simultaneously the same and not the same as the original, the insight into *ātman* renders the unique material, genetic, or psychic identity of the I secondary. "Neither is this (*ātman*) born nor does it die at any time, nor, having been, will it again come not to be. Birthless [*ajo*], eternal [*nityaḥ*], perpetual [*śāśvato*]" (BG 2.20). Births, deaths, and rebirths occur at an epiphenomenal level, which does not affect *ātman*; hence the prohibition of mourning directed toward those who are wise enough to realize this epiphenomenality—"the wise [*paṇḍitāḥ*] do not mourn for the dead or for the living" (BG 2.11)—which will become apparent in a different epoch and cultural context in the thought of Baruch Spinoza.[6]

Should we, then, not mourn species loss and the passing of human or nonhuman beings who are particularly dear to us? By cutting our attachments to life and to lives, our own and that of others, can we silently authorize environmental devastation in the name of the "birthless" and undying *ātman*, which remains unperturbed by empirical events in the world? Is the having-been of everything and everyone who has ever existed sufficient enough to ensure their (our) coming-to-be-again when the fragile conditions required for life are under threat?

According to Amerindian philosophies and some Christian doctrines (such as those of St. Hildegard of Bingen, whose works were discussed in chapter 5), an individual soul dons the body as a garment, which it takes off at death—the garment hiding, as well as expressing, the one who wears it. In the *Bhagavad Gītā*, *ātman* is the wearer of bodies as diverse as a blade of grass, a fly, an elephant, a palm tree, a human, a lotus flower: "As, after casting away worn out garments [*vāsāmsi jirṇāni*], a man later takes new ones, so, after casting away worn out bodies, *ātman* encounters other, new ones" (BG 2.22). A single world soul wears different bodies, which can be discarded, abandoned, or cast away (*vihāya*), as they age. The garment factory of material existence is not infinitely stocked, however, and its equipment as well as logistics have gone haywire. What if some or even most of these bodies-clothes are no longer available? Moreover, the garments may be manufactured as already worn out from the moment of their first fabrication, abandoned ab initio, defined by this abandon or by abandonability. Reincarnation is the donning of a new body or a piece of clothing by *ātman* (indeed, of a multitude of bodies/clothes that happen to be alive at a given time), but the novelty and renewability of the supply are far from guaranteed. The glitch of groundless hope that is operative in the phoenix complex is in equal measure present in the vision of the world concretized in *The Mahābhārata*.

The deaths and rebirths of different living bodies that *ātman* acquires find their parallel in the stages of life, undergone by the same organism: "Just as in the body childhood, adulthood, and old age happen to an embodied being, so also he (the embodied being) acquires another body [*dehāntara-prāptir*]" (BG 2.13). The cycle of reincarnations is due to the appropriation (*prāptis*) of bodies by the one who inhabits them, the embodied self. My body as a child, as an adult, and an old man is, in fact, three distinct bodies appropriated by *me*. I am reincarnated in myself as an adult, after the child that I was is no longer, and as an elderly person, after the adult, too, passes away. My adulthood is the child of my childhood; my elderly body is the offspring of me as adult, the same and other from its predecessor. I die in myself and I am reborn from myself, coming close to the figure of the phoenix or

153   *Death, Rebirth, and Beyond in Hindu Traditions*

Garuḍa, as much as to the nature of Kṛṣṇa himself as revealed to Arjuna: "I am the father of the universe, the mother, the establisher, the grandfather" (BG 9.17); "I am . . . the origin, the dissolution and the foundation [*prabhavaḥ pralayaḥ sthāanam*]" (BG 9.18); "I am both immortality and death, being and nonbeing [*amṛtam cāiva mṛtyuśca, sad asac cāham*]" (BG 9.19). Millennia later, the American poet Walt Whitman will convey something of this idea in his "Song of Myself," included in *Leaves of Grass.*

In the microcosm of my existence, the macrocosm of *ātman* makes itself known: within the span of that which I call my life, I am perpetually reborn and I constantly die. The moment of my death, conventionally considered, is yet another link in the endless chain of such events. That is why, once again, mourning is out of place: "And moreover even if you think this, to be eternally born [*nityajātam*] or eternally dead [*nityam . . . mṛtam*], even then you should not mourn for this, Arjuna" (BG 2.26). The overall orientation of the phoenix complex prohibits mourning: it is absurd to mourn a life that will remake itself, or one that, "eternally born" (of itself), stretches in an infinite chain of self-renewal, beginning ever afresh. The "eternally dead" is also unmournable, since it has never been alive, and so has never slipped out of life and, having never been, will not ever be. Death is vanquished by its negation in immortality as much as by its confinement in eternity.

*

When we turn to the hymns compiled in *The Ṛg Veda*, the goddess Uṣas (Dawn) personifies the idea of perpetual rebirth and of the ever-young beauty. While she is one of the few feminine deities in the hymns, "cognate with the Greek goddess Eos and the Latin goddess Aurora" (and, through Aurora, with the Virgin Mary, as presented by St. Hildegard of Bingen),[7] Uṣas belongs, together with the phoenix, in Gilbert Durand's category of the "spectacular symbols" of the diurnal order (Durand observes that *divinity* as such is diurnal, celestial, and spectacular—"in Sanskrit the root *div*, which means 'to shine' and 'day', gives *Dyaus, dios* and *deivos*, or the Latin *divus.*" And he adds that "the *Upaniṣads* . . . are full of luminous symbols: God is called the 'Shining One,' [while] 'Brilliance and Light of all lights and what is shining is merely a shadow of its brilliance.'"[8]) Entwined with the dark of

154   *Chapter 6*

night, the time of dawn is a transitional, limitrophe figure between death, on the one hand, and the new life and light of day, on the other.[9] Thus, in a hymn dedicated to Indra, it is sung that "from of old [*sanāt*], the two young girls of distinct forms, ever regenerating, go around heaven and earth along their own courses—Night with her black, Dawn with her gleaming white shapes, progress one after the other" (RV 1.62.8).[10] Remarkably, not only life regenerates each time but also death resurfaces and regenerates, circling heaven and earth along its course. Or, perhaps, it is the twin movement of renewed life and death that is subject to regeneration, while keeping the "distinct forms" of the two sisters who participate in this movement.

The *complexio oppositorum* (the conjunction of opposites in the matrix of the phoenix complex) is glaring in the Vedic construction of the time that has run out and the time that is dispensed, graciously, after the end; of black and white; of darkness and the new light. In fact, the unity of opposites is pronounced both between Dawn and Night and within Dawn herself. So, in the hymn dedicated to Uṣas, we read: "Having a gleaming calf, herself gleaming white, she has come here. The black one has left behind her seats for her. Having the same kin-bonds, immortal, following one upon the other, the two, Day and Night, keep exchanging their color. The road is the same for the two sisters—unending. They proceed on it, one after the other, commanded by the gods. They do not oppose each other, nor do they stand still, though well grounded—Night and Dawn, of like mind but different form" (RV 1.113.2–3). Death and rebirth, corresponding to Night and Dawn, belong to an immortality that is not stagnant, that is marked by a constant rotation or exchange of places and colors, that travels along the same unending road. The two sisters' difference in form echoes the same idea from the other hymn I have cited, but, given the dynamism of the exchanges, of positional changes (one follows the other, and then the first follows the second), and nonoppositional arrangement, this difference and each of these forms, too, are in motion. Even the twin of Night is not constant: at times, she is Day; at other times, she is Dawn, in the same way that the other of death is sometimes life and sometimes (re)birth.

The activity proper to Uṣas is "dawning forth" and "awakening" all creatures to life, the activity, through which she "hold[s] sway over every earthly

155   *Death, Rebirth, and Beyond in Hindu Traditions*

good" (RV 1.113.7). These awakenings are singularly adjusted for a plethora of creatures called forth into life ("Living beings are not alike in what they have in view. Dawn has awakened all creatures" [RV 1.113.6]); whereas dawning forth is everywhere the same, the dawn is different for each. A bridge between finite lives, this activity is, itself, infinite: "Over and over in the past the goddess Dawn dawned forth. And today she has dawned forth here, the bounteous one. And she will dawn forth through later days. Unaging, immortal, she proceeds according to her own customs" (RV 1.113.13). Viewed from the vantage point of such repetitions, Uṣas traces continuous lines along a discontinuous path, punctuated by the night. She is the forerunner of the fire ("you have caused fire to be kindled" [RV 1.113.9]), to which the aging phoenix entrusts himself, in order to rejuvenate from the ashes in the dominant versions of the myth. But, in line with the alternating sequences of the following and the preceding, she, who awakens all creatures to being, is also convoked into being by fire: "the hoarse-voiced singer [=Agni, the god of fire], himself being praised, arouses the radiant dawns" (RV 1.113.17).

When, in a hymn addressed to all the gods, it is sung, "Might this earth [*kṣāḥ*] here be like (the place) of the dawns" (RV 10.31.5), the hope is that the earth would be ever fresh and ever refreshed, recovering its youth every day, at daybreak, like the dawn. Of course, we are dealing with the conjunction of opposites in this verse, which wishes for the chthonic domain (the Greek word for earth as *chthōn*, or the underworld, derives from the same Proto-Indo-European root as *kṣāḥ*) to be or to become akin to the place of dawn, of the birth and rebirth of light in its incomplete separation from darkness. Diurnal and nocturnal orders intermix.[11] But the renewal of the earth, in all its impenetrable obscurity as *kṣāḥ*, will have come to pass not so much by the brilliance of light shed upon it in the dawning of the place that it is; this renewal depends on the other dimension of fire, which is life-giving heat, stimulating a more complete awakening than light alone. Isn't Jesus's exclamation in Luke 12:49 reminiscent of this Vedic verse, even if it sounds more abrupt than this ancient text: "I came to send fire on the earth, and how I wish it were kindled already!"?[12]

156   *Chapter 6*

The gifts of Dawn are those of rebirth, of the extension of life across and despite its discontinuities or intermittencies. As in the phoenix complex, the apotheoses of her gifts are the offspring who outlive their parents, in whom or through whom parents outlive themselves: "Today, then, o bounteous one, dawn for the one who sings; for us shine down a lifetime full of offspring" (RV 1.113.17). Thanks to the intimate connection between Uṣas and Agni, who in *The Mahābhārata* treats Garuḍa as his equal, her gifts are sacrificial. That is why she is "the beacon of sacrifice" (RV 1.113.19), opening through her own retreat the path for the rising sun: "She has left a path for the sun to drive on. We have come to where they lengthen lifetime" (RV 1.113.16). Why have to "come to where they lengthen lifetime" at this exact point, at which Uṣas is no longer (at least for now) and at which the sun can take over, traveling along the itinerary pre-delineated by her? Because the retreat in question is not a mere absence but a giving withdrawal that, in the measure that the retreating one disappears, charts a possible path for those who will come afterwards—the offspring, above all.

In this spirit, the Vedic tradition ascribes a protective capacity to sacrifice and to its main deity, Agni, who preserves, rather than destroys, whatever is burned. The phoenix presents us with an afterglow of this ancient sacrificial logic. In effect, Agni imparts something of his own immortality to the offerings he receives: in a hymn dedicated to him, he is revered as "immortal Agni [*agnir amṛtān*] among mortals" (RV 7.4.4). Imploring cremation fire to be just right, perfectly adjusted for receiving the dead, another hymn sings: "Don't burn him through, Agni; don't scorch him; don't singe his skin, nor his body. When you make him cooked to readiness, Jātavedas, then impel him forth to the forefathers" (RV 10.16.1).

Besides preserving, fire spans the worlds of mortals and immortals, the present and the past, the offspring and the ancestral realm. Its minute adjustments are the expressions of elemental justice, dispensing parts of the body, the senses, and breath itself back to their proper elements: "Let your eye go to the sun, your life-breath to the wind. Go to heaven and to earth as is fitting. Or go to the waters, if it has been fixed for you there. Take your stand in the plants with your limbs" (RV 10.16.3). The luminosity of vision returns to

157   *Death, Rebirth, and Beyond in Hindu Traditions*

the sun; the airiness of breath floats back to the wind. The body is distributed among various elements (through the element of fire), reuniting with the immensity of life; its parts are not claimed by one domain alone but are allocated to the realms above and below, "to heaven and to earth as is fitting." It doesn't take long for a quiet vegetal resurrection to be announced, either. The motif that begins with "take your stand in the plants with your limbs" returns at the end of the hymn: "The one whom you have entirely burnt, Agni, that one extinguish in turn. Let the *kiyāmbu* plant grow here and the *pākadurvā* and the *vyalkaśā*" (RV 10.16.13). Plant growth is the cooling down of fire and, at the same time, the continuation of fire in what no longer shares its hot and fiery nature, the extinguishing that promises a new life.

(I must add, parenthetically and in a rather telegraphic style, that the cosmic justice of fire is predicated on its wisdom, which lends to Agni the epithet Jātavedas, or having understanding and insight (*veda*) of all existence (*jāta*). Fire has its own material discernment, singularly fitting each thing it burns or melts at various speeds, analyzing it to its basic components. The just dispensation of each part to its proper element depends on fire's wise approach to and embrace of the body it burns—or cooks. The hymnic imploration of funereal fire, "Don't burn him through, Agni," is meant only to remind Jātavedas of his own discernments, to call fire back to its just and wise self.)

Rather than aiming to preserve the unique material form of a finite being, as in the Greek and Latin phoenix narratives, Vedic Hinduism, at least in some of its strands, focuses on the return of the body to the elements and on the continuation of life in other, unrecognizable configurations. Aside from identity, the vectors of this continuation are scrambled and temporal sequences are, consequently, disrupted. With the inversion of the relative positions of following and preceding, the very sense of resurrection or reincarnation swings toward indeterminacy, the future melting into the past. We have witnessed Agni's and Uṣas's intricate dance of precession and succession; now it turns out that Agni is "the son born before his two parents [the kindling sticks]" (RV 10.31.10). The kindling sticks are none other than heaven and earth, which earlier in the same hymn, were to meet, to touch, intermingle, and receive one another with the mediation of dawn.[13] To rebirth

158 *Chapter 6*

after death, we are obliged to add that one is born before one is born and that one dies after one has died. Thus, in a hymn to Yama, the god of the underworld and of death, the last line reads, "The base was stretched out in front and the 'coming forth' [*nirayaṇam*: 'afterbirth'] was made behind" (RV 10.135.6).

*

Other Vedic hymns throw into relief a transcultural dimension of the phoenix complex, according to which the power of death is eroded by one's afterlife in one's progeny. In a direct conjuring (away) of death, a hymn begins with the line: "Depart, Death, along the further path, which is your own, different from the one leading to the gods. To you who possess eyes and who listen, to you I speak: do not harm [*mā . . . ririṣaḥ*] our offspring nor our heroes" (RV 10.18.1). The idiosyncratic path of death is the farthest when it does not lead to another life (say, of dwelling with the gods) but culminates in death. Such a path is also its own destination, which is why it is so long as to be virtually infinite. Personified, though, death itself is alive with its sense organs and their corresponding activities: it possesses eyes and listens. And the harm it is urged not to inflict has to do with the possibilities of biological and cultural survival, affecting primarily the offspring and the heroes—survival as the rebirth of the individual and the collective in the progeny and in mythic archetypes.

The second line of the same hymn spells out the meaning of "effacing the footprint of death," which is the aim of the entire phoenix complex. "Effacing the footprint of death when you have gone, establishing for yourselves a longer, more extended lifetime, swelling up with offspring and wealth, become cleansed and purified, o you who are worthy of the sacrifice" (RV 10.18.2). This effacement is not a total negation of death; it happens "when you have gone," having been claimed by death for itself. How is this possible? The extension of a lifetime, mentioned in this verse, refers, once again, to biological and cultural legacies—to survival in one's offspring and wealth, which has now supplanted the heroes. It entails a discontinuous continuation of life after death, which effaces, precisely, the trace of death felt in oblivion and nonexistence. When in another Vedic hymn, singers beseech

Mitra and Varuṇa (called Rudras with reference to Rudra the "healer but also a terrifying archer"[14]) to protect them, they ask to be safeguarded from the effects of death that pivot on its trace as the erasure of all traces. What they fear the most is that "we in our own persons not endure (becoming) the specter of a nobody, either in our remains or in our lineage" (RV 5.70.4).

The sober recognition that is everywhere present in *The Ṛg Veda* is that death itself is ineffaceable, that, according to a line from the hymn to the god Ādityas, "We are men, whose kinsman is death" (RV 8.18.22). Rather than an external menace, death is a close relative of mortals, so much so that there are no bonds of kinship without it. But, despite the undeniable and proximate reality of death, this and numerous other hymns make a bid for a continuation of life, for survival after death: "For even though we are men, whose kinsman is death, o Ādityas, extend our lifetime for us to live" (RV 8.18.22). The simultaneous acknowledgment and repudiation of death, concentrated in the words "even though," is the crux of the phoenix complex. In the hymn to Ādityas, this conjunction is possible due to the rebirth of the supplicants in their "progeny and posterity"—"For the sake of progeny and posterity, make for us a longer lifetime to live, o very great Ādityas" (RV 8.18.18). "A longer lifetime to live" would then be made *for us*, but it will not be lived *by us*, within the limits of our fragile bodies.

In a text traditionally interpreted as priest Bṛhaduktha's funereal hymn sung on the occasion of his son Vājin's death, the logic of finite existence trouncing its own finitude is reduced to its bare bones. "All living beings," sings Bṛhaduktha, "are held down within their bodies, but they have extended themselves by multiplying through their offspring" (RV 10.56.5). The act of generating offspring challenges the spatial and temporal limits of the body, which, without this creative overflow that is also manifest in the senses and in how they reach out to the world, would have been a prison (we are "held down within" our bodies, the Vedic text says). The following verse elaborates on the extension beyond oneself, which goes two ways: from posterity to the ancestors and from the ancestors to posterity. "Sons set up their lord [father] as a finder of the sun. . . . And their forefathers have established their own offspring as their paternal power, as their 'stretched thread' among the later generations" (RV 10.56.5). The patriarchal overtones are glaring here, from

160   *Chapter 6*

the father–sons relation to the solar fetish associated with paternal power. Nevertheless, the stretching on of a thread of life is illustrated with the backward-looking cult of the ancestors and the forward-looking ordering of the descendants. A phoenix-like rebirth is conditional on both twines of the "stretched thread."

The idea of birth from death, which animates the phoenix complex, is also anticipated in Vedic Hinduism. In a hymnic reflection on cosmogony, it is sung that "in the first generation of gods, what exists [*sát*] was born from what does not exist [*ásat*]" (RV 10.72.3) And just as at the origin of the world existence is generated ex nihilo from nonexistence, so the birth of mortals is from a "dead egg." The goddess Aditi becomes the mother of immortals and of mortals, her eight sons. "With seven she went forth to the gods. She cast away the one stemming from a dead egg" (RV 10.72.8), and that one was the first mortal being.[15] Born *from* death, the mortal son of Aditi is also born *for* death, as well as for procreation that delays the finality of this fate and that allows this tragic (miscarried?) act of generation to be repeated time and again: "With seven sons Aditi went forth to the ancient generation. For procreation but also for death, she brought here again the one stemming from a dead egg" (RV 10.72.9).

The god of the underworld, Yama, renders the notion of being born from death literal. Although he is born immortal,[16] Yama freely elected death over immortality in order to honor the rest of the gods with his sacrifice: "For the sake of the gods, he chose death and for the sake of offspring he did not choose immortality. . . . Yama left behind his own dear body (as offspring)" (RV 10.13.4). Whereas choosing death and not choosing immortality are formally identical, subjectively there is a tremendous difference between the two expressions. For the sake of the gods, the choice of death is intelligible entirely within a sacrificial frame of reference. For the sake of offspring, not choosing immortality is a double negative that opens the time and the space for a punctuated, rugged continuation of life despite death. Astoundingly, reborn from the threshold of death, Yama is his own progenitor and his own offspring: he "left behind his own dear body (as offspring)." This theme, too, will recur in those phoenix narratives, where the rejuvenated bird is born from the dead body of its predecessor.

161 *Death, Rebirth, and Beyond in Hindu Traditions*

A hymn dedicated to an unnamed god known only as "who" (*ká*), expresses the entanglement of mortality and immortality in a more laconic mode yet. "*Who* is the giver of breath, the giver of strength" and one "whose shadow is immortality, whose shadow is death [*yasya chāyā amṛtam yasya mṛtyuḥ*]" (RV 10.121.2). If divinity is brilliance, diurnal and spectacular, then its shadow is much more than a mere privation of this defining feature in nocturnal darkness; the shadow is also an effect of divine bright glow, the shadow *of* brilliance as brilliance, that makes this glow what it is. It is in this sense that Chāyā, or Shadow, is a goddess, who is the consort of the sun god, Sūrya.[17] In her shape, representative of other chthonic gods, the divine resides in the shadows and as the shadows too. Furthermore, the unnamed god is the giver of breath and a giver of death, where the sense of the two gifts is far from certain (nor is it certain that these gifts are two, and not one). To give breath, to bring mortal beings to life, is already to deliver them over to a death to come. To give death is not to bring to a determinate end a body that, in any event, does not rest within its limits and that extends itself into the other or others through its fecundity. The same goes for rebirth: its concept is incomplete without the idea of redeath (*punar mṛtyu*), initially formulated in the Vedic *Brāhmaṇas* and in the *Upaniṣads*.[18]

The brilliance of light—in line with the brightness of the funereal fire and the flames, in which the phoenix is rejuvenated—provides guidance to those who are dead and are soon to be reborn. Let us go back to Bṛhaduktha's hymn to register the mechanisms, the mechanics and machinations, that direct textual spotlights onto these lights. "Here is one (light) of yours, and far away is another one. Merge with the third light. At the merging of your body, be one cherished and dear to the gods at this highest means of begetting" (RV 10.56.1). Presumably, the Vedic verse under our consideration spells out the meaning of a much more cryptic exhortation to the dead in an earlier funeral hymn, "Unite with your body in your full luster" (RV 10.14.8). Merging, uniting your light and other lights with the third is rejoining the shine of divinity through "the highest means of begetting." In the process, the body is not absent, as it also merges together with divine light, is born into the light. "In your full luster" likely refers to the karmic balance of actions performed in the past life and determining the brightness

162   *Chapter 6*

of your shining, even though this sense of "karma" does not get consolidated until the composition of the *Upaniṣads*. Still, the question remains: how does the merging of lights happen?

The answer is indicated in the second verse of the same hymn: "Unswerving, in order to uphold the great gods, you should exchange your own light as if for the light in heaven" (RV 10.56.2). These are the mechanics and machinations of life's reproducibility in the Vedas: whereas in the ancient Greek world an aging finite being replaces itself with another who is younger and formed in its image, in *The Ṛg Veda* an afterlife ideally involves an exchange of the personal for the universal, of your own light for the light in heaven. The actual impossibility of such an exchange does not escape the author of Vedic verse. The operation is to be carried out with the awareness of its nature as a transcendental illusion, signaled by the words "as if." Your own light and the light in heaven are incommensurable and, therefore, cannot be exchanged one for the other. But you are to act as if this were possible, regardless. In the later developments of Hindu traditions, notably of yogic practices and the notion of *ātman*, with which these practices strive to reconnect, the exchange will be effectuated already in this life. Schematically, we might say that what the discipline of yoga teaches is how to dim down the glare of your own light so as to let the other light shine through, including from within you.

*

As for the doctrine of reincarnation, of rebirth that is in equal measure a redeath, its formulations, like the sense of karmic action tied to the balance of good and bad deeds, first appear in the *Upaniṣads*. Take, for instance, Kauṣitaki Upaniṣad, which states: "When people depart from this world, it is to the moon that they all go. . . . Now the moon is the door to the heavenly world. It allows those who answer its question to pass. As to those who do not answer its question, after they have become rain, it rains them down here on earth, where they are born again in these various conditions—as a worm, an insect, a fish, a bird, a lion, a boar, a rhinoceros, a tiger, a man, or some other creature—each in accordance with his actions and his knowledge" (1.2).[19] The moon's "simple" question is *Who are you?* pertaining to the realm of self-knowledge, as opposed to other kinds of knowledge. The answer that serves

163   *Death, Rebirth, and Beyond in Hindu Traditions*

as a pass is *I am you*. Once this answer is given, "he gets on the path leading to the gods and reaches first the world of fire, then the world of wind, then the world of Varuṇa, then the world of Indra, then the world of Prajāpati, and finally the world of *brahman*" (1.3).

There are, then, two general paths that may be followed after death: the path of reincarnation down on earth and the path "leading to the gods" that rehashes the Vedic merging of lights. The moon functions as a hinge, turned both upward and downward, raining those to be reborn on earth and sending those on the way to *brahman* to the world of fire. It is, in the first instance, an elemental hinge separating water from fire, even though, according to one version of Agni's genealogy, he is "the child of waters [*apām napāt*]" (RV 3.1). Passage through fire is a step on the second, divine path, which is also reserved, in keeping with this logic, for the phoenix in versions of the myth that emphasize her fiery rebirth. But the region of (cosmic) fire in the *Upaniṣads* is more complex: "A fire—that's what the region up there is. . . . Its firewood is the sun; its smoke is the sunbeams; its flame is the day; its embers are the moon; and its sparks are the constellations" (Chāndogya Upaniṣad 5.4.1). While fire down below reflects cosmic fire, the moon (that together with the funeral pyre serves as a gateway for the deceased) is an ember within the elemental paradigm of the cosmic blaze. Both paths, therefore, begin from the end, with the rests of firewood and fire itself dying out.

The delivery of a dead body to fire repeats the instance of fiery birth, dispensing the deceased to his "native" element. "When he has departed, when he has reached his appointed time—they take him to the very fire from which he came, from which he sprang. Now, the people who know this, and the people here in the wilderness who venerate this: 'Austerity is faith'—they pass into the flame, from the flame into the day. . . . This is the path leading to the gods" (Chāndogya Upaniṣad 5.9–10). A birth, death, and rebirth in fire is the lot of those "who know this" and who favor a life of austerity in the wilderness. A certain merging with outside nature, as opposed to life in the village described in the next verse (5.10.3), is the prerequisite for passing through the flame and embarking on another path to an afterlife that eschews reincarnation here below. We are, most likely, privy to an attempt to reconcile in the same text two clashing traditions: on the one hand, an older idea regarding the fate of those who are born out of fire to return to the same element at the time of their death, and, on the other, freshly paid attention to the (karmic) balance of actions in this life, the place where life is spent, and the way of worshipping appropriate to this life.

The path, passing through fire and leading to the gods, is further outlined in Kaṭha Upaniṣad. To be sure, this path does not end with the gods; it winds on beyond the brightest of light (and beyond its opposition to or pairing with shadows and darkness) to nothing (3.11). Although it commences with the element of fire, in which the phoenix—in its iconic renditions—is reborn, the higher path does not arrive, in a circular manner, at yet another rebirth: "When a man lacks understanding, is unmindful and always impure; he does not reach that final step, but gets on the round of rebirth. But when a man has understanding, is mindful and always pure; he does reach that final step, from which he is not reborn again" (3.7–8). As the question posed by the moon demonstrates, the supreme understanding is a self-understanding that ultimately liberates one from the cycles of *saṃsāra*—rebirth, as much as redeath. Such liberation is the essence of *mokṣa*, cognate with the Buddhist *nirvāṇa*, which, in Śvetāśvatara Upaniṣad, bristles with the promise of "freedom from all fetters" (6.13). (Earlier, in the same Upaniṣad, an appeal is made to "the one God who covers himself with things issuing from the primal source, from his own inherent nature, as a spider, with threads," the appeal that plainly says, "may he procure us dissolution in *brahman*" [6.10]).

The phoenix complex trembles with the introduction of the other path, also prominent in Jainism, that does not crave rebirth, the extension of finite existence past its due date, preferably in an identical form. Its mechanisms—its mechanics and machinations—are incapable of processing a disruption of this magnitude. Already the doctrine of reincarnation withdraws the guarantees that rebirth would take place in the same kind of existence as that of the deceased. Only the exceptional cases of karmic stagnation (neither its increase nor decrease) account for the replication of being in its former kind: a horse in a horse, a fig tree in a fig tree, a human in a human. The phoenix's unchanging shape after its rebirth means that its actions throughout the long stretch of its life do not matter, the form of its existence indifferent to its content. The phoenix is what it is only genetically, by virtue of its birth, which

165   *Death, Rebirth, and Beyond in Hindu Traditions*

is always and necessarily a birth from death. This is what Graeco-Roman nature is as *phusis* and especially as *natura*, shaped from the beginning to the end by birth. Conversely, in the world of the Upaniṣads, the natural order, with its tides of rebirth and singular retreats from the cycle of reincarnation, is contingent on moral uprightness. *Dharma* belongs together with *karma*: what or who one is depends on how one acts, that is, on how one acted in one's past life. The acceptance of ethics as first philosophy in Plato's *epekeina tes ousias*, or the idea of the good beyond being, in certain mystical traditions (such as the medieval book of *Zohar* in kabbalistic Judaism), and in Levinas's thought are the closest Western approximations to this paradigm.

In order to process the disruptive influence of *mokṣa*, the phoenix complex mobilizes the discourse of nihilism, accusing Hindu traditions of throwing the baby out with the bathwater. Or, as Wendy Doniger has put it, of "throwing away not merely the present life but all those potential future lives as well, committing a kind of multiple proleptic suicide, a preventative euthanasia."[20] Nevertheless, the moment of liberation from the cycles of rebirth and redeath is not an embrace of nothingness (the *nihil* of nihilism) in a negation of being. The dialectic of being and nothing is wholly included in the dynamics of reincarnation as the two interlocking circles, the two rings—rebirth, redeath—show, unless they are one and the same ring examined from different sides. "Higher than the immense self [*mahān ātmā*]" and "higher than the unmanifest [*avyakta*]" (Kaṭha Upaniṣad 3.11) is not the absence of being; it is *Puruṣa* (spirit), in which the nothing is (nondialectically) cut from the same cloth as everything, its pale afterglow still detectable in Schelling's infinite that exists before, within, and after the world.[21] In the formula of the *Bhagavad Gītā*, it is the amalgam of "the existent, the nonexistent, and that which is beyond both [*tatparaṁ yat*]" (11.37).

What is more, an anonymous god—perhaps, the very same as the unnamed god of *The Ṛg Veda*—watches over both paths that await finite beings after their death. If the moon is the border crossing point for the deceased, regardless of their destination, then this god is their common point of departure, the cause of the desire to persevere in existence (clinging to it and to its interruptions, awash in suffering, by old age and death) and of the pacification of this desire. This mysterious god is "the architect of time; the one without qualities; the one with all knowledge; the lord of both the primal source and of individual souls; the ruler over the qualities; and the cause of liberation from, remaining within, and bondage to the rebirth cycle" (Śvetāśvatara Upaniṣad 6.16). In a recap of divine brilliance and darkness that *shadow* one another, the god without qualities orchestrates the operations of the phoenix complex and its disassembly. These lines from Śvetāśvatara Upaniṣad give us yet another clue, corroborating the intuition that the way out of the complex ought to be sought within it.

*

The name of Brahmā, the creator god in Indian cosmogonies, is "thought to derive from the root *bṛh* which means 'grow' or 'evolve.'"[22] Its semantic purview by and large overlaps with that of the Greek verb *phuein* (to grow, to appear), which, as I have already remarked, is formative of the nouns *phusis* (nature as the ensemble of everything that grows and appears in the light) and *phuton* (plant, comprehended as a growing being). What grows out of Brahmā's creative act is the world as an *aśvattha* tree (modeled on a sacred fig or a banyan; it was under this tree that Prince Gautama attained enlightenment and became the Buddha) that is, simultaneously, a tree of life and of knowledge. The *Bhagavad Gītā* describes *aśvattha* as "having its roots above and branches below, whose leaves are the (Vedic) hymns" (BG 15.1). Immediately, though, this hierarchical arrangement is put into question: "Below and above [*adhaścordhvaṁ*] its branches spread, nourished by the qualities, with objects of the senses as sprouts; and below its roots stretch forth, engendering action in the world of men" (BG 15.2). The realms above and below merge into a single domain above-below (*adhaścordhvaṁ*), just as living and knowing, sensing-thinking, and acting are different parts of the same vegetal being.

The practices of liberation from the cycles of redeath and rebirth, how-ever, must sweep aside the leaves, branches, and roots of the cosmic tree. The tree itself is left unharmed; one only distances oneself from it. That is why, although "its form is not perceptible here in the world, nor its end, nor its beginning, nor its existence," the one on the path of liberation must "cut this *aśvattha*, with its well grown root, by the strong axe of non-attachment [*asaṅga*]" (BG 15.3). The process leading to *mokṣa* requires one to cut oneself loose from the tree of nature with its sense objects and objects of knowing, desires and bonds tethering one to one's own existence (what Spinoza will much later call *conatus essendi*), as well as actions aiming at final outcomes. Particularly with respect to the latter, the *Bhagavad Gītā* continues to deploy a vegetal analogy, which is worth exploring in greater depth.

The core idea behind the practices of nonattachment is not, as it may first seem, that of absolute renunciation, the strictest asceticism, self-denial, and abstention from action. (In the development of Buddhism, the path of absolute renunciation is, likewise, renounced as a dead-end street, a deviation from the road to the enlightenment, which is "the Middle Way.") Rather, in the yoga of action (*karmayoga*), one engages in deeds without attachment, "unattached [*asaktaḥ*]" either to their outcomes or to the judgments thereof as good or bad, successful or failing (BG 3.7). If the outcome of an action is its coming to fruition, then active nonattachment consists in cutting off the fruit, while persevering in a practice without end in sight, reveling in lush greenness. It means being and acting in the middle.

In a contrast between "the ignorant ones" and "the wise ones," the *Bhagavad Gītā* sharpens the sense of positively fruitless action with an eye to the problematic of rebirth. The ignorant ones are "full of desires, intent on heaven" and "they offer rebirth as the fruit of action [*janmakarmaphalapradām*]" (BG 2.43). Rebirth is the fruit of fruit, the horizon, unsurpassable from the standpoint of sheer ignorance, for all activity in this life. It is, moreover, a fruit that does not signify completion and accomplishment, since it is exclusively focused on the re-initiation of existence after its end. This quality of fruit—its fruitness, as it were—is consistent with the unbridled desirous nature of the ignorant, for whom nothing is ever enough. The wise, for their part, "who have abandoned fruit [*phalaṁ tyaktvā*] born of action, are freed from the bondage of rebirth [*janmabandhavinirmiktāḥ*], [and] go to the place that is free from pain" (BG 2.51). Indifferent to success or failure, unmoved by desire, having cast aside the fruit, they are similarly aloof to the seed of new life it contains. Paradoxically, perseverance in the middle of an action without any regard to its outcome is more relevant to finality than fretting about end results that invite renewed actions, existences, or births.

The phoenix complex is inconceivable without an obsession with fruit. Not only because *phoenix* may be a designation of a bird and of a tree (namely, date palm), but also because the rejuvenation of finite existence it promises is conditional on fruition—of a new life from death, of oneself from oneself as the same and other to oneself. The uniqueness and independence of the phoenix are the products of its self-generation, mediated by fire or by spontaneous arising from decay. Kṛṣṇa is ambiguous on this point. He affirms, "Although I am birthless [*ajo*] and my nature is imperishable [*avyayātmā*], although I am the lord of all beings, yet, by controlling my own material nature, I come into being [*sambhavāmi*] by my own power" (BG 4.6). Birthless, the god subtracts himself from the order of nature, and the designation "imperishable" is a logical complement of this subtraction. Coming into being by means other than birth, he practices an essentially supernatural mode of appearance made possible by his "own power." His unborn appearance is, nevertheless, a periodic (perhaps rhythmic) reappearance: "For the sake of establishing righteousness, I come into being from age to age [*sambhavāmi yuge yuge*]" (BG 4.8). And in the next verse, this mode of appearance is denominated "divine birth": "He who knows in truth my divine birth and action [*janma karma ca me divyam*], having left his body, he is not reborn; he comes to me, Arjuna" (BG 4.9). What is going on here?

Divine birth is a birth without birth, without the fruit or coming to fruition, and in this sense, resembling the nature without nature of the Plotinian One. Kṛṣṇa groups it with divine action, which is similarly an action without action and without fruit ("Although I am the creator, know me to be the eternal non-doer [*viddhyakartām avyayam*]" [BG 4.13]). A phoenix is reborn from an external medium (fire or the ashes, a fertilized nest, etc.) or from its own (or its predecessor's) dead body. Born purely of himself, Kṛṣṇa is born without being born, his origin self-grounded and, therefore, ungrounded and abyssal, like that of nature itself. Indeed, he declares, "This, my highest nature, is the origin (or the womb) of all creatures [*etadyonini bhūtāni sarvāṇity*]" (BG 7.6). He is the unrooted root of existence and of liberation from the bonds of existence. Freedom from rebirth is granted upon the revelation and the "knowledge in truth" of divine birth, to the extent that the knower gets in touch with this abyssal ground. Can we not—already

169   *Death, Rebirth, and Beyond in Hindu Traditions*

or still—accept such birth without birth and, more broadly, nature without nature, having rid ourselves of the fear to fall into naive naturalism or conventional (that is to say, *not* natural) nature/culture oppositions?

When it comes to nature, the *Bhagavad Gītā* gives its readers an insight into the concept, interpreted in an admittedly narrow sense, as the inherent being or essence of things, their being- or becoming-their-own: *svabhāvas*. Nature unfolds in "(1) the means of action; (2) the actions of people; and (3) the union of action with its fruit [*karmaphalasaṁyogaṁ*]" (5.14). The disciplined rejection of fruit has in its crosshairs the third element of nature, undoing "the union of action with its fruit." What remains and what is cultivated on the path of liberation from the cycle of redeath and rebirth are the actions themselves and the means of action, pure means without ends.

Yogic discipline acts against another *yoga* (the Sanskrit word meaning *union* or *yoke*) tying together the means and the ends, which, never final, coil into the means for further ends. Cutting off the fruit that will become a placeholder for any sort of attachment, including the attachment to and love of one's life, the path of liberation (also from the phoenix complex) calls for an intervention into the order of nature, denaturing it. Seen from another angle, though, nature is inherently denatured. It is in the very nature of nature to be denatured, insofar as the union of action with its fruit, of the doing and that for the sake of which something is done, is not straightforward. Such a union presupposes, first, a meshwork of hermeneutical and semiotic (above all, biosemiotic) tools forged out of intentions, reasons, motivations, desires, calculations that stitch together the deed, the means of doing it, and the accomplishment held in view in the doing. Second, it is thought that the self is the doer of actions, while the doing lies exclusively on the side of material existence: "All actions are performed exclusively by material existence [*prakr̥tyāiva*], and thus the self is not the doer" (BG 13.29).[23] Third, the accomplishment is chronically unaccomplished, as the presumed end twists into a new means. This meshwork, this illusion of agency, and this unending end smuggle into things what is not their own, what is not proper to them, counteracting the movement of *svabhāvas*.

The self-denaturing of nature that results from the operations of *karmaphalasaṁyogaṁ* (or the union of action with its fruit) is the target of yogic

170   *Chapter 6*

discipline, which, "having abandoned the fruit of action [*karmaphalasaṁ*], attains steady peace [*śāntimāpnoti*]" (BG 5.12). Strange as it may seem, a "steady peace" is to be experienced in the world of pure means, of means without ends. It emanates from the transformation of insatiable desire (the desire symbolized by the flame: "The form of desire . . . is insatiable fire [*duṣpūreṇānalena*]" [BG 3.39]) into the desireless, the quenching of the fire without falling into the stupor of inactivity.

*

In the verses of the *Bhagavad Gītā*, the logistics of reincarnation also appear in a new light. According to Kṛṣṇa, "Action is known as the creative power (of the individual, which causes him to be reborn in this or that condition of being) [*visargaḥ karmasaṁjñitaḥ*]" (BG 8.3). The performative character of action is astoundingly far-reaching: through it, we create and re-create ourselves in this life, which has repercussions for the next, molding the form of existence to be assumed in reincarnation. *Visargas* (the creative power of action) is projected well beyond the immediate results—the fruit, or the accomplishments—from which it is to be detached on a path of liberation. Through objective accomplishments, one accomplishes *oneself*, the material form one would assume in future existence. Not by chance, *visargas* means "sending forth" or "discharging"; the creative power of action propels one on a trajectory of rebirth that is consistent with the specific contents of that action. But *karma* can also refer to the procreative act, as Rāmājuna explains: "*Karman* (action) is the procreative act connected with a woman which causes a human being, etc., to originate."[24] The discharge of *visargas* has a different semantic tinge here, imbuing the *procreative* act with creative power and inserting the text into the scheme of biological reproduction.

The other engine of reincarnation is memory: "Whatever state of being he remembers [*smaran bhāvaṁ*] when he gives up the body at the end, he goes respectively to that state of being, Arjuna, transformed into that state of being" (BG 8.6). The future of incarnation depends on the past, be it past actions or a memory that conjures up a certain state of being in the final moments of one's present existence. What is sent forth into the future, projected or discharged, is the past: the cumulative effects of *karma* or a momentary mental flashback to the being of a worm, a tree, an insect, a tiger, and any other living beings. To train the mind in focusing on that which these states of being express, a lifetime of practice is necessary, the practice, in which action is decoupled from its fruit. And that which they express is fundamentally the same: "The wise see the same [*samadarśinaḥ*] in a brahman endowed with wisdom and cultivation, in a cow, in an elephant, and even in a dog or an outcaste" (BG 5.18). Biological and social hierarchies collapse when, seeing *through* different states of being, the wise see being itself: they see with impartiality (*sama*), with the same regard, the shared existence of all. As the next verse concludes, "Even here on earth, rebirth is conquered by those whose mind is established in impartiality [*sāmye*: in equality, sameness, equitability, disinterestedness]" (BG 5.19). The chain of reincarnations stops. Instead of remembering this or that particular state of being, one remembers being itself, which is what one becomes, merging with it as with the "third light" in *The Ṛg Veda*.

Seeing the same where difference seems to prevail is a signature gesture of metaphysics, whether in its Western or its Eastern installments. The sameness of the phoenix reborn, comprehending all of nature by means a powerful synecdoche or by blurring classificatory distinctions among types of beings, is a case in point of metaphysical homogenization. Nevertheless, in the phoenix complex, the same is reactivated, or re-instantiated, across immense time spans, such as the Great Year, or the Sothic period. Although Garuda similarly marks the end of "the revolutions of the Eon" (possibly alluding to the day of Brahma[25]), the effect of spotting metaphysical sameness in the *Bhagavad Gītā* is the exact opposite: there is no more rebirth, as time stops for the one who merges with being itself. Beyond the discharges, transfers, and deliveries from one state of being to another, release into being is release as such: "The sage, whose highest course is release [*mokṣaparāyanaḥ*]; whose senses, mind and intellect are controlled; from whom desire, fear and anger have departed, is forever liberated [*sadā mukta*]" (BG 5.28).

Mukti is the consequence of *mokṣa*: release into being entails liberation from reincarnation in beings. Whereas Western philosophy continually suppresses and incompletely eliminates differences in the self-reproduction of the same, Hindu traditions let difference be and teach how to disengage from

172   *Chapter 6*

it. Free of desire, fear, and anger, the one on a path that ends in *mukti* lets difference stay ahead of, or for, others as *their* ultimate reality. What is totally dense and opaque for them—the destination of their gaze—is a transparent medium to see through, fixing one's gaze on that which is typically obscured by difference. The opaque becomes transparent for the practitioner skilled in fruitless practice: nothing befalls difference other than that. But there is no incarnation or reincarnation in the transparent, in the medium. Liberation from the cycle of redeaths and rebirths ensues.

Book 9 of the *Bhagavad Gītā* highlights the primacy of death (or redeath) over birth in the cycle of reincarnations: "Men who have no faith in this law [*dharmasyāsya*], Arjuna, not attaining to me, are born again in the path of death and transmigration [*mṛtyusaṁsāravartmani*]" (9.3). Rebirth is a birth for renewed death as a result of turning one's back on the cosmic law and order of sameness underlying all difference, the *dharma* (meaning not only *law* but also *rectitude* and *uprightness*) that holds up those who uphold it and rescues one from the circle of *saṁsāra*. Without seeing through difference, one drowns in "the ocean of death and transmigration [*mṛtyusaṁsārasāgarāt*]" (BG 12.7); what initially presented itself as a trodden path turns out to be as overwhelming as an ocean, where one is adrift. The true way—indeed, the only way—is a path of no return, a one-way ticket for a journey, where there is "no turning back [*na nivartanti*: also 'no returning']" (BG 8.21; 15.4).

Not to detract from the aforementioned observations, the logistics or the mechanics of reincarnation and transmigration are at their clearest in the final Book 18 of the *Bhagavad Gītā*. There, Kṛṣṇa unveils before Arjuna a *machina mundi* (a world machine), to resort to an expression used by Lucretius and, later on, by Pico della Mirandola, Nicholas of Cusas, Robert Grosseteste, Copernicus, and others.[26] In contrast to organic figures and images prevalent in the rest of the text, this verse really speaks of a machine or a mechanism, *yantra*, which is both our innermost part and a universally prevalent phenomenon.[27] The mechanism makes the world go round, or, more exactly, it makes world*s* go round, rotating in cycles of redeath and rebirth: "The lord abides in the hearts of all beings, Arjuna," says Kṛṣṇa, "causing all beings to revolve, by the power of illusion, as if fixed on a machine [*yantrārūḍhāni*]" (BG 18.61).

The power of illusion—also known as "divine . . . illusion [*dāivī . . . māyā*]" (BG 7.14)—beguiles with the finality of difference (including the difference that you are), its nontransparency that hides from view the underlying sameness. This illusion is nature itself, appearing in a multiplicity of living and inorganic forms. Like the shadows irradiating from divine brilliance, the illusory ultimacy of difference emanates from a higher truth. By clinging to one's own difference, or to the illusion pertaining to it, one keeps coming back to it, desperately endeavoring to propel this idiosyncratic difference into the future. The divine machine, thus, consists of two main parts: a bobbin and a spindle, weaving the illusion and causing the worlds to go round under its spell. The mechanism prompts whomever it processes to desire survival across the gap of dead time, to yearn (consciously or unconsciously) for the preservation of something of oneself in the period following one's immediate biological existence, to crave another life—and, with it, another birth and another death.

The world machine from the *Bhagavad Gītā* finds an uncanny double in the mechanism (*mechanē*) by means of which the finite becomes infinite in Plato's *Symposium*. Except that the ancient Indian text is acutely aware of the illusory nature of this becoming, while Socrates and other participants in the ancient Greek dialogue are convinced that the mechanism actually allows mortals to partake of immortality. (Since Diotima's position is summarized by Socrates in her absence, we cannot know with any degree of certainty if her teaching was ironic and if she, herself, was skeptical about the contraption she pinpointed.) Needless to say, the crux of the mechanism, its innermost nucleus or core, is the phoenix complex. The Hindu text laments the replaceability of lives, of existents and modes of existence, while also taking responsibility for this state of affairs instilled in the form of a desire in the very "heart" (*hṛddeśe*) of being. However deeply ingrained in all that lives, the phoenix complex is not our absolute destiny. The world machine we (together with mosquitoes and rose bushes, bacteria and lions, cod and seaweeds) construct with the materials it supplies can be made to malfunction from within, culminating in *mokṣa* and *mukti*, release and liberation.

174   *Chapter 6*

7 GENERATIVITY AND GENERATIONALITY IN CONFUCIANISM

In the nineteenth century, British scholars introduced a division between Western and Eastern phoenixes, between the Egyptian sources that fed into Greek and Roman mythical traditions, on the one hand, and the Chinese bird *fenghuang* (鳳凰), on the other. A key figure in this differentiation was nineteenth-century Scottish missionary to the Far East and translator of *Annals of the Bamboo Books* (dating back to the beginnings of the Zhou dynasty in the eighth and seventh centuries BCE), James Legge.[1] This was probably the greatest scandal in the cultural history of the phoenix: not only does the (undeniably colonial) system of classifications homogenize heterogeneous myths, narratives, concepts, and representations, rather than consider the phoenix in terms of an affective, ideational, imagistic, cross-cultural *complex*, but it also draws a geographical—indeed, a geopolitical—boundary (East/ West), without asking how this line of demarcation is affected by the logic of the phoenix. After all, within the latter, the West is the place of decline and sunset, of death and transcendence to the realm beyond: ancient Egyptians, among others, were abreast of this association, as they buried their dead on the Western bank of the Nile. The East is, conversely, the site of the new dawn and of life, of rebirth and regeneration. "Western phoenix" is, therefore, a contradiction in terms, seeing that in its promises and inclinations, mechanics, machinations, and other kinds of maneuvering the figure of the phoenix always leans on the East.

We might say that the entry *"fenghuang"* in *Encyclopedia Britannica*, which notes that this "immortal bird whose rare appearance is said to be an omen foretelling harmony at the ascent to the throne of a new emperor" is also called "(misleadingly) Chinese phoenix" is a right step albeit in the wrong direction, as Slavoj Žižek once expressed it.[2] The political connotations of *fenghuang* that are so prominent in China distinguish it from the phoenix:[3] although the sightings of the latter are also signs of momentous occasions and although Lactantius and Claudian, among other classical authors and even Roman emperors, endow the symbolism of the phoenix with the sense of absolute, sovereign power, in the Western tradition, these are very marginal attributes. But, while *fenghuang* is not a phoenix, the two mythical birds share recognizable traits, such as an ambiguous sex, as the same entry confirms: "Its name is a combination of the words *feng* representing the male aspect and *huang* the female." It is misleading to call *fenghuang* "Chinese phoenix," and yet to deafen oneself to a veritable *rappel des oiseaux* (bird call) between this bird and the permutations of Egyptian *bennu* would be simply unforgivable.[4]

The political associations of *fenghuang* with sovereignty, as well as with peace and harmony, shed new light onto the relation of political philosophy and a philosophy of nature. At stake in political and biological life is the process of reproduction, of a bubbling vital force that generates the new and, at the same time, repeats the old, stabilizing itself in living forms, be they organisms or institutions, and destabilizing itself by making possible another beginning, a multitude of fresh starts. The dilemma of the same and the other in the phoenix's offspring appears differently in the regal splendor of *fenghuang*. And it is this process of reproducing life itself, as opposed to the living forms, at the biopolitical and biophysiological levels, that is submitted to a serious stress test in the twenty-first century, the test it fails miserably. Succinctly put, whatever is generated today—what has been generated for some time in a long "today" that is finally coming to an end, even if we keep receiving reassurances from the phoenix complex that the reports of its demise are greatly exaggerated: *andrà tutto bene* (everything will be alright)— bars the regeneration of existence. We are caught in the perspective of short-sighted survival that undercuts the very conditions of possibility for survival.

Fenghuang, too, reassures the lucky few, to whom it reveals itself, with the signs of harmony and peace, starting with the harmonious coexistence

176   *Chapter 7*

of the sexes, the yin and yang of *feng* and *huang*. According to the *Classic of Mountains and Seas (Shānhǎijīng)*, this bird—"the king of the 360 species of birds"—comprehends all of nature, represented by the five elements and an equal number of moral ideals espoused in Confucianism: "Of the five elements, its green head represented wood, its white neck metal, its red back fire, its black chest water, and its yellow feet earth. Its feathers were patterned to represent written characters: on its head, a 德 for 'virtue' (*de*); on each of its wings, a 義 for 'righteousness' (*yi*); on its back, a 禮 for 'courtesy' (*li*); on its chest, a 仁 for 'benevolence' (*ren*); on its belly, a 信 for 'trustworthiness' (*xin*)" (1:11).[5] This description problematizes efforts, such as those of Jean-Pierre Diény with which this chapter began, aimed at discriminating between the phoenix and *fenghuang* based on the cosmological significance of the former and the political sense of the latter, a discrimination that is thoroughly modern and inapplicable either to ancient Chinese or to ancient Greek thought. As the first in the books of the *Classic of Mountains and Seas (Nánshānjīng*, "Classic of Mountains: South") makes amply clear, both dimensions are mapped onto the bird's body, with five moral ideals corresponding to the five physical elements. A more sensible distinction between the phoenix and *fenghuang* would have been the mode of universalization each of them deploys. Whereas the phoenix is an exceptional singularity that universalizes itself by means of a synecdoche, *fenghuang* gathers portions of cosmic and social orders by means of symbolic (color) and semiotic (feathers shaped as inscriptions) representations.

The porous boundaries, traversed in the very corporeity of *fenghuang*, between cosmology, on the one hand, and virtues, on the other, make Confucianism a perfect candidate for the examination of the phoenix complex in Chinese traditions. There are several reasons behind this choice. First, the characters spelled by the bird's feathers are the central values of Confucianism. For instance, *ren*, variously translated as benevolence, humaneness, or the Good, is "in some respects the most important [moral concept] in the *Analects*."[6] The position of *ren* on the chest of the mythical creature—the place that corresponds to the color black and to water in the cosmological scheme—bespeaks the animating function of the Good, seeing that water is taken to be the source of life. Likewise, trustworthiness (*xin*: a combination

177   *Generativity and Generationality in Confucianism*

of *ren*, the good, and *yán*, speech, yielding "good speech") is crucial to social relations as Confucius construes them: "Young people should be filial at home, brotherly with others, circumspect, and trustworthy" (1.6). The place of trust on *fenghuang*'s belly implies the intimacy and vulnerability that go along with this sentiment.

Second, Confucius himself is called *feng* (the male portion of *fenghuang*) in Book 18 of the *Analects*: "Jie Yu, the madman of Chu, passed by Confucius, singing these words: *Feng, feng, / how your virtue has ebbed away! / What's past has gone beyond mending / but what's to come is still within reach. / Leave off! Leave off! / Danger [a]waits those who work at governing today!*" (18.5)[7] For Diény, this is an important contrast: the phoenix is always connected, in one way or another, to divinity and the power of resurrection; *fenghuang* represents "the Confucian sage and the Taoist saint."[8] But what happens when the sage is actually hailed as the mythical bird, by a madman of all people, as in the passage I have just cited? Rather than a good omen, this moment is sorrowfully expressed as one of collapse and breakdown: "how your virtue has ebbed away!" signals nothing less than the beheading of the mythical bird, since the body part housing virtue is the head. The sage identified with *fenghuang* is a sage without the head, without the organ of thought or reason, not coincidentally referring to plant matter—wood—in the overlapping cosmological scheme. Worse still, the renovative, reproductive mechanism of the phoenix complex has failed: "what's past has gone beyond mending." The appearance of the sage-*feng* is belated; there is nothing to be done but to take flight again and to leave.

Third, traditionally read as a work of ancient moral, social, or political philosophy, the *Analects*' full scope is disclosed bearing the phoenix complex in mind. Its main concern is what the madman announces as the disaster that has already taken place—the impossibility of reproducing the existing order of things, or of perpetuating it into the future. Everything that Confucius and his interlocutors say is meant to ensure the ongoing regeneration of society, its past identity projected into the future, from family relations to state sovereignty. Once one works through the thick undergrowth of rules and injunctions that (quite frustratingly) sound like moralizing pronouncements, the root of the thought peers through from the cultural soil wherein

178   *Chapter 7*

it grows: the question of life, 生 (*shēng*). It is far from obvious, based on the overt themes of its most prominent writings, that Confucianism is, by and large, preoccupied with life in its biological, ethical, social, political instantiations, which is why there is broad consensus among commentators that the most enigmatic statement ascribed to Confucius is the one he utters standing by a stream: "It flows on like this—does it not?—never ceasing, day or night" (9.17).[9] Assuming that the reference here is to life, its ceaseless flow sweeps into its midst vitality and death, whether "day or night": "both survival and death are life, and life, like water, flows endlessly."[10] And so, Confucius will wonder, between the lines of the text: How to stabilize, if only temporarily, the flow of life? How to deal with its generativity and generationality, the birthing of the ever-new and continuity in the succession of the old?

*

The Chinese concept of life is so multifaceted that I cannot hope to do justice to it in the following pages. (The Confucius of the *Analects* retorts, immediately: "When you don't yet understand life, how can you understand death?" [11.12].) At minimum, readers should be aware of the tripartite division of life in Chinese thought into 精 (*jīng*), or essence; 氣 (*qi*), or vital breath, which condenses and disperses, congeals into temporary forms and dissolves;[11] and 神 (*shen*), or spirit. The doubling of life 生 (*shēng*) in the concept of 生生 (*shēng shēng*) yields "vitality," the production and reproduction, generation and regeneration of existence that is at the core of the phoenix complex. *Shēng shēng* may be defined "as the cycles of eternal change and endless creation in the universe."[12] In view of such conceptions of life, the chief problem in Confucianism is how to discern and to preserve the forms of life, with their fixed patterns, that are always subject to life's own destabilizing, ever-flowing, ever-changing momentum. In other words, how can night give rise to a new day, both the same as and different from yesterday, in the family, the society, and the polity?

The formal answer to this question is to be sought in the notion and practice of rituals, particularly of death rites and the cult of the ancestors. Hence, in the *Analects*, "Zizhang questioned the Master, saying, Can we know how things will be ten generations from now? The master said, Yin

179   *Generativity and Generationality in Confucianism*

followed the rites of Xia, and we know in what ways Yin added to or subtracted from them. Zhou follows the rites of Yin, and we know in what ways it added to or subtracted from them. Whoever carries on from Zhou, we can know how things will be even a hundred generations from now" (2.23). Rituals structure social and political life by submitting this life's new sprouts to a form that is honed (and, indeed, created) by repetition. In English, we might say that they negotiate between generation and generation—not only between one generation and the next but also between generation conceived as a novel emergence and generation as a carrier of genetic inheritance from the past it both alters and preserves. Rituals are bridges spanning the abyss of vital energy dispersed in death—the bridges spanning the past and the future that reiterates that past, one ephemeral congealment of *qi* (vital breath) and another. They are the chief instruments of the Confucian phoenix complex, the mechanics and machinations of social and political reproduction that regulate, as its valves, the otherwise unruly flow of life.

In the more intimate sphere of the family, death rites and the cult of the ancestors discharge an analogous duty, guaranteeing the stability of reproduction in the familial phoenix complex as it merges with that of the people as a whole. So, "Master Zeng said, Tend carefully to death rites, and pay reverence to those long departed, and the people will in the end be rich in virtue" (1.9). And again, "The Master said, While his father is alive, observe his intentions. After his father is dead, observe his actions. If after three years he hasn't changed his father's way of doing things, then you can call him filial [孝 (*xiao*)]" (1.11). The model father–son relation, as Confucius and his companions interpret it, is one where (ideally) nothing changes despite the death of the father; it is one, where the father is reborn like a phoenix in his son. If, before the father's death, the son may fulfill his wishes but harbor intentions that are inconsistent with those, afterwards, without an outward constraint, it is the son's actions that are of the essence.

Filiality is the persistence of the same conduct despite the change of actors, a transgenerational conjunction of sameness and otherness that is the main feature of the phoenix complex. The very term 君子 (*junzi*), which "originally meant 'lord's child' and referred to offspring of the ruling elite,"[13] frames the model ethical subject (the "gentleman"), whom Confucius

180   *Chapter 7*

invokes throughout the *Analects*, as a father reincarnated in the son. To be sure, Confucius "denied that birth alone entitled one to rulership and reinterpreted the term *junzi* to mean someone whose moral standards and superior understanding entitled him, if not to actual rulership, at least to high official position under a hereditary ruler."[14] This correction does not change things drastically; it only introduces, surreptitiously, the theme of a second, spiritual, birth, or of a rebirth into the world of virtue and understanding. The phoenix complex persists along the biological and social veins of existence so long as different kinds of reproduction are grasped as relations of replacement, substituting the unique with itself as other to itself.

To return to death rites, in Confucianism these are not empty, formalistic procedures; they are the repositories of virtue, with which the head of *fenghuang* is branded and which, we are told, are "the root of humaneness [*ren*]" (1.2). Properly tending to death and to the dead reinvigorates a life full of virtue, fulfilling this life. In the ancient Greek context Antigone is the embodiment of this traditional axiom, without which there is no tradition. The dead are subtly present in the lives of descendants through rituals and sacrifices, their meaning overfull, to the point of being inexhaustible: "Someone asked about the meaning of the ancestral sacrifice. The Master said, I don't know. Someone who knew its meaning would understand all the affairs of the world as if they were displayed right here—and he pointed to his palm" (3.11). In their singularity, ancestral sacrifices encapsulate universal knowing and the understanding of "all the affairs of the world." In this, they correspond to the scheme of universalizing singularity in the phoenix complex. And yet, there are no clear lines of transmission between the singular and the universal, no determinate and univocal meaning to be ascribed to the practices associated with the cult of ancestors that would serve as a key to opening the mystery of everything. That is why Confucius, like Socrates after him, professes his lack of knowledge (intricately balanced with the possibility of knowing the future ten or even a hundred generations ahead), as the only plausible response to the question of "the meaning of everything."

Ritual, 禮 (*li*), is the dynamic (and, as we've just seen, not at all formalistic) form of the phoenix, the form that transcends the distinction between life and death and, in so doing, performs the basic operations of the phoenix complex. Nor is it a purely mechanical, repetitive action, but, rather, a harmonizing factor, mending the world, reestablishing the "ideal of harmony" that is achievable here below and that requires the living to "work for it" (1.12). If ritual is capable of regulating the balance of forces between life and death *within life itself*, that is because it immanently transcends this distinction, as it does in the case of filial devotion (*xiao*): "The Master said, While they [the parents] are alive, serve them according to ritual. When they die, bury them according to ritual, and sacrifice to them in accord with ritual" (2.5). A ritualistic-sounding repetition of the words "according to ritual" practically exemplifies what it says: ritual stays constant in the phrase itself and throughout the intermittencies of life, death, and afterlife, marked, respectively, by the serving, burying, and sacrificing to one's parents. Its continuity is what weaves these three moments together, despite all the gaps between them, into a grand unity of life.

In the Confucian paradigm, ritual does not fall on the side of artificiality but on that of life itself. "The Master said, Courtesy without ritual becomes labored; caution without ritual becomes timidity; daring without ritual becomes righteousness; directness without ritual becomes obtrusiveness" (8.2). One way to receive these words is to detect in ritual something like second nature, the naturalization of the unwritten social rules by force of habit and repeated practice. Then rulebound conduct becomes automatic, merging with physiological processes. But the concept of life that is in the conceptual backdrop of the *Analects* suggests an alternative reading. What Confucius is saying—again, rhetorically and quasi-ritualistically accentuating the same words over and over again—is that "without ritual," hardly anything remains. His message is the opposite of the modern assumption that ritual formalizes human behavior, emptied of substance; rather, it is ritual that makes courtesy, caution, daring, and directness what they actually are. Sincerity is in step with the basics of ritual: "In funeral rites, rather than thoroughness, better real grief" (3.4). Why? Because ritual is the ligament holding together, more or less organically, life and the living, the torrents of vitality and vital breath temporarily stabilized in particular formations. Without ritualistic stabilizing structures, nothing or almost nothing is left, the nothing that is life without the living, the river that flows on "never ceasing, day and night," but with neither water nor a riverbed nor banks.

Taking the side of ritual and tradition that epitomize the phoenix complex, Confucius goes so far as to identify himself with their function: "The Master said, A transmitter and not a maker, trusting in and loving antiquity, I venture to compare myself with our Old Peng" (7.1). While commentators disagree as to who Old Peng is, one hypothesis states that this was a person who lived under the Yin dynasty and who, instead of composing new narratives, had a predilection for the transmission of ancient tales.[15] As a transmitter, too, Confucius would be echoed across centuries and continents by Socrates, who claimed in *Theaetetus* that he was not an original thinker, but the "midwife of ideas." Even in his nonoriginality, Confucius intimates, he is not original; as the comparison suggests, he copies Old Peng, putting himself in the position of the ancient transmitter's offspring, a phoenix incarnate. At bottom, transmission is the sense of tradition, of saving from oblivion and passing along what would have been otherwise lost, dissolved into the stream of life.[16] And the one who transmits passes along (trustingly and lovingly!) formed matter—neither empty forms nor formless matter. It is their combination that Confucius trusts and loves, wishing to see the formed matter from the past projected into the future, bestowed upon subsequent generations across the unpredictable twists and turns of life and death.

*

Trust in and love of the tradition coexist in Confucius with respect for the future. "The Master said, Respect those younger than yourself. How do you know that the coming generation may not prove as good as our present one?" (9.23). If the mechanics and machinations of the phoenix complex work as they should and, through ritual and related means, the future generation replaces the present as another but also as the same, then its representatives are potentially as worthy of respect as our contemporaries. These are the foundations of Confucian intergenerational ethics, which transforms filiality (*xiao*) into a symmetrical (that is to say, reciprocal) sentiment. No wonder then that master Zeng states in the *Analects* that "the Master's Way consists of loyalty and reciprocity alone" (4.15).[17]

183 *Generativity and Generationality in Confucianism*

While it is impossible to ascertain in advance that the reproductive logic of the phoenix complex would be carried to fruition, the mere possibility of a positive transgenerational comparison is sufficient for Confucius to demand respect for the young. This attitude does not, however, hold outside human society; it is inapplicable to nonhuman nature. As Confucius says (with a sigh, expressing regret?) later on in the text, "One cannot simply live with the birds and beasts. If I am not to join with my fellow men, who am I to join with? If the Way, 道 (*dao*) prevailed in the world, I would not try to change things" (18.6).[18]

When the Way prevails in the world, the machinery of the phoenix functions smoothly, particularly insofar as the substitution of one generation with another is concerned. And, conversely, "When the Way no longer prevails in the world, rites, music, and punitive expeditions proceed from the feudal lords, and rarely does this situation continue for ten generations before failure ensues" (16.2). The Way is what keeps generations from degenerating, and the evidently standard ten-generation mark is the historical limit of the continuation of social, cultural, if not biological, existence in the absence of the rectitude—or of the rectifying tendencies—of the Way. In such dire times, *fenghuang* does not appear, which also means that there is neither balance and harmony nor a sage in the world to steer it back toward the Way.

Confucius leans toward the hypothesis that he and his contemporaries live in an epoch when the world and the Way are lost. As he laments, "*Fenghuang* does not appear; the river puts forth no chart. It is all over with me, is it not?" (9.9). Besides personal reasons for Confucius's despair noted by Joseph Nigg—"The fact that the *fenghuang* reputedly appeared around the time of his birth . . . makes the bird's absence all the more personal to the Master"[19]— the lament is voiced at the very moment when Confucius questions his own wisdom that does not offer any special kind of knowledge but instead affords rigorous questioning. "The Master said, Do I have knowledge? I have no special knowledge. But if an uneducated fellow comes to me with a question, I attack it with all sincerity, exploring it from end to end until I've exhausted it" (9.8). The nonappearance of *fenghuang*, which would have been a sign that there is a sage in the world, makes Confucius interrogate his own craft, his epistemic practice, throwing into doubt the figure and the meaning of the sage (also of himself), associated with *fenghuang*.

In turn, regeneration commences at the root, which may be dormant (for instance, as a flower bulb) and which concentrates in itself the essence (*jīng*) of life. That is why *junzi* (the gentleman), or the moral subject of the *Analects* who is also the father reincarnated in the son, is said to operate at the root: "The gentleman operates at the root. When the root is firm, then the Way may proceed. Filial and brotherly conduct—these are the root of humaneness, are they not?" (1.2). The root is what secures the unbroken chain of generations, each following the path of the preceding ones not because they imitate their ancestors but because they are nourished, spiritually and physically, from the same source, the same basic life force and ethical desire. The root is what is shared and what renders humaneness (*ren*) co-human. It is what stays in place when the leaves fall in autumn or new buds and flowers open up in the spring. Its "firmness" evokes both spatial support and temporal constancy irrespective of climatic conditions and seasonal variations (the deaths of older and the births of newer generations). Both transgenerational stability and phoenix-like rebirth of the parent in the offspring go back to the root. Or, as one of the Confucian odes in Ezra Pound's rendition goes: "O omen peach, that art so frail and young, / giving us promise of such solid fruit, / going to man and house / to be true root."[20]

*

Attributed to the grandson of Confucius, Kong Ji (also known as Master Zisi), the *Doctrine of the Mean* (*Zhongyong*) is part of the four books and five classics of Confucianism.[21] The inseparability of metaphysical and ethical, social, and political themes in this work is evident from the very first phrase: "What heaven, 天 (*tian*) has ordained is called our nature, 性 (*xing*); an accordance with this nature is called the Way, 道 (*dao*); to cultivate the *dao* is called the teaching, 教 (*jiao*)" (1). That "our" nature is conferred by *tian* does not make it wholly heavenly though; what is conferred must be received by the one upon whom or by that upon which it is conferred—in this case, by the earth, 坤 (*k'un*), which is, according to the *Book of Changes* (*I ching*), the receptive element (1.2).[22] Everything hinges on how what is

185 *Generativity and Generationality in Confucianism*

conferred is received: whether it is accepted in accordance with the Way or contrary to it. And this is where the sage, who is identified with the *fenghuang* in Chinese traditions, becomes active in cultivating the Way and gauging possible divergences from it.

Lest we be under the impression that the sage had a purely instrumental function of discerning dangerous deviations from the *dao*, Zisi explains (indeed, exclaims), "How great is the *dao* of the sage! Brimming, it nurtures the things of the world, and towering, reaches the pole of heaven" (27). He relates the words of Confucius, for whom the model sages were Yao and Shun, the inaugural legendary rulers of the Warring States period, comparable to "heaven and earth" and "the succession of the four seasons, or the alternating brilliance of the sun and moon, or the things of the world, which are nourished side by side and do not harm one another" (30). It follows that Confucius and Zisi after him treated the figure of the sage in its full cosmic scope as embodying celestial brilliance, earthly nourishment, and everything in between. In his singularity, the sage stood for the whole of nature and, more than that, for that which ordained or bestowed nature, namely *tian*, itself composed of the Mandarin characters for "vast" and "unity": "As arching vastness, he is like the heavens. As depthless springs, he is like the deep" (31). The synecdoche of the phoenix is distinctly visible in these cosmic descriptions of a singular being taking on universal significance.

The *dao* of *junzi*, which is more down-to-earth, also rises to universality, to the extent that it "cleaves to the mean in action" (2, 11). But, in contrast to the sage, *junzi* neither shines brightly as a light to the world nor does he necessarily practice virtue in the open, as a singular but universalizable example. *Junzi* abides in anonymity and in a certain invisibility: "The *dao* of *junzi* is broad yet hidden" (12). On the obscure side of the phoenix complex, it is the anonymity of the unique that admits of replacing and being replaced in its singularity, thanks to filiality (*xiao*): "The filial son extends well the intentions of his father and carries on his father's affairs" (19). But, considering the cosmic scope of the matters Zisi is touching upon here, the hiddenness of *junzi*'s virtuous conduct is not limited to mere modesty, self-effacement, or indifference toward the opinions of others. On the one hand, the concealment of *junzi*'s Way is the concealment of the root; it is appropriate to the earth, to the receiving medium and subterranean nourishment that this medium signifies before the illumination and warmth it receives from the creative power of heaven.[23] On the other hand, the hiddenness of *junzi*'s actions and existence is close to the hiddenness of the source, from which everything emanates, as opposed to its emanations that are in the open; or to life itself, as opposed to the living. And yet, Zisi will upend the contrast between the sage and *junzi*, as much as between the heavens and the earth, asserting that "nothing is more visible than the obscure, nothing is plainer than the subtle. Hence, *junzi* is cautious in his solitude" (1).

It is in the faint, auroral or crepuscular light of this upending that one should approach the relation of filiality, in which, stretched beyond its time limits, the finite is replaced by itself as both the same and the other. "To occupy his post," Zisi writes, "to carry out his rituals, to perform his music, to respect what he honored, to love what he cherished, to treat the dead as one treats the living, to treat the departed as one treats those who remain: this is the ultimate of filiality" (19). Properly carried out, ritual treats the dead as if they were living and, in keeping with the rule of reciprocity, the living as if they were the (replacements of the) dead. "The ultimate of filiality" rebels against the ultimacy of death, denying death the last word. The price paid for this denial is a life lived not so much with the subtle presence as with the heavy weight of the dead.

The circle of existence where the end and a new beginning meet, consistent with the logic of the phoenix, rotates in *Zhongyong* under the sign of "genuineness" (真, *zhen*): "Perfect genuineness spontaneously completes things; the *dao* spontaneously guides them. Perfect genuineness is the cycle of things ending and beginning anew. Without genuineness there would be no things" (25). Further, "the utmost of perfect genuineness never ceases. Never ceasing, it endures. Enduring, it is manifest" (26).

By genuineness, the Confucian author understands much more than the authenticity or sincerity, to which a patently modern attitude reduces it.[24] It seems that *zhen*, as formulated in the *Doctrine of the Mean*, has to do with being on the verge of appearance: about to disappear from existence or having just become appearent. Its sense is first phenomenological and only subsequently moral, emotive, let alone normative. There are (or would be) no things without it, because at their spatial and temporal edges, things flash, shine forth, manifest, show themselves as what they are, and *that* is genuineness. That is, also, the territory of the phoenix, where endurance implies ceaseless movement and where renewal happens—things "beginning anew"—whether in a flash of rejuvenating fire or through the slower metamorphoses of decomposition, decay, and preparation of fresh growth. Beyond authenticity and inauthenticity, the obscurity of *junzi* is not incompatible with *zhen*: a life well lived, for *junzi*, is the life perennially on the verge, always on edge (in solitude, absolute filiality, and so forth) and *it is this verge or edge that, rather than averageness or mediocrity, is at the heart of the* Doctrine of the Mean.

Since I have briefly treated the subject of genuineness in Confucianism, this is a good place to revisit a recommendation or a wish Confucius makes in the *Analects*. In a conversation with Zilu, Confucius responds to the question of what he would do first if he were to take charge of government affairs in the following fashion: "If I had to name my first action, I would rectify names. . . . If names are not rectified, then speech will not function properly, and if speech does not function properly, then undertakings will not succeed" (13.3).

The rectification of names directly concerns trustworthiness (*xin*), a composite of *ren* and *yán* meaning "good speech." But the only way to gauge trustworthiness is through genuineness (*zhen*). In a commonsense interpretation, rectified speech becomes genuine and, therefore, trustworthy thanks to the establishment or reestablishment of correspondences between things and words, so that names really and truly designate that which they name. Note, however, that Confucius does not speak of things in the sense of physical objects; he invokes nothing more and nothing less than the proper functioning of speech itself and the success of undertakings (affairs in the practical-pragmatic sense of things). The imputation of the correspondence theory of truth to Confucius does not hold water, as Christopher Hancock has also recognized recently.[25] So then what does the rectification of speech entail? Assuming that genuineness spotlights spatiotemporal edges or verges, Confucius's first hypothetical action, permitting all further genuine action, would be to reconstitute language itself from the standpoint of the edge, to renew language or to let it rejuvenate itself by tapping into the unceasing cycles of endings and new beginnings. In other words, to allow language to participate in the phoenix of nature.

*

The starting point of the *Great Learning (Daxue)*, which is another classic of Confucianism on a par with the *Doctrine of the Mean*, this time attributed to Confucius's disciple Zengzi, is that of renovation and rejuvenation, of "renewing the people." Whatever this injunction means, it, too, requires going to the root, tapping into genuineness, and concentrating on the spatiotemporal edges, the beginnings and ends of things, themselves revolving in an endless cycle. Hence, "The Way of the great learning lies in letting one's inborn luminous virtue shine forth, in renewing the people, and in coming to rest in perfect goodness" (1).[26]

Of particular interest among the three inaugural guidelines of the treatise is the renewal of the people, which is not a demand for qualitative novelty but, rather, the process of becoming young again, guided by the logic of the phoenix. One of the classical commentaries on this section of *Daxue* relies on the "Basin Inscription of Tang," who was the founder of the Shang dynasty around 1600 BCE: "Day after day renew; make each day new again."[27] Such renewal thanks to the daily rebirth of the sun at dawn and, with it, of the day itself repeated in its identity as "day" and yet refreshed each time anew, is a hallmark of the phoenix complex. The idea is that the great learning would impart this capacity to the people, after the inborn virtue of each is allowed to shine forth and before the whole—individual and collective—comes to rest in perfect goodness. It is fitting that this stage be situated in the middle, not only as a mediator between the individual shine of virtue and the all-embracing good, but also, and more pertinently for our argument, as the transition between the end and the new beginning: the end of one day and the beginning of the next, the aging and the rejuvenation of the people.

At the same time, the knowledge of beginnings and ends (that is to say, in keeping with its interpretation by Zhu Xi, the metaphysical knowledge of first and last things, as it is also construed in the West) matters the most for following the Way: "Things have their roots and branches; affairs have a beginning and an end. One comes near the Way in knowing what to put first and what to put last" (3). To know beginnings and ends, in the right placement of roots and branches, is to be aware, in the first instance, of their relativity, since, from the end, further beginnings germinate. If date palm is the vegetal phoenix species, then the root is the vegetal phoenix organ.

It was both at the birth of a sage and at the time of political renewal, when a new emperor assumed power, that *fenghuang* was said to appear. The *Great Learning* advocates ethical renewal from below, rather than from above, from the root and the new day that would shine forth thanks to the shared luminocity of the innate virtue of each. As the *Analects* have shown, *junzi* "operates at the root," through filial and brotherly conduct that is "the root of humaneness [*ren*]." According to the ideals of the *Great Learning*, the root, now referring to self-cultivation, should be accessible to each: "From the Son of Heaven [i.e., the emperor, MM] on down to commoners, all without exception should regard self-cultivation [修身, *xiushen*] as the root" (6). Swerving back to the opening statement of the treatise, this root is where one's inborn luminous virtue, or humaneness, shines forth: the root, imagined in the dynamic shape of self-cultivation, is aglow and, therefore, celestial despite its mundane, down-to-earth formation![28] The democratization of virtue, first, by postulating the inborn ethical capacity present in each person and, second, by commending self-cultivation as a recipe for the actualization of this capacity, disseminates the figure and function of the phoenix in the people, universalizing its singularity ("without exception").

The renewal of the people goes in tandem with the renovation of imperial power, just as it complements the notion of biological regeneration with ethical and political generativity. Via the root of self-cultivation, each person is a phoenix reborn in the luminosity of innate virtue actualized, brought to appearance, exposed in the light of day, and making this very light what it is. From there, harmony spreads to the family and on to the state: "The mind becomes set in the right; the mind so set, the person becomes cultivated; the person being cultivated, harmony is established in the household; household harmony established, the state becomes well governed" (5). Repose—"coming to rest in perfect goodness"—is not paralysis, but perpetual movement in the circle of beginnings and ends in keeping with the Way, now permeating the fabric of individual existence, the family, and the state. It is the phoenix complex actualized in every stratum of being. What else could be the point of rest in filiality or even in self-cultivation, replacing the one with the other and oneself with a deeper and, simultaneously, a more luminous version of the self?

*

The naturalism of the analogies that Confucius and those close to him deploy goes well beyond the common rhetorical devices prevalent in the Chinese tradition:[29] it gives readers clues as to the nexus of ethical and political programs, on the one hand, and the program of biological reproduction and the natural order of existence, on the other. Even if this was "an important principle for the Song Confucians who related the creativity of life to the moral creativity of *ren*,"[30] the nexus does not in any way imply congruence: the celestial connotations of the root that is virtue shining forth complicate any efforts to find a simple parallelism between these domains.

Aside from roots and branches, Confucius's own commentary of the *Great Learning*'s section on repose in perfect goodness cites the *Book of Poetry* (the Confucian odes): "The silky warble runs in the yellow throat, / Bird comes to rest by the angle of the hill,"[31] only to wonder, "'Comes to rest'— they [the birds, MM] know where to come to rest. Can we believe that human beings are not so good as birds?" It is inconceivable for Confucius that human beings would not measure up to birds in their coming to rest in goodness, yet, the entire apparatus of the *Great Learning* needs to be activated, step by painstaking step, for the potentialities of a uniquely human good to become actual. Another bird analogy from the odes also demands of us tremendous efforts of self-cultivation: "A bird can circle high over cloud, / A man's mind will lift above the crowd."[32]

One of the links between the different orders of reproduction, generation, regeneration, and generativity itself is the phoenix complex, absorbing into itself psychophysiology, politics, society, culture, as well as what is called nature. In the "Great Appendix" to *I ching*, or the *Book of Changes*, completed by Zhu Xi, a Song dynasty revivalist of Confucianism, the alternations of yin and yang constitute the Way (A.5.1).[33] Further, "embracing all things, it [the Way] is called the Great Work [大業, *da ye*]. Renewing itself daily, it is called flourishing virtue" (5.5). Blending the ontological ("all things") and the ethical ("flourishing virtue"),[34] the Way, consisting of constant alternations, obeys the law of daily renewal, which traverses the movement of actualization, or the Great Work. So long as the alterations of yin and yang are happening, *da ye* is unaccomplished. What, then, is the meaning of this unaccomplished ever-actualizing movement? Zhu Xi responds in A.5.6: "Life and growth [production and reproduction, generation and regeneration: 生生 (*shēng shēng*)] are the meaning of change."

Shēng shēng is a phoenix concept: double in one, uncontainable in itself, the same and the other in replicative repetition after a gap that incorporates death into itself. In it, through it, finitude splits open and spills over into potential infinity. The Cheng brothers (who are equally the two authors of *Er Cheng cuiyan*, or "Perfect Words of the Two Cheng Brothers," also dating back to the Song dynasty) formalize this insight in their famous dictum, "The Way is life and growth without cessation [生生不息, *shēng shēng bu xi*]" (149).[35] Natural generation is already regeneration, folded, from the get-go, into the creativity of heavens and the receptivity of the earth, the origin itself split down the middle into two. In other words, birth is rebirth; it already contains rebirth in itself potentially, in the weakest sense, and actually, in the strong sense of everything staying alive only by being reborn from the ashes of itself (and of the other) in every single moment. Thus, inasmuch as life is generative, it is generational. And this, for Confucian authors, is *good*: an expression of the *dao*, which, "renewing itself daily, . . . is called flourishing virtue."

Does the regeneration that is life itself have its own figure in Chinese thought? It should be recalled that, according to the complex outlined in the course of this investigation, the phoenix is a figuration of nature and, by implication of life, because all of nature (even the inorganic kind) is alive in the premodern mindset (and it comes alive again at the dusk of modernity, with the revival of ancient animisms alongside the newfangled interrelation of matter and energy in relativity theory and quantum physics). In older

192   *Chapter 7*

Chinese texts, "nature" (*xing*) was written as "life" (*shēng*), taking on the sense of being born or giving birth, which is congruent with the later Latin *natura*.[36] In its turn, 生 (*shēng*) was written in Classical Chinese as a combination of 屮 (*che*), or freshly germinated grass on top, and 土 (*tu*), or the soil below.[37] Foregrounding vegetality in the dynamics of life, this way of thinking will resonate across centuries and vast geographical distances with St. Hildegard's notion of *viriditas*, the green phoenix par excellence. Spring returns and, with it, the first sprouts of grass: this is life in its indomitable re-initiation. *Shēng shēng*, or vitality, repeats the repetition already inherent in *shēng*, its fecund excess over and above itself: life and death, the germinating grass and the soil constituted by the remnants of past life it has received. Its doubling raises this excess to the power of infinity.

The phoenix movement of return in nature—the movement that is vitality and nature as such—is designated by hexagram 24 in the *Book of Changes*: 復 or ䷗ (*fù*, "returning, the turning point"). With the receptive earth (*k'un*) above and the arousing thunder (*chēn*) below, the turning point occurs "after the dark lines have pushed all of the lines of light upward. . . . The time of darkness is past. The winter solstice brings the victory of light. . . . After a time of decay comes the turning point. . . . The old is discarded and the new is introduced" (1.24).[38] Growth is the offshoot of a peculiar return, of seasonal and cosmic turns, in which the initial cosmological perspective is overturned: the receptive earth is now on top, in the position of heaven, and the inner impulse of *chēn* pushes the germinating seed from underneath. But, since vegetal growth in particular both underlies and expresses (via a synecdoche as pervasive in ancient Greece as it was in China) life and vitality, what this means is that life is a return from death, the revitalization of new growth by decay, from which and into which it will return.

One of the Cheng brothers, Cheng Yi, comments on hexagram 24 as follows: "One *yang* returning to the bottom is the mind of heaven and earth to generate things [生物, *shēng wu*]."[39] The "mind" of heaven and earth is the cosmic soul (recall the *zōon empsuchon* in Plato's *Timaeus*) that operates in a cyclical manner, generating and regenerating beings without end across the gaps that, at the same time, symbolize their mortality and a reopening toward the light within the five upper horizontal broken lines of the hexagram (☷). The cosmic soul is, in fact, the relation between these two opposite spheres, between the earthly and the celestial, the receptacle and the creative one that, upon contact, generate everything in between. Every time such a relation is initiated anew, it overflows with finite beings, who are the issue of heaven and earth touching in the thin layer of the habitable world bounded by the soil and the bottom of the troposphere. Plants are the most immediate instantiations of this generative contact and, for this very reason, they are good barometers for its iterative, seasonal, turning and returning rhythms.

What is intriguing in this scheme of things is what takes place in between in the contact zone of the extremes, as well as between *shēng* and *shēng* that, haltingly, without a trace of automatism, indebted to the "mind of heaven and earth" finding expression in conditions that are just right (and it is not a given that these conditions will always be optimal for the projection of vitality into the future), regenerate the world. Recently, Sun Xiangcheng has taken a close look at the concept of *shēng shēng*, tying its generativity to the generational emphasis of Confucian ethics, on the one hand, and Heidegger's notion of being-in-the-world, on the other.[40] Besides the consonance of his approach with the tenets of Confucianism, according to which ethics is inseparable from ontology and natural philosophy from political theory and practice, what I find most promising in Sun Xiangcheng's s text is the focus not on the generations themselves but on that which is between them.

It is, indeed, *between* generations that the phoenix complex falters or thrives, in a place and a time (if place and time these still are) where and when nothing is generated. Filial devotion (*xiao*) and all the other pious affects and dispositions, whether symmetrical or not, belong there, but subtending them is an interval, a gap, a break. The main purpose of the phoenix complex, in its various guises, is to assuage the fear that the interval would last indefinitely, the gap expanding and swallowing up all that is. All our representations of environmental and societal collapse together with their corresponding affects derive from this gap quickly dilating until it turns into an unfathomable chasm. As a reaction to the sense of dread it provokes, as old as the consciousness of mortality itself, the image of indefatigable, ceaselessly

194   *Chapter 7*

proliferating, endlessly birthing and growing nature emerges, ensuring the seamlessness of biological reproduction and of the reproduction of social and political relations. But, since the site of the phoenix complex is in between, the interval is not sealed off; it is not erased, but sparks off fecund conflations between the supplanting and the supplanted, who are, strictly speaking, neither the one nor the other and both the one and the other. It is high time to take the *inter-* of intergenerationality seriously and soberly, discarding the prism of the phoenix complex, through which it has been viewed thus far, and accounting for the promises and dangers, the oppressive and the liberating tendencies, that it harbors.

8 UNIVERSAL RESURRECTION IN RUSSIAN COSMISM

Russian philosopher Nikolai Fedorovich Fedorov (1829–1903) was ardently committed to the task of universal resurrection. So much so that a contemporary commentator states that this was "the one idea" Fedorov had, being "a thinker with one vast idea," which was itself replete with multiple ramifications.[1] Heidegger once noted that all genuine thinkers think one momentous thought throughout their lifetime, that "to think is to confine yourself to a single thought that one day stands still like a star in the world's sky."[2] On this view, rather than a philosopher with a limited scope of interests and concerns, Fedorov is a genuine thinker. But merely thinking the thought of universal resurrection, or even positing it as a desideratum for "mature" humanity, is not sufficient—above all, for Fedorov himself. Impatient with the rift between theory and practice, the Russian philosopher advocated the reorientation of all human endeavors (and especially of scientific and technological undertakings) toward the task of achieving immortality for everyone, whether currently living or long dead.

With an unwavering dedication to the task of universal resurrection, Fedorov was a proponent of what, in this book, I have been calling *the phoenix complex*. Yet, he demonstrates a fair degree of ambivalence with regard to the actual figure and symbolism of the phoenix. There are only three instances in which Fedorov mentions the phoenix, and all three are to be found in a long essay on *sobor*, which, more than *cathedral*, means gathering into a community that is the living body of Christ (*sobornost'*).

The first reference to the mythic bird in the essay on *sobor* presents itself in the context of the depictions of phoenixes and peacocks in the catacombs that served as burial sites for early Christians and, later on, as the foundations for churches. They are, without a doubt, the symbols of resurrection, but what catches Fedorov's attention is the artistic medium of their depiction, designated with the Russian word *zhivopis'* (drawing, or, literally, life-writing) that, though it is "often deemed a kind of learning for the unlearned," is just as often difficult to interpret for the learned, as well.[3] The subject of drawing is written into life, reinscribed back into the fold of vitality, and so, on a very formal level, resurrected. It is necessary to read the symbol in order to receive the writing of life itself that it contains and then to act upon it so that the writing passes from representation to actuality. Notable here is the fact that Fedorov associates himself with the unlearned not only in the long subtitle of his programmatic text, "The Question of Brotherhood," which is presented as "notes from the uneducated to the educated," but also in his lifelong position that has earned him the nickname "the Socrates of Moscow." The implication is that it is easier for the uneducated to engage with the realm of *zhivopis'*, to read life-writing and resurrect the senses it alludes to (*prima facie* vision, though not only), than it is for those who possess formal academic degrees and credentials, something that Fedorov himself eschewed.

The second reference to the phoenix follows on the heels of the first and is highly ironic. To help viewers read the life-writing of the catacombs, Fedorov fantasizes about chimeras: "If these symbols of resurrection (i.e., the phoenix and the peacock) were given human faces, then, despite the monstrosity of such depictions, the sense of the symbols they point toward would have been clarified."[4] It would have been possible then to interpret the symbols of resurrection in an entirely human key, as an aspiration to restore the lives of those buried in the tombs that bear the images. But why a human face? Is this narrow interpretation justifiable within the framework of Christianity and of Fedorov's own thought? The efforts to bring about a truly universal resurrection cannot be circumscribed to the human species alone. The phoenix as a figuration of nature, the season of rebirth that is the spring, and Fedorov's proposals to restore kinship among humans as well as between human and nonhuman natures are indicative of how precipitous and indefensible the anthropomorphized chimera would be.

The third and final reference to the phoenix in the essay on *sobor* is at once more complex and more critical of the bird's symbolism. Contemplating Paul Chenavard's commissioned decorations of the Parisian Pantheon, Fedorov writes, "Opposite the upper part, depicting the light of creation, we see a fire below, the burial pyre, into which geniuses throw the last corpses. Yet, this funereal pyre of the world is not the end; it expresses not despair but unreasonable hope placed into fire (instead of rational labor), since out of the flames a phoenix will arise, the son of its own ashes. And this phoenix will meet the same end; therefore, here we do not have the answer, but the repetition of the same question."[5]

In retrospect, my persistent critique of the phoenix complex partly echoes Fedorov: the hope that the world would revive from the ashes, time and again, is pernicious to the point of being lethal. Fedorov, however, is happy to substitute for fire's (currently) uncontrollable and irrational force the joint activity of labor that would seek the ways and means for resurrecting the dead. What equally irks the Russian thinker is the recurrence of the phoenix's death and rebirth that, instead of solving the problem of mortality once and for all, engages in an endless "repetition of the same question." For Fedorov, it is essential to vanquish the absolute evil of death *as much as* the cyclicality of life and death, which, as a movement, is symptomatic of our subjection to unconscious and automatic natural processes. A victory over death would free life from its bondage to finitude and render nature itself conscious by way of a mature humanity that would learn to "regulate meteorological processes"[6] and become autotrophic (plantlike in its capacity to procure energy from the sky, from solar power), no longer needing to feed on the remains of the dead.[7] Fedorov sees in this transformation of nature its transition from a blind and mortiferous force to an enlivening synergetic activity. Before we criticize him for the intensification of Enlightenment hubris, albeit with an unusual Russian Orthodox twist, also echoing some themes in Hindu thought, it is advisable to take a closer look at his conception of nature (*priroda*), without which the "common task" (*obschee delo*) of universal resurrection is impenetrable.

*

199   *Universal Resurrection in Russian Cosmism*

The Russian word for nature, *priroda*, is close to the Latin *natura*: it means "at-birth" (*pri* = at; *rodit'sya* = to be born). The prefix (*pri-*) should not be overlooked, however, since it names a presence—being in attendance, continually being at the side of something or someone—but a presence that is not static, one that dynamically gives itself anew, without representing itself. Being-at does not happen only once in the event of birth; the prefix suggests the sense of nature as being-at-birthing, in relation to which the incremental (evolutionary) or the more abrupt (catastrophic/revolutionary) developments in natural history are derivative. The grammatical root -*rod*-, with which this prefix is articulated, is also semantically rich: in addition to forming the verb "to be born" (*rodit'sya*), it is featured in "sex" or "kind" (*rod*), "kin" (*rodnya, rodstvo*), "relatives" (*rodstevnniki*), "kindred being" (*rodstvennost'*), "parents" (*roditeli*), and "genealogy" (*rodoslovnaya*).

All of the above are significations that are important to Fedorov. It is in this respect that we should examine the full title of his major work, "The Question of Brotherhood, or Kinship [*rodstve*]; the Reasons for the Unbrotherly, Non-Kindred [*nerodstvennogo*], i.e., Non-Peaceful Condition of the World; and the Means of Reestablishing Kinship [*rodstva*]—A Note from the Unlearned to the Learned, the Spiritual and the Secular, Believers and Unbelievers." Already the title homes in on the question of kinship beyond its limited human reach; it bemoans the "non-kindred [*nerodstrennoe*] . . . condition of the world," which, in one way or another, involves all of nature (*priroda*). In the non-kindred condition, nature is (already or yet) not itself. Fedorov confirms this reading in his text, where he defines "the agrarian question" as "firstly, the question of the non-kindred relations among people [*o nerodstvennom otnoshenii lyudei mezhdu soboy*], who have forgotten, due to ignorance, their kinship [*svoyo rodstvo*], and, secondly, the question of non-kindred relation of nature toward people [*o nerodstvennom otnoshenii prirody k lyudyam*], that is, of non-kindred being [*o nerodstvennosti*], which is felt if not exclusively then predominantly in villages that bear directly the brunt of this blind force; in turn, city-dwellers, who are far from nature [*daleko ot prirody*], may think that they are living the same life as it [nature] does for this very reason."[8]

200 *Chapter 8*

Non-kindred being (*nerodstvennost'*) is the negation of nature (*priroda*), which is subsequently reduced to a conjunction of blind forces, both within and outside the human domain. The reestablishment of kinship is akin to the Platonic *anamnesis*, remembering, or, more accurately, unforgetting the family ties binding us to each other and to the nonhuman world. For Fedorov, *anamnesis* cannot be a purely theoretical or imaginative exercise; it must have the practical component that lends it actuality. Universal resurrection is the necessary practical component for "the relation . . . of the descendant to the ancestor, which entails not only knowledge but also feeling and which is not limited to thought or representation, demands vision, a personal relation, being face-to-face; that is why kindred-being [*rodstvennost'*] as a criterion requires resurrection."[9] Impersonal transactions, with which civil society and civilization replace kinship,[10] deface the sphere of relationality as a whole, making it anonymous. The effacement of nature as our kin is a corollary of this defacement.

Since, carefully avoiding the fashionable discourse of alienation, Fedorov aligns non-kindred relations among humans with those between human beings and the rest of the natural world, the overcoming of divisions would have to apply to both spheres. In other words, the universality of resurrection would need to encompass, beyond humankind (*chelovecheskiy rod*), all those to whom we feel kinship (*rodstvennost'*), including all of nature (*priroda*). Fedorov stops short of taking his argument to its logical conclusion though. He writes, "A consequence of the loss of feeling is non-kindred being [*nerodstvennost'*], that is to say, both the forgetting of the fathers and the lack of unity among the sons. (In its causes, non-kindred being embraces the whole nature, too [*nerodstvennost' obnimaet i vsyu prirodu*], as a blind force not directed by reason.) . . . on the other hand, the fullness of feeling is the unification of all the living (sons) . . . for the purpose of resurrecting all the dead (fathers), the gathering (*sobor*) of all who have been revived, or the unification of the born for the resurrection of those who have been deadened, deadened by birth and nourishment."[11] Just as "non-kindred being embraces the whole of nature," so kindred being would have to embrace the whole, in the first instance, at the level of feeling, rather than of reason guiding nature from its unconscious to conscious state. Actually, "the fullness of feeling," which Fedorov cites has a much wider scope than he is willing to admit: "The gathering of all who have been revived" does not emphasize any uniquely human characteristics, but reproductive and nutritive activities, harkening back to the Aristotelian vegetative soul, shared by all organisms and responsible, at the same time, for the life-process and for the demise of each living being.

The theoretical and practical sense of nature as kin (*rodstvo s prirodoy*) is yet to be achieved in Fedorov's writings as well. In his critique of philosophy in general Fedorov is aware of the hard work such an achievement requires. In the essay on "Philosophy as the Expression of Non-Kindred Being and Kinship [*Filosofiya kak vyrazhenie nerodstvennosti i rodstvo*]," he states that the discipline "does not even acknowledge the question about the reasons of the non-kindred relation of nature toward us [*nerodstvennogo otnosheniya prirody k nam*]"[12] and pithily defines philosophy itself as "the science treating kindred and non-kindred being [*o rodstve i nerodstvennosti*], presented in a non-kindred form [*v nerodstvennoy forme*]."[13] Having led thought away from the relations of kin that are discernible in the mythic genealogies of creation or in the Trinitarian figure of divinity, philosophy still deals with the same relations of a second order, depersonalized, abstracted into likeness and unlikeness, sameness and difference, belonging and nonbelonging. Philosophy of nature thus intensifies the contradictions inherent in general theoretical philosophy: in the same "non-kindred [*nerodstvennaya*] form," it occupies itself with nature (*priroda*), in which we ought to recognize our kin, as the opposite—non-kin, a foreign element, the other vis-à-vis the human. In the twenty-first century, the thinking that has gone the furthest in restoring kindred being and form to the philosophy of nature is that of Donna Haraway.[14]

The practical sense of nature as kin is, following Fedorov, to be sought in the practice of resurrection, which, despite its theological provenance, fills with scientific content the technologies of salvation nestled in the phoenix complex. While Fedorov pursues his project of the universal resurrection of humankind, in "The Parents and the Resurrectors" he resorts to a language that admits a much vaster array of beings into the fold of revival. "The

202   *Chapter 8*

hypothesis of the recreation of the world," he argues there, "necessitates a shared experience [*trebuet opyta obschego*], embracing the entire globe of the earth in all its strata."[15] A shared experience is the outcome of discharging the common task (*obschee delo*) that is not only biological but also geological, atmospheric, and ultimately cosmic; in addition to humanity, the whole world is re-created via universal resurrection.

Fedorov's hands-on vision of the technologies of salvation, well ahead of nineteenth-century European science, underwrites the global scope of the task, which is far from species-specific. "The science of infinitesimal molecular movements . . . will search for the molecules that used to be part of the creatures, who gave us life. [The process will] unfold under the influence of the rays of light that will no longer be blind, like thermal rays; they will not be coldly indifferent. Chemical rays will be able to make choices, to discern, i.e., under their influence, kindred particles [*srodnoe*] will be reunited, while the foreign elements will be distanced."[16] Later on, Fedorov will compare the process of vegetal growth and that of the regrowth or return of a bygone life: "The process, through which mold or vegetal forms were produced *unconsciously*, will, *with consciousness*, become the aggregator of particles into living bodies, to which these particles belonged."[17]

There is no reason to limit the consciously directed synthesis of particles to human forms alone; in the soil, organic matter derived from dead plants and animals will have been mixed. Further, "the creatures who gave us life" are not limited to our parents, grandparents, and all the other human ancestors. If nourishment is added to reproduction as the two animating vectors of the life process (something that has been done ever since Aristotle and that continues in Fedorov, who aims to reshape both of these vectors beyond recognition), then the plants and animals who served as food for generations upon generations of humans, as well as the putrefied and decomposed organic matter in which plants have grown, are to be included in the debt that can be repaid only by means of resurrection. Fedorov, however, considers that we owe this debt to no one but our human predecessors. "At present," he notes, "we live on account of our ancestors, drawing food and clothing from their remains," calling such survival "a hidden cannibalism."[18] This may be true at the level of culture, with new productions cannibalizing on the old ones, but not at the level of organic life, in which human biomass is a drop in the ocean compared to that of other animals and, even more so, plants. So, drawing the radical lesson of a truly universal (i.e., not indexed to a single species) resurrection from Fedorov, we could visualize nature as a phoenix, reborn never to die again.

The above poses another problem: What will plants grow in, after all the compost on earth has been revived, receiving its vegetal, animal, and human forms back? That human and, perhaps, animal natality would be fixed at zero once the task of universal resurrection is accomplished is a logical conclusion of Fedorov's thought experiment, at the end of which the sex drive (reductively) serving reproductive purposes is finally quelled, becoming superfluous. But plant growth, vegetal life, is inseparable either from a perpetual birthing of itself or from the substratum of death and decay, from which it draws one of its sources of energy. More than a marginal issue associated with vegetal vitality, this is a blind spot in Fedorov's overall thinking, which is resistant to the double movement of change, namely metabolism and metamorphosis. For Fedorov, resurrection has sense on the condition that the deceased will return in the same form, will have the same look as they had when they were alive, making the vis-à-vis with the living descendants possible. Needless to say, each individual drastically changes throughout their lifetime, so that it is unclear what that desired look of the resurrected would be like. The same as the moment before death? That of a newborn regenerated from what we would now call recovered DNA materials? Who would be raising these ancestral children? Their descendants, which is to say, all of us, united by the common task? How contemporary would the resurrecting and the resurrected be, given the gaps of individual and historical development and maturation?

*

The configuration of the phoenix complex in Fedorov's thought is as idiosyncratic as his philosophy itself: he intensifies certain aspects of the complex, while watering others down. For example, Fedorov rejects both old age and decay. "To follow nature [*sledovat' prirode*]," he notes, "means to participate in the natural-sexual struggle for mating, to wage a struggle for

204   *Chapter 8*

survival and to accept all the consequences of this struggle, i.e., old age and death, bowing down to and serving a blind force. Old age is the fall, and the old age of Christianity will arrive if the evangelical message does not lead to the unification of humanity in the common task; the old age of humanity, the extinction and old age of the world, is its end."[19] Fedorov shares his distaste for aging with the phoenix complex, but, by snubbing the reproductive logic of replacing the aging individual with a younger copy, he disactivates the complex's mechanism, its mechanics and machinations. In the system of coordinates determined by universal resurrection, the one who is reborn is not a replacement, not a substitute, for the deceased: the debt of resurrection "demands the return of the identical, not of the similar [*trebuet vozvrascheniya tozhdestvennogo, a ne podobnogo*]."[20] These words have an ethical ring to them, which is missing in the phoenix complex. Whereas the phoenix is identical to itself across the flaming gap of its death, the immediate combination of sameness and otherness in classical accounts of its demise and rebirth powers the reproductive mechanics of replacement ever since Diotima's teaching. The ethical tenor of Fedorov's repudiation of these mechanics has to do with the irreplaceability of the deceased, of everyone who has ever lived and died.

Disgust with decay is another sentiment Fedorov shares with the phoenix complex, the sentiment that is purged from the accounts of the phoenix's rebirth through slow metamorphoses and instances of spontaneous generation out of rotting flesh. With an unmistakably Platonic ring to his words, the Russian thinker concludes, "Resurrection is also a duty, given that storage is impossible. To store or to keep [*hranit*] is to consign to decay; every stoppage is a fall; stagnation is destruction."[21] Stoppage joins old age as a condition of the fall, of fallenness into the material order of things, dictated by "blind" nature, where it is a moment of transition toward death and nonbeing. Sounding suspiciously like a champion of progress, the ideology he frequently chided for its immature outlook, Fedorov (who is the keeper par excellence: an excellent librarian, a proponent of living museums and of an amalgamated necropolis-acropolis) nonetheless rehashes Diotima's line of thinking, according to which finite beings cannot keep themselves forever the same as they are and must let go of themselves in order to recover themselves in the other. Remarkably, the Russian verb *hranit'* (to store, to keep) is nearly identical to *horonit'* (to bury), with both alluding to the Greek word for time (*chronos*), itself derived from the verb *chronizō* (to tarry, linger, delay). Finite, time is a delay of the end, postponing the final moment, keeping it at bay for a while; to store and to bury (*hranit'* and *horonit'*) is to hand the buried and the stored to *chronos*, to time and its signature activity of delaying and detaining, even in the course of decay. Fedorov's allergy to decay is the other side of the coin of his impatience with finitude and with time itself.

That said, in the essay "On the Question of Time [*K voprosu o vremeni, kogda dolzhno sovershit'sya voskreshenie*]," Fedorov leans toward a gradual transition that is closer to the alternative versions of the phoenix narrative than to the dominant account of the bird's miraculous rebirth. The essay begins with these lines: "Concerning the question of time, in which the 'task of resurrection' may be accomplished, we should say, first of all, that it cannot be accomplished in an *indivisible instant* [*nerazdel'nyiy mig*]—that what is necessary is a *succession* [*posledovatel'nost'*], which may attain *rather high speeds*, in contrast to the blind pace and unconscious development of the world."[22] Fedorov thus recovers time both in the Kantian sense of a succession and as a tarrying along, the postponement of and noncoincidence with the end. But this is just the initial state or stage of the gradual accomplishment of universal resurrection, which accelerates with every increase in technoscientific capacity. The time of resurrection ultimately strives to zero, emulating the model of hegemonic phoenix narratives.

The universality of resurrection, mirrored in the common task of humanity working together to bring it about, faithfully corresponds to the singularity and uniqueness of the phoenix. With reference to the time required to discharge this task, Fedorov pictures humanity as a single actor, restoring its own past life. Here, planetary time becomes the time of a united humanity, capable of regulating its own rhythms: "When humankind [*rod chelovecheskiy*], as one son of man [*syn chelovecheskiy*], acts upon the earth as a single whole, making earthly time its own action, it will be capable of slowing down and accelerating time's movement, whether diurnal or annual, based on the oscillations of the axis, lengthening one season and shortening

206   *Chapter 8*

another, as well as the year itself."[23] The regulation of planetary time is more intimately connected to the self-regulation of the human phoenix, of humanity as a phoenix, than is the space-based climatic regulation, which Fedorov envisions elsewhere.[24] The actions of a singular-universal humanity are synchronized with the singular-universal earth ("acted upon . . . as a single whole"), the universality of resurrection spilling over the boundaries of the human species. But what exactly does the phoenix-like singularity and uniqueness of humanity look like in Fedorov? Is it in agreement with the Jewish fantasy of the cosmic Adam or the Platonic idea of *makro anthrōpos* (the Great Human)?

We can distinguish three main axes in the unitary being of humanity as Fedorov sees it. The first is temporal: "its complete makeup, the gathering of all generations [*v polnom svoyom sostave, v sovokupnosti pokoleniy*]."[25] The second is spatial: inhabiting the earth and extraterrestrial worlds as "one creature [*vseedinoe suschestvo*]."[26] The third is categorial: the individual and the collective, the one and the many, are not subjugated to one another but given free expression through each other. The categorial axis spells out the highest meaning of kinship (*rodstvo*) for Fedorov: "Only in the teaching of kinship is the question of the crowd and personality resolved: unity does not swallow up [*edinstvo ne poglaschaet*], but aggrandizes each unit [*kazhduyu edinitsu*], while the difference of personalities only strengthens unity."[27]

The point at which all three axes intersect (the origin of the coordinate system they constitute) is the Trinitarian notion of God, who is both one and not-one, who is a "clan God" (*rodovoy Bog*),[28] the God of kinship. The creation of humanity in divine image is not an external given, but a mission to be carried out in a conscious realization of kinship as unity in multiplicity and multiplicity in unity. It is within the context of the Trinity, and despite the ambiguities of the phoenix's sex (or sexlessness) and even species belonging, that the generationality of the mythic creature is comprehended in Christian theology as a father–son relation and, moreover, as a relation, in which the phoenix is his own son and his own father. With fire and other elements mediating between the generations of the phoenix, the third participant enters the relation, precisely as the substantiation of its very relationality, the participant analogous to the Holy Spirit in Trinitarian theology. It

207   *Universal Resurrection in Russian Cosmism*

completes what Fedorov refers to as "the Trinity of agreement and the Trinity of revivification [*Troitsa soglasiya i Troitsa ozhivleniya*]."[29]

By dint of his shorthand reference to "fathers and sons," Fedorov's critics have read him "as the most patriarchal of Russian thinkers" and as "an authoritarian."[30] To the extent that Fedorov exhibits patriarchal tendencies, his thought is aligned with the dominant version of the story of the phoenix, in which fire and other solar accoutrements of the bird are the elemental symbols of masculinity, of the phallus and its erection. But the sweeping nature of the accusation is hardly justified. Fedorov would not have been able to insist on the universality of resurrection were he to have limited it to the sons and not to the daughters; as a matter of fact, he argues that the "Triune God" (*Bog Triedinyyi*) is "the deification of the inseparability of sons and daughters from fathers and their non-fusion with the latter."[31] This is the cornerstone of *vsemirnost'* (the whole-worldness, which should not be conflated with globality) of the project that renders concrete its sense of universality. Nor are the mothers left out of the picture: "The matriarchal and patriarchal conditions [of society and civilization] are already a restauration, albeit not yet complete."[32]

More than that, "the relation of sons and daughters, or, more generally of progeny (which is dual [*dvoystvennoe*], consisting of sons and daughters) toward parents, fathers and mothers (who represent for children one, rather than two principles [*sostavlyayuschim dlya detey odno, a ne dva nachala*]) must replace all other relationships, and cannot be limited to remembrance alone."[33] The dual nature of the progeny does not match, according to Fedorov, the sexed division among the parents, because, *pace* Freud, sexuality is absent from filial ties. The merging of two principles into one, with the addition of asexual being of filial relations somehow exempt from the dynamics of the fall, strongly resonates with the phoenix narratives, where sexual differences and the very difference between sexual and asexual modes of reproduction are blurry, backgrounded, or both. The universality of the common task exacts the grouping of all ancestors in "one principle," a single cause of the descendants' existence, without sacrificing the bonds of filial love between this cause and its effects. (Filial duty, we might recall, is an important motivating factor in those accounts of the phoenix, where the hatchling who encounters the predecessor's dead body in the nest must travel far away—typically, to Heliopolis—in order to give the parent proper burial rites.) In this way, Fedorov imagines himself writing an obituary of sexuality, which would become antiquated, a relic of our animal past, with the realization of universal resurrection, also because there would no longer be a need in conceiving and giving birth to new human beings: "The sexual feeling and birth [*polovoe chuvstvo i rozhdenie*] amount but to a temporary condition, a remnant of animal condition, which will be destroyed when the ancestral task becomes that of resurrection."[34] (A Platonic question can be raised in this respect: Would cultural productions also cease, given that they are the other way, on a par with biological reproduction, for mortal human beings to participate in immortality?)

As for the universality of resurrection in Fedorov, it is a singular universality, recalling the phoenix as a synecdoche of the whole of nature. Of course, Fedorov restricts this universality to humankind, because it is only for the human that death is a problem, in the face of which, regardless of all technical or technological progress, our understanding is resourceless: "We are perplexed before the phenomenon of death, and our perplexity continues to this day."[35] The organic connection between understanding and action, between theory and practice, in Fedorov means that we cannot really act on that which we do not understand, or, in a more positive key, that we can only act on life (and on its restoration), which is what we do understand. The phoenix complex as a whole reflects this failure of understanding death, of accepting and honoring it, which is why, even in the shape of a more or less brief interval between lives, death still appears as a higher vitality (fire, generative rotting, etc.). Within the mass of humankind, though, aspirations to "a privileged immortality [*privilegirovannoye bessmertie*]" are "disgusting,"[36] a sign of "the greatest egoism."[37] Rather than single out some humans who would be more worthy of resurrection than others, the singularity in question spotlights the personal affective ties (above all, of filial-parental love), out of which kinship is universally forged: universal in and through the singular.

The motif of fire is relatively rare in Fedorov, but when it appears, it sparkles with allusions to the phoenix. For instance: "The universal resurrection

209   *Universal Resurrection in Russian Cosmism*

is not just artistic creation out of stone, on a canvas, etc.; it is not the unconscious birth either, but a recreation out of us, as fire out of fire [*vosproizvedenie iz nas, kak ogon' ot ognya*], with the mediation of everything that is in the sky and on earth, of all the past generations."[38] The project of universal resurrection neither works on foreign materials, as a sculptor does on stone, nor does it enable the reproduction of our own flesh, guided by instinct. Neither artistic nor purely natural (and both at once), it is symbolized by the element of fire, the fire of life devolved from the future to the past generations. The fiery medium of the phoenix's rebirth could be produced internally (say, from the warmth of the decomposing body of the bird), externally (from lightning striking its nest), or from the interaction of the two (as in the case of the phoenix's wings rapidly beating the nest). The fire of resurrection, dispensing life back to the dead, arises in this space of an overlap between the internal and external, between the common task of humankind and "everything that is in the sky and on earth." The whole universe participates in and is transformed by the fulfillment of this task, since mediation is already participation. Nature (*priroda*) itself is reborn (*pererozhdaetsya*)—not as a metaphysical ideal but as kinship (*rodstvo*) realized.

The flame of universal resurrection does not burn out as it should according to the laws of thermodynamics, of force (*sila*), which "is heat, the energy of heat, the force of expansion and detachment . . . which is why life could appear only in gradual burning out or extinction, in gradual deadening."[39] The fire that doesn't burn forth into the future, but back into the past, so to speak, reverses not only the chronology of thermic exhaustion but also, and by the same token, the expansive and dissociative dynamics of energy: it concentrates, contracts into a unity, interrelating the resurrecting and the resurrected. The cosmic dimension of Fedorov's vision goes against the inevitability of the Big Bang and the subsequent entropy of an expanding universe it gives rise to. Instead, Fedorov implicitly postulates a notion of energy that increases in the measure in which it is actualized, restoring life and rebinding the intergenerational and interpersonal ties of humankind (the rebinding of the ties is the deepest sense of religion as an act of *religare*). It is for this reason that the Russian thinker can say that "the very representation of the

210   *Chapter 8*

elements was untrue in the past, and it is insufficient and underthought in the present."[40]

*

As Boris Groys notes in the introduction to the anthology of Russian cosmism, this philosophical strand "does not contain a unified or comprehensive doctrine. Rather, it has to do with a circle of authors from the end of the nineteenth and the beginning of the twentieth centuries, for whom the visible cosmos became the sole habitat for humanity."[41] One of the most interesting among its strands is anarchic biocosmism, associated with Aleksandr Svyatogor (Agienko, 1886–1937, who wrote both in Russian and in his native Ukrainian), Aleksandr Yaroslavsky, and brothers Aba and Wolf Gordin.

Fiery imagery permeates Svyatogor's poetic writings and manifestoes during World War I and the revolutionary period in Russian history. In his 1917 booklet *The Rooster of the Revolution*, Svyatogor advances the poetic and intellectual movement of volcanism, calling for the planetary-scale practice of "the highest culture," bent on "creating a new landscape and a new sky [*sozdat' novyi rel'yef zemli i novoe nebo*]."[42] Nature in its entirety, including the atmosphere, is to be reshaped by the power of fire that, breaking out from the molten core of the planet, renews the aging upper crusts of the earth. Although he does not explicitly refer to the phoenix, but rather to the rooster who signals the dawn of a new day, Svyatogor alludes to the solar bird who completes from above the work that volcanism initiates from below: "At dawn the rooster screams: / A volcanic day is starting. / The sun is in its daring nakedness / And its mighty flaring. / The sun is a celestial Faraway-giant [*Solntse—nebnyi Dalekan*]. / It flies, falling unto the earth, / So as to burn through earthly hardness / In the holiest of combustions."[43] Further, the volcanic day is not a twenty-four-hour period but a duration similar to the Great Year, measuring the phoenix's lifetime. "Learn to count . . . / By millennia, as God used to do it,"[44] Svyatogor appeals to his readers in the hopes of inaugurating, or of going back to, the time and space of cosmic existence.

211   *Universal Resurrection in Russian Cosmism*

The theme of millennial catastrophes and renewals returns in Svyatogor's later writings, such as the 1924 essay, "The Holy Cycle of Millennia [*Svyaschennyyi krugovorot tysyacheletiy*]," where the author finds himself in agreement with the Biblical hypothesis that worldwide upheavals are repeated with the frequency of a thousand years. After such upheavals, "a new Millennial Day" dawns in history, signaling the periodic renewal of humanity.[45] The cycles of death and rebirth confer the status of a phoenix on humankind, even as they exceed human history and ultimately involve the cosmic environs of life.

Already Svyatogor's volcanism envisions the fresh (and fiery: "*v svoyom ognennom detstve*") childhood of humanity in a cosmic age, when "cosmic infinity would serve them [the volcanic giants of new humanity] as a child's playground" and when, "having conquered death, they would knead with their own hands, like sculptors knead clay, the spirit and matter of the world, so as to create an absolutely new cosmos [*vozdvignut' sovershenno novyyi kosmos*]."[46] If we look closely, we will see an image of Plato's cosmic phoenix, or the phoenix as cosmos, redoubled in Schelling's *Weltalter* (the ages of the world), flash by our eyes in these lines. The chronology of phoenix's life, whether referring to the history of humanity or natural history, is a revolutionary timeline, both in the sense of abrupt changes and cataclysms, rather than incremental evolutionary development, and in the sense of a rotation, in which the end is followed by a new beginning. (Not by accident, the text where Svyatogor makes this point is titled "Volcanorevolution [*Vulkanrevolyutsiya*].") The cycles of destruction and creation, of the phoenix burning itself to ash and rising again, thus represent a victory over finite time and limited space, the victory that "will reunite us with cosmic life, with cosmic art."[47]

Similar to the idea of a permanent revolution, human participation in cosmic life involves the desire and the capacity to exist in and with fire, to lead what ancient Greeks called *purobios*, seeing that the cosmos *is* this very everlasting fire (*pur aeizōon*), kindling and extinguishing "in measures," as Heraclitus has it.[48] In contrast to the dominant version of the myth of the phoenix, where fire reduces the aged body to ash and offers a glimpse of a higher life, biocosmism demands the seemingly impossible: living on in the fiery medium. That is why Svyatogor craves speaking in "a fiery tongue

212   *Chapter 8*

[*govorit' ognennym yazykom*], which, emerging out of the depths of spirit, licks the blue of the atmosphere, burns the moons, cuts the tails of comets, and threatens the final frontiers of the world."[49]

*

Whenever Svyatogor approaches the work of Fedorov, he stresses the features of his own biocosmism that distinguish it from the "uncritical doctrine of the fathers."[50] Besides the patriarchal and Russian Orthodox influences that Svyatogor passionately rejects, what he most objects to in Fedorov's cosmism in a lengthy footnote to his essay "'The Doctrine of the Fathers' and Anarcho-Biocosmism ['*Doktrina otsov' i anarḥizm-biokosmizm*]" is the "mechanical restoration [*meḥanicheskoe vosstanovlenie*]," as opposed to a "creative transformation [*tvorcheskoe preobrazḥenie*]," of the dead.[51] At bottom, the complaint against Fedorov rehashes the Hegelian critique of the phoenix as a purely natural repetition, in which nothing changes, that is, in which, after another cycle, nature is complete and everything is restored in a figure, which is identical to the past. Nevertheless, since its Socratic utilization in his (or, better, Diotima's) rendition of the phoenix complex, *mechanē* has stood for much more than mechanics; the means that it names has gathered into itself the procedures, methods, and machinations of substitution— above all, those of self-substitution and of the substitution of the nonsubstitutable. Certain elements of "creative transformation" reside in "mechanical restoration," however concealed they might be. This indwelling of the creative in the mechanical and of transformation in restoration explains the mind-boggling (for Svyatogor, in the first instance) and "hopeless balancing act between Russian Orthodoxy and atomism"[52] in Fedorov's thought.

"Creative transformation," for its part, carries a very specific meaning for Svyatogor. It is true that Fedorov's notion of individual resurrection contains insistence on the recovery of dead human beings in their old living forms—the insistence that is, simultaneously, resistance to metabolism and metamorphosis. The assumed unity and uniqueness of the phoenix that each human is to become do not challenge the limits of bourgeois individuality, and this "narrowing down of the personality principle is a fundamental error of the doctrines of anarchism."[53] Positing "the instinct of immortality [*instinkt bessmertiya*]" as the basis of "the living human personality,"[54] Svyatogor radically undermines the equation of personality and identity, because the immortal is not the eternal, not that which is forever the same or self-identical, but, on the contrary, the other, the ever-altering, metamorphosing, and metabolizing. Succinctly put, "We have always discussed individuality in terms of a great dynamism. We have not talked of an identity, but of werewolfism and bestialism."[55]

Svyatogor presents us with yet another path, moving through the phoenix complex, represented by "the instinct of immortality," beyond it. The property relations upended by the Russian revolution cannot help but affect the revolution in spirit that he wishes for a mature biocosmism. What is the sense of "my" body and "my" mind in a communist society that is neither national nor international, but interplanetary in scope? How can one preserve the relations that are essential to private property (not to mention, the first appropriation of oneself, of one's body and mind) in such a society? And in which ways is a dynamic individuality constituted in biocosmism?

It has not escaped Svyatogor's commentators that his version of biological immortality is predicated on bodily transformations, or even "bodily deviations," such as bestialism and anabiosis.[56] What is curious, though, is that Svyatogor interprets individual and social life (the Greek *bios*, also at the root of biocosmism) through the lens of biological life (the Greek *zōē*). This interpretation gives traction to the idea of the dynamic individuality that persists in immortality, rid of private property relations and freed from the strict limits of an identity, as when Svyatogor writes that "human being is not a proprietor, but the capacity to become other—to get on all fours, to bark and croak."[57] Here, our author is in complete agreement with the Aristotle of *The Poetics*, for whom the defining feature of the human is our mimetic capacity: the human is the animal most capable of imitating all other animals. This, too, is the gist of Svyatogor's early poem, where the first strophe reads, "Who am I?—A werewolf. / My spirit lives within five dimensions. / On a weekday and on Saturday / I go through rows of transformations."[58]

In his poetry and prose alike, Svyatogor creates a short circuit, bypassing the humanist notion of the human, between the bestialism of biocosmic existence and the technological achievements that make it practically possible.

214   *Chapter 8*

In a Nietzschean vein, he contends that "the thirst for personal immortality is a beastly and hot love of oneself. . . . It is the speed of a bird, passing over into the speed of a spaceship engine. . . . One ought to learn the absolute sense of smell from a dog, instinct from insects, hedonism from a lizard, a victory over the dark forces from a rooster."[59] The same short circuit passes between animality and divinity: "That is why we refer to the human as to an animal . . . and to an animal as to a human and even as to a god."[60] The unanswered question in both of these short circuits is, Can the "thirst for personal immortality" manifest itself in animality, unless one supposes that the animal craving immortality is conscious of death? Recalling the distinction between eternity and immortality, we might say that animals are like gods because they are eternal—not deathless, but unperturbed by the problem of death as such. And, vice versa, only a human can experience the thirst for immortality, especially that of personality, broadly conceived.

Svyatogor's phoenix combines in itself cosmic and psychic dimensions, a little like the ensouled creature (*zōon empsuchon*) in Plato's *Timaeus*, albeit a creature in whom biological life (*zōē*) passes over into individual and social existence (*bios*). (It is, by the way, this passage of one type of vitality into the other that allows Svyatogor to learn from animals and to accept their deification, to the point of stating that "types of animals are higher than human types [*tipy zver'ya vyshe tipov chelovecheskih*]."[61]) The nonpossessive, nonproprietary personality that aspires toward immortality finds itself at home in cosmos as a whole. This, finally, is the meaning of biocosmism, "a new ideology, the cornerstone of which is the notion of personality, growing in its power and creativity up to its self-affirmation in immortality and in the cosmos."[62]

*

The group that Svyatogor established in Moscow in the 1920s bore a revealing name, "The Creatorium of Biocosmists [*Kreatoriy biokosmistov*]."[63] Reflecting on this name, Svyatogor writes, "We have already established The Creatorium of Biocosmists. To the ignorant, *creatorium* sounds like *crematorium*—and they are probably right to come to this conclusion. Indeed, we need to burn quite a lot, if not everything. After all, biocosmism commences a completely new era."[64] The cleansing and sacrificial power of fire retains its relevance for Svyatogor, as does its capacity to reinitiate life, transitioning between the end of an old age and the beginning of the new. The phoenix complex is easily recognizable in this flaming regeneration of humanity and of cosmos itself in acts of creation that are indefatigably foreshadowed by acts of cremation.

Among things to be burnt in the biocosmist Creatorium was not only the oppressive past and the present but also the future of the Futurists and of all the utopian projects that deferred, often indefinitely, the achievements on which biocosmism insisted in its revolutionary *now*. As early as the volcanist manifestoes, Svyatogor pitted volcanism against "temporism," announcing that "for volcanism, freedom is higher than time. . . . Freedom and time are eternal enemies."[65] A conceptual allergy to time is the telltale sign of the phoenix complex, and it is quite pronounced in biocosmist thought. The varied forms this allergy takes are worth attending to; in addition to fleshing out the biocosmist worldview, they shed light on finer issues associated with temporality in the phoenix complex.

The first stratum of protest against time has to do with an individual life hemmed in on two sides with birth and death. The finite time of human existence is seen as a curse, in that "fear for one's life gives rise to cowardliness."[66] In the second stratum, which partly coincides with the first, the temporal and spatial limits of individual and communal life introduce divisions within and between communities, among those currently living, as well as between the living and those long dead on the one hand and those yet unborn on the other. "This localism in time (death)," notes Svyatogor, "is the permanent basis for the spiritual and material decomposition of personality and society."[67] The revolutionary impulsion of volcanism and biocosmism is directed primarily against the conservatism of "the facts of life and history," and, in more philosophical terms, against the facticity of finite existence. In the third stratum of critique, time as such is imagined as a cage containing the modalities of the past, the present, and the future as its grid, modalities that are represented by the intellectual and aesthetic movements of perfectism, presentism, and futurism: "But time is not a kindly mother, who liberates

216   *Chapter 8*

her children from her womb. Time is a skeletal freak, letting her babies fester in her belly."[68]

Svyatogor's prescriptions for liberation from the yoke of time differ depending on the stratum one opposes. Individual life is extended beyond "natural" temporal limits by means of the technically realized dream of immortality and resurrection, which is, according to Svyatogor's modification of Fedorov's doctrine, not restoration but a creative transformation. Localism in time and space is countered via cosmic existence, whereby one becomes "a citizen of the cosmos" capable of interplanetary travels.[69] In each of these cases, the emphasis is on destroying the (biological, geographic, historical) limits that convert every finite determination into a prison-house of the infinite. With the battle against time itself, something changes, however: when Svyatogor states that "freedom and time are eternal enemies," he makes the pronouncement no longer from within the imploding or exploding temporal limits but from the metaphysical standpoint of eternity—*sub specie aeternitatis*, as Spinoza would say. Cosmic time is not exempt from an all-encompassing struggle against temporality, dissolved into the infinity of space. That is to say, Svyatogor uses a mixed arsenal of immortality and eternity to achieve the suppression of time characteristic of the phoenix complex, "to spit in the face of time [*plyunut' v litso vremeni*]."[70]

Another obligatory component of the complex ever-present in Svyatogor's writings is the disgust with (and the fear of) decay. In the poem "The Committees of Immortality [*Bessmert'ya komitety*]," the author is unable to accept the "stupid" situation, in which "I live and create—and, all of a sudden, I am a stinky corpse." He continues: "When death drives me into a grave, / The palms of my hands, my heart and lips, / As well as my brain, where wings are daringly flapping, / Will be gulped down by a hoard of horrible worms."[71] The conundrum is a paradox of spirit confined to the world of matter, which, nonetheless, has its own mode of deathlessness at the scale of atoms. For Svyatogor, as also for the rest of cosmists, the impersonal immortality congruent with matter is insufficient; the very relation between spirit and matter would have to be transfigured in the achievement of an immortal but "dynamic" individuality, alongside "an absolutely new cosmos."

217   *Universal Resurrection in Russian Cosmism*

Given the cosmists' distaste for decay, what sort of dynamism do they propose? Svyatogor, to be sure, jumps headlong into a series of metamorphoses, distinguishing his thought from that of Fedorov, but they remain sterile without the power of decomposition. As he conveys in a poem, "On an early June morning / I will become a clairvoyant oriole, / And at noon I will pass over the plains / As a menacing cloud. / In the evening, I will settle among the willows / And sing there as a magpie; / I will be suspended in the night sky as a waning moon, / And teach you a melancholy prayer."[72] If Svyatogor's elemental and animal metamorphoses exclude vegetation, which persists as a mere backdrop setting and habitat, that is because the capacities for growth and decay are highly concentrated in plants. The metabolic half of transformations is where rotting and decay with all their fetidness are operative, but Svyatogor entrusts metabolism to fire that reduces matter to a bare minimum and speeds up—to the point of obviating—the processes of putrefaction. The phoenix complex is particularly apparent in the wedge he drives between the two aspects of becoming, which is dematerialized in the evanescence of decay.

218   *Chapter 8*

9 POLITICAL RENAISSANCE FROM THE ROMAN EMPIRE TO THE THOUGHT OF HANNAH ARENDT

"Political renaissance" is something of a misleading term. The idea it evokes is that, no matter the political regime (democracy or monarchy, oligarchy or a mixed constitutional arrangement), politics *is* renaissance, the rebirth of life itself and of the political system of governance either in its current format or in a new shape as a consequence of revolutionary transformation. The phoenix complex lies at the very heart of politics, but the accent it places on life and death, birth and rebirth, is not necessarily a sign of vitalism or biologism transposed onto the political domain. What it reveals is that, far from a secondary issue, reproduction is the fulcrum of political form and existence; that political life is actually produced through its reproduction, with all the mechanics and machinations of substitution (including the substitution of the irreplaceable) built into the phoenix complex. The idea and the practice of rebirth, then, spawns both the content and the form of politics in the full spectrum of regimes, from autocratic to democratic.

In the Roman Empire, the phoenix signaled a periodic return of the golden ("happy") age (*Felicium temporum reparatio*) as bronze coins dating back to the co-emperors Constans I (337–350) and Constantius II (337–361) and bearing the image of the mythic bird show.[1] *Vita Constantini*, a panegyric text written in honor of their predecessor by Eusebius of Caesaria, likens Constantine the Great (306–337) to Christ, with the intermediary figure of the phoenix, mentioned and immediately rejected as a term of comparison: "He is not like the Egyptian bird, which they say has a unique nature, and dies among aromatic herbs, making itself its own sacrifice, then revives from the ash and, as it flies up, turns into what it was before. He is more like his Saviour." (4.72).[2] Tentatively appearing in the negative, under erasure so to speak, the phoenix synthesizes imperial renewal and Christian resurrection, along with the pre-Christian idea, already present in Virgil, of the past idyll of peace and tranquility, the legendary *Saeculum aureum*. It plays the role of a symbolic bond, tying together political and religious powers that last—that are said to be ever-lasting, like *Roma aeterna* itself[3]— thanks to their unshakable self-regenerating capacity.

The rebirth, which phoenix heralds at the behest of the Roman Empire, is twofold. On the one hand, it is the renaissance of time itself, conducting the ideal past (the golden age, *Saeculum aureum*) into the present and the future. The end of the old era and the beginning of the new unfold within a framework where an older era is still reincarnated in the incipient rule. On the other hand, the phoenix-modeled rebirth is the revival of political authority in the emperor after the death of his precedessor. And, in fact, according to the logic of the Roman phoenix complex, the renaissance of time is accomplished *by means of* the revival of imperial authority. Freshly minted emperors (pun intended) went out of their way to demonstrate that an epoch of peace, prosperity, and happiness had as its initial moment their inauguration—that the previous long cycle when auspicious times gave way to decline and final decadence ended with the death of their predecessors. Such a cycle had, therefore, to match the Great Year that was the lifetime of the phoenix, who would be reborn at the exact historical moment when the new emperor assumed power.[4]

For the fourth Roman emperor Claudius (41–54), it was particularly important to distance himself from the previous emperor, his nephew Caligula (37–41), whose reign was marked by a financial crisis, famine, feuds with the Senate, and general insanity. That is, probably, why it was claimed that a phoenix appeared in Egypt at the start of Claudius's reign and was then transported to Rome to mark 800 years since the founding of the city.[5] Pliny the Elder, who reports these events, has no doubt that the phoenix is a fake one, not least because the bird allowed itself to be captured: "It [the phoenix] was even brought to Rome in the Censorship of the Emperor Claudius in the year of the 800th anniversary of the city, and displayed in the Comitium, a fact attested by the Records, although nobody would doubt

220   *Chapter 9*

that this phoenix was a fake one [*in urbem Claudii principis censura anno urbis DCCC et in comitio propositus, quod actis testatum est, sed quem falsum esse nemo dubitaret*]" (*Historia naturalis* 10.ii.5).

Whatever the barefaced ideological machinations and manipulations of the phoenix narrative for the sake of the powers that be, the radical change that the emperor-phoenix augurs in the order of time and the course of the world broadens the range of his power well beyond the field of human affairs. The return of the golden age, coinciding with the beginning of an emperor's reign, leans back on a paradisiac more-than-human idyll and looks forward to the eschatological situation, described, for instance in Isaiah 11:6–8: "Then the wolf shall dwell with the lamb, and the leopard shall lie down with the kid." The emperor is presented as the guarantor of peace and felicity for all his subjects and, by extension, in the nonhuman realm.

Third- and fourth-century Latin writers built a conceptual bridge between the political authority of the phoenix and the respect she commanded among other avian species. Lactantius writes that, at the return of the phoenix, "every breed of fowl unites in the assemblage: no bird has thoughts of prey nor yet of fear [*nec praedae memor est ulla nec ulla metus*]. Attended by a chorus of winged creatures, she flits through the high air and the band escorts her, gladdened by their pious task" (*De ave phoenice* 155–160). By virtue of uniting around the phoenix, birds no longer fear predators nor think of preying on other animals: the reign of the phoenix is the reign of avian peace. Claudian echoes the topic of *pax aviana*: as the young phoenix flies to Egypt with the burned remains of his progenitor, "Birds innumerable accompany him, and whole flocks thereof throng in airy flight. . . . But from among so vast an assemblage none dares outstrip the leader [*duci*]; all follow respectfully in the balmy wake of their king [*sed regis iter fragrantis adorant*]. Neither the fierce hawk nor the eagle, Jove's own armour-bearer, fall to fighting; in honour of their common master a truce is observed by all" (*Carmina minora* 27.76–82). The phoenix is the "leader" and the "king" of the birds, who, outshining them in his singularity, ensures that, in his presence, they observe a truce.

To be fair, the conceptual bridge in question had been prepared before the third and fourth centuries CE and outside the Latin-speaking world.

In ancient China, the bird *fenghuang* was a symbol of the emperor or the empress (given that the bird combines male and female elements already in its name). During the Qin dynasty of 221–207 BCE, "empresses wore ceremonial 'phoenix crowns.'"[6] More than that, *fenghuang* was "honored as the emperor of birds," who was "followed in its flight by the other 359 species of its adoring kind."[7] Still before that, in Confucian *Analects*, a work which we have discussed at length, a virtuous government is likened to "the North Star standing in its place, with all other stars paying court to it" (2.1) in an emulation of *fenghuang*. The imperial overtones of the bird, or the celestial body associated with it, and the procession it headed, leading other avian species or stars, are the shared political elements in the construction of the Latin phoenix and the Chinese *fenghuang* that preceded the latter by nearly five hundred years. Hardly a fortuitous parallel, there is probably plenty of cultural cross-pollination going on between Chinese and Roman, or, earlier still, Chinese and Egyptian political representations of the mythical bird.

The power of the emperor, symbolized by the phoenix (and, in the Chinese context, by *fenghuang*) is power exercised not only *in* time, but also *over* time. Making time turn back, letting a past golden age return, the emperor no longer just controls beings; his jurisdiction and dominion extend to their very being. This tendency is particularly pronounced in the case of coins bearing the emperor's profile on one side and the phoenix on the other, accompanied by inscriptions, such as *Saeculum aureum* and *Felicium temporum reparatio, Aeternitas* and *Aiōn*.[8] To include a symbol of resurrection and of power's own rebirth on money is to mirror, symbolically, the operation that money is entrusted with carrying out: the value of the coin survives beyond the spatiotemporal limits of any given transaction and anticipates the repetition of exchange for another piece of merchandise in the future. This monetary value is, in other words, a phoenix—both economic and ontological—inasmuch as it outlives the moment of "death," or extinction in the relation of exchange, and is reborn for subsequent transactions constituting the movement of economic circulation. The political authority of the emperor, who is equated to the phoenix, warrants the validity of the

222   *Chapter 9*

transaction and, above all, transact*ability*, the rebirth of value, power (including purchasing power), and meaning in future exchanges.

*

At one point in his monumental study, *The King's Two Bodies*, Ernst Kantorowicz transports us to Elizabethan England, observing that "coins, or coin-like productions, of the sixteenth and seventeenth centuries displaying a Phoenix are not rare. The mythological bird was, for example, an emblem of Queen Elizabeth signifying her virginity as well as her singularity: *Sola Phoenix* is the inscription on some of her coins, and as *Unica Phoenix* she is celebrated in a medallion issued in the year of her demise, 1603."[9] Kantorowicz does not mention the Roman precedents of identifying the sovereign with the phoenix, but, in keeping with the historical range of his work, he excavates the medieval sources behind the papal and monarchic uses of the phoenix, notably in the concept of *dignitas*.

With respect to Elizabeth I, her comparison (and, especially, her self-comparison) to the phoenix is justifiable based on at least three factors.

First, several classical authors—Lactantius among them—treated the phoenix in the feminine. In other strands of the classical tradition, the phoenix is an androgynous figure, a portrayal that is exceptionally apt with respect to Queen Elizabeth. Kantorowicz does not comment on the gendered and sexually ambiguous status of the phoenix, even though this status calls for a broadening of his book's title. How do "the king's two bodies" relate to "the queen's two bodies"? It may be too precipitous to assume that the king stands for the king *and* the queen in what is yet another doubling of the regal body. Instead, Elizabeth I inverts the gendered dynamics of incorporation and corporeal representation. Just think of her famous 1588 speech to the troops at Tilbury: "I know I have the body of a weak and feeble woman; but I have the heart and stomach of a king, and of a king of England too."[10]

Second, the phoenix's virginity corresponds to the cult of Elizabeth as the Virgin Queen. Kantorowicz glosses on this correspondence without, however, examining it more closely.[11] Self-begotten, the phoenix does not participate in the dynamics of sexual reproduction. Virginity, for medieval authors such as St. Hildegard, is not mere abstinence; it is a stance that sacrifices physical self-replication in order to attain spiritual rebirth and an actively taken decision, reaffirmed every single day. Elizabeth's symbolic marriage to the country she ruled over was more than a refusal to split her loyalties between the private and the public spheres; it was a wholesale transplantation of the phoenix complex from bodily realities to the spiritual domain.[12] Whereas in hereditary monarchies physical progeny is the conditio sine qua non for securing spiritual-political survival and rebirth, the Elizabethan phoenix cuts the ligatures between the two types of reproduction. Nature is no longer a vehicle, the means for perpetuating a metaphysical claim of long-lasting, if not everlasting, authority; it stains and de-absolutizes this authority's metaphysical foundations.[13]

Third, the singularity of the phoenix is encapsulated in the adjectives *unica* and *sola* applied to Elizabeth I. For Kantorowicz, the conceptual relation of the phoenix's singular genus will be of paramount significance for the integration of the king's two bodies. But I suspect that the phoenix's uniqueness is doing another sort of work in Elizabethan numismatics and ways of thinking. Since the Virgin Queen was not going to produce a physical heir, she would be, in line with the figure of the phoenix, the heir of herself. (According to Ambrose, who echoes Lactantius, the phoenix "is made heir to its body and its ashes [*sui heres corporis et cineris sui factus*]" [*Expos. Ps.* cxviii.19.13]). Such ratiocination would be her secret response to "The Petition of the Lords" made to Elizabeth I in November 1566 "upon the two great Matters of Marriage and Succession," the petition voicing concern with what would happen "if God should call your Highness without Heir to your Body."[14]

Self-begotten and self-begetting, the phoenix does not resort to mating and the other biological ingredients of "marriage and succession," because it is not a being in, or even of, nature but the being of nature as such. By the same token, Elizabeth I would see herself not as a being in, or of, the political landscape of England but as the being of England as such, which is why, by the way, she could say that she was married to the Realm. Hers is not exactly the position of the absolutist monarch in the style of Louis XIV, *le Roi Soleil* (the Sun King: the solar associations of the phoenix are not fortuitous here)

224 *Chapter 9*

who claimed "*L'État, c'est moi*" (the State is me). If the Virgin Queen *marries* the country of which she is the sovereign, she does not substitute herself for it, opting instead for a rebirth in the spiritual fabric of England. This is what I mean by a cut in "the ligatures between the two types of reproduction," the biological and the spiritual, made by the Elizabethan phoenix.

On Kantorowicz's reading, the unity, unicity, and uniqueness of the phoenix that allow its species to be wholly exhausted in one individual living at a time provided a formula accommodating the mortal and the immortal bodies of theological and political authority figures. The medieval basis for this formula is the decretal of Pope Alexander III (1215), differentiating between the official role (*facta dignitati*) and the person occupying this role (*facta personae*). With reference to the Abbot of Winchester, for instance, it was not necessary to mention the individual name, safely omitting *facta personae* from ordinances and, most crucially, from the degrees of succession and substitution.[15] The principle was that of the replaceability of individuals within any given role, which assumed a life of its own as a "fictitious person" or a "corporation by succession," constructed by jurists.[16] But it will not be until 1245 that the comparison of the fictitious person consisting of a string of individual lives with the phoenix is made in the glossa of Italian canonist Bernard of Parma, who "said that a Dignity—as, for example: Abbot of Winchester—was not the proper name of a person, but only singled a person out; it designated 'a singular, like the *Phoenix*, and [was] likewise an appellative.'"[17]

Kantorowicz provides a wealth of historical documents for the utilization of the phoenix complex in the chapter of his book titled "The King Never Dies," a title that is mirrored in another gloss on the decretal by Pope Alexander III by canonist Damasus, "The Dignity never perishes [*Dignitas nunquam perit*], although individuals die every day."[18] Everything pivots on this "although": instead of insisting on eternity and immortality, the challenge that medieval theological and political thought faced was to reconcile the certainty of individual demise with the ideal perdurance of the occupied position. A familiar instance of the idea of imperishable *dignitas* or *auctoritas* (authority) is the French pronouncement upon the death of Charles VI, more than two centuries after the papal decretal, "*Le roi est mort, vive le roi!*"

"The king is dead, long live the king!" The king both dies and doesn't die, the life of the royal phoenix extended after the death of the previous "specimen," having leapt across the gap of dead time and mended what appears to be discontinuous at the level of physical existence. Where but a comma separates death from life, there is no time for transformative decay to set in and reshape the institution of monarchy from within. The allergy to time and the disgust with decomposition that mark the canonical version of the phoenix complex find their political outlet here. That is why "the successor to the French throne [was] occasionally called *Le petit Phénix.*"[19]

The persons who are at any given time the Abbot of Winchester, the Pope, or the King are utterly replaceable; abbotship, papacy, and kingship continue, unaltered by the change of actual flesh-and-blood individuals who play the official role. Given that the reborn phoenix is both the same as and other than its progenitor (most emblematically in classical texts by Tertullian and Lactantius), ipseity and alterity are now allocated to different registers of being: *facta dignitati* and *facta personae* (the role and its occupant). In a similar mode—deploying the mechanics and machinations of the phoenix complex—uniqueness and seriality are distributed along the two dimensions of what Kant will term *the transcendental aesthetic*, namely space and time: while spatially unique, the Abbot of Winchester is temporally a plurality of individuals occupying this position.[20] Corporation by succession is the creation of the imaginary body of the Abbot of Winchester out of a long line of actual people who served, one after another, as this Abbot.

Later glossators (and postglossators) who interpreted both the original papal decretal and the commentary by Bernard of Parma deepened the phoenix analogy with *dignitas* or *auctoritas.* Kantorowicz cites fourteenth-century Italian jurist Baldus de Ubaldis in this context: "The phoenix is a unique and most singular bird in which the whole kind (*genus*) is conserved in the individual," adding, "The species, of course, was immortal; the individual, mortal."[21] Biological thinking is exploited, deployed toward political legitimization: if the immortality of the species is analogous to the perpetuity of *dignitas*, then the mortality of the individual corresponds to the finite nature of the flesh-and-blood "dignitary." Survival and rebirth hinge upon the condensation of the species in a new specimen, or of an official role in the new incumbent. On this amalgamated biological-political plane,[22] the formal uniqueness and singularity of the phoenix cohabit with the material nondifferentiation among its successive instantiations. *This* mouse and *this* oak tree are ontologically and ethically insignificant compared to the species they are the members of; *this* Abbot of Winchester is so inconsequential, compared to the *dignitas* of abbotship, that his proper name can and should be safely omitted, in keeping with Pope Alexander III decretal. Aristotle's first *ousia* (*this* being) is eclipsed by the second *ousia* (*this* being understood as *that*). The phoenix's singularity justifies its very opposite (nonsingularity, generic character) when considering any given phoenix.

And this is not the sole instance of uniqueness being flipped into what is not unique under the aegis of the phoenix complex. The phoenix's species and the individual are one and the same, but their identity is maintained only in a particular epoch, which is equivalent to the life span of the phoenix. Singularity is self-negated, bifurcating, splitting into two, in an inner contradiction that, unacknowledged as such, becomes the engine in the apparatus of ancient and medieval legal, theological, and political thought. Kantorowicz diagnoses this dualism, without, however, spotting the tensions it foments in relation to the phoenix's traditional descriptions: "The ancient mythographers and apologetics thus clearly recognized that some kind of duality was an essential feature of the Phoenix; but when expanding on that duality, they thought chiefly of the bird's androgynous character."[23]

*

The centrality of rebirth, mediated by the phoenix, in ancient and medieval political philosophy and practice survives well into modernity; under the heading of natality, the concept of birth lends a distinctive flavor to the thought of Hannah Arendt. Although she famously claims that she is not a philosopher, but a political theorist,[24] Arendt gives us a *concept* of birth—that is to say, a philosophical point of access to the phenomenon—and ventures into the area of philosophy of nature. Natality is this concept, formalized in a Latin, or Latinate, word and, at the same time, related to the world of action (rather than labor or work). As she puts it in *The Human Condition*, "Action has the closest connection with the human condition of natality;

the new beginning inherent in birth can make itself felt in the world only because the newcomer possesses the capacity of beginning something anew, that is, of acting. In this sense of initiative, an element of action, and therefore of natality, is inherent in all human activities. Moreover, since action is the political activity par excellence, natality, and not mortality, may be the central category of political, as distinguished from metaphysical, thought."[25]

Natality, then, is not identical to birth; it is the principle "inherent in" birth, which turns out to be the very principle of principle, the arising of a new beginning.[26] Moreover, the principle persists: natality is "the central category of political . . . thought" because in any initiative or initiation of action, the beginning returns, making its comeback in the act of giving birth to oneself (better: to ourselves, in the plural), the act, in which, once again, "natality is inherent." The iterations of natality in a rebirth contribute to its idealization, not only as a concept and a principle but also as a repeatable event, as the matrix of repeatability, irrespective of claims that the unforeseen beginnings it brings forth break through the otherwise stale routines of the natural order. This is the "second birth," which is mentioned later in the text: "With word and deed we insert ourselves into the human world, and this insertion is like a second birth, in which we confirm and take upon ourselves the naked fact of our original physical appearance. This insertion is not forced upon us by necessity, like labor, and it is not prompted by utility, like work. It may be stimulated by the presence of others whose company we may wish to join, but it is never conditioned by them."[27]

Despite railing against metaphysical philosophers, Arendt joins *their* company when she subscribes to the notion of the second birth. Ever since Plato's allegory of the cave, another birth into the world of thinking or being with others unmediated by blood or family ties has been the holy grail of philosophers. (Fedorov is a curious exception here: he, too, advocates another birth in the common work geared toward universal resurrection, but the affective motivation behind it is thoroughly mediated by the filial-parental and fraternal relationships.) Philosophy has been closely linked to the task of self-begetting. Through this other birth—similar to "the other beginning," into which it metamorphosed in Heidegger's thought—human beings consciously and actively assume their unconscious and unchosen

228   *Chapter 9*

first beginning. Heidegger's distinction between world and earth remains intact here too: the second birth is an appearance, "with word and deed," in the human world, in contrast to the emergence of a newborn's body on earth at the event of the first birth. Ultimately, like a phoenix, the speaking and acting "we" gathered in a free association that is unmediated by either necessity or utility gives birth to itself, is born of itself, completing the movement of natality.

The first birth of each happens only once; the second birth of all is not a one-time event, but one that recurs to the power of infinity with every new initiative, action, or gathering. As a *re*birth, the second birth reenacts the first otherwise and anticipates a multiplicity of such reenactments.[28] While it might be tempting to analogize the first and the second births to the first and second natures, Arendt is adamant that what she calls "the human condition"—not least, the unconditioned, free element of this condition—is not to be conflated with human nature.[29] She is right, though not for the reason she herself cites, namely that the existential character of the human condition does not amount to an objectively determinable human essence. It seems to me, rather, that natality as Arendt articulates it approximates nature as such, without the obligatory references to human exceptionalism within the biological order, scattered all over her body of writing.

At the surface of the word itself, which is far from insignificant, both *natura* and *natality* point back to *natus*, the past participle of the verb *nascere* (to be born). Nature is that which is born (and reborn) out of itself, viewed as a totality of generation, growth, decay, and regeneration. Biologically, human beings are born from the other, who is the mother, and have their origin and genetic inheritance split between two progenitors. But since biological birth does not exhaust the sense of natality—since a second birth must be added for humans to emerge in the world through word and deed— origination from the other is not the only horizon of a specifically human beginning. Paradoxically, the second birth, which has all the trappings of a denatured, purely cultural, social, or political arising, is in syntony with nature to the extent that it evinces the subject's (individual or collective) arising out of itself. It moderates the passivity of being born with the active giving of birth, which is action itself. Natality is, in this respect, a mix of

229 *Political Renaissance from the Roman Empire to the Thought of Hannah Arendt*

natura naturata and *natura naturans*, transposed onto the abyssal terrain of the human condition.

Interweaving two kinds of birth, the concept of natality is internally complicated; it gathers into itself the *complex* of Arendt's thought, which in many ways telescopes the *phoenix complex*. Here are just three detailed features in the portrait of its complexity.

1. The first birth is disclosed and overviewed (and even then, only partially so) from the standpoint of the second birth. Hence, the first beginning is not strictly speaking first, and it is largely absent. We interpret, accept, or reject our unwilled and unchosen biological emergence without ever being able to thematize or represent it to ourselves. It is the most idiomatic, idiotic, impenetrable portion of our lives, like a piece of private property that is inseparable from ourselves, from our self-conception. As Arendt writes, "The sacredness of this privacy [of family property in Ancient Greece] was like the sacredness of the hidden, namely, of birth and death, the beginning and the end of the mortals, who, like all living creatures, grow out of and return to the darkness of an underworld."[30] The darkness of the beginning cannot be illuminated by any public act or deed that claims to reinitiate it, freely and together with others. The eidetic light, in which the ideal second birth was supposed to unfold, cannot dispel the obscurity of a messy and wordless emergence. Within the world, the earth is not quite earth: "the darkness of an underworld" is a metaphor for the corpse's burial in the soil, while the dimness of existence in a womb is an analogy for vegetal rootedness and germination. Such analogies and metaphors are deployed to substitute for the impossible representation of the first beginning.

2. The second beginning is also the third, the fourth, and so on, constituted, on the one hand, by repetitions of the absent origin and, on the other, by future iterations. Repeated, it is also, and more significantly, repeatable, idealizable, embracing rebirth both in its content and in its dynamic form.[31] But the change it promises is, itself, changeless. "It is in the nature of the beginning," Arendt writes, "that something new is started which cannot be expected from whatever may have happened

230   *Chapter 9*

before. This character of startling unexpectedness is inherent in all beginnings and in all origins."[32] Formally speaking, if the second beginning is empirically as much as transcendentally repeatable, it is to be expected that the unexpected would recur. More concretely, though, the novelty of each new beginning that is the beginner her- or himself[33] is neutralized the moment it is made to conform to the preexisting structures of the world and urged to behave in rather expected ways. (Mental asylums are, sadly, the institutions meant to deal with truly "startling unexpectedness.")

3. The *capacity* of beginning something anew stresses the potentiality of novelty, as opposed to its actuality. The first birth is to the second as the potential is to the actual, but even the second birth is only potentially an actual beginning. "With each new birth, a new beginning is born into the world, a new world has *potentially* come into being."[34] The potentiality of natality is, potentially, an impotentiality, never to be realized. Nothing guarantees a smooth passage from this potentiality to the actuality of a new world. This world stays the same when it seems that everything is changing, but the inverse is also true: the world is changing when everything seems to remain unaltered. "The fact of natality," as Arendt formulates it, is "that we have all come into the world by being born and that this world is constantly renewed through birth."[35] The world is a phoenix, reborn with each wave of "newcomers," who are themselves reborn in word and deed (*logos* and *praxis*) that supersede their biological birth. Does the capacity to begin, to be a new beginning, not bear any scars of the past? Are Arendt's newborns, newcomers, or natals (as she proposes to rename mortals[36]) equal—potentially or actually—in their capacity to begin? Are they unscathed by the original sin, which, besides its familiar Judeo-Christian connotations, has to do with the very humanity of the human condition? Implicitly, yet obstinately, Arendt insists on the innocence of the first birth and its sublimation in the second. Her natals are, like Elizabeth I, the incarnations of the phoenix—the only creature, who, according to the Jewish tradition, refused to eat the forbidden fruit and who, thanks to this refusal, gained eternal life.[37]

*

231   *Political Renaissance from the Roman Empire to the Thought of Hannah Arendt*

As she reconstructs the Greek understanding of history and its relation to nature, starting with Herodotus, Arendt notes that "his understanding of the task of history—to save human deeds from the futility that comes from oblivion—was rooted in the Greek concept and experience of nature, which comprehended all things that come into being by themselves without assistance from men or gods . . . and therefore are immortal. . . . Aristotle explicitly assures us that man, insofar as he is a natural being and belongs to the species of mankind, possesses immortality; through the recurrent cycle of life, nature assures the same kind of being-forever to things that are born and die as to things that are and do not change."[38]

The cyclical time of nature sets it on the trajectory of the phoenix thanks to a constant rotation and recurrence of birth and death that approximate immortal existence. Human beings participate in the cycle of life at the level of their species-being, giving rise to new generations and burying the old. The Platonic recipe for how finite beings can participate in the infinite (by generating other beings like them) still holds. Yet action—the freest of human endeavors—does not (automatically) fall under this heading; it is, in Arendt's words, in danger of incurring the curse of "futility that comes from oblivion." A deep fissure forms between the two technologies of salvation Plato outlined with reference to Socrates and Diotima in his *Symposium*: the biological pregnancy in the body and the cultural-intellectual pregnancy in the soul, which is supposed to achieve immortality through the works (and, above all, the laws).

The human being, for Arendt, is a tense combination of two temporalities, one of them moving in a circle and the other in a straight line. "The mortality of man," she writes, "lies in the fact that individual life, a *bios* with a recognizable life-story from birth to death, arises out of biological life, *zōē*. This individual life is distinguished from all other things by the rectilinear course of its movement, which, so to speak, cuts through the circular movements of biological life."[39] To be human is to keep trying to square the circle, to reconcile "the circular movements of biological life" with the straight line of biographical consciousness and narrative. Action belongs on this line at a point where it intersects with the circle and puts its own incompatibility

232   *Chapter 9*

with the trajectory of circular movement on display; hence the disruptive character of action in the ambit of daily existence.[40]

With minor variations, Arendt will repeat the same story of circular and rectilinear temporalities in several of her books and even on the pages of the same book. Her writing itself becomes strangely recursive, as it circles back to this simultaneity of merging and being at loggerheads of a circle and a straight line in the being of human beings. So, besides the already cited passages from *Between Past and Future*, in *The Human Condition*, she contrasts animal and divine immortality to human mortality, which is movement "along a rectilinear line in a universe where everything, if it moves at all, moves in a cyclical order."[41] In the same work, she comments that "from the standpoint of nature, the rectilinear movement of man's life-span between birth and death looks like a peculiar deviation from the common natural rule of cyclical movement."[42] In volume 1 of *The Life of the Mind*, Arendt assimilates the two trajectories of time to "sheer change," arguing that "it is the insertion of man with his limited life-span that transforms the continuously flowing stream of sheer change—which we can conceive cyclically as well as in the form of rectilinear motion without ever being able to conceive of an absolute beginning or an absolute end—into time as we know it."[43] And so forth.

Arendt's solution to the problem of time (and especially to the possible futility of action) is the discovery of circularity in the apparently rectilinear sequence of human life from birth to death. The second birth in and through action draws a circle where a straight line should have emanated from birth as a singular, unrepeatable event. Natality is Arendt's way of squaring the circle. With this theoretical gesture, she transposes the phoenix structure of nature's cyclical time of growth, decay, and regeneration onto the time of human history. After the alleged immortality of the species (which is doubtful, to say the least, given the ever-accelerating processes of extinction and species extermination) and the mortality of individual life, rebirth in deed and in speech recovers a supra-individual stratum of existence, albeit in another way, where being in common does not erase but lends the fullness of actual expression to the individual. The political field is a sublimation of

233   *Political Renaissance from the Roman Empire to the Thought of Hannah Arendt*

the biological, its ideal repetition of the event of birth equally modeled on the figure of the phoenix.

Mind you, the only extant mention of the phoenix in Arendt's work is negative, and it touches on the *immediate coincidence* of political and biological spheres, rather than the sublimation of the latter in the former. In her reflections "On the Nature of Totalitarianism," included in *Essays in Understanding*, Arendt chastises "the ideologies of racism and dialectical materialism that transformed Nature and History from the firm soil supporting human life and action into supra-gigantic forces whose movements race through humanity, dragging every individual willy-nilly with them." Both ideologies arrive at "the same 'law' of elimination of individuals for the sake of the process or progress of the species. From the elimination of harmful or superfluous individuals, the result of natural or historical movement rises like the phoenix from its own ashes; but unlike the fabulous bird, this mankind which is the end and at the same time the embodiment of the movement of either History or Nature requires permanent sacrifices, the permanent elimination of hostile or parasitic or unhealthy classes or races in order to enter upon its bloody eternity."[44]

Totalitarian Nature and History preclude action—something that is particularly tragic with regard to history that consists of actions remembered, saved from oblivion, and, therefore, granted a share of immortality, modest as it may be, by analogy with the self-reproduction of the species. Nevertheless, history and nature (as much as Nature and History) course through and establish themselves via bodies and actions, which they cannot purge once and for all. That is why individuals are, at the same time, "harmful or superfluous" and necessary, like the ashes that are the by-products and the building blocks of the phoenix's self-reconstitution. Where Arendt's comparison diverges from the myth of the phoenix, as she is quick to acknowledge, is in the fate of the ashes that are to be endlessly eliminated and sacrificed in a totalitarian assemblage, not incorporated into the renewed existence of the whole. (Given that the logic of the phoenix is sacrificial—better, self-sacrificial—this divergence assumes the air of a common trait, shared by the totalitarian phoenix and its mythical predecessor.) A movement of continual rebirth is thereby upended and transformed into a process of ongoing

234   *Chapter 9*

redeath, notably the elimination and consignment to oblivion of those who would stand in the way of the nearly automatic erection of the historical or biological totality.

The mechanics and machinations of the phoenix's self-reproduction in its natural and historical renditions boil down, for Arendt, to a certain automatism. "No doubt," she concludes in *Between Past and Future*, "human life, placed on the earth, is surrounded by automatic processes—by the natural processes of the earth, which, in turn, are surrounded by cosmic processes, and we ourselves are driven by similar forces insofar as we too are a part of organic nature."[45] The key to the circular (and even the elliptical) iterations of biological and cosmic time is this automatism that makes everything follow a predetermined course, where the end meets and reiterates the beginning. The cycles of capital mimic such movements, as do totalitarian rotations of Nature and History, which Arendt decries. In fact, she finds a good dose of automatism in all processes, "which is why no single act, and no single event, can ever, once and for all, deliver and save a man, or a nation or mankind."[46] That said, acts and events that live up to their names temporarily suspend the automatic workings of the world machine, raising the demand for freedom: their raison d'être is this disruption, which, in the last instance, is always a disruption of circulation, reproduction, or the phoenix's self-reconstitution and a reanimation of life beyond the phoenix complex. "Once man-made, historical processes have become automatic, they are no less ruinous than the natural life process that drives our organism and which in its own terms, that is, biologically, leads from being to non-being, from birth to death."[47]

Guided by the associations of automatism with external determination and unfreedom that are rife in industrial modernity, Arendt forgets the ancient sense of *automaton* as something or someone "self-acting," "self-animated," moving, or learning, or thinking of its own will and accord. This ancient sense, involving freedom and spontaneity, is the exact opposite of the modern notion of automatism, where both the product and the process rely on a preprogrammed set of instructions. Were Arendt to have recalled the semantic and philosophical origins of *automaton* (for instance, in the works of Aristotle), she would have, perhaps, articulated her thought differently: what is at stake is not a clash between free action and predetermined natural,

235 *Political Renaissance from the Roman Empire to the Thought of Hannah Arendt*

historical, social, or political processes but a finer distinction between two types of *automata*. The suspension of circular automatism, be it of nature or of history, is due to a temporary inactivation of its mechanics and machinations, of the mechanism ensuring the self-reproduction, self-replication, and self-replacement of its component parts. But this inactivation is the most intense expression of action, of an *automaton* without *mechanē*, bereft of any means, shorn of the apparatus of execution, of instrumental rationality.

In our terms, we might say that what Arendt wants is to close and not to close the sublimated circle of politics in the second birth we give to ourselves in words and deeds. She wants the phoenix without the complex, or—since she is not so naive as to assume that life without processes and "bad" automatisms would be possible—without the assurance that regeneration will inevitably happen just as it did in the past. Assuming that it did invariably happen in this way, regeneration would be a deadening, a self-ruination of the life process that inherently "leads from being to nonbeing, from birth to death." Though not a fan of Hegel by any stretch of the imagination, Arendt is following a strictly dialectical logic here: death is simultaneously affirmed and denied in the affirmative denial of life that is the process of living.[48]

The postmetaphysical position Arendt defends should have avoided an oversimplified head-on opposition between free spontaneity and predetermined necessity, seeking instead an inner contradiction in automatism (which rehashes the inner contradiction of repetition, pitting the cycles of nature and natural activity against not a straight line but the circle of first and second births).[49] But we do not find this more nuanced approach in her works. "The promise of politics," announced in the title of one of Arendt's books, lies in the capacity of politics to resist the totalitarian drive, determinism, and automatism that are at the antipodes of freedom: "What stands in opposition to all possible predetermination and knowledge of the future is the fact that the world is daily renewed through birth and is constantly dragged into what is unpredictably new by the spontaneity of each new arrival. Only if we rob the newborn of their spontaneity, their right to begin something new, can the course of the world be defined deterministically and predicted."[50] The underside of this diagnosis is that the daily renewal of

236   *Chapter 9*

the world through birth is, in equal measure, its daily (and nightly) renewal through death, the extremes that coincide in the phoenix complex. Moreover, the *fact* of the world's periodic renewal keeps the form constant, and constantly repeated, sent into the future, while the content varies. The beginning of something new by each new arrival is not an actual state of affairs; it is a right, itself formal and abstract. The passage from the first to the second birth is not a smooth-sailing one; empirically speaking, it is aborted in a vast majority of cases. By implication, the promise of politics forged on the basis of the right to bring novelty into the world, if not to birth a new world, remains a formal and abstract vow.

Arendt's astuteness is still evident in her (quasi-dialectical) thesis that each of the two time frames—the circular and the rectilinear—is mediated through the other. The cycle of nature, the cycle that *is* nature grasped in temporal terms, only presents itself as such thanks to a distinction we draw between growth and decay, arranging the two movements in succession and, therefore, in a rectilinear pattern. Arendt writes in *The Human Condition*, "Nature and the cyclical movement into which she forces all living things know neither birth nor death as we understand them. . . . It is only within the human world that nature's cyclical movement manifests itself as growth and decay. Like birth and death, they, too, are not natural occurrences, properly speaking; they have no place in the unceasing, indefatigable cycle in which the whole household of nature swings perpetually. Only when they enter the man-made world can nature's processes be characterized by growth and decay."[51]

According to Arendt's original line of thinking—I would say her *most* original line of thinking—births and deaths conceived as beginnings and ends are not present in nature; they are introduced into its circulation and recycling of the overall becoming of everything retroactively, from the perspective of human beings, who are natals (or mortals). Growing and decaying happen simultaneously and nourish one another, as they do in the case of a tree and the soil, in which it grows and into which decays. The cycle as such comes to visibility for observers moving in a rectilinear fashion: becoming becomes what it is for those partially excluded from its regimen. But this means that nature as the birth, birthing, or self-birthing of everything is not a natural category, since "birth and death . . . are not natural occurrences." And, if there is no birth as such in nature, there is really no nature in nature.

Just as the circle presupposes a straight line and becomes a circle with the mediation of this line, so a rectilinear trajectory presupposes a circle. This trajectory is what has been individuated from the circle, extracted or abstracted from its "automatic" rotations: "Only if we consider nature's products, this tree or this dog, as individual things, thereby already removing them from their 'natural' surroundings and putting them into our world, do they begin to grow and decay."[52] This tree and this dog are as unnatural as birth and death, or growth and decay, because we affix *this* to them (Aristotle's category of first *ousia*); they join us on the line moving from beginning to end by virtue of this singularizing, at once ethical and highly lethal, extraction. Within our world, they are no longer claimed entirely by the earth.

Arendt stays too close to Heidegger to question the worldlessness (or the poverty in the world) of a tree or an animal, that is, to entertain the possibility of *their* worlds, irreducible either to ours or to the elemental fold of the earth. For her, there is only biological life, which is mute and coterminous with death in the perpetual swings of becoming, and "life in its non-biological sense," as "the span of time each man has between birth and death," the life that "manifests itself in action and speech, both of which share with life its essential futility."[53] Through and beyond Heidegger's thought, she wholeheartedly subscribes to the ancient division between the biological *zōē* and the more-than-biological *bios*. The phoenix complex gets off the ground once we revisit biological life from within the sphere of "life in its non-biological sense." The rebirth, with which it seduces us, involves plenty of prior conceptual work, beginning with the birth of birth itself. There is no nature before the inception of the phoenix complex, for the same reason that there is neither birth nor death before the excision of natals and mortals from cycles of anonymous becoming.

*

Arendt's concerns with political foundations and constitutions cannot be decoupled from her take on natality. Having dismissed biological reproduction as the model for continuity (to the point of achieving immortality or

238   *Chapter 9*

participating in the infinite) in politics, Arendt postulates that political foundation is to be thought of "in terms of the re-establishment of a beginning which, as an absolute beginning, remains perpetually shrouded in mystery."[54] If there is any continuity here, it is a continuity in—or across—multiple discontinuities. Every foundation is a refounding devoid of a clearly demarcated origin, a rebirth folded into the very concept of natality, which operates between two births: the first and the second that has no other choice but to carry out an open-ended reconstruction of the first. Rome is, in this sense, not the gold standard and absolute point of reference in constitutional or foundational endeavors; it is the origin of a self-conscious displacement of the origin, of explicitly assuming the task of foundation as the task of tireless refoundation.[55]

In the context of Rome's political self-consciousness, Arendt cites a line from Virgil's Fourth *Eclogue, Magnus ab integro saeclorum nascitur ordo*, "The great cycle of periods is born anew" (4.5).[56] We can easily recognize *annus magnus* (the Great Year) associated with the phoenix's life span in these words, not to mention the theme of rebirth that is central in narratives about this mythic bird. Virgil himself had in mind the reign of Octavian, later known as Augustus, who established the Roman Empire, promising in this inaugural gesture nothing less than the re-institution of an earlier golden age.[57] In the European Renaissance, the phrase (and the idea) was adopted by the Medicis. Among the elaborate temporary structures created for the marriage of Cosimo I de' Medici and Eleonora of Toledo in 1539, there was one that depicted "the auspicious nativity of the most illustrious Duke Cosimo, as the new beginning of a happier age [*como nuouo principio di piu felice secolo*]; this was clearly demonstrated by the architrave, which had in its round a phoenix with these letters: 'The great sequence of ages is born anew [*Magnus ab integro saeclorum nascitur ordo*].'"[58] Later still, in 1782, the design of the Great Seal of the United States, was finalized by Secretary of Congress Charles Thomson, who included on its reverse side the words *Novus ordo seclorum*,[59] from which, in the spirit of nascent modernity, all allusions to rebirth are eliminated. There, as also on the dollar bill, the phoenix was replaced by a pyramid, the symbol of eternity, rather than resurrection.

To return to Arendt: the infinite displacement of the origin drives the no less infinitely expended efforts at its reconstitution. An absent foundation, bespeaking the absence of stability and objectively firm grounds, instigates the movement of ongoing political refounding. The political enterprise mirrors and gives the fullest expression to a conspicuously existential theme of the abyssal experience of human life as distinct from biological vitality, "the notion of life between two absences, before it arrives in birth and after it passes away in death." Such a life is "the lingering between two absences and a sojourn in the realm of errancy."[60] But the first birth and death are also absences that bookend a life seen in the light of autobiography. The repetition of the first birth in the second does not fill a lacuna, does not erase an absence nor convert it into a presence. Instead, this repetition is marshaled against the other absence, that is, death, which is also double: first, a biological cessation of life or disappearance, and, second, social, cultural, or political oblivion. Refounding is remembering, which is yet another leitmotif of Arendt's thought; it is rebirth aiming to neutralize redeath.

Tellingly, cultural history, according to Arendt, follows the same itinerary as political practice. "Far from being new, the phenomenon of re-birth or renaissance, from the fifteenth and sixteenth centuries onward, had dominated the cultural development of Europe and had been preceded by a whole series of minor renascences that terminated the few centuries of what really were 'dark ages,' between the sack of Rome and the Carolingian renaissance. Each of these re-births, consist[ed] in a Revival of Learning."[61] Rebirth is, in this view, a dynamic form of political and cultural existence, albeit a form that is not automatically reproduced but spontaneously implemented in keeping with the freedom of human natality. Nevertheless, the form of the phoenix Arendt is envisioning is conditioned by a determinate context and content—the "development of Europe." Does the rest of the world have the right to be reborn and to revive by the grace of the phoenix of the West? What is remembered, salvaged from death, in this rebirth? If the form of the cultural and political phoenix is molded by its European content, isn't the content that is sifted through it elsewhere, in turn, selectively admitted into and kept out of the form?

240   *Chapter 9*

AFTERWORD
ASHES TO ASHES . . .

"The Cult of the Phoenix," a rather cryptic short story by Jorge Luis Borges, begins with the following lines: "Those who write that the cult of the Phoenix had its origin in Heliopolis, and claim that it derives from the religious restoration that followed the death of the reformer Amenhotep IV, cite the writings of Herodotus and Tacitus and the inscriptions on Egyptian monuments, but they are unaware, perhaps willfully unaware, that the cult's designation as 'the cult of the Phoenix' can be traced back no farther than to Hrabanus Maurus and that the earliest sources (the *Saturnalia*, say, or Flavius Josephus) speak only of 'the People of the Practice' or 'the People of the Secret.'"[1]

In fact, in his magnum opus *De universo* (8.6; *PL* 111.246a-b), the eighth-century Benedictine monk and theologian Hrabanus Maurus lists the phoenix as part of a bestiary, which, in no way pertaining to a *cult*, is but an encyclopedic compendium of different species of animals. What he includes there is limited to a repetition of earlier descriptions of the marvelous bird that is "in the whole world singular and unique [*quod sit in toto orbe singularis et unica*]," that "is called 'phoenix' by the Arabs [*nam Arabes phoenicem vocant*]," and that "when it feels the approach of old age, collects aromatic twigs to construct a nest for itself and, having caught a ray of the sun in its wings, voluntarily sets itself on fire [*voluntarium sibi incendium nutrit*] only to rise from the ashes afterwards." It turns out that Hrabanus Maurus reiterates the words, precisely, of Herodotus and Tacitus and many, many other classical authors transfixed by the phoenix.

Everything, then, begins with a repetition—the repetition of the story of the phoenix and of nature, of the cult (or culture) of the phoenix, of its birth and death. Beginning with repetition, every birth is a rebirth, a renaissance, or a resurrection. Death, too, is redeath. The one who, or that which, is "singular and unique" is replicated, reduplicated, rehearsed at the beginning and in the end, at both its ends. It is and is not "singular and unique." Is this rehearsal the practice that lends "the People of the Practice" their name in Borges's narrative, one that turns out to be synonymous with "the cult of the Phoenix"? What do its members practice? Rebirth and redeath? Is this hypothesis really so far-fetched in light of the sexual innuendos on the subject of the cult scattered throughout Borges's short text?

The phoenix complex absorbs repetition in its own content and in its dynamic form. From the very depths of our unconscious, it reassures us that repetition will keep repeating itself, that the combined chamber of the present and the past it creates will reverberate with echoes of the future. (Borges again: "It is odd that the Secret [of the Phoenix, MM] did not die out long ago; but in spite of the world's vicissitudes, in spite of wars and exoduses, it does, in its full awesomeness, come to all the faithful. Someone has even dared to claim that by now it is instinctive."[2]) This reassurance motivates us to live and it prevents us from living; it lulls us into a near certainty that finitude—our own and that of the world—is inexhaustible, its *no more* mutating into *still more* (of the same). It motivates us to live on the condition that we would not cherish nor so much as pay attention to the finite in its finitude.

The mechanics and the machinations of the phoenix complex convert finite beings into mere shells for the invaluable molten kernel of infinity, of infinite replicability that overflows them, their reproductive potential, their energies, pleasures, or knowledges rushing outward and into the future in a steady stream. Finite existence thus appears under the aspect of nonidentity, its noncoincidence with itself. Since, untamable and uncontainable, infinity bursts out of the finite, there is no need to exert any force in order to extract this kernel, as, say, in the case of natural gas, coal, or petroleum stored beneath the surface of the earth. If anything, the infinite, welling over the edges of the finite, is taken to be a sign of communion with the divine, of the limited way in which mortals can participate in immortality. Despite—or thanks to—its free outpouring, the overflow is harnessed to the perpetuation of what is extraneous to the finite beings themselves. It matters little if exteriority refers to the infinity they are striving toward or the economic, political, or metaphysical systems they are a part of; truth be told, the conflation of diverse things that occupy the placeholder of exteriority is advantageous for systems that tie their own fate to the infinite or the immortal. (I harbor no illusions: the same mechanics and machinations also apply to my works, including the book you are now reading.)

An antidote to this pernicious perspective is for the finite to be appreciated in its finitude, that is to say, for nature, the world, the beings populating it, and being itself to be affirmed and valued as nonrenewable. The change of perspective, as theoretical as it is practical, does not spell out a return to the strict confines of identities, beyond which it would be impossible to venture. To some extent, this gesture repeats a certain program Jean-Luc Nancy has outlined in the collection *Finite Thinking*, where what he terms "finite thinking" is "not a thinking of relativity, which implies the Absolute, but a thinking of *absolute finitude*: absolutely detached from all infinite and senseless completion or achievement. [It is] not a thinking of limitation, which implies the unlimitedness of a beyond, but a thinking of the limit as that on which, infinitely finite, existence arises, and to which it is exposed."[3]

With the help of absolute finitude (or else, finite finitude, albeit without apocalyptic or eschatological connotations: the apocalyptic brooding about the end and the damnation of everyone and everything in existence often betrays *the end of a particular mode of thinking incapable of imagining the existence and viability of other such modes*) it might be possible to put the phoenix complex to rest, to untie its bonds and double or triple binds. It might be possible, finally, to get a sense of singularity, beyond that intimated by the "singular and unique" phoenix, in the finite being that corresponds to a finite thinking, "not a thinking of the abyss and of nothingness," in the continuation of Nancy's line of thought, "but a thinking of the un-grounding of being: of this 'being,' the only one, whose *existence* exhausts all its substance and all its possibility."[4] I cannot think of a stronger way of putting it: "This 'being' . . . whose *existence* exhausts all its possibility." It is the existence that

243   *Afterword*

exhausts all the possibility of a being that makes this being unique, "the only one," or, in a negative vein, nonrenewable. A uniqueness the phoenix and its associated complex could not have dreamt of.

How to conceive of nature in the light of absolute finitude, nonrenewable existence, and exhausted or exhaustible possibility? Such a nature would be one in which birth would not be overshadowed by rebirth in a mechanic (and a broken, to boot) cycle promising infinite repetition. Only then will each birth, each being that is born (*nato*) and is, therefore, natural, be an event, a gift, a unique instance of grace free from a productive or reproductive necessity. The notion of nature as grace dovetails with the Hindu sense of *mokṣa* or *mukti* signaling liberation from the cycles of redeath and rebirth on the wheel of *saṃsāra*. But it also bears saying that the concept of nonrenewable nature, free of the nonidentity that the phoenix complex confers on it—indeed, the concept of nature *as* nonrenewability and the nonrenewable destiny of nature's conceptualization—this concept becomes possible, in its multiple senses, against the horizon of historico-environmental nonrenewability, expressed in the currently ongoing sixth mass extinction, the depletion of fossil sources of energy, ocean acidification, the intensifying droughts and forest fires, the impoverishment and erosion of topsoils around the world, deforestation and desertification.

In light of objections to renewability, it is worthwhile to take a moment to consider what this word, rarely (if ever) treated as a concept, actually means. In fact, renewability is a highly condensed form of the phoenix complex, through which the old is rendered new *again*: renewed or renovated, rejuvenated or reinvigorated. Above all, it is supposed to contain the possibility of potentially infinite reinvigorations in a future, indefinitely repeating the past (as *re-*, "again" is a very specific mode of connecting the future to the past). Renewability is replaceability that overcomes time constraints, that substitutes for an aging, an old, or a dying being a new version of that being, *as though* old age and death had no effect. It is, more than the replacement of one being with another, the replacement of this being—"the only one," as Nancy has it—with the possibility of this being, inexhaustible in the existence of particular beings.

244   *Afterword*

Renewability also adapts the phoenix complex to the logic of resources, insofar as whatever or whoever is renewable is restocked without any glitches or delays, the storehouse of nature continually filled with fresh supplies of the same. The possibility that seduces us in the phoenix complex is not even existential; it is not ensconced in the finitude of actual existence but unfastened from the finite as finite and made fit for ledgers that, besides keeping track of the current stockpiles (of raw materials, energy resources, and so forth), prognosticate their steady abundance. Renewability bets on the reproducibility of life as the foundation for the replaceability of the living. Conversely, finitude implies, far from the secular ideology of the end of times and universal damnation, the possibility of life's reinvention—rather than its reproduction—amid the planetary trauma of extinction. For, doesn't evolutionary evidence suggest that in the aftermath of each mass extinction and catastrophic collapse of biodiversity there has been an equally spectacular resurgence of new life-forms?

Neither fatalism nor nihilism, a philosophy of nature beyond the phoenix complex (including the fast and the slow lanes it allots to rebirth, as well as the discourses and practices of renewability) is the only one adequate to the challenges of the twenty-first century. It commits the body of thought emblazoned with the phoenix to the ground, as *The Book of Common Prayer* stipulates for burial rites—"earthe to earthe, ashes to ashes, dust to dust"— but shorn of the "sure and certein hope of the resurrection to eternall lyfe."[5] This philosophy discovers a nature where birth does not dissolve in the routines of rebirth, where generations are not links in the chain of regeneration, where life emerges in its fragility, in its tenuousness as much as its strange tenacity. Although nonrenewability is not necessarily an empirical feature of life-forms, species, ecosystems, or lines of biological inheritance, it is the limit (not unlike the one invoked by Nancy), from which they receive their sense.

At the limit of nonrenewability, an apt question to raise is how to transform the negative finitude of extinction and the exhaustion of the earth and its resources into the positive finitude of existence. The self-reinvention of life in what Henri Bergson calls "creative evolution" is one aspect of this budding positivity. In turn, the ethical ramifications of a philosophy of nature rid of the phoenix complex are many, and every single one of them dares respond, in its own fashion, to this question. For example, the "renewable" sources of energy are not a better option than the "nonrenewable" sources not only because, often enough, the former damage the environment more than the latter (as in the case of biodiesel derived through the cultivation of mono-cultures in recently deforested areas, depletion of the soil, and massive com-bustion), but also because the certainty of their renewability, projecting the current state into the future, is false. Further, practices that cherish and preserve ecological assemblages should be justified not with respect to "our debt to future generations" but with reference to our debt to those now par-ticipating in the creation of these assemblages, including ourselves. Finally, and most importantly, care for the finite in its finitude pays extreme atten-tion not to the potential, which finite being contains, but to what and how it dynamically *is*. Ethical action needs no reasons that exceed its recipient, and least of all does it need to rely on the inner excess of the future, of the recipient's fecundity or renewability. Practiced beyond the matrix of the phoenix complex, ethics meets the world as it is, refusing to be blinded by the shimmer of the heavenly or earthly world to come; it encounters being on the brink of nonbeing and draws sense from this encounter.

246   *Afterword*

Notes

PREFACE

1. For a defense of a certain notion of essence, consult my "Musings on Vegetality," in *Botanical Speculations: Plants in Contemporary Art*, ed. Giovanni Aloi (Newcastle upon Tyne: Cambridge Scholars, 2021), pp. 19–27. For a defense of the phenomenological notion of truth, refer to my "Betrayal: A Philosophy," *Research in Phenomenology* 50 (2020): pp. 79–98.

2. This is not a sheer coincidence: despite their oppositional framing, nature and spirit presuppose one another, as Hegel showed, without necessarily drawing the right conclusions from the insight he stumbled upon.

3. Timothy Morton, *Ecology without Nature: Rethinking Environmental Aesthetics* (Cambridge, MA: Harvard University Press, 2007), p. 1.

4. Lorraine Daston, *Against Nature* (Cambridge, MA: MIT Press, 2019), p. 7.

5. Daston, *Against Nature*, p. 13.

6. For an antidote, consult Hans Jonas, *The Phenomenon of Life: Toward a Philosophical Biology* (Evanston, IL: Northwestern University Press, 2001).

7. R. G. Collingwood, *The Idea of Nature* (Oxford: Oxford University Press, 1945), p. 43.

8. In a more restricted sense, Elizabeth Spragins uses the term *necroepistemology* in her recent book, *A Grammar of the Corpse: Necroepistemology in the Early Modern Mediterranean* (New York: Fordham University Press, 2022).

9. William Arthur Heidel, "*Peri Phuseos*: A Study of the Conception of Nature among the Pre-Socratics," *Proceedings of the American Academy of Arts and Sciences* 45, no. 4: (1909): p. 129. In this, it might not be so different from all other materials processed by the cognitive machinery of understanding.

10. In turn, many of the contemporary negative reactions to nature are rejecting the largely Latin or Latinate heritage of this concept, without touching on its older and more heterogeneous layers.

11. The distinction of note here is more subtle than a banal contrast between darkness and light. Whereas, designated as *phusis*, nature is awash in active verbal connotations (it *loves to hide*: two verbs), philosophy falls on the substantive side (*a love* of *wisdom*: two nouns combined). Nature and philosophy, then, embody two forms of energy—activity and actuality—united around a double hinge—love/to love and that which hides/to hide. The task of articulating them is none other than the endeavor to reunite the cleaved halves of energy, emitted by love and by hiding.

12. F. W. J. Schelling, *First Outline of a System of the Philosophy of Nature*, trans. Keith R. Peterson (Albany: SUNY Press, 2004), p. 14.

13. This is essentially what Engels says in his *Dialectics of Nature*: "The metaphysical conception has become impossible in natural science owing to the very development of the latter." Friedrich Engels: *Dialectics of Nature*, Karl Marx and Friedrich Engels, Collected Works, vol. 25 (New York: International Publishers, 1987), p. 313.

14. Gilles Deleuze and Felix Guattari, *What Is Philosophy?* trans. Hugh Tomlinson and Graham Burchell (New York: Columbia University Press, 1994), p. 5.

15. Reiner Schürmann, *Broken Hegemonies*, trans. Reginald Lilly (Bloomington: Indiana University Press, 2003), p. 514.

16. An earlier version of this preface and the conclusion was published under the title "Is a Philosophy of Nature Still Tenable?" in *The Harvard Review of Philosophy*, XXIX, 2022.

CHAPTER 1

1. Michael Marder, *Pyropolitics in the World Ablaze* (Lanham, MD: Rowman & Littlefield, 2020), p. 149.

2. Likewise, this term alludes to a short story by Jorge Luis Borges, titled "La secta del Fénix." Jorge Luis Borges, "The Cult of the Phoenix," in *Collected Fictions*, trans. Andrew Hurley (London: Penguin Books, 1999), pp. 171–173, which will be discussed in the conclusion of the present study.

3. Heraclitus, frag. 90, "All things are an equal exchange for fire and fire for all things [*puros te antamoibē ta panta kai pur apantōn*], as goods are for gold and gold for goods," in G. S. Kirk and J. E. Raven, *The Presocratic Philosophers: A Critical History with a Selection of Texts* (Cambridge: Cambridge University Press, 1963), p. 199.

4. Gaston Bachelard, *The Psychoanalysis of Fire*, trans. Alan Ross (Boston: Beacon Press, 1964), p. 12.

5. Bachelard, *Psychoanalysis of Fire*, p. 16.

6. Pedro Sanchez et al., "Alternatives to Slash and Burn," in *Slash-and-Burn Agriculture: The Search for Alternatives*, ed. Cheryl Palm et al. (New York: Columbia University Press, 2005), p. 5.

7. The expression "green phoenix" was used by Paul Lurquin in *The Green Phoenix: A History of Genetically Modified Plants* (New York: Columbia University Press, 2001) and by William

Allen in *Green Phoenix: Restoring the Tropical Forests of Guanacaste, Costa Rica* (Oxford: Oxford University Press, 2003). It also serves as the title for a 1972 novel by Thomas Burnett Swann.

8. François Ruf and Frederic Lançon, "Innovations in the Indonesian Upland," in *From Slash and Burn to Replanting: Green Revolutions in the Indonesia Uplands*, ed. François Ruf and Frederic Lançon (Washington, DC: The World Bank, 2004), p. 2.

9. Spanish: "La esperanza es lo último que muere"; German: "die Hoffnung stirbt zuletzt"; Russian: "Надежда умирает последней"; Portuguese: "A esperança é a última que morre."

10. Sigmund Freud, *The Interpretation of Dreams*, trans. and ed. James Starchey (New York: Basic Books, 2010), p. 468.

11. All references to Spinoza's works rely on Baruch Spinoza, *Spinoza: Complete Works*, ed. Michael L. Morgan (Indianapolis: Hackett, 2002). Henceforth, abbreviated as *CW*.

12. Carl Jung calls their figural dimension "archetypes."

13. Not surprisingly, this is Freud's interpretation of the phoenix. Already the bird that feeds on the liver of chained Prometheus is understood in terms of masculine desire, with liver being the traditional "seat of passion." "A short step further brings us to the phoenix, the bird which, as often as it is consumed by fire, emerges rejuvenated once more, and which probably bore the significance of a penis revivified after its collapse rather than, and earlier than, that of the sun setting in the glow of evening and afterwards rising once again." Sigmund Freud, "The Acquisition and Control of Fire," in *New Introductory Lectures on Psycho-Analysis and Other Works*, standard ed., vol. 22 (1932–1936), ed. James Starchey et al. (London: Vintage Classics, 2001), pp. 190–191.

14. "The rising sun is, moreover, very often compared to a bird. In Egypt, the god Atum is called "the great Phoenix who lives in Heliopolis" and prides himself on "having placed the crown of feathers on his own head." Gilbert Durand, *The Anthropological Structures of the Imaginary*, trans. Margaret Sankey and Judith Hatten (Brisbane: Boombana Publications, 1999), p. 145. See also Roel van den Broek, *The Myth of the Phoenix According to Classical and Early Christian Traditions* (Leiden: Brill, 1972), p. 15. For a more recent cultural-intellectual (and popularized) history of the phoenix, including its derivation from the Egyptian *bennu* and relation to the Chinese *fenghuang*, refer to Joseph Nigg, *The Phoenix: An Unnatural Biography of a Mystical Beast* (Chicago: University of Chicago Press, 2016). *Bennu* articulates the primordial mound, *Benben*, with the the watery abyss *Nu*, whence it rises. The mound is revered as the dwelling place of the god Atum.

15. Porphyry, *On Aristotle's Categories*, trans. Steven K. Strange (London: Bloomsbury, 2014), p. 68.

16. Here, Phoenix is the name of a genus comprising fourteen species. Refer to Reem A. Al-Alawi et al., "Date Palm Tree (*Phoenix dactylifera* L.): Natural Products and Therapeutic Options," *Frontiers in Plant Science* (May 2017), doi: 10.3389/fpls.2017.00845. In the Egyptian tradition, the bird *bennu* is also associated with a sacred tree—the tree of life, *ished*, or the evergreen persea (*Mimusops schimperi*).

17. Refer to Nigg, *The Phoenix*, p. 7.

18. In this respect, Roel van den Broek notes that "the homonymy of phoenix and palm caused confusion even in Classical times," in *Myth of the Phoenix*, p. 57.

19. Along with the daily sunrise, the cycle of the seasons, and the germination of seeds, among other things, the phoenix supplies one of the emblematic "proofs" of resurrection (*insignia resurrectionis*) in Clement of Rome, Tertullian, Ambrose of Milan, Zeno of Verona, and Cyril of Jerusalem.

20. Laurence Gosserez expresses such astonishment in the section of his introductory chapter, "The Phoenix and Time, between Reality and Fiction" ["Le phénix, le temps et l'éternité"], in *Le Phénix et son autre: Poétique d'un mythe des origines au XVI siècle*, ed. Laurence Gosserez (Rennes: Presses Universitaires de Rennes, 2013), p. 37.

21. In this respect, it bears mentioning that eco-phenomenology implicitly positions itself at antipodes to the phoenix complex. For the roots of this alternative mode of relation to ecology and nature, see Hans Jonas, *The Phenomenon of Life: Toward a Philosophical Biology* (Evanston, IL: Northwestern University Press, 2001). More recent studies in this vein include *Rethinking Nature: Essays in Environmental Philosophy*, ed. Bruce V. Foltz and Robert Frodeman (Bloomington: Indiana University Press, 2004); works on Merleau-Ponty, such as Ted Toadvine, *Merleau-Ponty's Philosophy of Nature* (Evanston, IL: Northwestern University Press, 2009) or David Morris, *Merleau-Ponty's Developmental Ontology* (Evanston, IL: Northwestern University Press, 2018); and collections on ecology and deconstruction, such as Matthias Fritsch, Philippe Lynes, and David Wood, eds., *Eco-Deconstruction: Derrida and Environmental Philosophy* (New York: Fordham University Press, 2018).

22. We will explore this "highway" in chapter 2 of this book.

23. Due to the intricacies of the phoenix's sexuation (and, at times, asexual nature), I will alternate the use of pronouns "she," "he," and "it" throughout this text, unless a particular author under discussion insists on one of these pronouns. For a detailed discussion of the phoenix's "uncertain sex," see Françoise Lecocq, "Le sexe incertain du phénix : De la zoologie à la théologie," in *Le Phénix et son autre: Poétique d'un mythe des origines au XVI siècle*, ed. Laurence Gosserez (Rennes : Presses Universitaires de Rennes, 2013), pp. 187–210.

24. G. W. F. Hegel, *Philosophy of Nature: Encyclopedia of the Philosophical Sciences*, pt. 2, trans. A. V. Miller (Oxford: Oxford University Press, 2004), p. 305.

25. According to Gosserez, "*le symbolisme du phénix est . . . lié à la renaissance de la végétation lors des crues du Nil* [the symbolism of the phoenix . . . is tied to the rebirth of vegetation after the floods of the Nile]." Gosserez, "Le phénix, le temps et l'éternité," p. 27.

26. Michael Marder, *The Philosopher's Plant: An Intellectual Herbarium* (New York: Columbia University Press, 2014), p. 179.

27. Although the sunray is a classical phallus replacement, in Tzetzes we find a rather castrated version of the phallic substitute that retains only one of the two main powers of solar fire, namely heat. The absence of the other power—light—from this description removes the

regenerative impetus from the sphere of visibility and preserves the chthonic character of rebirth through decay.

28. Kirk and Raven, *The Presocratic Philosophers*, p. 199.

29. Like the oriental phoenix, the Egyptian *bennu* is a "star-bird," *astre-oiseau*, replete with a "cosmic and divine dimension [*une dimension cosmique et divine*]." Gosserez, "Le phénix, le temps et l'éternité," p. 27.

30. Timothy Mousseau et al., "Highly Reduced Mass Loss Rates and Increased Litter Layer in Radioactively Contaminated Areas" *Oekologia* 175 (2014): pp. 429–437.

31. V. I. Yoschenko et al., "Resuspension and Redistribution of Radionuclides during Grassland and Forest Fires in the Chernobyl Exclusion Zone: Part I. Fire Experiments" *Journal of Environmental Radioactivity* 86, no. 2 (2006): pp. 143–163.

32. van den Broek, *Myth of the Phoenix*, p. 205.

33. Thomas of Cantimpré expresses the same basic idea in book 17 of his *Liber de natura rerum*, pp. xlv, 8–10. Having built for itself "a nest-like altar [*altare quasi nidum*]" atop a beautiful tree, the phoenix whips up a solar storm with its wings, creating an aureole around itself and casting the sun's heat down to the nest, which is thus ignited: "*fervidos solis orbes alarum agitatione in se concitans super struem ruit et solis ardore accensis aromatibus ipsa partier accensa comburitur.*"

34. In its contemporary configuration, the technology of artefacts claims for itself the status of a secular technology of salvation.

35. Bernard Stiegler, *Technics & Time I: The Fault of Epimetheus*, trans. Richard Beardsworth and George Collins (Stanford: Stanford University Press, 1998), p. 142.

36. For more on this theme, refer to Michael Marder, *Dump Philosophy: A Phenomenology of Devastation* (London: Bloomsbury, 2020).

37. ——. "Ageing." *United Nations: Global Issues*, 2019. https://www.un.org/en/global-issues /ageing

38. See Hegel, *Philosophy of Nature*, p. 106.

39. Hildegard von Bingen, *Hildegardis Bingensis Epistolarium*, pt. 2, XCI-CCLr, ed. L. Van Acker, Corpus Christianorum, Continuatio Mediaevalis, vol. 91A (Turnhout: Brepols, 1993), p. 484.

40. Paul Guyer and Allen Wood's English translation of Kant's *Critique of Pure Reason* gives this example in a footnote. Refer to Immanuel Kant, *Critique of Pure Reason (The Cambridge Edition of the Works of Immanuel Kant)*, ed. and trans. Paul Guyer and Allen W. Wood (Cambridge: Cambridge University Press, 1999), p. 264.

41. Frank Heynick, *Jews and Medicine: An Epic Saga* (Hoboken, NJ: Ktav, 2002), p. 238.

42. In a later passage in *De generatione animalium*, Aristotle writes, "Those animals which are formed as a result of the copulation of animals of the same kind, themselves generate in turn

after their own kind; those, however, which arise not from living animals but from putrescent matter [*ek sēpomenēs tēs hulēs*], although they generate, produce something that is different in kind, and the product is neither male nor female" (715b).

43. In Portuguese, sunrise retains a literal trace of rebirth: *o nascer do sol*, "the birth of the sun."

44. This last designation may be found in Gosserez, "Le phénix, le temps et l'éternité," p. 44.

45. van den Broek, *The Myth of the Phoenix*, pp. 151ff.

46. A version of chapter 1 was published as an essay titled "The Phoenix Complex" in the special issue 22(2) of *CR: New Centennial Review* on "(In)Finite Ecologies."

CHAPTER 2

1. The replaceability of speakers, who inherit arguments from others, is a common strategy Plato resorts to, for example, in *Philebus*, where Protarchus steps in to flesh out the thesis of Philebus concerning the goodness of pleasure for living beings. Performatively, Plato implements in his own philosophical practice the very principle that the characters are discussing. Nonetheless, the structure of the relation Socrates/Diotima as played out in *Symposium* is not only that of *supplanting* but also that of *supplementing*. According to Frisbee Sheffield, "Diotima embodies the euporetic aspect of *eros* which transcends the limitations of a mortal, deficient, nature," represented by Socrates. Frisbee C. C. Sheffield, *Plato's* Symposium: *The Ethics of Desire* (Oxford: Oxford University Press, 2009), p. 67.

2. One exception to this general rule is the warrior Er, from a myth believed to be original to Plato and narrated at the end of *The Republic*. Er is killed during battle, his body staying uncorrupted on the battlefield for eleven days. On the twelfth day, "at the moment of his funeral, as he lay upon the pyre [*epi tē pura keinomenos*], he revived, and after coming to life [*anabious*] related what, he said, he had seen in the world beyond" (614b). Although Er is not actually burned, the position of his corpse on a funereal pyre, its incorruptibility, and its subsequent revival are evocative of the myth of the phoenix. And although he comes back to life in the same shape as before (as does the phoenix), his narrative revolves around the transformations of vitality; around the cyclicality of life, death, and a return to life; and around the allotment of life's shapes to various souls that return in the guise of the other, in a variety of animal forms. For more on the myth of Er, consult Claudia Baracchi, "Animals and Angels: The Myth of Life as a Whole in *Republic* 10," in *Plato's Animals: Gadflies, Horses, Swans, and Other Philosophical Beasts*, ed. Jeremy Bell and Michael Naas (Bloomington: Indiana University Press, 2015), pp. 209–224.

3. Of course, in sexual reproduction, qualitative novelty arises from new genetic combinations, since there are two (and now, with cutting-edge reproductive technologies, potentially more than two) progenitors, rather than one.

4. See Stella Sandford, "'All Human Beings Are Pregnant, Both in Body and in Soul': The Bisexual Imaginary in Plato's *Symposium*," in *Embodied Selves*, ed. Stella Gonzalez-Arnal, Gill Jagger, and Kathleen Lennon (Basingstoke: Palgrave, 2012), p. 56.

5. The semantic provenance of the word I am translating as "harmonious ordering," *diakosmēsis*, is the verb *kosmeo*, from which *kosmos* also derives. Claudio D. Conenna and Kyriaki Tsoukala, "Ethic and Ornament in the Modern and Contemporary Age," in *Intersections of Space and Ethos*, ed. Kyriaki Tsoukala, Nikolaos-Ion Terzoglou, and Charikleia Pantelidou (London: Routledge, 2015), p. 41. Connoting adornment, harmony, a good order, *diakosmēsis* is directly linked to beauty, which, for Diotima, is the universal object of love. The shining, indeed fiery, nature of the ornament-order that is the Greek *kosmos* places it in the vicinity of the phoenix, as we will see in the next chapter.

6. Edward Cohen, *The Athenian Nation* (Princeton: Princeton University Press, 2000), pp. 38–39.

7. Maria A. Liston and Susan I. Rotroff, "Babies in the Well: Archaeological Evidence for Newborn Disposal in Hellenistic Greece," in *The Oxford Handbook of Childhood and Education in the Classical World*, ed. Judith Evans Grubbs, Tim Parkin, and Roslynne Bell (Oxford: Oxford University Press, 2013), p. 77.

8. Roel van den Broek, *The Myth of the Phoenix According to Classical and Early Christian Traditions* (Leiden: Brill, 1972), p. 72. See *Timaeus* 39c-d. In the classical world, there was no consensus regarding the life span of the phoenix, which, nevertheless, was an important issue. The earliest extant mention of the phoenix by Hesiod focuses exclusively on its longevity and the exact life span. Refer to Sister Mary Francis McDonald, "Phoenix Redivivus," *Phoenix* 14, no. 4 (Winter 1960): p. 187.

9. In Portuguese, the same word is used for "new" and "young": *novo / nova*.

10. Refer to Joseph Nigg, *The Phoenix: An Unnatural Biography of a Mystical Beast* (Chicago: University of Chicago Press, 2016), pp. 61ff and van den Broek, *The Myth of the Phoenix*, pp. 27ff.

11. Nigg, *The Phoenix*, pp. 19ff. For more on *fenghuang*, consult chapter 7 of the present study.

12. W. Carl Rufus and Hsing-Chih Tien, *The Soochow Astronomical Chart* (Ann Arbor: University of Michigan Press, 1945), p. 5.

13. The perfect number is a geometric number, divisible without remainder and computed with the help of "the smallest numbers with which the theorem of Pythagoras can be proved" (van den Broek, *The Myth of the Phoenix*, p. 99).

14. As John Sallis puts it, "Timaeus' description of *poiēsis* (making, fabricating, production) brings to light its mimetic structure. In fabricating something, the maker looks to the model or paradigm (*paradeigma*) in order to form the product, to fashion its look and its capability, in such a way that it looks like the paradigm and has the capacity for whatever functions belong to something with such a look. Looking in advance to the paradigm, the maker gives the work the same look." John Sallis, *Chorology: On Beginning in Plato's* Timaeus (Bloomington: Indiana University Press, 2020), p. 51.

15. "Time imitates eternity and circles round according to number [*chronou tauta aiōna te mimoumenou kai kat' arithmon kukloumenou gegonen eidē*]" (*Timaeus* 38b).

253   *Notes*

16. van den Broek, *The Myth of the Phoenix*, p. 43.

17. There are many reasons for discussing Levinas side by side with Plato. One of them is that the former thinker characterized the project of his *Totality and Infinity* as "a return to Platonism." Quoted in Francisco J. Gonzalez, "Levinas Questioning Plato on Eros and Maieutics," in *Levinas and the Ancients*, ed. Brian Schroeder and Silvia Benso (Bloomington: Indiana University Press, 2008), p. 40.

18. As Stella Sanford puts it, in Levinas's works, "each time fecundity is said to overflow its purely biological signification, the biological origin of the concept is nevertheless affirmed." Stella Sanford, "Masculine Mothers? Maternity in Levinas and Plato," in *Feminist Interpretations of Emmanuel Levinas*, ed. Tina Chanter (University Park: Pennsylvania State University Press, 2001), p. 189].

19. Emmanuel Levinas, *Totality and Infinity: An Essay on Exteriority*, trans. Alphonso Lingis (Pittsburgh: Duquesne University Press, 1969), p. 267[299].

20. Levinas, *Totality and Infinity*, p. 268[301].

21. Levinas, *Totality and Infinity*, p. 284[317].

22. Levinas, *Totality and Infinity*, p. 282[314].

23. Levinas, *Totality and Infinity*, p. 268[301].

24. Levinas, *Totality and Infinity*, p. 268[300].

25. Levinas, *Totality and Infinity*, p. 277[310].

26. Claire Elise Katz adds that Levinas "writes from the position of a Jew—specifically, a Jewish man." Claire Elise Katz, *Levinas, Judaism, and the Feminine: The Silent Footsteps of Rebecca* (Bloomington: Indiana University Press, 2003), p. 71.

27. I mean the Oedipus and the Electra complexes.

28. Levinas, *Totality and Infinity*, pp. 278–279[311].

29. Levinas, *Totality and Infinity*, p. 269[301].

30. Levinas, *Totality and Infinity*, p. 272[306], translation slightly modified.

31. Emmanuel Levinas, *Otherwise Than Being, or Beyond Essence* (Pittsburgh: Duquesne University Press, 1973), p. 13[29].

32. Emmanuel Levinas, *On Escape*, trans. Bettina Bergo (Stanford: Stanford University Press, 2003).

33. Levinas, *Otherwise Than Being*, p. 56[95].

34. Levinas confirms this line of thinking later on in the book: "What can it [the passivity of a recurrence] be but a substitution of me for the others? It is, however, not an alienation, because the other in the same is my substitution for the other through responsibility, for which I am summoned as someone irreplaceable." Levinas, *Otherwise Than Being*, p. 114. Again, the sense of responsibility and of response as *t'shuvah* is paramount here.

35. Levinas, *Otherwise Than Being*, pp. 110–111[175].

36. Levinas, *Otherwise Than Being*, p. 57[95].

37. Levinas, *Otherwise Than Being*, p. 52[88].

38. Levinas, *Otherwise Than Being*, p. 54[91].

39. Levinas, *Otherwise Than Being*, pp. 75–76[121].

40. But *mediation* is not to be conflated with the middle, here or elsewhere!

41. Levinas, *Otherwise Than Being*, p. 105[165].

42. Emmanuel Levinas, "Enigma and Phenomenon," in *Emmanuel Levinas: Basic Philosophical Writings*, ed. Adriaan Peperzak, Simon Critchley, and Robert Bernasconi (Bloomington: Indiana University Press, 1996), p. 77.

43. Emmanuel Levinas, *Entre Nous: Thinking-of-the-Other*, trans. Michael Smith and Barbara Harshav (New York: Columbia University Press, 1998), p. 88.

44. Emmanuel Levinas, *Nine Talmudic Readings*, trans. Annette Aronowicz (Bloomington: Indiana University Press, 1990), p. 187[165]

45. van den Broek, *The Myth of the Phoenix*, pp. 59ff. The reference to sand (an inorganic, loose multiplicity, containing, among other things, remnants of past life) harks back to the blessing of Abraham, whose issue will be as numerous as the stars in the sky or sand on the seashore (Genesis 22:17). The context is extremely important here: the luxuriance of biological reproduction, with which God blesses Abraham, is a reward for his unconditional obedience in heeding God's command to sacrifice his only son, Isaac. We have the logic of the phoenix in reverse in this story: by agreeing to sacrifice the future, rather than the past or a life nearly at its limit, Abraham gains a wider foothold in that future.

46. Levinas, *Nine Talmudic Readings*, p. 188[165].

47. Levinas, *Entre Nous*, pp. 92–93.

48. Emmanuel Levinas, *Difficult Freedom: Essays on Judaism*, trans. Sean Hand (Baltimore: Johns Hopkins University Press, 1997), p. 53[89].

49. Levinas, *Difficult Freedom*, p. 263[391].

50. Levinas, *Difficult Freedom*, p. 263[391], translation lightly modified.

51. Levinas, *Difficult Freedom*, p. 262[390].

CHAPTER 3

1. Roel van den Broek, *The Myth of the Phoenix According to Classical and Early Christian Traditions* (Leiden: Brill, 1972), p. 144. As van den Broek notes, "In the later symbolism the phoenix was the paramount symbol of the fate of the soul after death" (p. 145). The same idea is echoed in the *Eclogues* of Asonius (Bk. 7). This is also the myth that Plato recasts in his own manner in Book 10 of *The Republic*, narrating the story of Er.

2. On this point, consult Jean Hubaux and Maxime Leroy, *Le Mythe du phénix dans les littératures grecque et latine* (Paris: E. Droz, 1939), p. 73.

3. Amelie Rorty calls this approach "philosophical bio-psychology." Amelie Rorty, "*De Anima*: Its Agenda and Its Recent Interpreters," in *Essays on Aristotle's* De Anima, ed. Martha Nussbaum and Amelie O. Rorty (Oxford: Oxford University Press, 1992), p. 7. Along similar lines, Claudia Baracchi writes that *psuchē* "names the vitality of the living being, including the automatic metabolic processes, whereby life is maintained, and unconscious emotional contents, feelings, thoughts, and so on." Claudia Baracchi, *Aristotle's Ethics as First Philosophy* (Cambridge: Cambridge University Press, 2008), p. 110. That Aristotle elaborates a "philosophical bio-psychology" is only half of the story; he also develops a philosophical biophysics, fastened to his psychology through a shared concept of *bios*, life.

4. For more on this inversion, see Michael Marder, *Energy Dreams: Of Actuality* (New York: Columbia University Press, 2017).

5. That is why Aristotle often equivocates between *to threptikon* (the nourishing faculty) and *to genetikon* (the reproductive faculty), reducing the latter to the former: a plant's reproduction of itself is already reproduction in the other, and vice versa. Hegel will later adopt this idea in his *Philosophy of Nature*.

6. Aristotle views semen, seeds, and fruit as residue, the by-products of the digestive process (see, for instance, *De generatione animalium* 725a.1–5).

7. "The greater part of *De Anima* is devoted to an analysis of how the psychological activities of living things are organized to maintain a specific sort of life. Psychological activities are individuated and identified not only by their contributions to sheer maintenance for survival, but also by their contributions to the organism's realizing the potentialities of its species" (Rorty, "*De Anima*," p. 10).

8. G. W. F. Hegel, *Philosophy of Nature: Encyclopedia of the Philosophical Sciences, Part II*, trans. A. V. Miller (Oxford: Oxford University Press, 2004), p. 344, translation slightly modified.

9. Hegel, *Philosophy of Nature*, p. 344.

10. "But the plant does not attain to a relationship between individuals as such but only to a difference, whose sides are not at the same time in themselves whole individuals, do not determine the whole individuality" (Hegel, *Philosophy of Nature*, p. 343). More generally, as Alison Stone notes, in Hegel's system, "Paradoxically, organisms at first are not properly 'alive' at all." Alison Stone, *Petrified Intelligence: Nature in Hegel's Philosophy* (Albany: SUNY Press, 2005), p. 51.

11. Hegel, *Philosophy of Nature*, p. 322.

12. Hegel, *Philosophy of Nature*, p. 343. Hegel affirms this point more clearly later on: "All that is necessary for the production and ripening of the buds is the arrest of luxuriant growth" (*Philosophy of Nature*, p. 346).

13. Hegel, *Philosophy of Nature*, p. 343.

14. Hegel, *Philosophy of Nature*, p. 346.

15. Hegel, *Philosophy of Nature*, p. 346.

16. Hegel, *Philosophy of Nature*, p. 350.

17. Hegel, *Philosophy of Nature*, p. 336.

18. Hegel, *Philosophy of Nature*, p. 351.

19. Hegel, *Philosophy of Nature*, pp. 336–337, translation modified.

20. G. W. F. Hegel, *Hegel's Phenomenology of Spirit*, trans. A. V. Miller (Oxford: Oxford University Press, 1977), p. 420. For more on "God as Light," consult Jon Stewart, *The Unity of Hegel's "Phenomenology of Spirit": A Systematic Interpretation* (Evanston: Northwestern University Press, 2000), pp. 392ff.

21. Hegel, *Philosophy of Nature*, p. 351.

22. Hegel, *Phenomenology of Spirit*, p. 438.

23. Hegel, *Phenomenology of Spirit*, p. 438.

24. G. W. F. Hegel, *Lectures on the Philosophy of Religion*, vol. 2, *Determinate Religion*, ed. Peter C. Hodgson (Oxford: Clarendon Press, 2007), p. 744.

25. Hegel, *Lectures on the Philosophy of Religion*, vol. 2, p. 453.

26. On fire as the material medium of ideality and "liberated negativity," consult Hegel, *Philosophy of Nature*, pp. 106ff and Michael Marder, *Pyropolitics*, passim.

27. Hegel, *Lectures on the Philosophy of Religion*, vol. 2, p. 453.

28. Hegel, *Lectures on the Philosophy of Religion*, vol. 2, p. 453.

29. Hegel, *Lectures on the Philosophy of Religion*, vol. 2, p. 743. Differently put, "if [divine] power and substance are to become spirit, this moment of antithesis [anguish in a finite subject] and its resolution are indispensable" (p. 742).

30. Hegel, *Lectures on the Philosophy of Religion*, vol. 2, p. 454.

31. Hegel, *Lectures on the Philosophy of Religion*, vol. 2, p. 743.

32. Hegel, *Lectures on the Philosophy of Religion*, vol. 2, p. 453.

33. G. W. F. Hegel, *Hegel's Philosophy of Nature*, ed. and trans. M. J. Petry, vol. 3 (London: Humanities Press, 1970), p. 212. This contrasts sharply with Terry Pinkard's argument about Hegel's *Naturphilosophie* to the effect that "as a whole, nature aims at nothing, even if there are some creatures in the natural order that do aim at some things. In fact, taken as a whole, nature does not constitute a genuine 'whole' at all, at least in the sense that nature 'as a whole' cannot be made fully intelligible to pure reason." Terry Pinkard, *Hegel's Naturalism: Mind, Nature, and the Final Ends of Life* (Oxford: Oxford University Press, 2021), p. 23.

34. G. W. F. Hegel, *Lectures on the Philosophy of World History*, ed. and trans. Robert Brown and Peter Hodgson, vol. 1, *Manuscripts of the Introduction and the Lectures of 1822–3* (Oxford: Clarendon Press, 2011), p. 142.

35. Hegel, *Lectures on the Philosophy of World History*, p. 142, translation modified.

36. Hegel, *Lectures on the Philosophy of World History*, p. 142, translation modified.

37. There is, then, a tinge of irony in assessments such as these: "Questions of what is 'living and dead' in Hegel's thought have been asked for over a century, yet before each wave of skepticism, his ideas seem to revive, Phoenix-like, and surprise with their continued relevance." Will D. Desmond, *Hegel's Antiquity* (Oxford: Oxford University Press, 2020), p. 2.

38. Hegel, *Lectures on the Philosophy of World History*, pp. 142–143, translation modified. In this sense, a total identification of Hegelian dialectics with the phoenix is wrong, or, at most, half-right. I have in mind Derrida's 1975–76 *Life Death* seminar, with its proclamation, in the very first session, that "the great syllogism of life at the end of Hegel's *Science of Logic* . . . follow[s] a movement that is everywhere marked in Hegel (let us call it the movement of the phoenix)." Jacques Derrida, *Life Death*, ed. Pascale-Anne Brault and Peggy Kamuf (Chicago: The University of Chicago Press, 2020), p. 2. Similarly, reading Levinas in "At This Very Moment in This Work Here I Am," Derrida exclaims in response to the "consummation [of subjectivity] for the other without the act being able to be reborn out of the ashes of that consummation": "I again interrupt: no Hegelian Phoenix after this consummation." Jacques Derrida, *Psyche: Inventions of the Other*, vol. 1, ed. Peggy Kamuf and Elizabeth Rottenberg (Stanford: Stanford University Press, 2007), p. 170. In a more political, rather than ethical, key, Shu-mei Shih endeavors to compare the Western and the Eastern, the Hegelian and the Chinese phoenixes: "While the Chinese phoenix had to die to be reborn a totally new being . . . , the Western phoenix in Hegel's conception draws strength from its previous incarnation to engender a new form." Shu-mei Shih, *The Lure of the Modern: Writing Modernism in Semicolonial China, 1917–1937* (Berkeley: University of California Press, 2001), p. 52. Nevertheless, the passage from *Lectures on the Philosophy of World History* that is under discussion here rejects wholesale "the conception of the phoenix" as suitable for Hegel's dialectics or for the Western idea of spirit.

39. G. W. F. Hegel, *Lectures on the History of Philosophy: Greek Philosophy to Plato*, trans. E. S. Haldane (Lincoln: University of Nebraska Press, 1995), p. 90.

40. Hegel, *Lectures on the History of Philosophy*, p. 90.

41. G. W. F Hegel, *Vorlesungen über die Philosophie der Kunst (1823)* (Hamburg: Felix Meiner Verlag, 2003), p. 3.

42. Hegel, *Vorlesungen über die Philosophie der Kunst (1823)*, p. 22.

43. G. W. F. Hegel, *The Science of Logic*, trans. and ed. George di Giovanni (Cambridge: Cambridge University Press, 2015), p. 677.

44. Hegel, *The Science of Logic*, p. 676.

45. Hegel, *The Science of Logic*, p. 677.

46. Hegel, *The Science of Logic*, p. 679.

47. Hegel, *The Science of Logic*, p. 687.

48. Hegel, *The Science of Logic*, p. 687.

49. Hegel, *The Science of Logic*, p. 687.

50. Hegel, *The Science of Logic*, p. 687.

51. Hegel, *The Science of Logic*, p. 688.

CHAPTER 4

1. John Donne, "The Canonization," in *The Complete Poems of John Donne*, ed. Robin Robbins (London: Longman, 2010), pp. 151–152.

2. Stephen Clark writes: "We know nothing about Plotinus's ancestry or early childhood. He does refer to native Egyptian practices and theories, but probably no more knowledgeably than should be expected of a resident of Egypt educated in the Hellenic tradition." Stephen Clark, *Plotinus: Myth, Metaphor, and Philosophical Practice* (Chicago: The University of Chicago Press, 2016) p. 4.

3. W. Spiegelberg, "Der Name des Phoenix," in *Strassburger Pestschrilt zur XLVI Versammlung deutscher Philologen und Schulmänner* (Strasburg: Karl J. Trübner, 1901), pp. 163–165.

4. Roel Van den Broek, *The Myth of the Phoenix According to Classical and Early Christian Traditions* (Leiden: Brill, 1972), p. 16.

5. Plotinus formulates the theme of the double most clearly in Ennead 2.3, "On Whether the Stars Are Causes." As he writes there, "Every man is double, one of him is the sort of compound being and one of him is himself; and the whole universe is, one part the composite of body and a sort of soul bound to body, and one the soul of the all which is not in the body but makes a trace of itself shine on that which is in the body" (2.3.9.28–34). Similarly, in Ennead 6.4, "The Presence of Being Everywhere," Plotinus advances a theory of "another man [*anthrōpos allos*]," who, "wishing to exist, approached that man [the authentic I]; and when he found us—for we were not outside the all—he wound himself round us and attached himself to that man who was then each one of us. . . . And we have come to be the pair of them" (6.6.14.20–30). For more on the theme of the double in Plotinus, see chapter 5 of Charles Stang's *Our Divine Double* (Cambridge, MA: Harvard University Press, 2016).

6. An "echo" of primordial nature's absolute quietude is apparent in the quietness of "things which are uniformly in accord with nature [*kata phusin echontōn hēremēsis*]" (3.4.4.12).

7. Concerning the soul "uttering and propounding" the rational principle with which it has reunited, Plotinus writes, "For it [this soul] is not full, but has something wanting in relation to what comes before it; yet it itself sees also quietly what it utters. For it does not go on uttering what it has uttered well already, but what it utters, it utters because of its deficiency, with a view to examining it, trying to learn through what it possesses" (3.8.6.25–30). For Plotinus, at the level of the soul as well, utterance is deficient compared to silence and quiet contemplation.

8. I touch on this theme in Michael Marder, *Energy Dreams: Of Actuality* (New York: Columbia University Press, 2017), pp. 42ff.

9. See also the designation of the eternal as *telos ameres*, "partless completion," or "indivisible perfection," in 3.7.3.19.

10. Apropos of this idea, Pierre Hadot writes that "concentrated in the original and absolute One, divine power is diffused and unfolds itself, first at the level of thought and then at that of the soul, which are unified multiplicities, to be then, finally, dispersed into the sensible world and in matter. We rediscover here, then, the representations of imperial ideology." Pierre Hadot, *The Selected Writings of Pierre Hadot: Philosophy as Practice*, trans. Matthew Sharpe and Federico Testa (London: Bloomsbury, 2020), p. 250.

11. The act of turning (around and toward oneself; later on, this act will signify conversion and a turn to God) raises the entity that so turns to "the theoretical and primary intellect [*theōrē-tikos nous kai prōtos*]," which "is what is in its own power in this way, that its work in no way depends on another, but it is all turned to itself and its work is itself [*to ergon autou autos*]" (6.8.6.31–34).

12. In this vein, Plotinus composes a short treatise against suicide (Ennead 1.9) and saves his disciple, Porphyry, from suicidal thoughts by sending him to Sicily.

13. Clark notes that "it was at least a widespread opinion, in his day, that souls transmigrated— and must therefore somehow retain their own identity through time and their distinctness from all other souls" (*Plotinus*, p. 31).

14. In Plato's probably original myth of Er, the determination of a future form of existence by habits in a past life is coupled with choice, the opportunity to select the kind of animal a soul prefers (*Rep.* 620a).

15. F. W. J. Schelling, "System of Philosophy in General and of the Philosophy of Nature in Particular," in *Idealism and the Endgame of Theory: Three Essays by F. W.J. Schelling*, trans. and ed. Thomas Pfau (Albany: SUNY Press, 1994), p. 153.

16. This passage is not included in the English translation of the text. For the original, consult F. W. J. Schelling, *von Schellings Sämmtliche Werke*, vol. 6 (Berlin: Total Verlag, 1997), p. 352.

17. F. W. J. Schelling, "Stuttgart Seminars," in *Idealism and the Endgame of Theory: Three Essays by F.W.J. Schelling*, trans. and ed. Thomas Pfau (Albany: SUNY Press, 1994), p. 218.

18. F. W. J. Schelling, *First Outline of a System of the Philosophy of Nature*, trans. Keith R. Peterson (Albany: SUNY Press, 2004), p. 29.

19. Schelling, *First Outline*, p. 29.

20. F. W. J. Schelling, *The Ages of the World*, trans. Jason M. Wirth (Albany: SUNY Press, 2000), p. 36, translation modified.

21. Schelling, *The Ages of the World*, p. 29.

22. On liberation from the cycle of rebirth in Jainism, see Brianne Donaldson and Ana Bajželj, *Insistent Life: Principles for Bioethics in the Jain Tradition* (Oakland: University of California Press, 2021), pp. 39ff.

23. Schelling, *The Ages of the World*, p. 27.

24. F. W. J. Schelling, "On the Nature of Philosophy as Science," in *German Idealist Philosophy*, ed. Rüdiger Bubner (London: Penguin Books, 1997), pp. 220–221.

25. Schelling, *First Outline*, p. 14.

26. Through his father, who taught him Hebrew, Schelling was familiar with Jewish theology and mysticism. In *The Ages of the World*, he interprets *netzach*, one of the *sefirot*, or the emanations of divinity in the Kabbalah, in keeping with the double sense of the Hebrew word as eternity and victory (over time, Schelling speculates) (p. 43). For more on Schelling's relation to mysticism, see Friedmann Horn, *Schelling & Swedenborg: Mysticism and German Idealism*, trans. George F. Dole (West Chester, PA: Swedenborg Foundation Publishers, 1997).

27. Schelling, *First Outline*, p. 15.

28. Schelling, *First Outline*, p. 14.

29. Schelling, *First Outline*, p. 40.

30. Also, as Schelling writes, "Since everything in Nature—or rather, here just that absolute product—is conceived continually in becoming, then it will neither be able to achieve absolute fluidity nor absolute nonfluidity (solidity). This will furnish the drama of a struggle between form and the formless." Schelling, *First Outline*, p. 28. This drama, too, is that of the phoenix complex.

31. Schelling, *First Outline*, p. 35.

32. Schelling, *First Outline*, p. 46.

33. Schelling, *First Outline*, p. 36. This assertion is applicable to other thinkers of sexual difference, including Jacques Derrida and Luce Irigaray. According to Slavoj Žižek, "It was possible for Schelling to accomplish the unheard-of step to radical contingency only in the guise of a 'regression' to the pre-modern mythology of a sexualized universe." Slavoj Žižek, *The Indivisible Remainder: On Schelling and Related Matters* (London: Verso, 2007), p. 73.

34. Werner Beierwaltes, "The Legacy of Neoplatonism in F.W.J. Schelling's Thought," *International Journal of Philosophical Studies* 10, no. 4 (2002): pp. 393–428.

35. Schelling, *First Outline*, p. 39.

36. Schelling, *First Outline*, p. 51.

37. Schelling, *First Outline*, p. 49.

38. "This absolute organism could not be presented through an individual product, but only through an infinity of individual products which, seen singly, depart infinitely from the ideal, but taken in the whole are congruent with it." Schelling, *First Outline*, pp. 49–50.

39. Schelling, *First Outline*, p. 64.

40. Schelling, *First Outline*, p. 58.

41. Schelling, *First Outline*, p. 59.

42. Schelling, *First Outline*, p. 95.

43. Schelling, *First Outline*, pp. 67–69.

44. Schelling, *First Outline*, p. 69.

45. Schelling, *The Ages of the World*, p. 43.

46. Schelling, *The Ages of the World*, p. 44.

47. F. W. J. Schelling, *Clara, or On Nature's Connection to the Spirit World*, trans. Fiona Steinkamp (Albany: SUNY Press, 2002), pp. 24–25.

48. Schelling, *The Ages of the World*, p. 20.

49. Schelling, *The Ages of the World*, pp. 20–21.

50. Schelling, *The Ages of the World*, p. 20.

51. Schelling, *First Outline*, p. 86.

52. Schelling, *The Ages of the World*, p. 21.

53. Schelling, *First Outline*, p. 86.

54. Refer to Michael Marder, *Dump Philosophy: A Phenomenology of Devastation* (London: Bloomsbury, 2020), and Michael Marder, "On Art as Planetary Metabolism," in *Reading by Osmosis: Nature Interprets Us*, ed. Sema Berikovic (Rotterdam: Nai010 Publishers, 2020).

55. Schelling, *The Ages of the World*, p. 11.

56. Schelling, *The Ages of the World*, p. 21.

57. Schelling, *First Outline*, p. 5.

58. Schelling, *First Outline*, p. 5.

59. Schelling, *First Outline*, p. 17.

60. Schelling, *The Ages of the World*, p. 5.

61. Schelling, *The Ages of the World*, p. 24.

62. Schelling, *The Ages of the World*, p. 16.

63. Schelling, *The Ages of the World*, p. 92.

64. Schelling, *The Ages of the World*, p. 94.

65. F. W. J. Schelling, *Ages of the World*, 2nd draft, trans. Judith Norman, in Slavoj Žižek / F. W. J. Schelling, *The Abyss of Freedom / Ages of the World* (Ann Arbor: The University of Michigan Press, 1997), p. 121.

66. Schelling, *Clara*, p. 81. At the everyday level, life is possible thanks to the "attenuation and suppression of that force which, when actuated (activated) or spiritualized, is a consuming fire." Schelling, *The Ages of the World*, p. 96. In turn, the phoenix is reborn, receiving a brand-new life thanks to its transformation in fire. Finally, when the previously concealed fire gains an upper hand over all external forms, it transforms the world into postworldly, spiritual existence. But this last possibility is already assumed in the description of everyday life that carries on thanks to the attenuation of the fiery force that, if given sway, spiritualizes reality and takes life itself to a new level.

67. Schelling, *The Ages of the World*, p. 96.

68. In line with the external and internal representations of the phoenix, the cosmic witness is reflected deep within the recesses of the soul, which, "eternally young," "must turn to an inner oracle, the only witness from a time before the world." Schelling, *Ages of the World*, 2nd draft, p. 114.

69. Schelling, *The Ages of the World*, pp. 96–97.

70. John Goodridge, *The Phoenix: An Essay* (London: Wells & Grosvenor, 1781), pp. 45–46. A bright star on some ancient Roman coins representing the phoenix may be a visual reference to a comet.

71. Schelling, *The Ages of the World*, p. 97.

72. Schelling, *The Ages of the World*, p. 97.

CHAPTER 5

1. All Latin citations from St. Hildegard's *Physica* are drawn from *Physica liber subtitilitatum diversarum naturarum creaturum*; Migne, PL 197, pp. 1117–1352. *Patrologiae cursus completus: series latina* (also known as *Patriologia Latina*), ed. J.-P. Migne, 221 vols. (Paris, 1841–1864) is cited as "PL."

2. Hildegard von Bingen, *Hildegardis Bingensis Epistolarium*, first part, 1–90, ed. L. Van Acker, Corpus Christianorum Continuatio Mediaevalis, vol. 91 (Turnhout: Brepols, 1991), cited as "CCCM 91."

3. Hildegard von Bingen, *Hildegardis Scivias*, ed. A. Führkötter, Corpus Christianorum Continuatio Mediaevalis, vol. 43 (Turnhout: Brepols, 1978), cited as "CCCM 43."

4. The expression *in viriditate animae* also appears in *Scivias* 3.3.12; CCCM 43, p. 387. There, it announces the patience and perseverance of believers in the face of adversity.

5. The apparent tautologies that keep cropping up here are justifiable with respect to the way Hildegard expresses her insights, as in a letter where she writes, "But life is in life. A tree flourishes from nothing else but *viriditas*, and even a stone is not without moisture, nor is any other creature without its power. For eternity itself is alive and not without floridity [*Sed vita est in vita. Arbor enim non floret, nisi de viriditate, nec lapis est sine humore, nec ulla creatura sine vi sua. Ipsa etiam vivens eternitas non est sine floriditate*]" (Epist. 31r, 18–21; CCCM 91,

p. 83). "Life is in life" means that the enlivening *viriditas* dwells within and animates living beings, not excluding even stones.

6. "A human is the edifice of God, in which he dwells because he sent a fiery soul into it, the soul that flies with rationality in expansion, just as a wall encompasses the breadth of a house [*Homo enim edificium Dei est, in quo ipse mansionem habet, quoniam igneam animam in illum misit, que cum rationalitate in dilatatione volat, quemadmodum murus latitudinem domus comprehendit*]" (Epist. 45, 10–13; CCCM 91, p. 114).

7. Hildegard von Bingen, *Ordo virtutum*, ed. P. Dronke, in *Hildegardis Bingensis Opera Minora*, Corpus Christianorum Continuatio Mediaevalis, vol. 226 (Turnhout: Brepols, 2007), pp. 503–521, cited as "CCCM 226."

8. Interestingly, Hildegard shares the understanding of the body as a garment of the soul with Hindu and Amerindian philosophies. Eduardo Viveiros de Castro notes that the "notion of the body as clothing can be found among the Makuna, the Yagua, the Piro, the Trio, and the Upper Xingu societies. The notion is very likely pan-American, having considerable symbolic yield for example in Northwest Coast cosmologies, if not of much wider distribution." Eduardo Viveiros de Castro, *Cosmological Perspectivism in Amazonia and Elsewhere* (Manchester: HAU, 2012), p. 48n4.

9. Hildegard von Bingen, *Symphonia: A Critical Edition of the "Symphonia Armonie Celestium Revelationum" (Symphony of the Harmony of Celestial Revelations)*, 2nd ed., ed. and trans. Barbara Newman (Ithaca: Cornell University Press, 1998), cited as "*Symph.*"

10. Hildegard von Bingen, *Hildegardis Bingensis Liber Divinorum Operum*, ed. A. Derolez and P. Dronke, Corpus Christianorum Continuatio Mediaevalis, vol. 226 (Turnhout: Brepols, 1996), cited as "CCCM 92" and abbreviated as "LDO."

11. Michael Marder, *Green Mass: The Ecological Theology of St. Hildegard of Bingen* (Stanford: Stanford University Press, 2021), p. 95.

12. Roel Van den Broek, *The Myth of the Phoenix According to Classical and Early Christian Traditions* (Leiden: Brill, 1972), p. 239.

13. It is not by chance that the extreme monotheism of Plotinus and Spinoza results in their commitment to philosophies of pure immanence. I cannot, however, agree with Lenn Goodman that "the fullest elaboration of the monotheistic idea [in Spinoza] will take normative rather than narrative form." Lenn Goodman, "What Does Spinoza's *Ethics* Contribute to Jewish Philosophy?" in *Jewish Themes in Spinoza's Philosophy*, ed. Heidi M. Ravven and Lenn E. Goodman (Albany: SUNY Press, 2002), p. 27.

14. When "our mind, as we have said, reproduces nature as closely as possible . . . , it possesses in the form of thought the essence, order and unity of nature" (*Emendations* 99; *CW* 27).

15. "'Part' and 'whole' are not true or real entities, but only 'things of reason,' and consequently there are in nature neither whole nor parts" (*CW* 44).

16. In *Emendations*, Spinoza specifies that "an idea is situated in the context of thought exactly as is its object in the context of reality. Therefore, if there were something in nature having

no interrelation with other things, and if there were also granted its objective essence (which must agree entirely with its formal essence), then this idea likewise would have no interrelation with other ideas [*nihil etiam commercii haberet cum aliis ideis*]; that is, we could make no inference regarding it" (41; *CW* 12). A lot could be said on the subject of this specification; here, I will limit myself to two crucial points. First, while Spinoza considers ideas and things in the respective contexts of thought and reality, he does not contemplate the idea and the thing that furnish and, indeed, *are* these contexts: God, substance, nature. (There is no context for the context is an implicit Spinozan axiom we should always keep in the back of our mind.) These are, at one and the same time, totally separated and intimately interrelated with everything they encompass. As a result, inferences about them are easily possible from all that is and entirely impossible in a mélange of intelligibility and unintelligibility that turns out to be a major roadblock on the path of Spinozan philosophy. Second, assuming, as Spinoza does, that to be interrelated with other things and ideas is to be produced and to produce the other ideas and things, only mediated (rather than immanent) causality is accounted for in this scheme of what in later philosophy will be called *the world*. The sites of meaning, generation, life and death, intelligibility and perceptibility are the interactions between the texts and the contexts of existence and of thinking, and it is there that the phoenix complex thrives, condensing their relation into a thought-image.

17. One of the paradoxical ways in which Spinoza defines nature, along these lines, is as an infinite extension without division (*CW* 44).

18. In his take on Spinoza's notion of beatitude, Deleuze intellectualizes love and desire forgetting a birth, a birthing, and a rebirth *through* love, rather than *of* love: "From the joy that flows from an adequate idea of ourselves is born a *desire*, a desire to know ever more things in their essence or *sub specie aeternitatis* [under the aspect of eternity]. And there is born, above all, a *love*." Gilles Deleuze, *Expressionism in Philosophy: Spinoza*, trans. Martin Joughin (New York: Zone Books, 1990), p. 305.

19. G. W. F. Hegel, *Phenomenology of Spirit*, trans. A. V. Miller (Oxford: Oxford University Press, 1977), p. 10, translation modified.

20. Refer also to *The Principles* 1.xii.pr: "God preserves all things; that is, he has created, and still continues to create, everything that exists" (*CW* 141).

21. This logic is most compellingly spelled out in Charles Stang's *Our Divine Double* (Cambridge, MA: Harvard University Press, 2016).

CHAPTER 6

1. Laurence Gosserez, "Le Phénix, le temps et l'éternité," in *Le Phénix et son autre: Poétique d'un mythe des origines au XVI siècle*, ed. Laurence Gosserez (Rennes: Presses Universitaires de Rennes, 2013) p. 21.

2. All citations from Book 1 of *The Mahābhārata* are drawn from the van Buitenen translation: *The Mahābhārata. I. The Book of the Beginning*, trans. and ed. J. A. B. van Buitenen (Chicago:

The University of Chicago Press, 1973). The title of *The Mahābhārata* is abbreviated as "M" for citation purposes.

3.   Christopher Key Chapple, "The Setting of The *Bhagavad Gītā*," in *The Bhagavad Gītā*, 25th anniversary ed., trans. Winthrop Sargeant, ed. Christopher Key Chapple (Albany: SUNY Press, 2009), p. 9.

4.   All citations from the *Bhagavad Gītā* are drawn from the Sargeant translation: *The Bhagavad Gītā*, 25th anniversary ed., trans. Winthrop Sargeant, ed. Christopher Key Chapple (Albany: SUNY Press, 2009). The title of the *Bhagavad Gītā* is abbreviated as "BG" for citation purposes.

5.   "The two words 'everlasting' and 'indestructible' are not repetitive, because everlastingness and indestructibility are of two kinds. As for instance, a body which is reduced to ashes and has disappeared is said to have been destroyed. (And) even while existing, when it becomes transfigured by being afflicted with diseases, etc. it is said to be 'destroyed.' That being so, by the two words 'everlasting' and 'indestructible' it is meant that It [*ātman*] is not subject to both kinds of destruction. Otherwise, the everlastingness of the Self would be like that of the earth, etc." *Bhagavad Gītā, with the Commentary of Śaṅkarācārya*, trans. Swami Gambhirananda (Kolkata: Advaita Ashrama, 2018), pp. 28–29.

6.   Refer to *Ethics* 5.lxvii: "A free man thinks of death least of all things, and his wisdom is a meditation of life, not of death" (*CW* 355).

7.   Stephanie W. Jamison and Joel P. Brereton, "Introduction," in *The Rigveda: The Earliest Religious Poetry of India*, trans. Stephanie W. Jamison and Joel P. Brereton (Oxford: Oxford University Press, 2014), p. 46; Klaus Klostermaier, *A Survey of Hinduism*, 3rd ed. (Albany: SUNY Press, 2007), p. 312.

8.   Gilbert Durand, *The Anthropological Structures of the Imaginary*, trans. Margaret Sankey and Judith Hatten (Brisbane: Boombana Publications, 1999), p. 142.

9.   "As the recurring dawn, Uṣas is not only celebrated for bringing light from darkness. She is also petitioned to grant long life, as she is a constant reminder of people's limited time on earth." David Kinsley, *Hindu Goddesses: Visions of the Divine Feminine in the Hindu Religious Tradition* (Berkeley: University of California Press, 1988), p. 8.

10.   All Vedic hymns are drawn from *The Rigveda: The Earliest Religious Poetry of India*, trans. Stephanie W. Jamison and Joel P. Brereton (Oxford: Oxford University Press, 2014). The title of *The Ṛg Veda* is abbreviated as "RV" for citation purposes.

11.   This is in line with the Heraclitus fragment 67: "God is day night [*o theos hemerē euphronē*], winter summer, war peace, satiety hunger; he undergoes alterations in the way that fire, when it is mixed with spices, is named according to the scent of each of them." G. S. Kirk and J. E. Raven, *The Presocratic Philosophers: A Critical History with a Selection of Texts* (Cambridge: Cambridge University Press, 1963), p. 191.

12.   For a detailed exegesis of this phrase, refer to Jean-Louis Chrétien, *L'Intelligence du Feu* (Paris: Bayard, 2003).

13. "What was the wood, and what the tree from which they carved out heaven and earth, the two that stand together, unageing and enduring? But the days, the many dawns, grow old" (10.31(857).7).

14. Stephanie W. Jamison and Joel P. Brereton, "Mitra and Varuna," in *The Rigveda: The Earliest Religious Poetry of India*, trans. Stephanie W. Jamison and Joel P. Brereton (Oxford: Oxford University Press, 2014), p. 752.

15. Karl Hoffmann, *Aufsätze sur Indoiranistik*, vol. 3, ed. S. Glauch, R. Plath, and S. Ziegler (Wiesbaden: Reichert, 1992), p. 723.

16. Refer to RV 1.83.5. See also Stephanie W. Jamison and Joel P. Brereton, "The Soma Carts," in *The Rigveda: The Earliest Religious Poetry of India*, trans. Stephanie W. Jamison and Joel P. Brereton (Oxford: Oxford University Press, 2014), p. 1388.

17. Wendy Doniger, *On Hinduism* (Oxford: Oxford University Press, 2014), pp. 277–278.

18. "What they [the authors of early Hindu texts, MM] feared most of all was what they called *punar mrityu*, recurrent death: how terrible to go on getting old and dying, over and over again. Re-death may have meant merely a series of ritual deaths within a natural lifespan, but it may have foreshadowed an actual series of rebirths and re-deaths." Doniger, *On Hinduism*, p. 92.

19. All citations from the *Upaniṣads* are drawn from the Patrick Olivelle translation: *The Early Upaniṣads: Annotated Text and Translation*, trans. and ed. Patrick Olivelle (Oxford: Oxford University Press, 1998). In the Graeco-Egyptian context, the riddle of the sphinx resonates with the Upaniṣadic question of the moon. Both pertain, in one way or another, to the problem of self-knowledge and to matters of life and death.

20. Doniger, *On Hinduism*, p. 92.

21. It could well be the case that *puruṣa* and *ātman* are used interchangeably. See P. T. Raju, *Structural Depths of Indian Thought* (Albany: SUNY Press, 1985), p. 29.

22. Chapple, "The Setting of *The Bhagavad Gītā*," p. 9. I wonder to what extent the Hebrew root *b.r.ā.*, meaning "to create" and appearing as the first verb in the Hebrew Bible, is cognate with the Sanskrit one.

23. This thought presages Nietzsche's famous assertion that "there is no 'being' behind the deed, its effect and what becomes of it; 'the doer' is invented as an afterthought—the doing is everything." Friedrich Nietzsche, *On the Genealogy of Morality*, ed. Keith Ansell-Pearson (Cambridge: Cambridge University Press, 2006), p. 26.

24. See the note by Chappel in *The Bhagavad Gītā*, p. 351.

25. This allusion is important in light of the phoenix's connection to the Great Year or cosmic seasonality. As the *Bhagavad Gītā* proclaims, "They who know that the day of Brahmā extends as far as a thousand yugas, and that the night of Brahma ends only in a thousand yugas; they are men who know day and night" (8.17). *Yuga* is an age of the world, a formative reference for Schelling. A thousand *yugas* last 4,320,000,000 years. Refer to the note by Chappel in *The Bhagavad Gītā*, p. 365.

26. Juergen Mittelstrass, "Nature and Science in the Renaissance," in *Metaphysics and Philosophy of Science in the 17th and 18th Centuries: Essays in Honor of Gerd Buchdahl*, ed. R. S. Woolhouse (Dordrecht: Kluwer, 1988), pp. 25ff.

27. Indeed, this is the only time that references to a machine or a mechanism are made in the *Bhagavad Gītā*.

CHAPTER 7

1. Joseph Nigg, *The Phoenix: An Unnatural Biography of a Mystical Beast* (Chicago: University of Chicago Press, 2016), p. 19.

2. "*Fenghuang* [Chinese mythology]," *Encyclopedia Britannica*, https://www.britannica.com /topic/fenghuang.

3. For more on this distinction, see Jean-Pierre Diény, "Le Fenghuang et le Phénix," *Cahiers d'Extrême-Asie*, 5 (1989–1990): pp. 1–13.

4. While writing this text, I was listening, on a loop, to Jean-Philippe Rameau's "Le rappel des oiseaux" in an incomparable rendition by Víkingur Ólafsson.

5. *Fantastic Creatures of the Mountains and Seas: A Chinese Classic*, trans. Howard Goldblatt (New York: Skyhorse Publishing, 2021).

6. Burton Watson, "Introduction," in *The Analects of Confucius*, trans. Burton Watson (New York: Columbia University Press, 2007), p. 11.

7. All translations of the *Analects* refer to *The Analects of Confucius*, trans. Burton Watson (New York: Columbia University Press, 2007).

8. Diény, "Le Fenghuang et le Phénix," p. 10.

9. Watson's bewildered commentary in a footnote to this passage is, "One of the most famous passages in the *Analects*. What does it mean?" *The Analects of Confucius*, p. 62n9].

10. Huang Yushun, *Life Confucianism as a New Philosophy: Love and Thought*, trans. Xuening Li and Meirong Yan (Los Angeles: Bridge21, 2020), p. 270.

11. Lee Dian Rainey, *Confucius and Confucianism: The Essentials* (Chichester, UK: Wiley, 2010), p. 164.

12. Todd Cameron Thacker, "*Sheng sheng*," in *Routledge Encyclopedia of Confucianism*, ed. Xinzhong Yao (London: Routledge, 2003), p. 546.

13. Watson, "Introduction," p. 9.

14. Watson, "Introduction," p. 9.

15. Confucius, *Analects, with Selections from Traditional Commentaries*, trans. Edward Slingerland (Indianapolis: Hackett, 2003), p. 64.

16. Needless to say, rescue from forgetting and, therefore, from nonbeing was also the Socratic mission in Plato's *Republic*. "And so, Glaucon, the tale was saved, as the saying is, and was not

lost [*muthos esōthē kai ouk apōleto*]. And it will save us if we believe it," (621b-c). Their scope exceeding the myth of Er about the reincarnations of the souls of dead heroes, these words hold for the vital impetus of Plato's thought, with the paradoxical twist that what is saved is *muthos*, rather than *logos*.

17. See also Zisi's "The Doctrine of the Mean," *Zhongyong* 13.

18. Here is how Watson explains the uniquely Confucian conception of the Way, or *dao*: "In the *Analects*, Confucius frequently employs the term *dao*, which means 'a path or a way' and, by extension, 'a method of doing things.' In some contexts, such as the writings of the Daoist school, the word has more metaphysical connotations. But in Confucius's pronouncements, it refers specifically to the characteristics of peaceful, benevolent, and culturally distinguished government typical of the periods of ideal rule, particularly that of the early years of the Zhou dynasty" (Watson, "Introduction," pp. 8–9). Nevertheless, as I have already succinctly argued, contrasts between metaphysical and practical/cultural/political conceptions are strained with regard to ancient philosophical traditions, not least Confucianism. There will always be a metaphysical foundation to ancient political thought, and, vice versa, ancient metaphysics is not easily distinguishable from ancient political notions.

19. Nigg, *The Phoenix*, p. 26.

20. Confucius, *The Confucian Odes: The Classical Anthology Defined by Confucius*, trans. Ezra Pound (Cambridge, MA: Harvard University Press, 1959), p. 3.

21. For the background and interpretation of this work, see *Focusing the Familiar: A Translation and Philosophical Interpretation of the* Zhongyong, ed. Roger T. Ames and David L. Hall (Honolulu: University of Hawai'i Press, 2001). Refer also to *Daxue and Zhongyong: Bilingual Edition*, trans. Ian Johnston and Wang Ping (Hong Kong: Chinese University Press, 2012).

22. All references to the *Book of Changes* are drawn from *The I Ching, or Book of Changes*, trans. Cary F. Baynes (Princeton, NJ: Princeton University Press, 1977), p. 10.

23. Of course, this is only a hypothetical division, given *Zhongyong* 26: "The *dao* of heaven and earth may be thoroughly described in a single phrase: As a thing, it possesses no duality, hence the way it gives birth to things cannot be fathomed. The *dao* of heaven and earth is broad, is deep, is high, is bright, is distant, is enduring."

24. This is as much the case in Western as in Chinese traditions. Consult Pauline C. Lee, *Li Zhi, Confucianism and the Virtue of Desire* (Albany: SUNY Press, 2012), particularly chapter 5, "Genuineness," pp. 101–114.

25. "It should by now be evident that Confucius's view of truth and truthfulness is quite different from empiricist 'referentialism,' or a 'correspondence theory' of truth. It is closer to Western ideas of truth as 'coherence' (Leibniz, Spinoza, Hegel, and F. H. Bradley), 'practice' (C. S. Pierce, William James, and John Dewey), and 'performance' (J. L. Austin, P. F. Strawson)." Christopher Hancock, *Christianity and Confucianism: Culture, Faith, and Politics* (Edinburgh: T&T Clark, 2022), p. 336.

26. For the translation of *The Great Learning*, I have relied on Daniel Gardner, *The Four Books: The Basic Teachings of the Later Confucian Tradition* (London: Hackett, 2007).

27. Kathryn A. Lowry, *The Tapestry of Popular Songs in 16th- and 17th-Century China: Reading, Imitation, and Desire* (Leiden: Brill, 2005), p. 222.

28. So, Legge adds to the opening words of the *Great Learning* traditional commentary from Tai Jia, a king from the Shang dynasty: "In the Tai Chia, it is said, 'He contemplated and studied the illustrious decrees of Heaven.'" Peter Liebregts, *Ezra Pound and Neoplatonism* (Madison: Fairleigh Dickinson University Press, 2004), p. 240. A simpler translation would be, "Regard this bright mandate of Tian." The decrees of Tian—heaven, the sky—are naturally luminous. Thus the luminosity of inborn virtue, cultivated here below as and at the root, emanates from the celestial sphere.

29. Gardner, *The Four Books*, p. 7.

30. Joseph A. Adler, "Introduction," in Zhu Xi, *The Original Meaning of the Yijing: Commentary on the Scripture of Change*, trans. and ed. Joseph A. Adler (New York: Columbia University Press, 2019), p. 23.

31. Confucius, *The Confucian Odes*, p. 143.

32. Confucius, *The Confucian Odes*, p. 139.

33. All renditions of the "Great Appendix" are from Zhu Xi, *The Original Meaning of the Yijing*.

34. In a similar blend of ontology and ethics, it is said that "the great virtue of heaven and earth is life [生, *shēng*]" (B.1.10.).

35. *Shēng shēng bu xi* "means that the very nature of cosmos is processive in nature, and that to have a cosmos means the generation of new and novel things and events." John Berthrong, *Expanding Process: Exploring Philosophical and Theological Transformations in China and the West* (Albany: SUNY Press, 2008), p. 69. Nevertheless, according to the original phrase, the generativity of the cosmos—the generativity that *is* the cosmos—is neither haphazard nor committed to the qualitatively new, but to generation as regeneration, to birthing as a ceaseless rebirthing.

36. Yushun, *Life Confucianism as a New Philosophy*, p. 82.

37. Jingyi Liu, "Questioning Metaphysics," in *A World in Discourse: Converging and Diverging Expressions of Value*, ed. Sydney Morrow and Matthew Izor (Newcastle upon Tyne: Cambridge Scholars Publishing, 2015), p. 55.

38. *The I Ching, or Book of Changes*, p. 97.

39. Adler, "Introduction," p. 23.

40. Refer to Sun Xiangcheng, "Sheng-Sheng (生生) as Being-Between-Generations: On the Existential Structure of Confucian Ethics," *Yearbook for Eastern and Western Philosophy*, 4 (2019), pp. 119–149.

CHAPTER 8

1. George Young, *The Russian Cosmists: The Esoteric Futurism of Nikolai Fedorov and His Followers* (Oxford: Oxford University Press, 2012), pp. 46–47.

2. Martin Heidegger, *Poetry, Language, Thought*, trans. Albert Hofstadter (New York: Perennial Classics, 2001), p. 4.

3. N. F. Fedorov, "Vopros o vosstanovlenii vsemirnogo rodstva. *Sobor*," in N. F. Fedorov, *Collected Works*, vol. 1 (Moscow: Progress, 1995), p. 315. This and all subsequent translations of the Russian text are mine.

4. Fedorov, "Vopros o vosstanovlenii vsemirnogo rodstva. *Sobor*," p. 316.

5. Fedorov, "Vopros o vosstanovlenii vsemirnogo rodstva. *Sobor*," p. 330.

6. N. F. Fedorov, "Vopros o bratstve ili rodstve . . . ," in N. F. Fedorov, *Collected Works*, vol. 1 (Moscow: Progress, 1995), p. 40.

7. Fedorov, "Vopros o bratstve ili rodstve . . . ," p. 97. On the autotrophic project of Russian cosmism, see A. D. Moskovchenko, *Russkiy kosmism: Avtotrofnoe chelovechestvo buduschego* (Tomsk: TUSURA, 2012).

8. Fedorov, "Vopros o bratstve ili rodstve . . . ," p. 41.

9. Fedorov, "Vopros o bratstve ili rodstve . . . ," p. 81.

10. Fedorov, "Vopros o bratstve ili rodstve . . . ," p. 43.

11. Fedorov, "Vopros o bratstve ili rodstve . . . ," p. 45.

12. Fedorov, "Filosofia kak vyrazhenie nerodstvennosti i rodstvo." In N. F. Fedorov, *Collected Works*, vol. 3 (Moscow: Traditsiya, 1997), p. 253.

13. Fedorov, "Filosofia kak vyrazhenie nerodstvennosti I rodstvo," p. 254. Elsewhere, Fedorov concludes: "the whole of philosophy is a representation of clan being [*rodovogo byta*] in an estranged form" (Fedorov, "Vopros o bratstve ili rodstve . . . ," p. 96).

14. Refer to Donna Haraway, *Staying with the Trouble: Making Kin in the Chthulucene* (Durham, NC & London: Duke University Press, 2016).

15. N.F. Fedorov, "Roditeli i voskresiteli." In N. F. Fedorov, *Collected Works*, Vol. II (Moscow: Progress, 1995), p. 259.

16. Fedorov, "Roditeli i voskresiteli," pp. 259–260.

17. Fedorov, "Roditeli i voskresiteli," p. 260.

18. Fedorov, "Vopros o bratstve ili rodstve . . . ," p. 109.

19. Fedorov, "Vopros o bratstve ili rodstve . . . ," p. 82.

20. Fedorov, "Vopros o bratstve ili rodstve . . . ," p. 107.

21. Fedorov, "Vopros o bratstve ili rodstve . . . ," pp. 108–109.

22. Fedorov, "K voprosu o vremeni . . . ," in N. F. Fedorov, *Collected Works*, vol. 3 (Moscow: Traditsiya, 1997), p. 360.

23. Fedorov, "K voprosu o vremeni . . . ," p. 360.

24. Fedorov, "Vopros o bratstve ili rodstve . . . ," p. 41. On this point, Dipesh Chakrabarty presents an alternative view: "My point here depends on the validity of a distinction often made between a necessary and a logical relationship between two entities and a contingent and historical relationship between the same. Making this distinction allows me to make room within my framework for planetary processes that work regardless of how human societies are internally structured. The surface temperature of the planet depends on the extent of greenhouse gasses emitted into the atmosphere. The atmosphere does not care whether the gases come from a massive volcanic eruption or internally unjust human societies." Dipesh Chakrabarty, *The Climate of History in a Planetary Age* (Chicago: University of Chicago Press, 2021), p. 57. Further down in this chapter, we will see that another Russian cosmist, Aleksandr Svyatogor, posits his ideal of creative humanity, precisely, in terms of a cultural, linguistic, political, and practical "volcanism."

25. Fedorov, "Vopros o bratstve ili rodstve . . . ," p. 101.

26. Fedorov, "Vopros o bratstve ili rodstve . . . ," p. 91.

27. Fedorov, "Vopros o bratstve ili rodstve . . . ," p. 44.

28. Fedorov, "Vopros o bratstve ili rodstve . . . ," p. 85.

29. Fedorov, "Vopros o bratstve ili rodstve . . . ," p. 89.

30. Bernice Glatzer Rosenthal, "Introduction," in *The Occult in Russian and Soviet Culture*, ed. Bernice Glatzer Rosenthal (Ithaca, NY: Cornell University Press, 1997), p. 11. A similar critique was already leveled in the Soviet Union in the 1960s and 1970s by Pobisk Kuznetzov.

31. Fedorov, "Vopros o bratstve ili rodstve . . . ," p. 71.

32. Fedorov, "Vopros o bratstve ili rodstve . . . ," p. 91.

33. Fedorov, "Vopros o bratstve ili rodstve . . . ," p. 99.

34. Fedorov, "Vopros o bratstve ili rodstve . . . ," p. 100.

35. Fedorov, "Vopros o vosstanovlenii vsemirnogo rodstva. *Sobor*," p. 318.

36. N. F. Fedorov, "Bessmertie kak privilegiya sverkhchelovekov," in N. F. Fedorov, *Collected Works*, vol. 2 (Moscow: Progress, 1995), p. 136.

37. Fedorov, "Bessmertie kak privilegiya sverkhchelovekov," p. 138.

38. Fedorov, "Vopros o bratstve ili rodstve . . . ," p. 101.

39. Fedorov, "Vopros o bratstve ili rodstve . . . ," p. 106.

40. Fedorov, "Vopros o vosstanovlenii vsemirnogo rodstva. *Sobor*," p. 324.

41. Boris Groys, "Russkiy kosmizm: biopolitika bessmertiya," in *Russkiy Kosmizm: Antologiya*, ed. Boris Groys (Moscow: Ad Marginem Press, 2015), p. 6.

42. Aleksandr Svyatogor, *Poetica, Biokosmizm, (A)teologia*, ed. Evgeniy Kurchinov (Moscow: Common place, 2017), p. 56. I thank the editor of Svyatogor's collected writings, Evgeniy Kuchinov, for sharing these and other unique archival materials with me. This and all subsequent translations of the Russian text are mine.

43. Svyatogor, *Poetica, Biokosmizm, (A)teologia*, p. 44.

44. Svyatogor, *Poetica, Biokosmizm, (A)teologia*, p. 53.

45. Svyatogor, *Poetica, Biokosmizm, (A)teologia*, pp. 184–185.

46. Svyatogor, *Poetica, Biokosmizm, (A)teologia*, p. 70.

47. Svyatogor, *Poetica, Biokosmizm, (A)teologia*, p. 77.

48. In Judaism, *ḥayyot esh* is a similar notion of "fiery beings" or "fiery animals." Refer to Babylonian Talmud (BT), *Ḥagigah* 13a-b and *Zohar* 2.82a.

49. Svyatogor, *Poetica, Biokosmizm, (A)teologia*, p. 71.

50. Svyatogor, *Poetica, Biokosmizm, (A)teologia*, p. 131.

51. Svyatogor, *Poetica, Biokosmizm, (A)teologia*, p. 149.

52. Svyatogor, *Poetica, Biokosmizm, (A)teologia*, p. 149.

53. Svyatogor, *Poetica, Biokosmizm, (A)teologia*, p. 143. It is worth noting that Svyatogor defines Fedorov's teaching as "uncritical unitary anarchism," *Poetica, Biokosmizm, (A)teologia*, p. 131.

54. Svyatogor, *Poetica, Biokosmizm, (A)teologia*, p. 144.

55. Svyatogor, *Poetica, Biokosmizm, (A)teologia*, p. 159.

56. Olga Burenina-Petrova, "Bessmertie cheloveka i telesnye metamorfozy v tvorchestve anarcho-biokosmistov," *Quaestio Rossica* 7, no. 1 (2019), p. 223.

57. Svyatogor, *Poetica, Biokosmizm, (A)teologia*, p. 159.

58. Svyatogor, *Poetica, Biokosmizm, (A)teologia*, p. 25.

59. Svyatogor, *Poetica, Biokosmizm, (A)teologia*, p. 117.

60. Svyatogor, *Poetica, Biokosmizm, (A)teologia*, p. 160.

61. Svyatogor, *Poetica, Biokosmizm, (A)teologia*, p. 92.

62. Svyatogor, *Poetica, Biokosmizm, (A)teologia*, p. 97.

63. Evgeniy Kurchatov, "Predislovie," in *Poetica, Biokosmizm, (A)teologia*, ed. Evgeniy Kurchinov (Moscow: Common Place, 2017), p. 11.

64. Svyatogor, *Poetica, Biokosmizm, (A)teologia*, p. 88.

65. Svyatogor, *Poetica, Biokosmizm, (A)teologia*, p. 68.

66. Svyatogor, *Poetica, Biokosmizm, (A)teologia*, p. 104.

67. Svyatogor, *Poetica, Biokosmizm, (A)teologia*, p. 104.

68. Svyatogor, *Poetica, Biokosmizm, (A)teologia*, p. 68.

69. Svyatogor, *Poetica, Biokosmizm, (A)teologia*, pp. 105, 106.

70. Svyatogor, *Poetica, Biokosmizm, (A)teologia*, p. 81.

71. Aleksandr Svyatogor, "Bessmert'ya komitety," in *Universal*, 3–4, 1921, pp. 15–16.

72. Svyatogor, *Poetica, Biokosmizm, (A)teologia*, p. 27.

CHAPTER 9

1. Roel Van den Broek, *The Myth of the Phoenix According to Classical and Early Christian Traditions* (Leiden: Brill, 1972), p. 181.

2. Eusebius, *Life of Constantine*, trans. Averil Cameron and Stuart G. Hall (Oxford: Oxford University Press, 1999), p. 181.

3. Laurence Gosserez, "Figurations Latines du Phénix de l'élégie érotique à l'épitaphe," in *Le Phénix et son autre: Poétique d'un mythe des origines au XVI siècle*, ed. Laurence Gosserez (Rennes: Presses Universitaires de Rennes, 2013), p. 50.

4. "The appearance of a new ruler on the scene and the beginning of a new era were seen as a return to the Golden Age, the fortunate state of things that prevailed at the beginning of the Great Year. This is clearly shown by the symbolism of the phoenix on a number of coins of Roman emperors" (van den Broek, *The Myth of the Phoenix*, p. 105).

5. van den Broek, *The Myth of the Phoenix*, pp. 115–116; Nigg, *The Phoenix*, pp. 54–55.

6. Joseph Nigg, *The Phoenix: An Unnatural Biography of a Mystical Beast* (Chicago: University of Chicago Press, 2016), p. 28. Compare this crown to the rayed, radiant nimbus traditionally depicted around the phoenix's head on Roman coins, epitaphs, and in other iconographic contexts. In the second century CE, Greek writer Achilles Tatius refers to the phoenix's headpiece as "the crown of feathers [which] is an image of the sun" (in van den Broek, *The Myth of the Phoenix*, p. 235n3).

7. Nigg, *The Phoenix*, p. 21.

8. In van den Broek, *The Myth of the Phoenix*, p. 417.

9. Ernst Kantorowicz, *The King's Two Bodies: A Study in Medieval Political Theology* (Princeton: Princeton University Press, 2016), p. 413. The words *unica phoenix* are, of course, borrowed from Lactantius.

10. Elizabeth I, *Elizabeth I: Collected Works*, ed. Leah Marcus et al. (Chicago: The University of Chicago Press, 2000), p. 326.

11. Refer to Kantorowicz, *The King's Two Bodies*, p. 388n245.

12. "Once I am [was] married already to the Realm of England when I was crowned with this ring, which I bear continually in token thereof. Howsoever it be, so long as I live, I shall be queen of England; when I am dead, they shall succeed that has most right. . . . I am sworn when I was married to the Realm not to alter the laws of it" (Elizabeth I, *Collected Works*, p. 65).

274 *Notes*

13. Shakespeare supports this line of thinking in *Henry VIII*: "Nor shall this peace sleep with her: but as when / The bird of wonder dies, the maiden phoenix, / Her ashes new create another heir, / As great in admiration as herself" (5.5).

14. *The Parliamentary or Constitutional History of England*, vol. 4 (London: Thomas Osborne, 1751), p. 67.

15. Kantorowicz, *The King's Two Bodies*, p. 385.

16. Kantorowicz, *The King's Two Bodies*, p. 387.

17. Kantorowicz, *The King's Two Bodies*, p. 388.

18. Kantorowicz, *The King's Two Bodies*, p. 385.

19. Kantorowicz, *The King's Two Bodies*, p. 394.

20. Kantorowicz, *The King's Two Bodies*, p. 387.

21. Kantorowicz, *The King's Two Bodies*, p. 389.

22. Commenting on Kantorowicz's analyses, Eric Santer calls this plane "royal physiology": "Much of the rest of Kantorowicz's study focuses on the ways these various virtual realities—dynasty, crown, dignity—were seen to enter into the constitution of the 'royal physiology,' which could then serve as the linchpin and the focal point guaranteeing the consistency and *undying nature* of the body politic." Ernst Kantorowicz, *The Royal Remains: The People's Two Bodies and the Endgames of Sovereignty* (Chicago: The University of Chicago Press, 2011), p. 42.

23. Kantorowicz, *The King's Two Bodies*, p. 391.

24. When in an interview Günter Gauss says, "I consider you to be a philosopher," Arendt immediately interrupts with a quip, "Well, I can't help that, but in my opinion I am not. In my opinion, I have said good-bye to philosophy once and for all. As you know, I studied philosophy, but that does not mean that I stayed with it." Hannah Arendt, *Essays in Understanding, 1930–1954: Formation, Exile, and Totalitarianism* (New York: Schocken Books, 1994), p. 2.

25. Hannah Arendt, *The Human Condition*, 2nd ed. (Chicago: The University of Chicago Press, 1958), p. 9. A sharp contrast between natality and mortality might not apply to the onto-theological rendering of these terms. As Kantorowicz reminds us, "The *natalicium* of saints and martyrs was the day of their death, and not their natural birthday." Kantorowicz, *The King's Two Bodies*, p. 391n255.

26. In this sense, natality is not reducible to the framework of biologism. See, for instance, Theodore Kisiel, "Rhetoric, Politics, Romance: Arendt and Heidegger, 1924–26," in *Extreme Beauty*, ed. James E. Swearingen and Joanne Cutting-Gray (London: Continuum, 2002), pp. 94–109.

27. Arendt, *The Human Condition*, pp. 176–177.

28. The time span separating the first from the second birth does not matter, or matters little. Seyla Benhabib identifies the second birth with the beginning of the child's linguistic development, but this contraction of the distance between the first and the second birth does not invalidate the structure of repetition and rebirth I am exploring here: "The birth of the human infant has a biological as well as a psychic-social dimension. The human infant becomes a self by learning speech and action in the human community into which it is born. Through this process, the infant also becomes an individual, that is, the unique initiator of these words and deeds, the carrier of this life story." Seyla Benhabib, *The Reluctant Modernity of Hannah Arendt* (Lanham, MD: Rowman & Littlefield, 2003), p. 109.

29. "To avoid misunderstanding: the human condition is not the same as human nature, and the sum total of human activities and capabilities which correspond to the human condition does not constitute anything like human nature." Arendt, *The Human Condition*, pp. 9–10.

30. Arendt, *The Human Condition*, p. 62.

31. This, according to Lenin, is the conditio sine qua non of "communists who have no illusions." Embodying the Leninist phoenix, they who "do not give way to despondency, and who preserve their strength and flexibility 'to begin from the beginning' over and over again in approaching an extremely difficult task, are not doomed (and in all probability will not perish)." V. I. Lenin, *Collected Works*, vol. 33: August 1921–March 1923 (Moscow: Progress, 1980), p. 203.

32. Arendt, *The Human Condition*, pp. 177–178.

33. Arendt, *The Human Condition*, p. 177.

34. Hannah Arendt, *The Origins of Totalitarianism*, new ed. (London: Harcourt, Brace, 1979), p. 465, emphasis added. In *Hannah Arendt and Human Rights: The Predicament of Common Responsibility* (Bloomington: Indiana University Press, 2006), Peg Birmingham takes exception to a reading of the relation of the first birth to the second on the basis of the relation of potentiality to actuality (pp. 83ff). It is true that Arendt is thinking more along the lines of existential possibility than the classical teleology of the potential and the actual; however, her language, operating with potentialities, is not to be so easily dismissed.

35. Hannah Arendt, *Between Past and Future: Six Exercises in Political Thought* (New York: Viking Press, 1961), p. 196.

36. Hannah Arendt, *The Life of the Mind*, vol. 2: *Willing*, one-volume ed. (London: Harcourt, Brace, 1978), p. 109.

37. Refer to *Bereshith Rabbah* 19.5; van den Broek, *The Myth of the Phoenix*, p. 59. Kantorowicz confirms that the "Rabbinic tradition, for example, ascribed to the bird immortality because it refused to share in Eve's sin by tasting of the forbidden fruit, and therewith preserved its paradisean state of innocence." Kantorowicz, *The King's Two Bodies*, p. 395.

38. Arendt, *Between Past and Future*, pp. 41–42.

39. Arendt, *Between Past and Future*, p. 42.

40. Arendt, *Between Past and Future*, p. 43.

41. Arendt, *The Human Condition*, pp. 18–19.

42. Arendt, *The Human Condition*, p. 246.

43. Hannah Arendt, *The Life of the Mind*, vol. 1: *Thinking*, one-volume ed. (London: Harcourt, Brace, 1978), p. 203.

44. Arendt, *Essays in Understanding*, p. 341.

45. Arendt, *Between Past and Future*, p. 168.

46. Arendt, *Between Past and Future*, p. 168.

47. Arendt, *Between Past and Future*, p. 168.

48. Anne O'Byrne accepts the prevalent view, according to which Arendt's thought is nondialectical: "What keeps Arendt's thought together *and* moving is the fact that it is a historical thinking that eschews both Hegelian dialectic and any Kantian notion that history is progressing toward perfection or completion." Anne O'Byrne, *Natality and Finitude* (Bloomington: Indiana University Press, 2010), p. 79. Nevertheless, some of the speculative reversals that happen at crucial junctions in Arendt's thought are, properly speaking, dialectical.

49. It is this problem of (metaphysically framed) spontaneity that prompts Steve Buckler to write that, in Arendt's thought, "spontaneous foundational agency would seem akin to lifting ourselves up by our own bootstraps. Spontaneity remains the central problem and an absolute must be found somewhere, whether in the form of the general will, natural law, or, later, the logic of history." Rather than refocus the problem in postmetaphysical terms, Buckler follows Arendt, who, in this, follows Heidegger, in identifying philosophy tout court with metaphysics. Hence, for Arendt, this problem "may be insoluble from a philosophical point of view, but she does not see it as a philosophical question; it is rather wholly a political one." Steve Buckler, *Hannah Arendt and Political Theory: Challenging the Tradition* (Edinburgh: Edinburgh University Press, 2011), p. 118.

50. Hannah Arendt, *The Promise of Politics* (New York: Schocken Books, 2005), p. 127.

51. Arendt, *The Human Condition*, pp. 96–97.

52. Arendt, *The Human Condition*, p. 98.

53. Arendt, *The Human Condition*, p. 173.

54. Arendt, *Life of the Mind*, vol. 2, p. 212.

55. While Rome was "the paradigmatic example of a successful foundation," "it was of the greatest importance . . . to find that even the foundation of Rome, as the Romans themselves had understood it, was not an absolutely new beginning. According to Virgil, it was the resurgence of Troy and the re-establishment of a city-state that had preceded Rome." Arendt, *Life of the Mind*, vol. 2, pp. 211–212).

56. Arendt, *Life of the Mind*, vol. 2, p. 212.

57. Arendt, *Life of the Mind*, vol. 2, p. 212.

58. Quoted in L. B. T. Houghton, *Virgil's Fourth Eclogue in the Italian Renaissance* (Cambridge: Cambridge University Press, 2019), p. 60.

59. *The Great Seal of the United States* (Washington, DC: US Department of State, 2003), p. 4, https://2009-2017.state.gov/documents/organization/27807.pdf.

60. Arendt, *Life of the Mind*, vol. 2, p. 193.

61. Arendt, *Life of the Mind*, vol. 2, p. 211.

AFTERWORD

1. Jorge Luis Borges, "The Cult of the Phoenix," in *Collected Fictions*, trans. Andrew Hurley (London: Penguin Books, 1999), p. 171.

2. Borges, "The Cult of the Phoenix," p. 173.

3. Jean-Luc Nancy, "A Finite Thinking," in *A Finite Thinking*, ed. Simon Sparks (Stanford: Stanford University Press, 2003), p. 27.

4. Nancy, "A Finite Thinking," p. 27.

5. *The Book of Common Prayer: The Texts of 1549, 1559, and 1662*, ed. Brian Cummings (Oxford: Oxford University Press, 2011), p. 172.

Index

Abraham, 255n45

Absolute, 11, 15, 18, 28, 46, 53, 80, 86, 89, 110, 111, 113, 114, 243, 244

Abstraction, xii, xviii, 85, 61, 73, 76, 86, 91

Actuality, 9, 63, 64–68, 87–88, 94–98, 145, 198, 201, 231, 248n11, 276n34

aeizōon (everlasting life, ever-living), 15, 16, 39, 212

Afterlife, xv, 19, 24, 30, 61, 77, 159, 163, 164, 182

Agriculture, 2, 3

Alterity, xix, 32, 45, 147, 226

Ambrose (of Milan), 6, 13, 18, 20, 23, 49, 71, 224, 250n19

Analects, 177–190, 222

Animality, 22, 90, 103, 215

Antigone, 54, 181

Appearance (coming to, coming-to-appearance) xii–xv, 36, 85, 111, 124, 169, 175, 178. *See* Birthing

Arendt, Hannah, xiv, 227–240

Aristotle, xix, 23, 24, 59–75, 96, 128, 130, 136, 203, 214, 232, 235

Artemidorus, 60

Atemporality, 99–100, 133

ātman (soul, world soul), 151–154, 163, 266n5, 267n21

Augustine (of Hippo), 21, 43, 129

Auschwitz, 55–57

Autocombustion, 5

Autopoiesis, xii, 100

Autotrophy, 76, 199

Avicenna, 61

Awakening, 155–156

Bachelard, Gaston, 1, 2, 4, 5

Baracchi, Claudia, 252n2, 256n3

Benhabib, Seyla, 274n28

Bennu (Egyptian mythological bird), 5, 15, 38, 92, 107, 139, 149, 150, 176, 249n14, 249n16, 251n29

Bergson, Henri, 245

Bernard (of Parma), 225, 226

Bhagavad Gītā, 151, 153, 166–174, 266n5

Biocosmism, 211–216

Birthing, xii–xiv, 13, 52, 65, 142, 179, 195, 200, 204, 237, 265n18, 270n35. *See also* Appearance (coming to)

Borges, Jorge Luis, 241, 242, 248n2

Brightness, 35, 133, 135, 136, 162

Broek, Roel (van den), 25, 250n18, 253n13, 255n45, 255n1

Burning, xx, 1, 3, 15, 19, 20, 21, 56, 57, 75, 115, 133, 210, 212

Cantimpré, Thomas (of), 251n33

Chakrabarty, Dipesh, 272n24

Change, xiii, 21, 82–84, 91, 95, 179, 192, 204, 230, 233
Cheng (brothers), 192, 193
Chernobyl, 17
Childhood, xv, 34, 45, 47–49, 69, 153, 164
Christ, 41, 43, 72, 133, 134, 135, 145, 197, 219. *See also* Jesus of Nazareth
Christianity, xix, 16, 30, 49, 59, 71, 77, 128, 198, 205
Chronos, 99, 101, 206
Chthonic, 25, 137, 156, 162, 176
Cicero, 59
Circularity, 37, 108, 114, 116, 119, 165, 232–237
Clark, Stephen, 259n2, 260n13
Claudius Aelianus, 8
Claudian, 7, 14, 16, 18, 60, 68, 70, 72, 123, 150, 176, 221
Combustion, 19, 20, 27, 44, 69, 106, 108, 115, 246
Coming-to-be-again, 153
Complexio oppositorum, 89, 155
Conatus, 138, 144, 146–147, 168
Confucius, 178–189, 191
Consciousness, 53, 54, 77, 78, 81, 82, 106, 194, 203, 232
Cosmism, xix, 197–218, 211, 213
Cosmos, 38, 39, 41, 42, 61, 92, 95, 98, 118, 125, 212, 215, 217, 252n5, 270n35
Creature, xv, 7, 39, 42, 43, 53, 71, 74, 104, 120, 131, 147, 151, 207, 215, 231, 263n5
Cyclicality, xix, 38, 40, 53, 94, 108, 119, 133, 151, 153, 170, 187, 199, 212, 220, 232, 237, 244, 250n19, 252n2, 261n22

Dao (道, the Way), 184–187, 192, 269, 198–201, 206, 283
Darkness, xiv, 93, 96, 136, 155, 156, 162, 165, 167, 193, 230, 248n11, 266n9
Daston, Lorraine, xiii

Dawn, 133, 135, 154, 155–158, 175, 189, 211
De-absolutization, 18, 108, 113, 224
Death of death, xx, 17
Decay, xv, 19, 21, 22, 26, 40, 65, 66, 67, 85, 137, 169, 188, 193, 204, 205, 206, 217, 218, 229, 237, 238
Deconstruction, 75, 131, 250n21
Deleuze, Gilles, xvii, 265n18
Derrida, Jacques, 258n38, 261n33
Destruction, xii, xx, 39, 58, 62, 77, 124, 150, 205, 212, 266n5
Devastation, xii, xx, 17, 38, 152, 31, 52, 166
Dialectics, 12, 49, 76, 78, 80–86, 234, 237, 258n38, 277n48
Diény, Jean-Pierre, 177, 178
Digestion, 68, 74, 75, 117, 119
Dionysius (of Alexandria), 6
Diotima, 11, 30, 32, 34, 62, 232, 252n1, 253n5
Disavowal, 12, 26, 40, 73, 121
Doniger, Wendy, 166, 267n18
Dracontius, 20, 72
Drive, xvii, 109, 120, 122, 204, 236
Dunamis, 68, 94, 96–98, 101, 105
Durand, Gilbert, 154, 249n14
Duration, 61, 62, 100, 143, 144, 211
Dying, xii, xiv, 10, 20, 22, 26, 32, 51, 52, 62, 64, 67, 77, 78, 117, 164
Dynamism, 60, 64, 115, 145, 155, 193, 210, 214, 218

Elizabeth I, (Queen of England), 223–225, 231
Encounter, 246
Engels, Friedrich, 248n13
Essence, xi, xvi, 33, 34, 36, 50, 51, 88, 141, 170, 179, 180, 185, 247n1, 264n16
Eternity, xix, 42, 91, 96, 97, 98–99, 101, 131, 132, 138, 154, 215, 217, 225, 239, 253n15, 263n5
Everlasting, 2, 15, 39, 61, 98, 212, 224, 266n5

Existence, 1, 2, 10, 13, 46, 48, 64, 67, 69, 76, 85, 114, 140, 165, 171, 216, 243, 245

Existential, 229, 240, 245, 276n34

Experience, 80, 81, 109, 203, 232

Extinction, 10, 19, 205, 210, 222, 233, 244, 245

Fecundity, 2, 11, 45–48, 51, 52, 54, 162, 246, 254n18

Fedorov, Nikolai Fedorovich, 197–213, 218, 228

Female, xiii, 5, 9, 11, 14, 15, 70–72, 133, 176, 222, 252n42

Feminine, 5, 11, 24, 89, 136, 154, 223

Fenghuang (Chinese mythological bird) 39, 149, 175–178, 181, 184–186, 190, 222, 249n14

Fermentation, 77, 78, 134, 135

Figuration, xiii, xviii, 5, 8, 16, 97, 110, 151, 192, 198

Finitude, xviii, xix, 2, 11, 12, 18, 19, 20, 25, 28, 29, 46, 54, 55, 62, 74, 81, 128, 139, 146, 192, 199, 206, 242, 243, 244, 245

Fire, 15–17, 19, 21, 27, 34, 39, 43, 57, 64, 72, 76, 92, 93, 95, 107, 108, 123, 136, 149, 156–158, 164, 210, 212, 241

Flesh, 14, 16, 20, 23, 34, 54, 59, 78, 102, 142, 205, 210, 226

Flower, 133–136, 153, 185

Fluidity, 14, 23, 24, 108, 112

Force, xvi, 18, 31, 32, 71, 110, 117, 132, 176, 185, 199, 201, 210, 263n66

Formation, 4, 13, 73, 74, 108, 113, 182

Freedom, 109–110, 111, 114, 118, 120–123, 165, 169, 235, 236, 240, 244

Freud, Sigmund, 4, 48, 208, 249n13

Fruit, 25, 68, 134, 168–169, 170, 256n6

Garuḍa (Indian mythological bird), 149–151, 152, 154, 157, 172

Gender, 11, 45, 48, 136, 223

Goodridge, John 124

Gosserez, Laurence, 149, 250n20, 250n25

Greenness, 128, 130, 132, 168

Gregory (of Tours), 14

Gregory Nazianzus, 72

Growth, xiv–xv, 1, 3, 67, 74, 90, 103, 107, 112, 158, 192, 193, 218, 237

Groys, Boris, 211

Guattari, Felix, xvii

Hadot, Pierre, 260n10

Haraway, Donna, 202

Harmony, 35, 176, 182, 190, 252n5

Heat, 17, 20, 26, 27, 68, 76, 77, 127, 128, 130, 136, 156, 210, 250n27

Hebrew, 19, 21, 55, 56, 150, 153, 261n26, 267n22

Hegel, Georg W. F. xix, 12, 13, 50, 72–88, 236, 247n2, 256n5, 256n10, 257n33, 258n38

Heidegger, Martin, xiii, 194, 197, 228, 238, 277n49

Heliopolis, 5, 9, 22, 25, 107, 209, 241, 249n14

Heraclitus, xv, 2, 15, 39, 118, 212, 248n3, 266n11

Herbs, 20, 21, 68, 135, 219

Herodotus, 20, 23, 54, 60, 232, 241

Hesiod, 59, 60, 130, 253n8

Hildegard (von Bingen), xix, 127–134, 136–137, 153, 154, 224, 263n5, 264n8

Homer, 23, 67

Hope, xix, xx, 1, 3, 56, 59, 108, 118, 151, 153, 199, 245, 213

Horapollo, 24, 25

Hrabanus Maurus, 241

Hulē, 43, 62, 63, 93, 96, 252n42

Humaneness (Chinese *ren*), 177, 181, 185, 190

Immanence, xix, 30, 32, 44, 45, 47, 48, 50, 52, 53, 54, 103, 133, 143, 144, 182, 264n13, 265n16

Immortality, xiii, xix, xx, 16, 31, 32, 33, 36, 104, 109, 150, 154, 161, 197, 209, 214–215, 217, 225, 232, 233, 238, 276n37
Impatience, 19, 20, 22, 23, 40, 42, 43, 206
Impulse (animating), 54, 56, 111, 113, 145, 193
Indestructibility, 58, 62, 152, 266n5
India, 2, 117, 149, 150, 151, 167, 174
Infinity, 2, 11, 20, 35, 45, 54, 112, 120, 121, 122, 139, 146, 192, 261n38
Irigaray, Luce, 261n33
Isidore (of Seville), 5, 6, 49
Iterability, 9, 10, 28, 34, 139, 194, 228, 230, 235

Jainism, 29, 109, 165, 261n22
Jesus of Nazareth, 7, 11, 128, 131–136. *See also* Christ
Jonas, Hans, 247n6, 250n21
Judaism, xix, 55, 56, 57, 137, 166, 207, 231, 261n26

Kant, Immanuel, 4, 206, 226, 251n40, 277
Kantorowicz, Ernst, 223–227, 275, 276n37
Karma, 163, 166, 169, 171
Kinship, 160, 198, 200–202, 207, 209, 210
Knowledge, xvi, 9, 44, 111, 141, 142, 163, 184, 189

Lactantius, 5, 6, 9, 11, 16, 20, 25, 27, 28, 32, 43, 45, 48, 49, 60, 64, 71, 97, 139, 176, 221, 223, 224, 226
Language, 133, 151, 188, 189, 202, 276n34
Lavoisier, Antoine, 116
Legge, James, 175, 270n28
Leibniz, Gottfried, 269n25
Lenin, Vladimir, I., 276n31
Levinas, Emmanuel, xix, 10, 45–58, 119, 143
Life, xii–xiv, xix, 4, 8, 10, 16–20, 85–88, 94–96,198, , 232–233, 238, 240, 252n2, 263n66, 263n5
  finitude (of), 29, 30, 32, 36, 52, 55–58, 60–70, 74–81, 203, 210, 216

Chinese (conception of), 179–185, 192–193
production (of) 40–44, 102–103, 108–110, 115–118, 120, 128, 131, 146, 154, 165
Light, xvi, 8, 16, 17, 20, 27, 29, 33, 35, 75–77, 92, 96, 136, 154, 155, 156, 162, 163, 187,190, 193, 203, 230, 248n11, 250n27
Logos, 37, 61, 71, 93, 231, 269n16
Love, xv–xviii, 30–31, 32, 33, 34, 35, 36, 48, 89, 133, 141, 142, 143, 144, 170, 187, 208,209, 248n11, 253n5, 265n18
Lucretius, 173
Lurquin, Paul, 248n7

Mahābhārata, 149, 151, 153, 157, 265n2
Masculinity, 5, 9, 13, 14, 48, 70, 71, 72, 89, 133, 176, 178, 208, 222, 249n13
Mary (Virgin), 128, 131, 133, 134, 135, 136, 154
Materiality, 20, 21, 26, 27, 28, 76, 77, 104, 105, 136
Maternity, 53, 254n18
Matter, 19, 20, 21, 26, 27, 28, 42, 43–45, 52, 63, 64, 66, 77, 79, 81, 93, 104–105, 112, 114, 115, 120, 123, 132, 135, 136, 145, 183, 192, 203, 212, 217, 252n42, 260n10
  vegetal, 2, 17, 33, 64, 65, 134, 136, 178
Mechanism, 30–34, 36, 50, 84, 111, 112, 117, 118, 119, 173, 174, 178, 236, 268n27
Medium, 2, 8, 19, 21, 35, 38, 64, 69, 71, 76, 79, 90, 92, 169, 173, 187, 198, 210, 212, 257n26
Merleau-Ponty, Maurice, 250n21
Metabolism, 101, 119, 204, 213, 218
Metamorphosis, 3, 22, 23, 26, 28, 40, 44, 66, 91, 95, 107, 134, 188, 204, 205, 214, 218, 228
Metaphysics, xviii, 31, 83, 172, 269n18, 277n49
Middle, xiv, 16, 46, 53, 86, 168, 189, 192, 255n40

282 *Index*

Modernity, xi, xix, 35, 51, 64, 111, 177, 182, 187, 192, 227, 235, 239

Moisture, 23, 24, 27, 61, 68, 76, 127, 128, 134, 263n5

Mortality, 11, 13, 20, 29, 70, 73, 113, 128, 134, 143, 162, 194, 199, 226, 228, 232, 233, 275n25

Morton, Timothy, xii

Movement, xii, 13, 44, 54, 61, 64, 66, 77, 79, 80, 86, 99, 110, 118, 122, 123, 125, 141, 146, 155, 192, 193, 229, 232–234, 235, 237, 258n38

Multiplicity, 48, 65, 66, 75, 89, 94, 96, 105, 114, 174, 207, 255n45, 260n10

Mysticism, 32, 127, 130,136, 137, 166, 261n26

Nancy, Jean-Luc, 243, 244, 245

Natality, xii, 2, 52, 227–232, 233, 238, 239, 275n25, 275n26

Nature (phoenix-nature), xx, 8, 9, 13, 49, 54, 65, 113, 141

Negation, 12, 26, 46, 50, 72, 79–80, 82, 84, 121, 154, 159

Negativity, 74, 75, 78, 80, 84, 245, 257n26

Newborn, 34, 37, 204, 236

Nietzsche, Friedrich, 215, 267n23

Nigg, Joseph, 184, 249n14, 274

Nihilism, 34, 44, 166, 245

Nonbeing, 109, 151, 154, 246, 268

Nonhuman, xix, 5, 29, 51, 81, 83, 152, 184, 198, 201

Non-kindred, 200–202

Nonrenewability, xviii, 243, 244–246

Nourishment, xiv, 63, 64, 67, 68, 76, 130, 131, 203

Odyssey, 23, 68

Oedipus, 4, 254n27

Offspring, 24, 36–37, 48, 64, 69, 157, 159–161, 180, 185

Organic, xii, 8, 77, 110, 112, 115, 119, 127, 203

Organism, 64, 73, 112, 113, 114, 119, 261n38

Origin, 47, 53, 75, 94, 95, 105, 161, 169, 192, 239, 240

Othering, 8, 48, 67, 79, 80, 97

Otherness, 10, 12, 32, 33, 79, 104, 138, 139, 180, 205

Overcoming, 11, 17, 22, 25, 45, 62, 74, 81, 117

Ovid, 20, 22, 23, 54, 68, 71

O'Byrne, Anne, 277n48

Palm (tree, date palm), 6, 60, 62, 76, 127, 128, 129, 132, 134, 136, 169, 190

Perfection, 39, 40, 41, 260n9

Perpetual, 8, 78, 98, 99, 166, 168, 205, 218, 252

Perpetuity, xviii, 51, 64, 84, 85, 139, 152, 154, 204, 224, 226, 238, 243

Perseverance, 109, 168

Phenomenality, xii, 15, 20, 64, 79, 114

Phenomenological, 40, 62, 70, 71, 201, 261

Phenomenology, 26, 48, 50, 56, 142, 187, 247n1//(eco-phenomenology)250n21

Philosophy of nature, xvi–xviii, xx, xxi, 51, 54, 85, 86, 119, 176, 202, 227, 245, 246

Phoenician, 78, 80

Phoenix-like, xx, 34, 41, 46, 86, 101, 114, 141, 161, 185, 207, 258n37

Phusis, xiv–xvii, 13, 61, 65, 89, 98, 101, 104, 166, 167, 248n11

Planetary, xiii, 119, 123, 206, 207, 211, 245, 272n24

Plant, 13, 62–63, 65, 73–77, 90, 102, 105, 107, 115, 256n10// (growing) xiv, 3, 52, 66, 94, 97, 158, 167, 204. *See also* Vegetal

Plantlike, 64, 76, 199

Plato, xvi, xix, 10, 11, 29–44, 58, 59, 92, 98, 101, 102, 119, 123, 129, 130, 136, 166, 174, 193, 212, 215, 228, 232, 252, 254, 255n1, 260n14, 269n16

Pliny the Elder, 6, 9, 14, 25, 31, 68, 220

283 *Index*

Plotinus, xix, 89, 90–106, 113, 136, 139, 259, 260, 264
Plutarch, 60, 128
Pomponius Mela, 11, 23, 70
Potentiality, 20, 35, 63–68, 88, 94, 96, 97, 128, 131, 145, 191, 231, 256n7, 276n34
Pound, Ezra, 185, 269n20
Presocratic, xiv, xv, xvii, 2, 247n9
Production, 46–51, 74, 75, 113, 256n12
Prometheus, 1, 2, 4, 5, 18, 34, 150, 249n13
Putrefaction, 23, 24, 105, 114, 203, 218, 252n42. *See* Rotting

Rameau, Jean-Philippe, 268n4
Redeath, 162, 163, 165, 166, 167, 170, 173, 235, 240, 242, 244
Reincarnation, 10, 29, 30, 103, 130, 153, 158, 163, 165, 166, 171, 172, 173
Religion, 77, 78, 80, 82, 137, 139, 210
Remains, xiv, 19, 23, 24, 27, 54, 98, 119, 160, 199, 203
Renaissance, 219, 220, 240, 242
Renewability, 10, 153, 244–246
Return, 50, 78, 80, 81, 103, 124, 158, 193, 203, 219, 221, 252n2
Revolution, 15, 55, 150, 172, 212, 214
Rigveda, 151, 154, 160, 163, 166, 172, 266n10
Rorty, Amelie, 256n3
Rotting, 17, 20, 22, 23, 24, 28, 114, 205, 209, 218. *See* Putrefaction

Sacrifice, 2, 24, 32, 56, 75, 106, 107, 122, 157, 161, 181, 255n45
Sallis, John, 253n14
Salvation, 18, 32, 46, 47, 56, 202, 203, 232, 234, 251n34
Sanford, Stella, 254n18
Schelling, Friedrich, xvi, xix, 106–124, 151, 261, 263, 2667n25
Schürmann, Reiner, vii, xix, xx
Science, 17, 110, 111, 202, 203, 248n13

Seed, 10, 13, 14, 27, 28, 93, 94, 96, 97, 168, 193
Sensibility, 20, 21, 43, 53, 66, 82, 91, 167
Sentiment, xiii, 42, 43, 178, 183, 205
Sexuation, 5, 12, 13, 14, 15, 24, 26, 70–73, 113, 114, 177, 207, 208, 250n23
Shakespeare, 275n13
Shēng (生, life), 179, 192–194
Singularity, 5, 6, 7, 17, 28, 38, 70, 72, 85, 89, 122, 125, 138, 147, 177, 181, 186, 207, 209, 223, 227, 243
Socrates, 11, 30, 32, 35, 36, 37, 41, 53, 174, 181, 183, 198, 232, 252n1
Sovereignty, 176, 178, 223, 225
Speciation, 5, 60, 70, 115, 203, 227
Speech, 178, 188, 276n28
Spinoza, Baruch, xix, 4, 137–147, 152, 168, 217, 264n13, 264n16, 265, 269n25
Spiritual, 48, 49, 57, 58, 70–72, 96, 106, 107, 111, 136, 142, 143, 145, 149, 156, 195, 214, 230, 238, 239, 277
Spiritualization, 43, 44, 57–58, 82, 93, 123, 224, 263n66
Spontaneity, 22, 23, 24, 98, 105, 169, 187, 235, 236, 277n49
Subjectivity, 47, 49–52, 54, 57, 76, 81, 122, 258n38
Substance, 47, 49, 51, 58, 81, 100, 115, 138–141, 143–144, 243, 265n16
Survival, 2, 64, 74, 77, 93, 117, 159, 176, 179, 203, 226, 256n7
Svyatogor, Aleksandr, 211–218
Symbol, 59, 60, 61, 70, 79, 81, 90, 132, 198, 222, 239, 255n1
Synecdoche, 7–9, 12, 13, 15, 17, 18–19, 22, 34, 40, 54, 60, 70, 72, 74, 85, 90, 101, 108, 113, 125, 129, 137, 139, 142, 172, 177, 186, 193, 209

Tacitus, 9, 14, 70, 71, 241
Technology, xiii, 5, 18, 19, 32, 34, 151, 197, 206, 209, 214, 251n34

Temporality, 30, 44, 46, 52, 74, 99, 133, 143, 207, 216, 217, 232, 233, 237
Tertullian, 7, 8, 9, 16, 32, 45, 59, 64, 226, 250
Theology, xix, 19, 29, 131, 133, 145, 207, 261n26
Thought-image, 85, 91, 145, 265n16
Transcendence, xix, 2, 30, 32, 44, 45, 47, 48, 49, 50, 52, 53, 54, 74, 133, 143, 175
Tzetzes, Johannes, 13, 14, 70, 250n27

Universality, 38, 85, 87, 88, 104, 106, 137, 186, 208, 209
Upaniṣads, 151, 154, 162, 163, 164, 166, 267n19

Veda, 165, 168–78, 180, 181, 186, 280
Vegetal, xiv, 13, 60, 62–68, 74, 75, 77, 90, 115, 136, 190, 203, 204, 230. *See also* Plant
Virgil, 220, 239, 277n55
Viriditas (greenness), 128–137, 144, 146, 193, 263n5
Vitality, 2, 15, 61, 63, 64, 66, 67, 95, 106, 109, 179, 182, 193, 252n2, 256n3
Viveiros de Castro, Eduardo, 264n8
Volcanism, 8, 106, 107, 211, 212, 216, 272n24

Watson, Burton, 268, 269
Western (thought), xviii, xix, 58, 83, 129, 151, 166, 172, 175, 258n38
Wisdom, xv, xvi, xviii, 8, 9, 152, 158, 168, 172, 184, 248n11, 266n6
Wood, 18, 43, 63, 64, 66, 132, 137, 177, 178, 267n13

Yoga, 163, 168, 170
Youth, 14, 20, 25, 38, 39, 41, 54, 63, 64, 132, 137, 156

Zeno (of Verona), 33, 36, 41, 71, 250n19
Zhongyong (*Doctrine of the Mean*), 185, 187, 269

Zhu Xi, 189, 192, 270
Zisi (Master, Kong Ji), 185–187
Žižek, Slavoj, 176, 261n33
Zohar (Book of), 166, 273n48

285 *Index*